BLACK WIND, WHITE SNOW

BLACK WIND, WHITE SNOW

THE RISE OF RUSSIA'S NEW NATIONALISM

CHARLES CLOVER

YALE UNIVERSITY PRESS
NEW HAVEN AND LONDON

For information about this and other Yale University Press publications, please contact:
U.S. Office: sales.press@yale.edu   yalebooks.com
Europe Office: sales@yaleup.co.uk   yalebooks.co.uk

Typeset in Minion Pro by IDSUK (DataConnection) Ltd
Printed in Great Britain by Gomer Press, Llandysul, Ceredigion, Wales

Library of Congress Cataloging-in-Publication Data

Clover, Charles, 1968–
Title: Black wind, white snow : the rise of Russia's new nationalism / Charles Clover.
Description: New Haven : Yale University Press, 2016. | Includes bibliographical references and index.
LCCN 2015037501 | ISBN 9780300120707 (hardback)
LCSH: Putin, Vladimir Vladimirovich, 1952—Political and social views. | Putin, Vladimir Vladimirovich, 1952—Friends and associates. | Eurasian school. | Nationalism–Russia (Federation) | Political culture–Russia (Federation) | Russia (Federation)–Politics and government–1991- | Russia (Federation)–Foreign relations–Philosophy. | BISAC: HISTORY / Europe / Russia & the Former Soviet Union. | HISTORY / Europe / Former Soviet Republics. | HISTORY / Modern / 21st Century.
Classification: LCC DK510.766.P87 C56 2016 | DDC 947.086/2092–dc23
LC record available at http://lccn.loc.gov/2015037501

A catalogue record for this book is available from the British Library.

10 9 8 7 6 5 4 3 2 1

To Rachel and Jaya

Now I held in my hands a vast methodical fragment of an unknown planet's entire history, with its architecture and its playing cards, with the dread of its mythologies and the murmur of its languages, with its emperors and its seas, with its minerals and its birds and its fish, with its algebra and its fire . . .

Jorge Luis Borges

CONTENTS

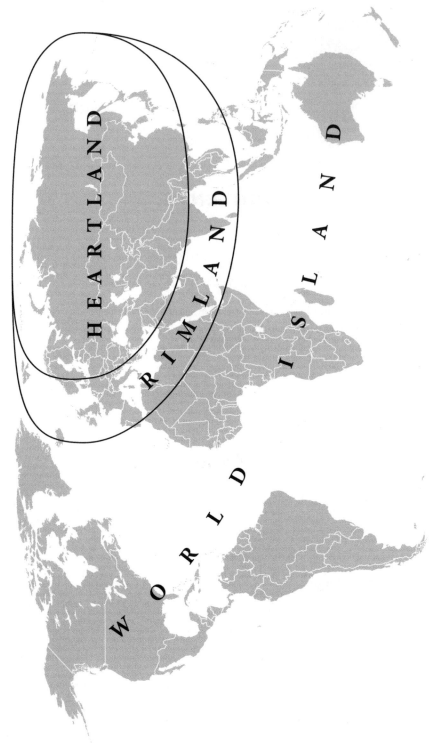

Map of Eurasia, first outlined by Sir Halford Mackinder in his 'The Geographical Pivot of History', and reproduced in Russian by Alexander Dugin in *The Foundations of Geopolitics* (1997).

PREFACE

This book grew out of a meeting I had in 1998, soon after I arrived in Ukraine as a rookie stringer for the *Financial Times*. After a few months of reporting from Kiev, the Foreign Ministry finally acceded to a request for an interview, putting forward their courtly, if rather severe, first deputy foreign minister, Anton Buteiko, to gently lobby me on some of my more persistent errors ('it's Lviv, not Lvov anymore') and to give me a bit of a steer politically.

Much of what he said was standard boilerplate about Ukraine's 'partnership' with Russia and its desire for 'integration' with 'Euro-Atlantic structures' – two objectives that at the time did not seem incompatible. But towards the end of the meeting, he mentioned an interesting tidbit.

A book had been published in Russia a few months previously, called *The Foundations of Geopolitics*. Its author, Alexander Dugin, was known to have the backing of conservative Russian hardliners, said Buteiko, and the book was produced with the help of Russia's Academy of the General Staff. It laid out plans for the dismemberment of Ukraine. It might be worth a read, he said, if I wanted to get an idea of what his former colleagues in Moscow were thinking.

The next day I went to the Lesya Ukrainka public library in Kiev and found a copy. (The book was not available in bookstores, for understandable reasons.) I was intrigued: on the cover was some sort of ancient Norse rune, plus a map of the former Soviet Union. And inside, sure enough, was a note thanking General Nikolay Klokotov, head of the department of strategy at the Academy of the General Staff, for his insightful analytical help with the project.

The book was an exposition of right-wing theories of nationalism; fascistic theories from interwar Nazis, like geopolitics; plus a political movement I had never heard of, known as Eurasianism. This appeared to describe a plan to put the Soviet Union back together again, *en route* to creating a world-dominating empire.

There was plenty to worry a Ukrainian foreign minister, including one passage that, in light of the events in Georgia and Ukraine over the past half-decade, deserves some attention:

> One absolute imperative of Russian geopolitics is the total and unfettered control of Moscow over the entire length of the Black Sea coast stretching from Ukrainian to Abkhazian territory . . . The north shore of the Black Sea should be exclusively Eurasian and centrally obey Moscow.

On my next visit to Moscow, I met Alexander Dugin, the book's author, at his office in a public library across from the golden onion domes and secluded ponds of the Novodevichy Convent in Moscow. A former dissident, who cranked out his manifestos in dingy basements and on Xerox machines, Dugin's search for freedom from totalitarian rule led him in a very different direction from many of his fellow Soviet-era intellectuals.

Russia's salvation, Dugin believed, lay in turning back the tide of democratic liberalism, re-establishing repressive central control, and bringing to power a regime of patriots, beholden to an imperial concept of Russia, a multinational, multi-ethnic, multi-confessional, but distinctly Russian and distinctly non-Western geopolitical space – 'Eurasia'.

Dugin's very existence is interesting, given the booming triumphalism which accompanied the end of the Cold War. He had spent his life wrestling with the chains of authoritarianism, only to embark on building a new type of authoritarianism when the old type finally fell. He reminded me of Shigalov, the character from Fedor Dostoevsky's novel *Demons* who said: 'Starting from unlimited freedom, I arrive at unlimited despotism.'

Dugin may have looked the part of a philosophy-crazed Dostoevsky-esque anchorite. But in fact he was a funny, hip and altogether likeable guy as well as being one of the most interesting, well-read intellectuals I have ever met. To this day I wonder: does he actually believe it or not? But I know that that is somehow irrelevant. Whether he is a true believer or is just playing a role, he carries both off equally well, flitting in and out of references to the occult, numerology, fascism, postmodernism and French cultural theory. But I was intrigued by the reference to the General Staff: in addition to being a conspiracy theorist, was Dugin actually part of a conspiracy? Or was he just a talented self-publicist? Dugin's answer confirmed both possibilities: 'There are high-level people within the state who support these views.'

When a piece of mine criticizing Dugin and his views ran in the arch-Atlanticist journal *Foreign Affairs* in 1999, Dugin did not take umbrage, and we soon became unlikely penpals.

Though I left Russia for the Middle East and South Asia soon after the 9/11 attacks, I continued to take an interest in Dugin and his Eurasianist movement. And when I returned to London, I resolved to write a book about what I had learned. That meant going back through a century's worth of writing, as well as conducting more interviews with contemporary figures.

That is the project which is now in your hands. It has gone through many changes since I originally conceived it in 2005 (and started writing it a few years later). It is, for many tragic reasons, more relevant. At the time I started, Dugin was a marginal crank, and the subject matter of Russia's imperial ambitions was largely theoretical. The book I envisaged was about the gradual inroads of a little-known philosophy into Russian politics, and about how a century of Russian history at its most capricious and cruel had given birth to a theoretical doppelgänger for communism.

But by the time I had finished the book, eight years after I started (five of them as the *FT*'s Moscow bureau chief), the phenomenon I had been writing about had transformed itself from a fringe idea written on pamphlets and sent out through grainy webcasts to a semi-official ideology of power, blaring from state TV channels and wielded by Vladimir Putin's Kremlin in the conquest of eastern Ukraine. Dugin was listed as one of *Foreign Policy* journal's top 100 global thinkers for 2014.[1]

I had not intended to write a book with a lot of hard news in it. Instead of grasping at straws in an attempt to connect the movement's esoteric writings to Russian reality, I was suddenly confronted by a new challenge – how to weave what I already had into the U-turn that Russian history had taken. This resulted in a very different book: it went from a vague meditation on the interconnection of life and ideas through a century of Russian history, to a more sensational work. And suddenly the last few pages had to get a lot longer. Also, while the book now has an ending, it is one that keeps changing every fortnight.

There are still a few glitches. One such is the transliteration from Cyrillic. For various reasons – including laziness, but mainly a desire to keep things simple and to preserve the best-known English versions of Russian names – there is no overall consistency: we have Jakobson (not Yakobson), Yeltsin (not Eltsin), Savitsky (not Savitskiy), etc.

Another problem some may find is my use of the word 'nationalism', particularly in the title. Many of the authors here would take grave exception to being labelled 'nationalist', which in Russian is akin to 'racist'; however, in English it has a wider meaning which I find appropriate. I have used 'nationalism' as a broad category to represent the civilizational identity that Eurasianism proposes. Like nationalism, it suggests a common culture and political boundaries, and may be used to justify conquest and irredentism.

While it is true that Eurasia is itself a 'multinational' unit, made up of Tatars, Russians and Yakuts (among others), its concept is in essence an imperial form of Russian nationalism, and its members have all joined in a Russian nationalist war of conquest in eastern Ukraine. Calling them nationalists is not a fudge, it is a fact. But it will be confusing later, when these nationalists criticize other nationalists for 'nationalism'. It can't be helped.

Literally a cast of thousands has helped me to write this book. The University of Michigan has provided an immense resource, as well as a delightful place to spend a year dabbling in the subject on a Knight Wallace Fellowship. Charles Eisendrath and Birgit Reick especially deserve my thanks. A special note of gratitude goes to LaVerne Prager, an incredibly generous woman who funded the fellowship that kept me at Ann Arbor for a year.

Jindrich Toman, head of Michigan's Department of Slavic Languages and an expert on the Prague School of Linguistics, spent a lot of time with me explaining phonology, Jakobson and Trubetskoy. Olga Maiorova, who taught a course in Russian orientalism while I was in Ann Arbor, was of immense assistance. Patrick Seriot of the University of Lausanne helped me hugely with Prague School linguistics and with the links between these theories and Eurasianism. I am also very grateful for a long telephone conversation with Anatoly Liberman of the University of Minnesota, who helped me with the same.

Robert C. Otto has been an immense resource to me on the modern period of Eurasianism and Russian politics in general. He kindly read my manuscript, made many helpful comments and corrected many errors. John Dunlop of the Hoover Institution provided a great deal of help with the history of the 1991 coup, Dugin and the modern infiltration of nationalism into Russian society.

Yitzhak Brudny of the Hebrew University of Jerusalem has likewise been incredibly generous with contacts on modern nationalism, Gumilev and the Soviet 'politics by culture' era of the 1960s to the 1980s, and also kindly read my manuscript.

Andreas Umland, who wrote his PhD dissertation on Alexander Dugin, has been similarly generous with his sources.

Andrew Weiss and Dmitri Trenin of the Moscow Carnegie Center were extremely helpful during my time as bureau chief in Moscow, and specifically in tracking the penetration of conservative ideas into the Russian mainstream.

Journalists Sergey Kanev and Nadezha Prusenkova of *Novaya Gazeta*, and Andrey Soldatov of Agentura.ru helped me hugely with sources, documents and – most of all – judgements.

Petr Suslov, formerly of the KGB's Vympel unit, kindly spent many hours with me discussing – in somewhat vague terms – the history of the KGB, the Chechen conflict, his own participation in Eurasianism and some of the odder coincidences of post-Soviet history. Vladimir Revsky, another Vympel veteran and former Suslov collaborator was also a great help.

Igor Rodionov, ex-commander of the 40th Army in Afghanistan and Russia's former defence minister, helped me both with his own history and with the ideological climate in the Russian military following the collapse of the USSR – a climate that geopolitical theory helped to shape.

Many of the participants in the 1980s Moscow bohemia (described in Part III) came forward to explain what was apparently the best party ever. Sergey Zhigalkin helped me to recreate, on a much tamer scale, a typical evening of the Moscow 'mystical underground' circa 1980 at his dacha, while Igor Dudinsky spent many hours showing me his photo albums, drinking cognac and recounting episodes of hard partying.

Gaidar Dzhemal sat with me for two hours, after which I realized that nothing I knew was actually true and I might as well live in a yurt.

Archimandrite Tikhon Shevkunov of the Sretensky monastery sat for two long interviews and some thoroughly enjoyable conversation that provided the basis for both a magazine feature in the *FT* and a chapter in this book. Thanks to him, to Father Pavel and to Oleg Leonov for helping to set it all up.

Mikhail Leontyev, anchor for the programme *Odnako*, was incredibly generous with his time in answering questions about Russian politics, and made himself available on numerous occasions, as did Maxim Shevchenko and Vladimir Pozner.

Thanks to Vladimir Yakunin, formerly head of Russian Railways, who gave me a number of (fairly vague) interviews on conservative thinking at the peak of Kremlin power.

Alain de Benoist, leader of the French Nouvelle Droite, was very patient with my attempts to understand the theory of the movement, and helpful.

Marina Kozyreva, the niece of Lev Gumilev's campmate who now runs the Lev Gumilev Apartment Museum in St Petersburg, sat with me for hours, on several different occasions, helping me with contacts and explaining Gumilev's legacy. I remain steadfastly grateful to her.

Alexey Bondarev, who has completed his PhD on Gumilev's theories, spent a day discussing Gumilev's philosophy and showing me around the palaces of St Petersburg. Many of his insights have found their way into the book.

Ivan Savický, son of Petr, generously spent a day with me in Prague speaking about his father and helped me access the archive of the elder Savitsky's correspondence in the Slavic Library.

Many thanks are due to the Russian Academy of Sciences Institute of Ethnography. In particular, Valery Tishkov, Anatoly Anokhin and Sergey Cheshko ran me through the criticism of 'Ethnogenesis' and the two-decade spat between the institute's former director Yulian Bromley and Gumilev.

Anatoly Chistobaev of the Leningrad University Institute of Geography, where Lev Gumilev taught for three decades, spent a day giving me a tour of the institute and regaling me with stories of Gumilev's time there.

Special thanks to Kseniya Ermishina of the Russian State Humanitarian University for sharing sources and her exhaustive knowledge of the 1920s. On that period, too, many thanks to Irina Troubetzkoy Booth, and Varvara Kühnelt-Leddihn, Nikolai Trubetskoi's grand-daughter, for much help locating sources on the family history of this exalted Russian lineage.

A former high-ranking Kremlin official who has requested anonymity was an immense help to me while I was Moscow bureau chief: he spent many hours explaining how things work and debunking my wilder theories about Alexander Dugin.

Which brings me to Dugin, without whom this book would not have been possible, but who, I fear, took a dislike to an early manuscript I showed him. I believe he became uneasy with my project and his participation in it, although we never really discussed this. I am grateful for the time he spent with me, and sorry that he has not had a chance to check the final manuscript for the inevitable errors – inevitable, since I was forced to rely mainly on the versions of his detractors, of whom there are quite a few.

Dugin's wife Natalya stepped in to help, and I thank her for the hours we spent discussing the history of the movement that her husband led.

Pavel Zarifullin and I downed many pints of lager at the John Bull Pub in Moscow, while discussing political theories, events and the history of the Eurasian Youth Union, which he led until 2009. Valery Korovin, Dugin's acolyte, Old Believer and theoretician of network wars, sat with me for a number of interviews, as did Leonid Savin.

Likewise Gleb Pavlovsky and Marat Guelman, spin doctors extraordinaire, were massively helpful both during my time as a journalist and in helping me to track the infiltration of nationalist ideas into the political mainstream.

Eduard Limonov, when he was not being stuffed into police paddy-wagons, was patient with my questions on the National Bolshevik Party.

Caroline Dawnay, my London agent, sat patiently with me while I waded through the process of deciding to write this, and believed in it enough to take it to Yale University Press. I am equally grateful to Zoe Pagnamenta, who represents me in the US, who found me by reading a magazine piece I had written about Fallujah and showed impeccable judgement in signing me up. I'm incredibly grateful to both for their patience and great ideas. Robert Baldock of Yale University Press was patient and pushy in the appropriate measures, and thanks to him this project is where it is. Also thanks to Yale's Rachael Lonsdale, Lauren Atherton and Bill Frucht, as well as to Clive Liddiard, who edited the manuscript and turned an incoherent jumble of gobbledygook into something resembling a book.

A posthumous thanks to Vladimir Pribylovsky, a critic of the Kremlin and specialist in Russian nationalism who spent several hours helping me with the subject matter. As I write comes the news that he has been found dead in his Moscow flat. I hope his death will be investigated.

I owe an immense debt of gratitude to Katerina Shaverdova and Elena Kokorina of the *Financial Times* Moscow office, who frankly made possible the research that went into this, tracking down impossible-to-find phone numbers, helping me set up interviews and locating interesting articles.

Thanks ever so much to my *FT* colleagues Catherine Belton, Courtney Weaver and Neil Buckley, who made coming to work every day a joy and a laugh, and who taught me to be a better journalist.

And most of all, thanks to the love of my life, Rachel, without whom I would never have had all these wonderful adventures. She has read various versions of this book, has given me much constructive criticism – and has made me promise not to write another one 'too soon'. And thanks to our lovely daughter Jaya, my father, Frank, the best professor I ever had, and my late mother, Dorothy, who I wish could have seen this.

INTRODUCTION

Vladimir Putin's annual address to the federal assembly, delivered every year in the glittering St George's hall of the Kremlin, is a festival of crystal-chandeliered, live televised grandeur. Over 600 dignitaries fill the room in costumed finery: sleek designer suits, minority nationality headdresses, lacquered towers of hair, Chanel gowns, cassocks, turbans, shoulder boards, braids of all sorts, and absurdly tall peaked caps. Sitting awkwardly on small, white, hard-backed chairs, the assembled dignitaries know they are in for three hours of gruelling oratory.

As the president takes the stage, the applause from the audience is rapturous and sustained. Russia's handpicked elite fill the room, all of whom know that their careers, their incomes, their property and their futures depend on one man, and that this speech will contain vital clues about which way these considerations are tending. Civil servants hang on Putin's every word to see which programmes will be funded and which will not. Kremlinologists watch to see who is seated next to whom. Journalists hope Putin will say something threatening or off colour (which he often does), and this will become a Twitter hashtag within seconds. And in December 2012, everyone was watching to see if Putin, who had limped noticeably during a meeting with Israeli President Shimon Peres and who was rumoured to be in ill health, would make it through the speech.

He did, but almost no one was paying attention to the most important thing: a fleeting reference to an obscure Russianized Latin term, which was flung into the speech at about minute 5: 'I would like all of us to understand clearly that the coming years will be decisive,' said Putin, vaguely hinting, as he did very frequently, at some great, massive, future calamity. 'Who will take the lead and who will remain on the periphery and inevitably lose their independence will depend not only on the economic potential, but primarily on the will of each nation, on its inner energy which Lev Gumilev termed *passionar-nost*: the ability to move forward and to embrace change.'

Putin's passing mention of the late Russian historian Lev Gumilev and this odd word, *passionarnost*, meant very little to the uninitiated; but to those familiar with the conservative theories of nationalism that have made dramatic inroads into Russian politics since the end of the Cold War, it indicated a lot – a classic Kremlin signal, known in US politics as a 'dog whistle', used to commu-nicate to certain groups a message which only they could hear. It was a way of announcing in deniable terms what Putin probably could not say outright – that certain circles within the state enjoyed his understanding and support.

The word *passionarnost* is resistant to easy translation (passionarity? passionism?), but the few who knew its provenance took immediate notice. It was seven months after Putin's inauguration for a third term as Russia's presi-dent, and he was sending a subtle signal to the elite that new ideas had swept to power along with him. Ideas that might, just a few years previously, have been considered both marginal and even barking mad were suddenly the anchor of his most important speech of the year. And these ideas would make themselves clearer 15 months later, when Russian soldiers quietly seized airports and transport chokepoints across Crimea, starting a domino effect that would lead to war in eastern Ukraine. Instead of the polite, non-ideological civic patri-otism of the previous two decades, Putin was extolling chest-thumping nation-alism, the martial virtues of sacrifice, discipline, loyalty and valour.

Putin's definition of passionarity (from the Latin word *passio*) was a slightly sanitized one. 'Moving forward and embracing change' was one way of putting what Gumilev meant, though more accurate would be something akin to 'capacity for suffering'. It was a word, with dramatic allusions to the New Testament, that had been dreamt up by Gumilev during his 14 years in Siberian prison camps. In 1939, while digging the White Sea canal and daily watching fellow inmates die of exhaustion and hypothermia, Gumilev invented his theory of *passionarnost*. It was a theory of the irrational in human history. The capacity of single individuals to make a sacrifice for the greater good, and therefore change history, he would later write, was the defining trait of great nations.

During the decades following his internment, Gumilev's eminently spir-itual vision became profoundly pessimistic, and his idea became the germ of a new idea of Russian nationalism. As a historian, working from the late 1950s to the end of his life in 1992, Gumilev became a renowned expert on the steppe tribes of inner Eurasia: the Scythians, the Xiongnu, the Huns, Turks, Khitai, Tanguts and Mongols. Such history did not record the progress of enlightenment and reason, but rather an endless cycle of migration, conquest and genocide, and death, repeating itself through eternity. Every few hundred years, primitive nomads would sweep out of the steppes, plunder the flourishing kingdoms of Europe, the Mideast or Asia, and then vanish into history's fog just as quickly as they had come. The victors in such history were not the societies that led the world in technology, wealth and reason. Instead, they had passionarity. Gumilev's work is echoed in the works of other scholars through the ages describing much the same phenomenon: Machiavelli used the term *virtù* to describe martial spirit, while the medieval Arab philosopher Ibn Khaldun described the tribal solidarity of nomadic raiders and plunderers of civilized cities as *asabiya*.

Gumilev's obsession with the steppe tribes may have been a reflection of his own life, of 14 years spent in the Siberian gulag, witnessing at close quarters the latest incarnation of a savage, millennium-old process of life-taking and ruin amid the icy continental vastness. Observing his fellow inmates stripped of all their civilization and forced to behave as beasts to survive taught him that man is not the master of nature, but is subject to it. The human virtues of society, friendship and brotherhood, he would later write, are not a mark of human advancement, but a biological natural impulse, the instinctual urge, common to all humans at all times, to distinguish 'us' from 'them'.

A staunch anti-communist, Gumilev was nonetheless surprisingly embittered by the collapse of the USSR, which occurred six months before his own death in 1992. Like many of his fellow prisoners, he later became possessed by an odd patriotism – an inexplicable loyalty to the homeland (and even the regime) that had stolen his health, his years and his friends. It was a type of Stockholm syndrome which produced some singularly odd scholarship: paeans to Russia's imperial greatness, the organic character of the Russian Empire (and later the Soviet Union) as a singular super-ethnos, or civilization, whose many nations willingly joined Russia not as conquests, but as voluntary subjects of the tsar's imperial greatness. Gumilev even purported to be able to quantify the amount of physical passionarity remaining in Russia, a civilization which, he predicted, was in the middle of its 1,200 year lifespan.

His theories, which he called 'Eurasianism' were drawn from a literature which preceded him by several decades, having been invented by a group of White Russian exiles in Europe in the 1920s. The word, popularized by Gumilev, became a favoured slogan among ideologues of reaction – both dissident nationalists and Soviet hardliners, who were increasingly finding common cause. Amid the death throes of the USSR, Gumilev became an odd, flag-waving Soviet patriot and denigrator of democrats in several perestroika-era interviews which even his lifelong friend Emma Gerstein called 'dreadful'.

Despite having suffered so much at its hands, no person of higher social standing glorified the Soviet empire more in its dying days of the late 1980s. He had spent his career studying the irrational bonds that tie nations and peoples together – the irony was that he himself, a former gulag prisoner who fought tooth and nail in his last days to save his beloved USSR, was exhibit A.

Such displaced anger is the hallmark of all the authors chronicled in this book who suffered mightily at the hands of Soviet power, and yet worked tirelessly to build a new ideology of imperial domination for its successor, a new authoritarian superstate.

Putin's mention of *passionarnost* in 2012 was part of a pattern of lacing his speeches and writings with a new vocabulary. Following his announcement the previous year that he would run for a third term as president, Putin embarked on a new political trajectory – a strikingly consistent appeal to Orthodox Church values and Russian nationalism; strident criticism of liberalism and Western values; and projects for reintegration with former Soviet neighbours. In speeches, TV talk shows and newspaper articles, he began to use new terminology. Referring to the West, for example, he began to use the term 'Atlantic'; and when he spoke of Russia's broader identity he used the term 'Eurasia'. When he refers to Russians, he increasingly frequently uses the term *Russky* (meaning ethnic Russians), rather than *Rossiisky* (referring to a more civic and inclusive definition of the Russian nation state).[1] He also replaced the term 'nation state' (with its liberal connotations) with 'civilization state', as more appropriate to the historical sweep of the Russian people. Later, unmistakably militaristic words started to enter his lexicon – 'national traitor' and 'fifth column'. When he spoke of patriotism he began to appeal to 'passionarity'.

These words were drawn from a literature which, until recently, had been the preserve of fringe radical nationalists, and signalled to close observers of Russian politics that their arguments had taken hold. Many of these were drawn from Gumilev's own works or those of proponents of his theory of Eurasianism, both earlier and later. Now, they are increasingly accepted by a ruling elite that has historically been susceptible to the temptations of philosophical dogma.

For 15 years of rule by Vladimir Putin and his circle, the Kremlin has drifted towards this idea, aimed not at mass mobilization behind public slogans, but at consolidating an elite behind a set of understood (if unspoken) truths, deniably vague statements and opaque policies; it is the subject not of booming speeches but of whispered codes. Gumilev's *passionarnost* will be a major theme of this book. The heroism, sacrifice, valour and tragedy of his life – as for all the authors I write about in these pages – were instrumental in the production of a particularly fateful theory of nationalism, one that seems destined to reproduce the tragic circumstances that gave birth to it.

* * *

As scholarship, Gumilev's work was generally regarded by his academic peers as gripping, talented fiction, but they mostly let him be – 'on account of his tragic life', in the words of one. But what controversy there was only helped his popularity in the late days of the USSR, when challenging any orthodoxy was a sure route to popularity and scholarly fame.

This is also a book about why bad ideas win out over good ones, or at least better ones. Why ideas which no one took seriously a decade ago are suddenly being enunciated from the tribune of Kremlin power. Even hopelessly abstruse ideas, ideas that have been soundly disproven, renounced by their creators as demagoguery, labelled 'fairy tales' in authoritative journals, censored (even for the right reasons) and proven to be forgeries can change the world. This is a case study of how an idea written on paper sacks in the midst of the Soviet gulag archipelago can one day be pronounced as a national idea by the modern-day heirs of the NKVD.

Ideas – both good and bad – play an underappreciated role in political life, a point made by John Maynard Keynes as far back as 1936: 'The ideas of economists and political philosophers, both when they are right and when they are wrong, are more powerful than is commonly understood. Indeed the world is ruled by little else ... Madmen in authority, who hear voices in the air, are distilling their frenzy from some academic scribbler of a few years back. I am sure that the power of vested interests is vastly exaggerated compared with the gradual encroachment of ideas.'[2]

This perhaps applies nowhere more than in Russia, a country which has been brimming with – and heavily swayed by the vagaries of – philosophy over the past 200 years. 'You must conceive', wrote philosopher Isaiah Berlin of nineteenth-century Russia, 'of an astonishingly impressionable society with an unheard of capacity for absorbing ideas.'[3] In many works of Russian fiction, ideas are treated as things that assume corporeal form. The fanatical Stavrogin, the protagonist in Fedor Dostoevsky's *The Possessed*, is 'eaten by an idea', while many of the nineteenth century's most famous novels were fictional illustrations of the virtues of the commitment to philosophy, or how it can go badly wrong. Dostoevsky's own *Crime and Punishment* was a criticism of just such a commitment – a meditation on how theory produces monsters: the main character, Raskolnikov, kills an old woman simply to prove a theory to himself. 'It's as well that you only killed the old woman. If you'd invented another theory you might perhaps have done something a thousand times more hideous', Raskolnikov's friend tells him at the end of the novel. This black humour would tragically foreshadow Russia's twentieth-century fate.

Serious scholarship has lately been devoted to the proposition that ideas have real corporeal existence and should be treated in a similar way to diseases or parasites, spreading and infecting hosts. Neurobiologist Roger Sperry argues that ideas have the ability to push around physical matter; they have 'infectivity' and 'spreading power'. 'Ideas cause ideas and help evolve new ideas. They interact with each other and with other mental forces in the same brain, in neighboring brains, and thanks to global communication, in far distant, foreign brains.'[4]

British evolutionary biologist Richard Dawkins has put forward a similar theory of 'memes' – which he describes as simple units of cultural information whose primary characteristic is the ability to replicate and spread virally through their interaction with other memes through a version of natural selection. As Dawkins puts it: 'When you plant a fertile meme in my mind you literally parasitize my brain.'[5] Truth and proof are barely criteria in the competition among memes – indeed Dawkins invented the theory to explain the persistence of religion in the face of science. Far more important is what US comic Stephen Colbert might call 'truthiness': the inherent catchiness of ideas like 'belief in God' or 'war on terror', spread without very much conscious action or explanatory power, or even understanding of their meaning.

This is what seems to explain the success of one of the most powerful memes today: nationalism, which has reshaped the world since it captured the imagination of nineteenth-century Europe, starting the most destructive wars in history and ending another global conflict – the Cold War – without a shot being fired. Ernest Gellner, perhaps the most respected scholar of nationalism in the twentieth century, observed that 'wherever nationalism has taken root, it has tended to prevail with ease over other modern ideologies.'[6] His statement is interesting because it presumes that nationalism is an 'it' – a subject in itself. Nationalism is not equivalent to the sum total of nationalists – the individuals who profess it and carry nationalist slogans and banners; rather, it is a separate and total thing in itself which has sociological reality and objective existence. Nationalism wins out not because nationalists are better, or stronger, or more capable, but because nationalism itself appears to possess inherent characteristics that allow it to vanquish other memes in a fair fight.

In country after country, nationalism has hijacked political debate. It does this with a suddenness that astounds seasoned political observers and that has helped convince some experts that nationalism is a ruse, a manipulation, which is created solely as a way to achieve political ends. Indeed, nationalism is arguably only 200 years old, and its inherent newness is hard to reconcile with the claim that the nationalists make to oldness. Ironically, nationalism's success is due in large part to its being judged more basic, more fundamental, more instinctual and more genuine than competing modern philosophies, although it actually antedates most of them.

The fact is that creativity, imagination and even outright dishonesty have never been far from the pens of all nationalists who aim to shed light on the ancient and immutable, but who are almost always aware of the arbitrary and paradoxical nature of their quest – that they are discovering or recovering something that was never there to begin with. But to say that nationalism is a cynical manipulation used for political ends is misleading. Founding a nation is a fundamentally creative and even selfless act that becomes useful to the cynical exploiters of it only later, after it is fully formed. Nations are, as a rule, the creation of writers and poets, not of leaders and generals. Nations existed in books and poems long before politicians began to exploit nationalism to kill kings, tear down empires and build new ones.

It would be difficult to find any real cynicism in the 'scribblers' detailed in this book, all of whom, like Gumilev, suffered tremendously for their efforts. The personal histories of the authors profiled in this book show how ideas can hijack people, not the reverse. In addition there is another objection to regarding nationalism as only a manipulation, because if it were so, it would be fairly simple to manipulate out of existence. But it is not. Nations are wispy, flighty, arbitrary things until they, with astonishing rapidity, become hardened facts, incapable of retraction. They take on a permanence that is hard to explain. Where nationalism takes root, in other words, it stays.

Today, politicians may reach for nationalism in a moment of crisis, in an effort to distract attention, or to mobilize or consolidate power. Many find that in doing so they lose control of it, empowering radical forces best left undisturbed. From then on, nationalism is 'wagging the dog' – when it takes root, statesmen have to behave according to its logic. This book argues that something akin to that happened to nationalism in Russia last century: invented by 'passionaries' (to use Gumilev's term) who mostly suffered for their efforts, it spread virally in the USSR, despite all efforts by the Soviet authorities to stamp it out. While its proponents went to the gulag, into exile or worse, their views came to be adopted, or co-opted, by the regime: first under Stalin, in an effort to harness nationalism to win the Second World War, and then under Khrushchev, who co-opted nationalists as a counterbalance to hardline orthodox Stalinists; then the Stalinists and the nationalists joined forces in the 1970s under Brezhnev, in the era of 'politics by culture'.[7] Finally ascendant, nationalism tore the Soviet Union apart in 1991, and in 1993 it again was defeated by a hegemonic ideological competitor – Liberal Democracy – in the streets of Moscow amid the military confrontation between Yeltsin and the Supreme Soviet (as parliament was called). But once again nationalism leapt from the vanquished to the victors, infiltrating the Yeltsin regime until it came to power under Putin. Now it has surged into Georgia, eastern and southern Ukraine and threatens other conquests in the service of Russia as 'Eurasia'. While nationalists were repressed and defeated at every turn, nationalism emerged victorious.

That nationalism is ubiquitous in modern societies is beyond question. But there is no rule as to how it manifests itself, no law to predict which of any number of competing nationalisms will settle in a given country. There are roughly 8,000 unique languages in the world, and roughly 200 countries. Add to this maybe an equal number of irredentist nationalist movements which have not yet achieved their dream of statehood, and it is clear that only a very few nations so conceived ever become political movements. This is the phenomenon referred to by Gellner as nations that 'failed to bark'; he was trying to explain how some nations get chosen for either historical greatness or for martyrdom, and why some get ignored. It is a problem to which no one has yet found a consistent formula. This speaks to the inherently creative and contingent way in which nationalism appears.

Further to this argument there is the opposite problem – the thoroughly fictitious nations which did 'bark': in other words, political movements expressing the shared desire for a common statehood of peoples who do not share a nation in any sense, who have virtually nothing in common and who are likely unaware of what is being pursued in their name. One of these is Eurasianism, the subject of this book. It is an audacious attempt to stitch together a unitary political entity out of a mythical steppe tribe ancestry and a great profusion of linguistic, cultural and anthropological data.

As serious scholarship, Eurasianists' scholarly arguments are barely credible and are best understood as a sort of metaphor. One useful comparison for Eurasianism is Serbian novelist Milorad Pavić's *Dictionary of the Khazars*, a surreal hypertext published in 1984 and devoted to a fictional account of the eponymous Central Asian tribe, which disappeared in the ninth century. Pavić, a Serbian nationalist, had actually written an allegory about Serbian nationalism: the Khazars were the Serbs, a lost tribe on the frontiers of Europe, maligned and misunderstood, with a foot in both the West and the East, the victims of acute cultural schizophrenia. In the same way, the Eurasianist ideas described in these pages is best understood not as real ethnographic or political theories, but as ciphers for a lost Russia, which most likely never existed; a metaphor for a national tragedy; and the precursor to a long, agonizing and bloody reckoning with the same demons as their Serbian cousins.

* * *

It is somehow appropriate that 'Eurasianism' – the version of Russian nationalism which concerns us – was originally an apocalyptic vision, authored by the survivors of the most violent half-decade ever recorded at the time. Eurasianism should be viewed in the context of the other ideological innovations of the interwar period in Europe, most of which turned out to be very bad: at no other time in history have ideas more violently altered or ended the lives of more people on earth than in the 1920s and 1930s.

Following the Bolshevik revolution and in the wake of the Russian Civil War, which had made them exiles, a group of two dozen Russian scholars – historians, linguists, composers, writers and even a priest – gathered in the capitals of Europe. They had seen Europe, the home of the Enlightenment and the envy of their generation, consumed by trenches and gas and slaughter on an industrial scale. The arrival of advanced European social theories in their relatively backward country brought further slaughter and the largest human refugee crisis in history. Their pet theory was born out of a collective questioning of the very value of civilization and progress. Paradoxically, this group found hope in all the carnage, seeing in the Bolshevik revolution something uniquely Russian.

'Russia in sin and godlessness, Russia in loathsomeness and filth. But Russia in search and struggle, in a bid for a city not of this world', wrote Petr Savitsky, one of the four original founders of the movement, in the group's founding document entitled *Exodus to the East*.[8] It was, in fact, trauma disguised as serious scholarly work and symbolized the soul-searching of the 1920s. They argued that their native Russia, rather than being a branch of the rationalistic West, was the descendant of the Mongol Horde – a legacy that the Bolshevik revolution, with all its savagery, seemed to confirm. They saw in the revolution some promise of a future – a shedding of slavish Western conformity and the rebirth of authentic Russianness, a Biblical event, a cataclysm that brings earthly beatitude.

The melding of the Bolshevik revolution with religious themes is something that was common to many intellectuals of the time. Many of them seemed to suffer from a version of Stockholm syndrome: identifying with the goals of the Bolshevik revolution, while being its awestruck victims. The greatest poem of the era, 'The Twelve', written in 1918 by Alexander Blok, reflects this urge to suffuse communism with Christianity. In the poem, 12 Red Guards patrolling Petrograd through the 'Black night, white snow' see a ghostly figure ahead of them:

soft-footed where the blizzard swirls,
invulnerable where bullets crossed –
crowned with a crown of
snowflake pearls,
a flowery diadem of frost,
ahead of them goes Jesus Christ.

The Eurasianists' ideas were not serious scientific theories but rather (like the poem) an analogy – an aesthetic attempt to reconcile Red Russia and White Russia. They saw in communism a transient version of Christianity which, when united with the Orthodox faith, leading the Red Guards through the snow, would be fit to govern a vast empire.

Top-heavy with cerebral energy, the group pronounced the discovery of an ancient continental Atlantis, submerged in the collective unconscious of the population of Inner Asia, a unique Eurasian civilization destined to be unitary, which has emerged in various incarnations as the Scythians, Huns, Turks and Mongols. The Russian Empire and its successor, the Soviet Union, had become the most recent expression of this timeless unity, the new organic host of the inner continent's steppeland and forests.

The theory they authored saw Russia as a natural 'ideocracy', destined to be governed by a party very much like the communist one – once communism collapsed under the weight of its own contradictions. The boundaries of the Russian Empire and the Soviet Union were the natural demarcations of a political unit destined to be whole. As Nikolay Trubetskoy, the movement's main intellectual, wrote in 1925: 'By its very nature, Eurasia is historically destined to be a single state entity.'[9]

Eurasianism was but a sideline to the group's serious academic work – the place where they 'poured' their dark side, a repository for their bitterness. It was more therapy than serious scholarship, and Trubetskoy was to come to regard his own political works not only as fakery, but as quite harmful fakery; he viewed Stalin's rule as the epitome of the political manifestos the group had been writing for a decade: 'our predictions, hitting the mark, turn out to be nightmares', he told a friend, eventually renouncing his own views.

* * *

Gumilev, whom we met at the beginning of the introduction, is the writer most often identified with the emergence of Eurasianism. He was a successor to the first wave, to which he looked for inspiration. He wrote 14 histories of Russia and the steppe nomads which accentuated the interrelations between the two groups and de-emphasized Russia's links to European culture. Indeed, the Mongols were presented in a positive light as frequent Russian allies, while the West European nationalities were portrayed as devious and wicked despoilers of Russia.

Gumilev himself was frank with his colleagues about the shortcomings of his history – much of which was written while he was in prison and had no access to books or sources. 'Thus I was forced to rely on my imagination and come to my own conclusions using, shall we say, my own logic', he told his fellow Eurasianist Petr Savitsky in a letter.[10] In his books, the steppe tribes appear more as historical allegory than as serious scholarship. The Xiongnu, the Huns, the Turks, the Mongols – all subjects of Gumilev's early histories – are isolated, perpetually maligned, backward societies historically prone to tragic, dramatic cycles of glory and ruin. In this, it appears, they serve mainly as metaphors for Gumilev's native Russia.

The son of two of the most famous poets of the twentieth century, Anna Akhmatova and Nikolay Gumilev, Lev was one of the most famous public intellectuals in the USSR during the perestroika era. Having created a theory of *passionarnost*, his own life became a case study. His theories were readily received in a country that was suspicious of any orthodoxy and that saw his suffering as a sign of authenticity. His celebrity status launched Eurasianism into Russia's post-Soviet mainstream culture, with the idea that Russia is not a nation but a civilization that has inherited the mantle of the Russian Empire and the Soviet Union, both of which were just transient permutations of some mystical unity that has possessed the inner continent since deep antiquity. As the Soviet hammer and sickle was lowered from the Kremlin mast for the last time in 1991, his theories were co-opted by elements of the old regime looking for a synthesis of internationalism with nationalism that would allow them to continue to rule as before, as the embodiment of the Eurasian empire he loved so neurotically towards the end of his life.

The old-style hardliners were swept away in the failed coup of August 1991. With them went any chance of 'Red Nationalism' directly succeeding communism. Instead, it was kept alive in basements and on cranky pamphlets by the efforts of a third man, Alexander Dugin, a former dissident, pamphleteer, hipster and guitar-playing poet, who emerged from the libertine era of pre-perestroika Muscovite bohemia to become a rabble-rousing intellectual, a lecturer at the military academy, and ultimately a Kremlin operative. His former associate Eduard Limonov playfully calls Dugin the 'St Cyril and Methodius of Fascism' for his importation of European extreme-right ideas into Russia, while in an interview with me Kremlin spin doctor Gleb Pavlovsky acidly poked fun at Dugin's influence over the so-called *siloviki* – the security men who came to power with Putin: 'He made a huge impression on people who never read any books.'

Throughout his career as a propagandist, ghostwriter, journalist and professional provocateur, Dugin has had a near monopoly on the production of the symbols, theories and pamphlets of a new hardline nationalism, which started in the dingy basements and cafés of perestroika Moscow. While Dugin himself never made the leap to big politics, his ideas did – for better or worse. Dugin's best-known book, *The Foundations of Geopolitics*, written at the nadir of Russia's post-Soviet slump in 1997, was a primer on world domination. It was eagerly received in a country for which that seemed such a distant goal. Running through the book is the idea that the Cold War was not a clash between communism and capitalism, but was rather a permanent conflict between two geographical realities – the world's greatest land power of 'Eurasia' and its natural opponent of 'Atlantic' sea power, represented first by Britain and then by the United States. As such, hidden from sight of all but the initiated, lies the fundamental esoteric truth of the post-Cold War era: the United States' most dangerous opponent is not radical Islam, nor China, nor an amorphous asymmetric failed state, nor a cyber virus. It was, is and will remain Russia, the impregnable bastion of land power, the Eurasian heartland. And unbeknownst to even its own population, the United States is working right now to destroy its foe.

The theory of geopolitics held that there were no rules for statecraft other than an age-old drive for conquest. Anything else – slogans like 'universal human rights' or 'democracy' – was mere window-dressing and propaganda. The reality was competition, warfare, alliances, buffer states, red lines, spheres of influence and empires. The message of *Foundations* was seductive for Russia's *siloviki* – the generals, security men, centurion guardians of the state – who had been consigned to irrelevance at the end of the Cold War by pronouncements about the 'end of history'. They wanted to be told that the fundamental reality of the world had not changed: nations still needed armies, spies, security services, strategic alliances and large defence budgets. In the same way as Machiavelli had electrified sixteenth-century Florence with his candid how-to guide to acquiring and keeping political power, *Foundations* had an aura of hidden wisdom which the ruling cabal of global plutocrats preferred to keep out of public reach. A more politically correct version of the tsarist-era *Protocols of the Elders of Zion*, it located the global conspiracy of chaos not in a Prague cemetery, but in the corridors of 'Atlanticism' in Washington and London.

Dugin's personal influence is widely dismissed in Russia, but there is good reason to pay him close attention: his dystopian vision oddly foreshadows major developments in a way that seems to demand explanation.

In 2009, in a nationalist prank, Dugin drew a map of a dismembered Ukraine, which included the fateful words 'Novorossiya' to signify the eastern provinces, which would ultimately break away after an armed uprising by Russian-backed separatists in 2014. His use of the tsarist-era term prefigured by five years Putin's use of the same label. In a YouTube video from that year, he gives an elaborate account of the breakup of Ukraine, predicting that 'these elections [the 2010 presidential elections] will be Ukraine's last as a unitary state'.[11] Dugin has been scarily, spookily right about the Ukraine conflict since it started. He was the first of the nationalist crowd to use the term 'Novorossiya' to reference eastern Ukraine in an interview on 3 March 2014, long before the occupation of Donetsk and Lugansk was launched,[12] and one and a half months before Putin used the same term in a call-in show. He predicted that militias in Donestk and Lugansk would declare independence weeks before they did. He correctly predicted the design of the flag of the Donetsk Republic – red with a blue St Andrew's cross – two months before a contest was held to decide it. He also predicted that Russia would introduce ground troops on a large scale, which it did in late August.

In more than ten years of acquaintance with Dugin, I have no reason to doubt his insistence that he has no direct connection to Putin – I have found none, though several of Putin's immediate circle footnote him, quote him and fund his projects. Rather than Cardinal Richelieu, the hidden hand on the tiller of state, Dugin seems more like a character in an Umberto Eco novel – a conspiracy theorist and pamphleteer who is just as surprised as everyone else when his creations leap off the page and into real life. 'It is not as though I am the adviser to Putin, that I am dictating to him and Putin is under the influence of these ideas', he explained in an interview on YouTube in July 2014.[13] 'We are simply acting according to the logic of Russian history and the laws of geopolitics', Dugin told the interviewer. 'That is, Putin and me, and Washington and Berlin are all being acted on by laws of history, laws of politics, and to some extent laws of elite behaviour.'

Dugin is, in equal parts, a monomaniacal nineteenth-century Slavophile conservative and a smug twenty-first-century postmodernist who expertly deconstructs his arguments as rapidly as he makes them. He can give impassioned speeches about Holy Russia and then, in an unguarded moment, joke about it or parody himself. 'There are only two real things in Russia', he once told me during a long conversation. 'Oil sales and theft. The rest of it is all a kind of theatre.' 'Is he serious or is he not? That is the whole postmodern question', pondered Andrey Karagodin, one of Dugin's former acolytes and now editor of the Russian edition of *Vogue*, over coffee in Moscow. 'The answer is both.'

Indeed, given the enthusiasm of Russian intellectuals for adopting and co-opting the latest intellectual fads from Europe (such as Hegel and Marx), it is all but predictable that the Russian elite would become carried away by a new philosophy wafting out of late-twentieth-century Europe, the essence of which is the denial of all philosophy. In the hyperreality that is Russian politics, where a parallel universe is amplified to deafening volume via state TV and talking heads like Dugin, all ideology is indeed mere language games or camouflaged power relations; all politics is simulacrum and spectacle; all 'discourses' are equal, as is all truth. Critical theory, postmodernism and post-structuralism, philosophies designed to criticize power, have been co-opted by the Kremlin's formidable 'political technology' machine and converted into an instrument of authoritarian rule. When John Kerry accused Putin of 'nineteenth-century thinking' following the Crimean invasion, he may have been missing the point. The Ukraine crisis owes more to the twenty-first-century simulacrum of Russia's state media bubble, than it does to sober assessment by nineteenth-century statesmen like Bismarck and Disraeli.

Dugin has been one of the pioneers of the postmodern revolution in Russian politics, an early adopter of the arch, ironic pose assumed by many in the Kremlin today. Many smile or wink when they use terminology like 'Eurasia' or 'Atlanticist', but they use them nonetheless. They may claim that there are no Russian soldiers in eastern Ukraine, but they regard this not as a crude propaganda lie, but rather a postmodern *geste*, made with the same self-congratulatory smugness as Jean Baudrillard's playful claim that 'the Gulf War did not take place'.

* * *

Today, unlike in the twentieth century, no state can afford publicly to espouse any system other than democracy, ethnic tolerance, self-determination, free trade and universal human rights – even if its rulers do not practise what they preach. Speaking openly of conquest and the subjugation of a neighbouring country is simply no longer acceptable in public. Wars are waged in the name of liberating and protecting, in the name of principles and values, not in the name of wanting someone else's land. That is why governments speak of these things in an assortment of 'dog whistles', shibboleths and codes. Many governments and political parties throughout the world have evolved a secret rhetoric for speaking about the unspeakable: 'war on terror' or 'the Chinese dream'. Russia is no different.

'Eurasia' serves a key function in Kremlin rhetoric as an extravagant *double entendre*. On 4 October 2011, a week after Putin announced that he would be running for the presidency for a third term, following four years as prime minister, readers of the *Izvestiya* newspaper found a full-page article by their former and future president describing his vision for a 'Eurasian Union' of old Soviet states to be in place by 2015. Putin insisted that the union was 'not like other previous unions' and was simply a trade organization analogous to the EU. Most were sceptical, particularly US Secretary of State Hillary Clinton, who raised squeals of indignation in Moscow when she accused the Kremlin of 'a move to re-Sovietize the region'. 'It's not going to be called that,' said Clinton. 'It's going to be called a customs union, it will be called Eurasian Union and all of that. But make no mistake, we know what the goal is and we are trying to figure out effective ways to slow down or prevent it.'[14] The Kremlin responded that Clinton had 'fundamentally misunderstood' Putin's vision – but this is how dog-whistle politics works: the leader keeps a deniable distance, while the initiates, cloistered away from the profane masses, interpret his esoteric meanings.

Another dog whistle was blown in a 23 January 2012 article, authored by Putin, in the newspaper *Nezavisimaya Gazeta*. In it, Putin referred to Russia using a new dog-whistle term, 'civilization state':

> The Great Russian mission is to unite, bind civilization. In this type of state-civilization there are no national minorities, and the principle of recognition of 'friend or foe' is defined as a common culture and shared values . . . This civilizational identity is based on the preservation of the Russian cultural dominance, the carriers of which are not only ethnic Russian, but all carriers of such identity regardless of nationality.

In other words, as long as you are 'culturally' Russian, you are friend. Others, it turns out, may not be. Putin added that the concept of 'nation state', burdened as it was with connotations of liberalism, should be eliminated from official vocabulary as inadequate for the Russian people: 'I am deeply convinced that the attempts to preach the idea of constructing a Russian "national" monoethnic state directly contradict our thousand-year history.'[15]

In September 2013, Putin again referred to Russia as a 'civilization state' in an address to the Valdai forum of journalists and Russia experts. He made his most specific comments yet about his vision for Eurasian integration: 'The twenty-first century promises to be the century of great change, the era of the formation of major continents of geopolitical, financial, economic, cultural, civilizational, political and military power. And because of this, our absolute priority is the tight integration with our neighbours.'[16] He described his proposed Eurasian Union not in strictly trade and economic terms (as he had in the past), but as 'a project for the preservation of identity of peoples, of historical Eurasia in the new century and a new world . . . Eurasian integration is a chance for the Former Soviet Union to become an independent centre of global development, rather than the periphery of Europe or Asia.' Putin's words appeared to indicate the true ambitions for 'Eurasia': that the future belonged to 'major continents of geopolitical, financial, economic, cultural, civilizational, political and military power.' In the coming century, in order to matter, you have to be big. In this context, it is significant that the Russian elite has chosen to talk about the idea of a 'civilization state' amid profound

disappointment with the post-Soviet 'nation state' era. And it is equally significant that (like Putin) the way they have chosen to talk about it is through
Eurasianism.

* * *

Putin's ambitions for 'Eurasia' – and, to be fair, the West's ambitions to thwart
him – directly provoked the war in Ukraine. Partly, it seems, in an effort to
complicate any plans for a 'Eurasian Union', the EU offered states of the former
Soviet Union association agreements in 2013. Due to concerns that these would
undermine Putin's plans, the Kremlin put immense pressure on heads of state
– such as Ukrainian President Yanukovich – to back out of the EU agreement
(which Yanukovich did). The Ukrainian president's fateful decision ignited the
'Euromaidan' protests in Kiev, aimed at toppling the Russia-centric government.
Following a brutal massacre of protesters by Ukrainian security forces in late
February, Yanukovich fled, leaving a constitutional vacuum for several days.
Russia exploited this by deploying troops from its Black Sea naval base in
Sevastopol, quietly seizing roads and chokepoints. Some months later, Russian
irregulars and mercenaries fanned out across eastern Ukraine – the Russian-
speaking heartland of Donetsk and Lugansk.

Russia has drawn a red line around its former imperial subjects – a sphere
of influence that delineates those countries that will not be allowed into
the Western orbit and those that Russia will grudgingly part with. It is interesting to examine this line and see where it passes: it appears to have bypassed
the Baltic states, which are immensely strategic, possessing large Russian populations that could be 'defended' from fascists and with Second World War
histories that leave them vulnerable to the Russian propaganda machine. These
could just as easily have been stirred up using the same technology that went
to work in Ukraine.

Yet the Baltic states were let into NATO in 2004. Meanwhile the Kremlin
chose to fight in 2008 to defend Abkhazia and South Ossetia, which are also
not inside its borders, after Georgia signed a membership action plan with
NATO (and attacked South Ossetia, giving Russia a clear casus belli). That
the Kremlin is driven to defend territories that are not in all cases Russian, but
does not 'defend' Russians in other states, is indicative: there are certain parts
of the former Russian Empire that are seen as 'ours' and certain parts that
are not. This dividing line appears to follow a strategic and cultural logic
strikingly in tune with the theories of the Eurasianists who drew cultural frontiers across Eastern Europe, approximately where the Kremlin seems to have
done the same.

Other attempts to discern logic in the Kremlin's recent behaviour tend to fall into two camps, both of which deny that Putin is following any sort of ideological or strategic doctrine. First the 'realist' camp, which sees Putin acting in accordance with a naked concept of Russia's interests, and which regards the invasion of eastern Ukraine as a clever gambit in the face of Western weakness (or else as the least bad option in the face of Western provocation). The second camp argues that rather than a rational and calculating chess master, Putin is an emotional, rash, short-term crisis manager who panders to Soviet nostalgia and is interested in accomplishing mainly internal political goals: keeping his reputation and propping up sagging approval ratings. It contends that there is nothing as coherent as a strategy.

Neither of these approaches tackles what Putin is hoping to achieve or credits the Kremlin with a strategy. The realists tend to be vague on the question of what Russia's interests actually are (aside from being whatever the Kremlin happens to be doing that particular day), making their observations hard to falsify, but also not very useful. They also fail to explain the sea-change that has occurred in Russian politics – formerly, the Kremlin trod lightly in the so-called 'near abroad', for fear of the economic consequences. But suddenly, a foothold in Ukraine is worth a plunging rouble and billions in sanctions-hit revenues.

The opposite point of view – which portrays Putin as a stopgap catastrophe delimiter, subsumed by knee-jerk imperial nostalgia – gives short shrift to the evident calculation that went into the conquest of Crimea. It was undertaken in the short space of the 48 hours when Ukraine was in the grip of a constitutional vacuum following the exit of President Yanukovich, itself provoked by the desertion – for reasons still not very convincingly explained – of his body-guards. It also does not explain the evident care that the Kremlin has taken in choosing which battles to fight and which not to – clearly 'Soviet' nostalgia is not the issue, because Russia has parted with some bits of the Soviet Union with relative equanimity. Russia has put a great deal of thought and calculation into its moves in the near abroad, moving with lightning speed in the case of both Crimea and South Ossetia and taking advantage of (or perhaps creating) once-in-a-lifetime windows of opportunity for conquest.

Looking at Russia's recent behaviour through the lens of Eurasianism – the goal of protecting Russia's civilizational identity – makes a lot of the current behaviour snap into focus and gives a consistent explanation as to which battles the Kremlin has chosen to fight, which ones it has chosen not to, and how it has fought them. Never mind that the whole idea of a civilizational identity is tendentious at best and totally contrived at worst. The most important aspect of Eurasianism is not its merits, but the consensus that it appears to enjoy across the Russian elite.

* * *

Speaking by phone with US President Barack Obama in the wake of Russia's invasion of Crimea, German Chancellor Angela Merkel reported that Vladimir Putin, with whom she had just come off the phone, was 'in another world'. The following day, Putin appeared on Russian television to rant about CIA subversion. 'They're sitting around a puddle in the US and playing with Ukraine like rats', he said. He went on to offer contradictory theories about the overthrow of President Vladimir Yanukovich and to deny that Russian soldiers had even occupied Crimea: 'You can buy those uniforms everywhere'. Any doubts about what was going on in Putin's head, however, were put to rest a year later when, in a documentary broadcast on 16 March 2015, the first anniversary of the Crimea occupation, he let on that he had known all along that the uniformed and balaclava-clad occupiers had been Russian troops, who had fanned out across Crimea on his orders.

No one, of course, was particularly shocked by the revelation. Putin is certainly not the first head of state to lie publicly about a military adventure. But his urge to come clean is curious and has few precedents. So is the public reaction: between 15 March and 22 March 2015 (i.e. the week in which Putin's comments were aired), polling by the Moscow-based Public Opinion Foundation showed that the number of Russians who said they had come to trust Putin more in the past month increased from 42 per cent to 44 per cent.[17]

It is certainly not obvious why it actually buttresses Putin's credibility to boast about lying, except in the hyperreal simulacrum of Russian politics: to borrow a term from Hegel, many Russians now live in a *verkehrte Welt*, an 'upside-down world', where black is white and up is down. In this world, Ukrainian fighter planes shot down Malaysian airliner MH17 over Donetsk, Russian soldiers are 'on vacation' in eastern Ukraine, and Kiev is in the grip of a fascist pro-NATO junta.

Putin has correctly surmised that lies unite rather than divide Russia's political class. The greater and more obvious the lie, the more his subjects demonstrate their loyalty by accepting it, and the more they participate in the great sacral mystery of Kremlin power by believing it.

Hannah Arendt, in her peerless study *The Origins of Totalitarianism*, explained the power of the lie, especially the obvious lie, in authoritarian regimes:

> One could make people believe the most fantastic statements one day, and trust that if the next day they were given irrefutable proof of their falsehood, they would take refuge in cynicism; instead of deserting the leaders who had lied to them, they would protest that they had known all along that the

statement was a lie and would admire the leaders for their superior tactical cleverness.

In this environment – where lies are accepted enthusiastically precisely because they are lies – it is easy to see how the largely discredited theory of Eurasianism could become a central ideological theme, not to mention a strategic doctrine enjoying broad authority among the political elite. In this way, loyalty to a man and a regime has now become supplemented by loyalty to an idea and a set of texts that possibly no one actually believes – not even the authors.

In a remarkable book, *Towards a Science of Belief Systems*, Oxford professor Edmund Griffiths includes a chapter on 'beliefs that are not meant to be wholly believed'; these include the category of 'alternative histories', such as Atlantis, UFOs or 9/11 'Truthers'. These movements, Griffiths argues, are more about punching a hole in establishment consensus than about creating new knowledge. As he puts it:

> The specific proposition A is thus supposed to be believed, but not wholly believed: its function is to dynamite the existing consensus, rather than to become the cornerstone of a new consensus that could, in its turn, come to be felt as monolithic and oppressive.[18]

Likewise, Eurasianism's success comes not from winning intellectual arguments but from poking holes in official epistemology, simply by sowing doubt. With some exceptions, few of the works I cite in this book are worth much in scholarly terms. Some are downright fiction; others are disowned by their authors soon after publication. All possess the telltale signs of a native Russian intellectual culture, in which the primary aim is to shock and self-publicize.

Unless one includes the original Eurasianists' works on linguistic structuralism in the canon of the movement, there is nothing that has survived serious scholarly scrutiny. The first works on Russia's Mongol inheritance were renounced by the author, Nikolay Trubetskoy, even before publication. Gumilev's works were popular and fabulously interesting, but hardly withstood peer review. Dugin's esoteric geopolitics is similarly an intriguing intellectual journey, but more so for its literary qualities (evoking the fictional Eurasia of George Orwell's *Nineteen Eighty-Four*) than for any recognizable objective reality.

Eurasia's appeal stems not from its accuracy or its explanatory power or its rigour (none of which it has), but from the way in which it exorcizes demons, heals psychic wounds and papers over ruptures in Russia's crude and disjointed history. Arendt wrote much about how conspiracies and totalizing theories are often preferable to empirical reality, because they offer order, predictability and an explanation for misfortune.

Eurasia was therapy for three generations of men who were buffeted by wars and repressions, and who wanted to find some sense in their suffering, in the brutal caprice of history as it unfolded underneath them. The first generation of writers sought to explain the *deus ex machina* of the Bolshevik revolution, which disenfranchised them and made them exiles; the second sought to deal with the awful Stalinist reality of the gulag archipelago; and the third faced the challenge of how to rationalize the very surreal collapse of the Soviet Union and the crushing decade of misery brought on by economic and political reform gone wrong. Over the course of a very dramatic century of Russian history, these scribblers dreamt – in exile, in labour camps or in their dissidents' basements – of a new utopian idea, which put the words in the mouths of a new generation of Kremlin autocrats.

This is a case study in how a fanciful and overly romantic idea, generated from nostalgia and bitterness, travelled from the pen of some cash-strapped academic in 1920s Prague, to a convict writing on paper sacks in a 1950s Siberian prison, to a filthy squat in the Yeltsin era of the 1990s, only to wind up a few short years later as a sort of half-baked and misunderstood Russian national idea, written into national speeches and official policy documents. Throughout the narrative, these stories intersect with the omnipresence of Russia's secret police, the OGPU, the NKVD, the KGB and their successor agencies of today. Those organizations joined the narrative as provocateurs, infiltrators, tormentors, killers, later as sponsors, and today apparently as consumers and clients of the writings of this group of thinkers.

Eurasianism threatens to become a new totalitarian idea that has come into the world largely due to the efforts of the victims of totalitarianism, who longed to see meaning in their misery. They thus created a theory which better answered the demands of the human mind, which longs for order, laws, consistency and meaning – demands that are at their most acute when reality is at its most random, capricious, wanton and cruel. That theory has been reached for in a moment of crisis by the Kremlin, which suffers from the same paranoia of persecution and trauma of loss as did its authors.

But for all that is wrong with the Eurasianists' scholarship, they were ultimately right. They predicted that communism would collapse, that the Russian Empire would be torn apart by ethnic nationalism, and that, on the verge of crisis, their ideas would come to power. This book will attempt to explain the parallel universe of Putin and his regime, how it was created, and by whom. Putin may indeed be living in another world, but one day in the not too distant future, we may all be living there, too.

PART I

CHAPTER ONE

THE MOST BORING ADVENTURE EVER

Over 100 boats were in the harbour of Sevastopol, on the southern tip of Crimea, on the morning of 14 November 1920, when Prince Nikolay Trubetskoy, a young professor of linguistics from one of the most aristocratic families in Russia, his wife Vera Petrovna, and their two-year-old daughter Elena, clambered aboard the US naval ship *Whipple*, which, along with the flotilla, had been sent to evacuate some of the thousands of White Russian refugees to Turkey. The previous week, the southern flank of the White forces, commanded by General Petr Wrangel, had collapsed and the Red Army was surging towards their final redoubt on the southern tip of the Crimea.

Trubetskoy and his family had been forced to flee with little more than a suitcase in October 1917, when they were surprised by the Bolshevik revolution while on vacation in the north Caucasus. Penniless and unable to return to Moscow, the prince and his family had wandered the war-scarred landscape of southern Russia through three years of civil war, through starving countryside and typhoid-ravaged cities, always just one step ahead of the Red Army. They had huddled in Crimea, and presumably the exalted Trubetskoy name had secured them three scarce places on the final allied boatlift across the Black Sea to Constantinople.

Sevastopol presented a grim picture: thousands of soldiers and refugees huddled under black coats and blankets, begging for passage; but most were left to their fate. Taking on passengers to the very last minute, the *Whipple* set sail for Turkey just as the Bolshevik forces broke into the town square and started firing at the retreating White Russians. It had been a very narrow escape for the Trubetskoys, the end of a harrowing three years; and according to Prince Trubetskoy, it had all been so desperately *boring*. As he wrote to his friend Roman Jakobson the following month, in his first letter after the ordeal:

'After the past few years spending a very stimulating life in Moscow, I was first in Kislovodsk, in the most remote provinces, and later in Rostov ... there was not a trace of intellectual life and not a soul with whom one could have discussed anything.'[1]

Jakobson and Trubetskoy had known each other since 1914, when they were both students of linguistics at Moscow University. Their destinies divided in 1917: while Trubetskoy fled south, Jakobson had stayed in Moscow during the revolution. He even briefly joined the Bolsheviks, for whom he worked as a propagandist. Then he found employment at a heating plant. In July 1920 he had made his way to Prague as the official translator of a Soviet diplomatic delegation, which he promptly left in order to join the university and complete his PhD.

Finding one another had been a stroke of good fortune for both: the two men were each looking for something from the past to anchor them amid the uncertainty of their flotsam-and-jetsam lives. Jakobson, a fellow exile, was in Prague, while Trubetskoy had made his way to Sofia, Bulgaria, where he found work at the local university. Before the revolution, the two men had belonged to an exalted group of young intellectuals known as the Moscow Linguistic Circle, which had pioneered modern-day literary criticism. So captivated were the pair by the theory of signs, the history of languages, and the difference between writing poetry and writing *about* it, that they would often tramp the lamp-lit streets of pre-revolutionary Moscow till dawn, finishing their discussion only when the sun came up.

Trubetskoy's letter was characteristic of the seriousness with which both men took their intellectual pursuits. Few people were so committed to scholarly life that surviving the Russian Civil War would seem like a waste of time. But this obsession with the cerebral was, in fact, fairly typical of many generations of upper-class Russians like Trubetskoy and Jakobson, who viewed philosophy and scholarly theories not as interesting conversation topics, but as total programmes for life and action. It would take the Bolshevik revolution – the ultimate application of theory to human beings – to reveal the terrifying consequences of this otherwise eccentric cultural foible.

We see this obsession with ideas borne out in the letters exchanged between Jakobson and Trubetskoy. Sure enough, having not seen his friend for three years, roughly a quarter of Trubetskoy's five-page initial letter was devoted to greetings, mutual acquaintances, and a fairly blasé account of his terrifying three-year ordeal. The other three-quarters were devoted to setting out his controversial but penetrating thoughts on linguistic theory. The spirit of scientific endeavour, it seems, had not deserted the prince, even when he contracted typhoid in Baku or had to escape Rostov under bombardment from the Red forces. The most stressful part of the whole ordeal, he told Jakobson, was that in fleeing that city he had been forced to abandon the notes for a new book he was working on (never published), titled *Prehistory of Slavic Languages*. He feared they were lost forever.

But all was not lost, wrote Trubetskoy. He had managed to reconstruct most of his models from memory and was working on them at that very moment. He would tell Jakobson more in the next letter. But come to think of it, the prince continued, he was keen to share with Jakobson a matter of extreme sensitivity: 'I was forced to split quite decisively with the dogma of the Moscow school. I was forced to break with other dogmas as well.'[2] He was concerned that the *Prehistory* was so revolutionary, so provocative, that once it was finished it may not be received too enthusiastically by their colleagues back in the philology department of Moscow University. The arguments he was making would be controversial, he knew. Scandalous, even. 'If my work is ever printed, it will, quite truly, provoke the bitterest attacks', Trubetskoy confided to Jakobson.

In fact, five years earlier, Trubetskoy's concern would not have been misplaced. The *Prehistory* was a direct broadside aimed at Alexey Shakhmatov, one of the most eminent philologists and historians at Moscow University and leader of the so-called 'Moscow School' (though he taught in St Petersburg). His 1915 work *Outline of the Oldest Period in the History of the Russian Language*[3] had sought to elaborately reconstruct the development of Russian and Slavic languages from their ancient roots. The upstart Trubetskoy, barely 30 years old, was calling the sage's methods into question.

But things in their homeland had changed a lot. In the winter of 1920, the *Prehistory of Slavic Languages* was probably about the furthest thing from any Muscovite's mind, philology department or no. Red Guards roamed the streets with orders to shoot dissenters on sight. Food and fuel were scarce, and famine cast a long shadow over the land. As it turns out, fate would forever cheat Trubetskoy of his longed-for duel with the Moscow School. Jakobson's very next letter to Trubetskoy contained the bad news that Shakhmatov was dead and many of the other members of the Moscow School who would certainly have bayed for Trubetskoy's blood had he published his heretical views five years previously were also either dead or in exile. To top it off, the entire philology department of Moscow University had been closed by the new Bolshevik regime. Those of its former members who remained alive probably had more pressing matters to attend to, such as finding food and not being shot.[4]

However, the one member of the Moscow School who could possibly still have been interested in the subject, happily, was Jakobson. Decades later, after

Trubetskoy was long dead and Jakobson was approaching the end of his life (he died in 1982), he would remember Trubetskoy as one of three men of genius he had come to know in his life. The others were Claude Lévi-Strauss, the great French anthropologist and inventor of structuralism, and the Russian poet Velimir Khlebnikov, who transformed Silver Age poetry with his radical *Zaum* verses. But Trubetskoy, said Jakobson, was in a class of his own:

> 'He made an immediate impression on me. I was dazzled after hearing only a few sentences he said at a meeting of the committee of folklore . . . I immediately said: This must be a man of genius; everything was clear to me.'[5]

Such was their bond that Trubetskoy and Jakobson are hard to separate intellectually. Their ideas were so eerily similar, and their breakthroughs anticipated each other so perfectly, that one is tempted to treat them as one scholarly mind rather than two. Even Jakobson noticed this, and in 1972 would tell French TV that given their voluminous and impassioned exchanges, he could no longer clearly distinguish between his own thinking and that of his friend: 'it was a surprising collaboration, we needed each other'.[6] Trubetskoy, for his part, dedicated his masterpiece, *The Principles of Phonology* (1939), to Jakobson, and wrote to their mutual friend Petr Suvchinsky: 'I am especially close to and united with Jakobson. In the sphere of scholarship he is, probably, the closest person to me.'[7]

Nevertheless, the two men could not have been more different: born in 1890, Trubetskoy was the scion of one of Russia's most prestigious aristocratic lineages; Jakobson, born six years later, was of Jewish Armenian origin. Trubetskoy was an aristocrat straight out of one of Dostoevsky's novels: forthright, earnest and monomaniacal. As linguist Anatoly Liberman put it in a biographical sketch: 'His tact, restraint and excellent manners were not a mask, but rather an invisible wall, which, like every wall, served as a protection and a barrier.'[8] At the same time he was 'a passionate, irascible man, prone to depression and nervous breakdowns, often insecure and shy'. Tall and imposing, never seen without his grey double-breasted suit and well-trimmed goatee, Trubetskoy was nonetheless rather stooped, as if made for listening rather than speaking.

Before 1917, the name Trubetskoy was practically synonymous with the Russian Empire. Descended from a fourteenth-century Lithuanian nobleman who married the sister of a Muscovite prince, the Trubetskoys were the hereditary lords of Trubetsk, near the border with Lithuania, and their bloodline was among the most venerable of the Russian aristocracy – older even than that of the Russian royal family, the Romanovs.

The nineteenth century was riven by debate between the Slavophiles (who believed in Russia's unique destiny and spoke out against westernizing reforms) and the westernizers (who believed that Europe was a model to be emulated). Intellectual seriousness of purpose was the order of the day – the Slavophiles wore traditional *murmolka* and *zipum*, peasant caps and coats, while westernizers were just as fanatical about dressing in the European style; the writer Alexander Herzen moaned in his memoirs about Russia's penchant for foppish conformity as a symptom of a national disease: 'If one were to show him the battalions of exactly similar, tightly buttoned frock coats of the fops on Nevksy Prospekt, an Englishman would take them for a squad of policemen.'[9] The fights that raged with the new-born intelligentsia were brutal and total: 'People avoided each other for weeks at a time because they disagreed about the definition of "all-embracing spirit" or had taken as a personal insult an opinion on "the absolute personality and its existence in itself"', wrote Herzen.

Nikolay's father Sergey and uncle Evgeny were both philosophers, and some of the most famed intellectuals of their time. Evgeny was a famous scholar of the Orthodox faith, while Nikolay's father was rector of Moscow University. Though they staunchly supported the monarchy and had a reputation as *grands seigneurs*, they had supported reform. Sergey, indeed, played a key historical role in the aftermath of the 1905 revolution, when he addressed Tsar Nicholas II on the need for political reform. The rejection of that petition would ultimately seal the monarchy's fate.

The two men, whom the young Nikolay idolized, epitomized the spiritual journey of their generation – a generation that would ultimately sire the Bolshevik revolutionaries. They questioned empiricism and idealism, searched for the place of faith in knowledge, and went through cycle after cycle of rejecting and then embracing the Orthodox Church. Uncle Evgeny describes in his memoirs growing up with a conservative Orthodox mother, and rebelling against that upbringing after reading French and English philosophers of positivism. Then, having absorbed German philosophy, which demolished the empiricism of the positivists, he at last conceded, reflecting the frustrations of his generation, that 'all the formulae which I believed blindly and dogmatically were shattered . . . childish self-assurance vanished and I realized that I had yet to develop a philosophy of life.'[10]

This spiritual indecisiveness was not a sign of irresoluteness; quite the contrary, it was a measure of just how seriously this generation took the search for truth. The actual ideas were secondary in significance to something much more important: the rigour with which they applied philosophical teachings to daily life. The romantic ideal of the nineteenth century demanded that one live in total conformity with one's beliefs; take the conclusions of those beliefs to the furthest extent possible; and apply those ideas in life, whatever the practicalities. Life demanded it, and anything less was a sign of moral cowardice. Philosophical ideas presented themselves to Russians of this period less as fanciful notions, and more as total programmes. Nikolay's uncle Evgeny Trubetskoy, himself an acclaimed philosopher, wrote of this preoccupation with the metaphysical in his autobiography of 1920: 'At some moment, a man possessed by a single thought, a single feeling, deaf to all else, infuses this single thought with a power of temperament and energy of will that knows no obstacles, and he therefore inevitably achieves his goal.'[11]

Russia, in short, was a country brimming with ideas and unique in its capacity to be totally carried away by them. Herzen encapsulated this tendency with typical sarcasm which tragically foreshadowed Russia's twentieth-century fate:

'We are great doctrinaires and raisonneurs. To this German capacity we add our own national . . . element, ruthless, fanatically dry: we are only too willing to cut off heads . . . With fearless step we march to the very limit, and go beyond it; never out of step with the dialectic, only with the truth.'[12]

Nikolay was born into this cerebral world on 16 April 1890.[13] His family lived in Moscow, in an apartment on Starokonyushenny Pereulok, off Arbat Street. They spent weekends and summers on their estate at Uzkoe just outside Moscow, its orchards and paths described lovingly by Boris Pasternak, later the Nobel Prize-winning author of the novel *Doctor Zhivago*, who was born the same year as Nikolay and was one of the prince's best friends at university. Uzkoe was the basis for his 1957 poem 'Linden Avenue':

A house of unimagined beauty
Is set in parkland, cool and dark;
Gates with an arch; then meadows, hillocks,
And oats and woods beyond the park.[14]

Serfdom had been abolished a year before Nikolay's father, Sergey Nikolaevich, was born. But the old social order still dominated life on the estate, and it dominated Nikolay's rather sheltered childhood. On 20 July, the day of celebration for 'Our Lady of Akhtyrka',[15] the Trubetskoy children would receive the children of the local village and hand out sweets, according to Evgeny's account, just as the ancient Trubetskoy landlords had always done.

Nikolay grew up amid the academic pageantry and prestige of his father and uncle; and just as they had delved into the intellectual currents of the day, so did he. Nikolay's father served as rector of Moscow University from 1904 until his death in 1905. Pasternak devoted several paragraphs of his autobiography to the family:

> The elder Trubetskoys, the father and the uncle of the student Nikolai were professors, one of jurisprudence while the other was rector of the university and a well known philosopher. Both were corpulent, and like two elephants, frock coats and all, without waists, would mount the rostrum and in a tone with which one might accost a deaf mute, in aristocratic burring imploring voices, delivered their brilliant courses.[16]

Sergey Trubetskoy realized that the foundations of the monarchy of Tsar Nicholas II were shaking, but his social position meant that the household could not avoid being swept along in the current of politics. On the night of 10 December 1904, Olga Nikolaevna Trubetskoy, Nikolay's aunt, wrote in her journal: 'Little by little, echoes of party differences begin to interfere with the peaceful and quiet flow of former social and family relations ... Even the children argue and quarrel, sometimes even fight – for or against autocracy.'[17]

Less than a month later, on 9 January 1905, the tsar's army smashed a peaceful demonstration in St Petersburg, killing at least 200 unarmed demonstrators, and touched off the savage violence of the 1905 revolution, which revolted and shocked Russia's upper classes. At the time, Nikolay's father tried to stay aloof from politics, but as rector of the university he was to play a role – one that ultimately may have catastrophically worsened his health and led to his untimely death. That year he met the tsar, as head of a delegation of local councils or *zemstvos*, in an attempt to convince Nicholas II to implement reforms that might have saved his throne, or at least saved Russia.

He failed. The only thing the intervention achieved was to earn the family the lasting enmity of Vladimir Lenin, who referred to Sergey Nikolaevich as the 'tsar's bourgeois flunkey' in a derisive obituary after his death that year. That would prove fateful in 1917, when Trubetskoy had to decide whether to return to Moscow or to flee.

The Silver Age

The period from 1905 until the final October revolution of 1917 would be one of political and artistic ferment. It was already clear that the monarchy's days were numbered, and Nikolay's generation would likely see its end. This was Russia's Silver Age, an exceptionally creative period in Russian art, literature and poetry, and a reaction to the science and Western philosophy of the nine-teenth century.

One of the chief influences of this period came from the writings of Nikolay's 'uncle Vladimir' – Vladimir Solovyev – who had died in 1900 on the Trubetskoy family's Uzkoe estate, attended by Nikolay's father. A mystic and religious philosopher (though not Nikolay's real uncle), Solovyev's philosophy was an extension of the nineteenth-century Slavophile tradition of idealism and metaphysics. A friend of Dostoevsky's, he was a model for the character Alesha Karamazov, the cerebral, naïve hero of *The Brothers Karamazov*. Solovyev's mysticism epitomized the Russian philosophical tradition at the end of the nineteenth century.

It was the maximalist era of Russian philosophy. Intellectuals like Solovyev were obsessed with the borderlands of reason, where it met the occult, the esoteric and the mystical. Nikolay Fedorov, an ascetic librarian and friend of Solovyev's, preached that humanity had to devote all its resources to over-coming death and to the resurrection of its ancestors, while Vladimir Vernadsky, a geologist, conceived the notion of the 'noosphere', the unity of human reason. Pavel Florensky attempted to unite mathematics and spirituality toward a mystical resolution of all antinomies and apparent contradictions. Solovyev, meanwhile, sought the establishment of a universal church, uniting Catholicism and Orthodoxy.

This was a trend that begat the artistic movement of symbolism, the idea that symbols possessed eternal, primal qualities, which led artists to an exploration of primitive themes and spiritual motifs. In Russia, Alexander Blok, one of Russia's most gifted poets (and nephew of Solovyev), was thrilled by the idea of apoca-lypse. His poetry was full of religion, pagan idolatry and eastern cultures. His 'Poetry of Spells and Incantations' of 1904 fascinated Nikolay and his peers. Solovyev meanwhile wrote 'Pan Mongolism', a poetic ode to eastern barbarians, one of his best-known works:

'Pan Mongolism! The name is monstrous
Yet it caresses my ear
As if filled with the portent
Of a grand divine fate.'

Eastern themes were no strangers to Russian art: the East mainly shows up in Russian nineteenth-century literature in the form of the wild tribes of the Caucasus mountains, where many a novel or poem was set. But what began to emerge in the Silver Age was something different: a generation of artists began to identify their homeland with the East, rather than using it only as an exotic backdrop for their creations. From the time of Peter the Great and his reforms, educated Russians had identified their land with Europe, and even those who criticized Europe (such as the Slavophiles) did so in a fraternal spirit. The 'East' for previous generations of Russians had always been a place that helped Russia to situate itself in the 'West'.

Not a single intellectual of the nineteenth century had identified Russia with Asia.[18] In literature and poetry, Western reason had always opposed Eastern mysticism; Western women versus Eastern slave girls; Eastern savagery versus Western mercy. This orientalist tradition in Russian literature was virtually the same as could be found in the West at the same time, and had seemingly been borrowed whole by Russia in the nineteenth century: Russia's 'East' was defined by Alexander Pushkin in 'Prisoner of the Caucasus', Mikhail Lermontov in *A Hero of Our Time* and Leo Tolstoy in *Hadji Murad*. The East presented itself in the garb of slaves and sultans, in barbarity and blood feuds; while Russian protagonists, appearing as quintessential rational Europeans, characterized the West.[19] Now, a generation of artists was questioning Russia's 'Westernness'. 'As for St Petersburg, it will sink,' wrote the great symbolist author Andrey Bely, of the city built by Peter the Great as Russia's 'Window to the West'. In *Petersburg*, his most famous novel, a Mongol horseman rides through the city, sowing chaos. Some believed that Russia's two-decade fascination with the East foretold an imminent catastrophe, the rejection of civilized Western ways and the coming savagery of the Bolshevik revolution and civil war. For others, the East was salvation, a counterweight to the excessive influence of Western scholastic rationalism.

Trubetskoy could not help but be influenced by this artistic and philosophical debate, given his family's closeness to Solovyev. Despite his elevated social status (he was taught by private tutors rather than in school), he could not remain completely aloof from the prevailing *air du temps*. He followed the trend towards the study of folk tales, myths and traditions, publishing his first scholarly article on folklore ('The Finnish Song "Kulto Neito" as the Survival of a Pagan Custom') when he was just 15; it was followed soon after by another article on the cult of a northwest Siberian pagan goddess: 'Zolotaya Baba'. Around the same time, in 1904, he began regularly to attend meetings of the Moscow Ethnographic Society, analogous to the Royal Geographical Society in Britain at the time. This was an elite club of aristocrats, adventurers and academics who would meet to ponder the latest discoveries of the age or argue about how to classify and organize the immense patchwork of peoples that stretched across Russia's empire, from Poland to Manchuria.[20]

The Trubetskoy name opened many doors. When Nikolay was 14, he decided that he wanted to meet the president of the Ethnographic Society,

Vsevolod Miller. He was quickly granted an audience, and Miller eventually invited him for two seasons to his summer home in the Caucasus to study local ethnology. In 1908, Trubetskoy enrolled at Moscow University, and declared his major to be in history. However, Trubetskoy rapidly became disenchanted with history and transferred in his third semester to linguistics. As he was to explain many years later:

> '[Linguistics] was the only branch of humanities that had a real scientific method, and . . . all the other branches of the science of man (ethnography, history of religion, cultural history) could move from their alchemic stage of development only if they followed the example of linguistics.'[21]

In 1912, Nikolay married Vera Petrovna Bazilevskaya, and the following year he was appointed a candidate professor in the department of comparative linguistics and Sanskrit on the recommendation of Viktor Porzhezinsky, the chairman. His letter of recommendation survives: 'His [Trubetskoy's] outstanding talent, wide reading in the literature of the subject, and finally, rare work ethic has shown itself in full measure in his various studies of linguistic science.' Nikolay's mentor also found it relevant to mention that he was the 'son of the deceased rector'.

* * *

If Trubetskoy was known for single-minded pursuit of scholarly enquiry, Jakobson was the opposite. He flitted between projects, ideas, books, friends and even women, with an almost compulsive randomness. Short, bespectacled and intense, he seemed to thrive on disorder and an upturned existence almost as much as Trubetskoy shunned it.

Jakobson was born in 1896 to a family of Jewish Armenian merchants that lived in the centre of Moscow at No. 3 Lubyansky Proezd, just off a main trolley line and right around the corner from the Russia Insurance Society (whose building would, in 1918, be transformed into the 'Lubyanka', the headquarters of the feared Soviet secret police). Before the revolution, Jakobson, six years younger than Trubetskoy, had been a charter member of Moscow's avant-garde scene. This was a time of thriving creativity, when movement after movement of artists – from symbolists to acmeists to suprematists to futurists – jostled for the limelight, denounced each other as poseurs and brawled with one another in the streets. Each had a more audacious project to reinvent the future, to pay homage to this or that legacy, to rediscover the primitive, and to (ever more feverishly) perform art in harmony with the great theoretical pronouncements of the day. Jakobson found himself surrounded by people with as great a sense of their own intellectual self-worth as his friend Trubetskoy.

Nor was Jakobson immune to the occasional excess of zeal in his desire to live life in harmony with his principles. Devoted to the theory of poetic formalism, for example, Jakobson avoided writing – and even speaking – in the first person, unless it was absolutely necessary or was under his artistic pseudonym 'Comrade Alyagrov'. This somewhat compulsive feature of his personality was remarked on by virtually all his students and biographers. It also annoyed his second wife, Krystyna Pomorska: 'A striking feature of his discourse is the strong tendency to avoid the first person singular . . . even when directly addressed.'[22] It made the process of writing his memoirs especially tricky: in one set of reminiscences, he quotes extensively from a letter from 'the poet, Alyagrov' – without ever mentioning that he was Alyagrov.[23] Or, as Jakobson wrote in 1962 of himself and his early linguistic interests: 'Proverbial sayings were jealously seized upon to cover empty calendar sheets . . . The six year old boy, fascinated by these intermediate forms between language and poetry, was compelled to stay on the watershed between language and linguistics.'[24]

Even more curious than the idea of a six-year-old boy being fascinated by 'intermediate forms between language and poetry' is that these sentences display the fundamental applications of his theory, which was aimed more than anything at questioning and obscuring the role of the individual author in literature and poetry. Thus he refers to himself, wherever possible, in the third person ('the six-year-old boy') or uses the passive voice ('Proverbial sayings were jealously seized upon'). According to one of Jakobson's biographers, Richard Bradford, Jakobson seems to have produced around 5,000 pages of prose while self-consciously avoiding any trace of the lyrical first person: 'This practice should not be dismissed as a mere eccentricity, rather it should be seen as silent testimony to his belief that the poetic function exerts a constant pressure on our linguistic presence.'[25] In the style of the true Russian intellectual, Jakobson proved his commitment to ideas by living according to them. If he had a theory of writing, it should be applied to all writing. 'Prose had to be prose', as a former student of his, Omry Ronen, put it.[26] And Jakobson considered the first person singular a poetic device. He avoided not only it, but also poetic flourishes in his writing – though he sometimes allowed himself the luxury of the first person in letters and reminiscences.

In his poetry, meanwhile, poetic devices (such as the first person) take on an almost obsessive prominence: his literary *nom de plume*, 'Alyagrov', under which he published poetry from 1914 until he left Moscow in 1920, was even a play on the first person singular in Russian (*ya*). In fact the *ya* in Alyagrov was deliberately emboldened to make the connection obvious: 'Аля**гров**'. Jakobson considered himself a poet first and foremost; but by his own admission, he was not a particularly noteworthy one. He was, however, a great theoretician and analyser of other people's poetry, and a promoter of other artists. He was intrigued by all things counterculture, bohemian and avant-garde in the moveable feast of pre-revolutionary Moscow.

Jakobson's philosophy of language, which would one day revolutionize academia, was born amid his musings on poetic criticism. He believed that the principle of poetic language applied more generally – that language was not simply a tool to represent meanings that were, in some sense, already there and were waiting to be named. As he would put it three decades later: 'language is composed of elements which are signifiers, yet at the same time signify nothing.'[27]

The suspicion cast on 'objects' in language was very much part of a new shift that was under way in how people viewed the world. The results of physics experiments, artistic inspiration, philosophical introspection and a host of other cerebral musings together and separately added up to what is known as modernism. Newtonian physics gave way to relativity; positivism gave way to phenomenology; in art, the realism of the nineteenth century gave way to futurism, cubism and suprematism. The linguistics of Jakobson and Trubetskoy was not above this trend. As Jakobson put it 50 years later, speaking of this period: 'The common denominator, both in science and art, is not the emphasis on the study of objects but, rather, the emphasis on the relations between objects.'[28] The two men were heavily influenced by Ferdinand de Saussure of the University of Geneva, who, in his posthumously published *Cours de linguistique générale* (1916), wrote in similar vein: 'In language there are only differences.'

In his linguistic studies, Trubetskoy focused on a new discipline called 'phonology', the study of the relationships between sounds in ordinary language and how they differentiate meaning – an exploration of the patterns and symmetries that lie at the unconscious base of the linguistic utterance. A phoneme was not a sound; it was not even a thing. It was a relationship, a difference, which could appear in almost any form. For instance, a line drawn midway between the Russian cities of Novocherkassk (near the Black Sea) and Pskov (up towards the Baltic), for example, separates Russian pronunciation into the northeast *g* and the southwest *h* – *gara* in the northeast is *hara* in the southwest.[29] While these are not the same sound, they are the same phoneme, so that however it is pronounced, the opposition between two words will be the same.

In fact, at several levels of theoretical abstraction, completely different sounds could be regarded as the same phonemes; this makes the task of keeping track of them exceedingly difficult and heavily theoretical, but it opened up an extremely exciting prospect for Trubetskoy; he believed the patterns and recurring rules he was finding to be evidence that linguistic evolution was not random, but had to be a small part of some much larger process of dynamic change. His soon-to-be one-sided duel with the soon-to-be-deceased Shakhmatov was to be fought over the significance of these patterns: Trubetskay's insights led to the idea that universal laws of language exist and are valid for all languages at all times, which would revolutionize twentieth-century linguistics.

Trubetskoy and Jakobson were part of a generation of Russians who were bursting with self-entitlement and privilege: the sons and daughters of Russia's Silver Age, that decade of artistic and intellectual ferment that produced poets like Alexander Blok and Anna Akhmatova, composers like Igor Stravinsky and Sergey Prokofiev, and painters like Kazimir Malevich. Theirs was an arrogant generation, convinced of its own superiority. Like many previous generations of Russians, it longed to drag the country into the modern age, but saw her weighed down by history and tradition. It was full of scorn for the old generations, and longed to create a new Russian science and scholarship. Had it not been for a tremendous accident of history, in the form of the Bolshevik revolution, it no doubt would have done so.

CHAPTER TWO

THE SHORT SUMMER

Russia's population turned out in droves to cheer Tsar Nicholas II when he declared Russia's entry into the First World War in 1914. But within just a few years, this optimism and public spirit had vanished. Casualties from fighting the Germans were horrific, and wartime shortages took their toll. Pre-war Russia had witnessed the zenith of the reforming monarchy, taking its first baby steps into the modern era; but the war erased all that progress. Soon, the only crowds that gathered were those demanding bread, an end to conscription and finally the abdication of the tsar and an end to monarchy.

Not everyone, however, was so distracted by the dramatic European events that would soon change their lives forever. Trubetskoy's autobiographical notes provide a good indication of what was occupying the prince's monomaniacal attention span for most of this period: his teaching qualifications. He spends pages describing in minute detail the composition of the qualifying exam he took to hold a professorship ('each of these questions had to be answered by a half hour of detailed discussion including the cogent literature. Each of the faculty members had the right to ask other questions on the same subject which had not been provided for in the program . . .').[1] He then lovingly lingers on his contributions to the scholarly work on 'north Caucasian fire abduction legends'. And, following a brief mention of his research trip to Leipzig in 1913, his coverage of European affairs is succinct: 'Soon after that the World War broke out.' He then picks up again with his efforts to pass his instructor's exam. Absorbed in his world of paleo-Siberian fricatives and Finnic folktales, Trubetskoy did not seem overly troubled by the carnage taking place in Europe and the upheavals in his own country.

His autobiographical notes break off in mid-1917, having failed to mention the end of the Romanov monarchy in March 1917, when Tsar Nicholas II abdicated and the short-lived provisional government came to power. His last thoughts, unsurprisingly, are of his plans to write his prehistory of Slavic languages: 'in it I planned to illustrate the process of development of the individual Slavic languages from Proto Slavic . . . by an improved method of reconstruction . . .'

Leaving Moscow in the summer of 1917 for a spa in the north Caucasus town of Kislovodsk, Trubetskoy had no inkling that he would never return to his native Moscow. The Bolshevik seizure of the Winter Palace in the renamed Petrograd in October, and the declaration of Soviet government apparently caught him off guard. But he knew he could not return to Moscow, as all members of his dynasty would be potential targets for the communists.

For the next three years, Trubetskoy, his wife and daughter wandered the war-ravaged landscape of southern Russia: first to Tbilisi, then to Baku, then to Rostov, then to Crimea, and across the Black Sea by ship to Constantinople (see chapter 1). Finally, the young prince's aristocratic connections proved useful in landing him a job in the Bulgarian capital Sofia teaching Slavic linguistics.

Jakobson, meanwhile, stayed on in Moscow, and even briefly joined the Bolsheviks, working for the bureau of propaganda – the imposingly named Commissariat of the Enlightenment. He even delivered a lecture entitled 'The Tasks of Artistic Propaganda' under his pseudonym, Alyagrov. Life in post-revolution Moscow was difficult: food was scarce, crime was rampant, and the Bolshevik regime, insecure and fighting a civil war across the breadth of Eurasia, was becoming increasingly intolerant of any dissenting views. As Jakobson wrote to a friend on his arrival in Prague in July 1920 (using the first person singular): 'Really, each one of us has lived through not one but ten lives in the last two years . . . In the last few years I, for example, was a counter-revolutionary, a scholar (not a bad one), scholarly secretary of the Director of the Department of the Arts, deserter, card player, irreplaceable specialist in a heating enterprise, man of letters, humorist, reporter, diplomat. Believe me, this all is an adventure story and that's all that there is to it, and so it is with almost every one of us.'[2]

Gradually, as the Bolsheviks consolidated their power, they began to quarrel with all who questioned orthodox Marxist views. The formalists' view that art is autonomous and independent of society pitted them squarely in ideological conflict with orthodox Marxism, which held that art is an expression of history and social forces and must be subordinated to political considerations. Asserting, as the avant-gardists did, that the social context of literature was irrelevant amounted to a rejection of what was fundamental to the philosophy of dialectical materialism. In the pluralistic atmosphere immediately after the revolution, when the Bolsheviks needed allies and tried to appeal to the intellectuals, formalism could be tolerated. But as time went by, any competition to the official state ideology began to be met with stiffer and stiffer resistance.

It was unclear why, in the spring of 1920, Jakobson suddenly felt that he needed to leave Moscow, but it may have been related to the turning of the tide – to the slow erosion of the position of the formalists. He landed a job as interpreter for one of the first groups of Soviet diplomats to be sent abroad. The 24-year-old was not a diplomat by training, and nor was he really a communist. Furthermore, his knowledge of Czech was limited to a one-semester class on the comparative grammar of Slavic languages at Moscow University. But competition for the job was not too stiff, he had been told by the man who recruited him, because 'everyone else was afraid the White army would blow them up as soon as they got over the border'.[3]

Whether it was because he was unafraid of this contingency or feared something worse if he stayed in Moscow – one way or the other, Jakobson embarked on a new life.

The people here are nice

Russia's exiles – 2 million of them – made their way to Europe, Turkey, Persia and China in what was, at the time, the largest human migration the world had ever seen. The newly exiled Russians were overwhelmingly from the aristocracy and the intelligentsia: educated, cultured and cosmopolitan, used to lives of privilege. But in postwar Europe, they were shorn of their status – and even of their citizenship. They were stateless, poor and desperate. Former princes could be found waiting tables in Paris or begging in the streets of Shanghai; ladies accustomed to silk evening gowns and costumed balls were now chambermaids and prostitutes.

They were nostalgic and bitter, clutching at any thread of their upended, pre-revolution lives. They gathered for weekly literary and poetry readings, transplanted Russian theatre and ballet to Paris and Berlin – all on a shoestring budget. Aristocrats and grandees who had been used to unlimited entitlement were now scraping by in humiliating poverty. As Vladimir Nabokov put it: 'Hardly palpable people who imitated in foreign cities a dead civilization, the remote, almost legendary, almost Sumerian mirages of St Petersburg and Moscow.'[4]

To the exiles, the Bolshevik revolution still seemed like a gigantic, cosmic accident – 'that trite *deus ex machina*', in the words of Nabokov – that would soon be righted. During the civil war, from 1917–20, propaganda newspapers published in Europe by the monarchist forces all gave optimistic accounts of the desperation faced by the Red forces. Even after the Red victory proved them all wrong, and even after the formation of the USSR, most of the émigré community believed that the new regime would not last more than a few years. They continued eagerly to read news of starvation and bad harvests. Believing that their exile would only be a matter of months – or a year at most – many were even reluctant to buy furniture. Few bothered to learn a new language. And while there were no barriers to their travel to the Americas, north or south, it is curious that so few elected to go there; the vast majority preferred to stay in countries that bordered on, or were close to, Russia.

What is remarkable in the accounts of many émigrés is this fervent belief that they would be returning imminently. For example, when the Czech government helped set up a Russian law school in Prague, it was aimed at émigrés whose sole purpose in studying was to prepare for a career as a civil servant or lawyer in post-communist Russia. It attracted over 500 students before its doors closed in 1927.

For the exiles, any contact with the homeland was a near sacred experience. For Trubetskoy in 1922, getting a piece of mail from Moscow was like 'getting a letter from the moon', as he wrote back to his friend Fedor Petrovsky, who had tracked him down in Sofia. Petrovsky had been a classmate of Trubetskoy's, a specialist in Latin, who had stayed behind in Moscow. Trubetskoy marvelled at the fact that the mail actually operated between Sofia and Moscow: 'Here we go this way and that and then in the end all we have to do is stick a stamp on an envelope.'[5]

Trubetskoy's life in Sofia was 'none too flashy', he wrote. The Bulgarian capital was clearly the 'result of a struggle between Vienna and Tula [a Russian provincial town], in which the latter got the better. Intellectual, artistic and spiritual pursuits here basically do not exist. In this lies the main distinction from Tula. But the people are nice.'[6]

Trubetskoy's disdain for his new home was typical of the Russian exiles in Europe. It was matched only by their breathless long-distance love affair with their homeland, a place that was alive in their memory, but to which it was for the most part impossible to return while the communists were in power. As Trubetskoy told Petrovsky:

You cannot imagine what happiness every stroke of the pen from our homeland brings to us, living among strangers. In general, all of my acquaintances abroad have more or less settled down and would all be happy, if there did not lie on each one of us a heavy stone of separation from Russia and from loved ones, and terrible concern over the fate of those close to us.[7]

Nowhere was the misguided optimism of the exiles more apparent than in politics. Everywhere, Russian émigrés were making preparations for the Bolsheviks' imminent collapse and their own triumphant return. Political parties – monarchists, socialists, fascists, liberals – all recruited members, published journals and newspapers, held congresses, created governments in exile, raised funds and jostled to be crowned rulers of post-communist Russia. These included the two main monarchist parties: one organized in 1922 by Grand Duke Cyril, who proclaimed himself 'emperor of all Russias'; the other formed by his cousin, Grand Duke Nikolay Nikolaevich. Non-monarchist parties of various stripes also sprang up like mushrooms. There were the Constitutional Democrats (the 'Kadets' for short), a liberal party established in tsarist Russia. And there was also the Socialist Revolutionary party (the SRs or 'Esers'), formed of moderate socialists. Both had been in power under the provisional government after the end of the monarchy in 1917, but before the Bolshevik coup of that October. Both presented themselves as the only alternative for Russia that would suit the twentieth century.

Trubetskoy – the scion of one of Russia's leading families, whose father had been rector of Moscow University, and who himself was a formidable public intellectual, despite his relative youth – could not remain aloof from the question of Russia's future. About the time he first wrote to Jakobson from exile, Trubetskoy was already moving in émigré circles, finding like-minded intellectuals and publishing his first political writings. For the next decade he would divide his time between his scholarly pursuits in linguistics and his political organizing.

His politics were partly moulded by his friendships, but his political views were clearly an expression of the scholarship that he and Jakobson were pioneering. Indeed, many of the concepts he and Jakobson would use to revolutionize linguistics were explored first in Trubetskoy's political writings. Like many Russian intellectuals before him, he pursued his conclusions to the farthest limit, turning a theory of linguistic meaning into a view of world history and grand political doctrine. The recurring theme in his political writings and in his scholarship was the primacy of culture. He saw culture through the lens of his linguistics studies – something essential, vibrant and real, rather than something ephemeral and decorative as the nineteenth century had held. The pre-war academic establishment had seen culture as something one could assign to various rungs on the ladder of human progress, some cultures more advanced than others. Trubetskoy saw all cultures as roughly equivalent, in the sense that their primary purpose was to communicate.

Culture in Trubetskoy's view was also something opposite to history. The nineteenth century had sought the origins of all things, from geology to music and language. Trubetskoy and Jakobson, however, believed that culture evolved exclusively due to cultural variables obeying their own inner logic, and not the random cause and effect of wars, migrations and the like. The origins, in other words, were less important than finding the rules, symmetries and systems by which cultural change occurred. In culture, Trubetskoy would attempt to find a third way between two opposing ideologies – Western liberal capitalism and Soviet communism – both premised, consciously or unconsciously, on the unyielding dogma of universal history.

CHAPTER THREE

FAMILY TREES

It seems that nostalgia for his old life was at least part of the reason that Trubetskoy, tracked down by Jakobson to Sofia in 1920, was so eager to engage on the subject of his *Prehistory* and his forthcoming riposte to his deceased mentor Shakhmatov.

Perusing the contents of other letters that Trubetskoy wrote to various friends during the early 1920s, one finds his *Prehistory* frequently to be a prominent subject – an obsession, one might be tempted to say. As he told his friend Petrovsky in a 1922 letter: 'I don't know if I will ever be able to finish this work, *The Prehistory of Slavic Languages*. If I manage to finish it, this book is going to create a "Grosses Schkandal" in Moscow, as they say' – the German used for dramatic emphasis. And in his next letter to Petrovsky: 'I am working still on *The Prehistory of Slavic Languages*. This will create such a scandal in Moscow when it is published!'

Trubetskoy's further letters to Jakobson are littered with seemingly random musings on sounds, vowels and patterns of sounds drawn in triangular and other shapes. Trubetskoy was pushing relentlessly towards something that he could not quite put his finger on, but – with Jakobson's help – he might be able to.

Clearly there was something about this work that weighed heavily on Trubetskoy. His urge to write a book did have a firm practical reason behind it: he needed to publish in order to get a professorship at a major European university. While in pre-revolutionary Russia that might have been assured by his family's connections, it was another matter now that he was an émigré wanderer in Europe. ('Due to the lightness of my printed scientific baggage, I can only count on, in truth, a job in the provinces, and not even a professor's position, but that of a docent.')[1]

But Trubetskoy turned down at least one offer by Jakobson – in the very next letter, it seems – to find such a publisher, responding that he needed more time. He wanted to know what the rush was. From then on, Trubetskoy's obsession with the book seems to have been mixed with a reluctance to be done with it. In a 1925 letter to Jakobson, he raised the subject again: 'The *Prehistory* again occupies my attention. I believe that the later I shall print it, the better; such things are to be nurtured.' Then, in 1926: 'I simply don't know when I will get to the *Prehistory*. I'm afraid it is overdue . . .'

Ultimately, Trubetskoy could never bring himself to finish his masterpiece. The manuscript of the book was in his flat in Vienna in 1938, when, following Germany's Anschluss of Austria, the Gestapo searched the premises and confiscated all his writings. Trubetskoy's friends believe the loss of this manuscript was what led to his heart attack and untimely death eight months later. But would Trubetskoy, Gestapo or not, ever have finished his masterwork? Eighteen years after he started it, he had only dribbled out parts of the book as scholarly articles and in his main work, *The Principles of Phonology*, published posthumously.

One explanation for both the obsession and the failure to see the end of it springs to mind: his attachment to the book may well have been driven by nostalgia, a simple yearning for the vanished Moscow of his youth. In Sofia, Trubetskoy did better than most exiles, but still found it hard to provide for his family on the meagre pay of a Bulgarian *privatdotsent*, an unsalaried professor dependent on contributions from his students. Even after he moved to Austria and got a full-time teaching position at the University of Vienna in 1923, he battled depression and ill health, and faced chronic financial difficulties. In one letter to Jakobson, for example, Trubetskoy said he was not able to make the trip to Prague for a conference because of lack of funds.

Those who knew Trubetskoy before the revolution as a grand aristocrat with unlimited self-entitlement formed a very different impression of the man from those who got to know him after his flight. In Europe he was prone to bouts of depression and self-doubt, sometimes isolating himself from friends and family, taking solace in his scholarly theories. 'In a strange land, Trubetskoy remained a stranger', wrote his colleague, the Danish linguist Louis Hjelmslev, in his 1939 obituary. He was 'naturally friendly with all people, modest and unassuming, but also a man who never overcame the inauspicious circumstances of his life'.[2]

For Trubetskoy, finishing the *Prehistory* would have meant letting go of the past, letting go of Moscow University, of the tuxedoed debates at the Ethnographic Society, of his oedipal rivalry with Shakhmatov, of the pleasant summers at his family estate at Akhtirka, in the Ukraine. These memories died hard for Trubetskoy – as they did for many Russian exiles like him. *The Prehistory of Slavic Languages* was indeed the last thread binding him to a dream life he had lost forever; but it was also the first hurdle in a scholarly steeplechase that would enlist Jakobson and that would last from the fateful December when they first got in touch until Trubetskoy's death in 1938.

Jakobson, for his part, expressed increasing excitement about Trubetskoy's obsession with the patterns he was finding in languages. True, Jakobson was himself looking for a professorship and probably figured that the patronage of Trubetskoy and his family connections could be useful in that endeavour. This ulterior motive might have justified a brief and indulgent correspondence with the prince, until it became clear that the latter had no useful contacts to speak of in European academic circles. But in fact Jakobson did not turn his flattery and encouragement elsewhere even after it became clear that Trubetskoy had no interest in finding him a job. Whatever it was about the book, it got Jakobson hooked as well, and he appeared genuinely to share Trubetskoy's passion for delving deeper into the study of human language.

Inner logic

The linguistics that the pair had been discussing before the war raised the fascinating question of how sounds, words and structure created meaning. But the orderly semantic oppositions they unearthed manifested themselves as a static, crystalline, unchanging universe of interconnected elements frozen at a single instant in time. They could not explain the one constant attribute of language which Trubetskoy was finding in his study of pre-Slavic dialects and in his quest to usurp Shakhmatov's mantle: change.

The rapidity of language change in history is astounding. Within a few hundred years a single language could split into two mutually unintelligible dialects. Poetry which rhymes in one decade can appear jarring and atonal a few dozen years later. Vulgar Latin's transformation into French, Italian and Spanish is thought to have taken only 400–500 years. While these changes had been exhaustively catalogued by previous generations of philologists, culminating with Shakhmatov, the reasons for language change had never been seriously considered. By default, it had been generally thought that languages shift due to external historical factors, such as the movement of peoples, the isolation of some elements and contact with other languages.

Both Jakobson and Trubetskoy challenged this view that language change was primarily the result of history, in the sense that history was a random occurrence of external events. Both believed that most linguistic evolution is internally motivated rather than the direct result of external interference. All that was required to prove this was some evidence of the regularity of linguistic change, which would yield universal laws that apply to all languages at all times.

Later in life, Jakobson was fond of telling his colleagues that the start of the linguistic revolution that he and Trubetskoy had initiated owed its inspiration to the theory of thermodynamics. The new notion of equilibrium in physics, discovered in the 1890s by Ludwig Boltzmann, created a robust theory of 'systems'. If gas from one chamber is released into another, or if an iron rod is heated at one end, these systems seek a 'rest state' – in other words, some gas will flow into the other chamber, or the heat becomes evenly distributed across the iron rod, which gradually cools. Jakobson credited Boltzmann's idea of the equilibrium of systems with 'the beginning of the new science and art, function and purpose rather than cause oriented'.[3]

A language, in other words, could be thought of as a container in Boltzmann's example: if a new element is introduced – for instance a new word, or a change in the pronunciation of an old word – the language functions like a system whose equilibrium has been disturbed. It seeks a new rest state. But the interconnectedness of language terms means that, for the system to accommodate a new or changed element, a lot of other elements need to change in order to compensate. Languages, like any system, seek 'equilibrium'. The research of Trubetskoy and Jakobson showed (and later research by other linguists confirmed) that changing some parts of a language caused a chain reaction. Their research was limited to sounds that differentiate meaning, or 'phonemes', rather than whole words; but it revealed a number of relationships between these phonemes that held, no matter what language they belonged to.

Trubetskoy's theory of phonology showed that certain phonological features are universally coupled with certain others, or are lost in the absence of others. In practice, these relationships are very abstract – it is almost impossible to describe them in layman's terms. For example, in all languages vowel length is irrelevant as a signifier of meaning unless stress becomes fixed, in which case vowel length does become significant.

The unintuitive nature of these changes makes them all the more intriguing, however, and they are difficult to explain without recourse to some notion that the unconscious language organ of our brains is a great deal more complicated and sophisticated than we thought. In fact, it was subsequently proved that sound changes always happen in groups, indicating that language changes are not isolated, but each necessitates a chain reaction of further changes to compensate for the original shift.[4]

Between 1350 and 1700, for example, virtually all vowels in Middle English became diphthongs, one after the other, in what has become known as the biggest documented 'chain shift' in modern linguistics, when several sounds move stepwise along a phonetic scale. Other such chain shifts were found in fifteenth- and sixteenth-century Germany: most famously, stop consonants became fricatives – i.e. *b* became *f*, *d* became *th* or *ts*, and *g* became *h*.[5] The regularity of sound changes indicated that there are pre-set paths that languages have to follow as they develop and change over time. This lent the notion of linguistic structuralism an almost metaphysical, teleological significance.[6]

'Many elements of the history of languages seem fortuitous,' wrote Trubetskoy to Jakobson,

> but history does not have the right to be satisfied with this explanation. The general outlines of the history of language, when one reflects upon them with a little attention and logic, never prove to be fortuitous. Consequently, the little details cannot be fortuitous either – their sense must simply be discovered. The rational character of the evolution of language stems directly from the fact that language is a system.[7]

As we have seen, Trubetskoy created his theory as an oddly obsessive riposte to the deceased Professor Shakhmatov, who, in 1915, had written a historical treatise on the reconstruction of 'Proto-Slavic' – what was proposed as the language that had existed before Russian, Belarusian and Ukrainian split into separate dialects and then languages, sometime in the Middle Ages.

Shakhmatov was 'never able to free himself from its influence: perhaps unwittingly, he always imagined the development of language as the branching of a family tree', according to Trubetskoy, who presented an elaborate reconstruction of the creation of Ukrainian, Belarusian and Russian in the thirteenth century through his advanced study of phonemes. He showed that from 1160 onwards, certain vowels shifted their pronunciation in the southern region of what is now Ukraine, a change that spread slowly to the north. According to a surviving manuscript that documented the sound shift, by the time it arrived there in 1282 other changes had already taken place in the southern region's pronunciation (the hardening of soft consonants before syllable-forming front vowels); and these prevented the spread of certain sound changes over the entire Old Russian language area, such as the transformation of *e* into *o* in Ukrainian. That was the beginning, Trubetskoy showed, of a separate Ukrainian dialect.[8]

Trubetskoy argued that the dialects of Ukrainian and Belarusian thus emerged for entirely internal linguistic reasons, and were not caused by some external historical factors, such as migration, war or politics. In his view, then, language repeatedly demonstrates that it moves on a completely separate plane of existence from history, changing, spreading, expanding and dying out according to its own internal 'systemic' logic, rather than being conditioned by the hurly-burly of physical cause and effect.

Trubetskoy and Jakobson both mused regularly that the systemic laws they were finding in language could apply to many other aspects of human culture as well. The same principles they discovered in phonemic systems might pertain to a vast system of communication and art, such as dance, music, folklore, literature, poetry and myth. As Trubetskoy wrote to Jakobson: 'There can be no doubt that some parallelism in the evolution of the various aspects of culture exists, so some law concerning parallelism also exists. Thus, for instance, the entire evolution of Russian poetry . . . has inner logic and meaning; no moment of this evolution should be derived from non literary facts.'

If taken to their furthest limits (and Russian intellectuals had a tendency to take their theories to the furthest limits), Trubetskoy's findings seemed to arrive at a paradox: because of the existence of universal linguistic laws, there were sufficient grounds to ask whether human culture was something universal itself.

Phonology was therefore the key to a new universe. Trubetskoy believed that culture, like nature, could have its own structuring principles, hidden and unconscious DNA, and that subtle variations at a deep genetic level could give rise to the different species that multiplied through nature, a regularized geometry of autonomous units – discrete cultures and linguistic groups, whose inner workings do not assimilate foreign elements in a straightforward manner. Each such creation would thus traverse its own autonomous path of development, spreading and existing entirely within an internally organized system. Culture was not a product of independent human minds, of chance or of external causal forces: it was an immanent system of laws and structures which decisively condition our cultural, artistic, literary and linguistic identities. Operating below the threshold of consciousness, this rule-bound system held up a mirror to the inner workings not just of the individual human mind, but also of the collective, simultaneous activity of communities and nations.

* * *

The academic work of Trubetskoy and Jakobson would ultimately result in what Jakobson termed the 'Eurasian Language Union' and the notion that inner Eurasia was one gigantic basin in which a system of interconnected languages flowed together, sharing more and more deep structural traits over time. Trubetskoy went a step further and proposed a 'Eurasian cultural conglomerate' – the notion that this boundary applied not just to languages but to overall culture. Within these boundaries nations and civilizations lived as hermetically sealed totalities, rather than sharing a common wellspring of universal nature with the rest of humanity.

This idea, that nations and civilizations exist as individual organisms, was particularly widespread in the aftermath of the First World War. With the horrific events of the previous decade, the shine had worn off European civilization, which no longer appeared to represent something universal and aspirational. Its moral authority had been questioned as never before by the carnage of the conflict, as had the values that Europe had championed since the Enlightenment: individual rights, freedom, democracy and the perfectibility of man. A number of interwar thinkers, such as Oswald Spengler, argued that non-Western civilizations have fundamentally equivalent (if incommensurate) moral and epistemological systems, and they fundamentally questioned the authority and singularity of the Enlightenment.

The destruction of the war, the millennial cataclysm of the Bolshevik revolution, the unprecedented population movements after the war, and the collapse of three major empires which had ruled for centuries – all this combined to create a mood where the most deeply embedded truths were suddenly open to question. It was in this environment that Trubetskoy began to pursue a sideline in political pamphleteering, which was tangentially related to his and Jakobson's academic work. In his political writings, he could not resist extending the metaphor of language as a self-regulating 'system' to culture generally, contending that cultures represent autonomous sealed universes of unconscious structure.

Trubetskoy, along with a number of other, better known interwar writers, questioned the idea – a dogma of Enlightenment thought – that humanity 'advances' at all; that such a thing as 'progress' exists. If the most advanced nations of the world could wage such a brutal war and extinguish so much life in so short a time, then what right did they have to cloak themselves in 'progress' and to teach other civilizations about its virtues?

The weakening consensus around the universal values preached by the Enlightenment was matched by the strengthening of elemental nationalism. Instead of the pinnacle of human reason, nationalism sold itself as the most primordial human instinct: the urge to reach back in time to secure identities that had lost their moorings because of the turmoil. Political parties across Europe immediately understood the power of this simple formula to mobilize profoundly alienated and demoralized populations.

This rise of nationalism was helped by the post-war deconstruction of the Russian, Ottoman and Habsburg empires. The new states that emerged in the wake of the Paris Peace Conference of 1919, such as Romania, Czechoslovakia and Hungary, were unlike the nation states of the eighteenth and nineteenth centuries. These new nation states were nations first, and states second. The right to citizenship was guaranteed only to members of the titular nationality, and it was felt that minorities needed protection under a treaty in order to enjoy full rights, until they could be assimilated.[9] Rights for the first time became equated with a nation rather than a state, and it was not long before Hitler declared that 'right is what is good for the German people' and rendered Germany's Jews stateless and rightless by stripping them of their nationality.[10]

It is noteworthy that the first to feel the bitter taste of this new xenophobia and bombast were Europe's refugees, and especially the Russian exiles. In the new postwar political climate, the stateless were the continent's most vulnerable: they had no recourse to embassies, no representation and no rights, and states found they could deal with this increasing mass of uprooted people through arbitrary police power. The stateless lived in constant fear of deportation; the only factor preventing this was that no other country would take them in. With their political rights attached to citizenship and nationality, the stateless Russians were, in a sense, the first subjects of the totalitarian regimes that were to come, even before these regimes took shape.

It was in this climate that Trubetskoy wrote his first political pamphlet – a blistering attack on Europe's claim to universalism and progress, called *Europe and Mankind*. It would eventually lead Trubetskoy to found the Eurasianist movement the following year with three other collaborators. For Trubetskoy, the Bolshevik revolution and the rapid disintegration of Russia provided proof that Russian efforts since the time of Peter the Great to Europeanize had weakened the country, and that Europe ('Romano Germanic civilization') did not deserve the prestige it arrogated to itself. As he wrote in the introduction to the pamphlet:

> The Great War and especially the subsequent 'peace' (which even now must be written in quotation marks) shook our faith in 'civilized mankind' and opened the eyes of many people. We were witness to the sudden collapse of what we used to call 'Russian culture'. Many of us were struck by the speed and ease with which this occurred, and many began to ponder the reasons for these events.

Trubetskoy's bitterness at Europe has to be understood in the context of his own personal situation as a stateless refugee; but he was also ploughing a well-worn furrow among Russian writers, who were only too happy to speak European languages, drink European wine and vacation in Europe, but who endlessly decried their country's slavish imitation of the West and proclaimed their desire to be free of it. The Russian writer to whom Trubetskoy most clearly owed a debt was Nikolay Danilevsky, whose *Russia and Europe*, printed in 1869, clearly inspired Trubetskoy's title and many of his ideas.

An avowed Russian imperialist, Danilevsky was a little-known fisheries expert and obscure pamphleteer, whose most famous work was a venomous assault on the prestige of European culture. His pen dripping with derision, he lambasted Russia's intelligentsia for its docility and anxiousness to reproduce the latest intellectual fashions of Paris and London salons in their own country. He argued that Russians were hesitant to assert themselves politically because they had internalized the view – promoted by Europe – that forceful and confrontational policy towards the West was immoral, narrowly nationalistic and non-humanitarian. This constituted implicit acceptance of Europe's claims that its civilization was the culmination of human history.

To be fair to Trubetskoy, *Europe and Mankind* was not sheer plagiarism of Danilevsky's ideas; but the young prince, without once attributing or even mentioning Danilevsky, was clearly profoundly influenced by the Pan-Slavist, right down to his choice of terminology: to describe civilization, Trubetskoy adapted the key term 'Romano German' from Danilevsky, who had called it 'Germano Roman'.

Like Danilevsky, Trubetskoy went on to chastise the Russian intelligentsia for their unquestioning belief that foreign ideas and cultural norms could be superior to native ones: 'The Romano Germans have always been so naively convinced that they alone are human beings that they have called themselves "humanity", their culture "universal human culture" and their chauvinism "cosmopolitanism". The ladder of progress was an illusion, and the reality, argued Trubetskoy, was that no foreign culture can ever be assimilated properly: 'Efforts to achieve complete Europeanization promise all non Romano Germanic nations a miserable and tragic future.'

Europe and Mankind was noteworthy for its clear and erudite style. This distinguished it from the political propaganda of the time that was being churned out by all major exile groups. Danilevsky's views, reproduced by Trubetskoy, may not have found their mark in the age of John Stuart Mill and Turgenev, when the prestige of European culture was at an all-time high. But by 1920, dismayed Russian exiles were more willing to countenance the increasingly popular view that the West was in decline. The pamphlet was also noticed for the exalted Trubetskoy name, which still held tremendous cachet among Russians. Though the pamphlet did not sell particularly well, it was reviewed in a number of prominent journals. One reviewer was a man named Petr Savitsky, who happened to arrive in Sofia at the same time as Trubetskoy. Savitsky wrote for the widely distributed liberal publication *Russkaya Mysl*. In his review of *Europe and Mankind*, he extrapolated from some of Trubetskoy's thoughts and added a few of his own ('the cultural emancipation of Russia-Eurasia from Eurocentric egotism').

Like Trubetskoy, Savitsky was an aristocrat, though with less blue blood. His family owned the estate of Savshchino in the Chernigov region of Ukraine, which at that time was part of the Russian Empire. They also owned a sugar mill. His father was chairman of the local *zemstvo*, a type of local council set up in the nineteenth century as an experiment in political reform. While the Trubetskoys were among the top five names in the court aristocracy of the tsar, the Savitskys were simply landed gentry.

Born in 1895, from an early age Petr took a huge interest in geography and soil studies. He attended St Petersburg Polytechnic University, where he fell under the influence of the remarkable professor and political figure Petr Struve, and soon became Struve's favourite student. After the Bolshevik seizure of power, Struve and Savitsky joined the White forces under General Petr Wrangel, who held the Crimea, and Struve was briefly Wrangel's foreign minister (with Savitsky as his deputy), until the interim government declared by the White forces collapsed and both Savitsky and his older patron found their way to Sofia.

Struve represented the old establishment, Savitsky the new avant-garde, some of whom had begun to believe that Russia should look forward and not back. The Bolshevik revolution was a fact, and it was ridiculous to claim otherwise – to pretend it had not happened. Savitsky evidently admired some of the achievements of the Bolsheviks: if not their communism, then at least their ability to quickly consolidate power and 'defend Russia from foreign interference', as he put it. He wrote this in a letter to his mentor at the end of 1921, initiating a final break between the two, as Savitsky joined Trubetskoy to work on Eurasianism.

His letter was a declaration of a fresh line of thinking within the new generation of younger émigrés. First and foremost, Savitsky said that the Bolshevik revolution represented a turning point in the history of Russia. It must be recognized, and the lessons must be learned: 'Changing the economic policy of Bolshevism is a condition for the life of Russia. Keeping its political apparatus is the condition for the strength of the country.' But Struve still felt that Bolshevism had to be condemned as unlawful and accidental,[11] and began to suspect Savitsky of being pro-Bolshevik. This led to a bitter schism between them. But by this time Savitsky had met Trubetskoy and had found a small but growing group that shared his views.

In 1920, following Savitsky's review of *Europe and Mankind*, Trubetskoy made contact with the reviewer, and joined with Petr Suvchinsky, a musicologist and heir to a Ukrainian sugar fortune, who was friends with Stravinsky and Prokofiev, and most importantly, owned a printing house. Suvchinsky published *Europe and Mankind*, and with Father Georgy Florovsky, an Orthodox priest, also in Sofia, the four published a stunning new book of essays, entitled *Exodus to the East*. Part scholarship and part apocalyptica, *Exodus* was the founding document of the Eurasianist movement, clothing it in the same religious imagery, the same eschatological significance, as the poetry of Blok and the prose of Bely. 'These are frightening times, terrifying epochs, like apocalyptic visions, times of great realizations of the Mystery, times frightening and blessed', wrote Suvchinsky in a characteristic passage from *Exodus*.[12]

The same distinctly Russian instinct that had brought the Bolsheviks to power – the incredible capacity for destruction and creativity – had been unleashed and would not lie quiet. The task now was to guide this formidable energy in positive directions: 'Russia in sin and godlessness, Russia in loathsomeness and filth. But Russia in search and struggle, in a bid for a city not of this world', wrote Savitsky. The civil war had cleansed Russia of the old; purged Russia of its lethargy; brought Russia's vitality to the surface; and answered the question of who 'we' are. According to the jointly written introduction to the book: 'Russians and those who belong to the peoples of "the Russian world" are neither Europeans nor Asians. Merging with the native element of culture and life which surrounds us, we are not ashamed to declare ourselves *Eurasians*.'

What emerged from the overly intellectual milieu was an utterly original attitude to the Bolshevik revolution. Every other major émigré party had announced its utter rejection of the revolution, and its desire to turn back the political clock: some to 1861, before the accession to the throne of Nicholas II; some to before February 1917, when Nicholas abdicated; and some to various points between February and October 1917, when Russia was ruled by a liberal (if extremely disorganized) provisional government. The Eurasianists were alone in their neutral attitude towards the revolution, which they saw as a half-finished 'Eurasian revolution' against the West. While it was indeed biblical in its savagery and bloodiness, they saw the religious, eschatological echoes of 1917 as a catastrophic culmination of the two-century-long westernizing trend of Russian intellectual history and its simultaneous exculpation.

Exodus was a pseudo-religious blend of reason and myth, steel and sentimentality, and was reminiscent of other totalitarian writings of that decade. The exact purpose of the violence, bloodshed and upheaval was not exactly addressed – instead it had a vague theological meaning. War, revolution and dictatorship were not a means to an end, but rather a transition to a new existential state – an 'end of days', to be followed by the reign of God on earth.

The focus on the 'East' was an original view. The East envisaged by Trubetskoy and his fellow émigrés was most clearly an expression of the art of Russia's Silver Age, with its symbolist influences such as Blok, who in 1918 wrote 'The Scythians', foretelling a savage conflict between Europe and Russia, presented as the descendants of Inner Asian nomads:

> You are millions. We are hordes and hordes and hordes.
> Try and take us on!
> Yes, we are Scythians! Yes, we are Asians –
> With slanted and greedy eyes![13]

While Russian historiography had mourned the thirteenth-century Mongol invasion as a historical tragedy severing Old Russia from the European and Byzantine culture of which it had formed a part, the Eurasianists celebrated it as a redemptive event in which 'the Tatars purged and sanctified' Russia. There was no contradiction in celebrating both Mongol heritage and the Orthodox Church as unique essences of Russian civilization: Bolshevism, like the Golden Horde, was a purge which foreclosed a Western future for Russia and established a separate civilization.

The Eurasianists' penchant for Mongol-centric history was, for the most part, not a serious ethnographic theory but rather a symbolic rejection of Russia's Western heritage and an embrace of the native and primitive. It was more an aesthetic element of their utopian theory than a serious attempt to reconcile the steppe cultures with Russian history. Of the original generation of Eurasianists, only historian Georgy Vernadsky, who would later emigrate to the United States and teach at Yale University, gave scholarly legitimacy to some of the more modest claims of the Eurasian movement vis-à-vis the Mongolian inheritance.

Trubetskoy wrote a fanciful essay on 'The Legacy of Genghis Khan', in which he claimed that Russia's historical penchant for ideocratic, authoritarian rule originated with the Mongols. However, this work was not taken seriously – not even by its author. In 1925, he wrote to Suvchinsky about the forthcoming article, which he described as 'tendentious': 'There is a big question as to whether we should hide this from public view . . . I fear that for serious historians this will present a big bull's eye.'[14] Ultimately it was published under a pseudonym. As Trubetskoy explained to Suvchinsky: 'I still would not want to put his name on this piece, which is clearly demagogic and dilettantish from a scientific point of view.'[15]

CHAPTER FOUR

COALS TO NEWCASTLE

In 1922, fortune smiled on Trubetskoy. He was offered a teaching post at the University of Vienna, in the Slavic department. It was a coincidence: the job had been offered to a more senior professor from Munich who had turned it down, and so it passed to Trubetskoy. He was obviously happy to be in Vienna, one of Europe's intellectual capitals; but evidently he found his appointment as a teacher of Slavic linguistics quite amusing, as he reminisced later, in 1933, to Jakobson: 'Being a refugee has taught us that when traveling to Tula, one must bring one's own samovar.' He was chuckling over the equivalent of 'bringing ice to Eskimos'.[1]

The lesson, he wrote, was that:

> in Paris immigrants should open fashionable boutiques or nightclubs. In Munich, beer halls. Russian Slavic specialists should, according to this principle, stick to Slavic countries. In other countries, Russian Slavists have not managed to make a go of it, not one, except me. And I am the exception that proves the rule: I was given a job not in the capacity of a Slavist, but that of a prince. And that in Vienna, which is already up to its eyeballs in princes!

The Vienna job was the start of an incredibly creative period for Trubetskoy, in both his political activism and his linguistic scholarship. He wrote to Jakobson in September 1922 that he was on a very productive 'streak' and 'went around like one possessed. I am choking, bursting with so many new ideas that I hardly manage to jot them down.' He provided Jakobson with the first detailed outline of (what else?) his proposed *Prehistory of Slavic Languages*.[2]

In 1925, Jakobson, Savitsky and Trubetskoy helped formed the Prague Linguistic Circle, along with some other Czech and Russian colleagues. This would pursue many of the theoretical questions that had interested the

Eurasianists, and gave them a more respectable theoretical gloss.[3] They would meet regularly in Prague, either at Savitsky's house or at the downtown café U Prince. Over beer and sausages, they would develop the outlines of a new theory that would revolutionize linguistics.[4]

Collectively, the writings of Trubetskoy, Jakobson and Savitsky sought to argue that cultures and civilizations have natural boundaries that delineate the extent of the unconscious architecture of a unique cultural geometry. They are characterized by an entire substratum of unconscious relationships between language sounds, music scales, folk dress, art and even architecture which will naturally occur over a certain territory and end at common geographical frontiers of common culture.[5] These delineate the boundaries of large-scale cultural change, much like a watershed, inside which culture and language flow towards each other.

The Eurasianists proposed that such a boundary runs roughly from the Russian city of Murmansk to the westernmost Belarusian city of Brest and on to the Romanian town of Galati, dividing Europe along a number of interesting criteria. On one side is the Orthodox world, on the other side the Catholic. On one side, many Russian songs are composed on the pentatonic scale, which is also widely in use among the Finnish and Turkic peoples of the Russian zone, but is barely to be found on the other side of the line.[6] The line also roughly divides some rather esoteric linguistic structures: on the Eurasian side of the line one finds the phonological correlation of consonants,[7] which is absent on the other side.[8] To Trubetskoy, that was the boundary of the Eurasian cultural conglomerate.

Savitsky argued that the territory of Inner Asia – Eurasia – occupied by the late Russian Empire and now the USSR, was a single, integrated geographical unit, forming one 'zone' due to the relatively flat terrain between western China and the Carpathian Mountains, where a strip of fertile land running east to west is joined vertically by six major river systems. Russia was, in Savitsky's formulation, a separate 'continent' surrounded by formidable barriers from the outside, but whose internal arrangement was conducive to the mingling and interdependency of its peoples.[9]

Trubetskoy's view of culture as a system was encapsulated in a number of articles devoted to the view that all the nations of the Russian Empire represented a single political unit by virtue of its singular culture. As he wrote in 1921:

Generally speaking, [Russian] culture comprises its own special zone and includes, besides the Russians, the Ugro-Finnic peoples and the Turkic peoples of the Volga Basin. Moving to the east and southeast, this culture merges almost imperceptibly with the Turko-Mongolian culture of the steppes, which links it in turn with the cultures of Asia.[10]

Nineteenth-century linguistics saw the evolution of languages as a process of divergence from a common ancestor – just as French and Italian were descended from the common original Latin, or Indo-European languages descended from Sanskrit. But it had trouble explaining why all Balkan languages, for example, despite being from different ancestries, had come to resemble each other over time.

Trubetskoy and Jakobson drew on their phonological research to argue that acquired language traits are not acquired by accident, but result from the internal workings of a language's systemic ordering principles. This gave 'convergence zones' like the Balkans and inner Eurasia, where languages of different origins grew more alike over time, a mystical, teleological significance or purpose. As Jakobson phrased it in 1929: 'The question of "to where" has become more important than "from where".'[11] While Trubetskoy wrote: 'The evolution of a phonemic system at any given moment is directed by the tendency towards a goal . . .'[12]

For both men, the act of becoming was never random. It had a sense, a reason, which was quite beyond the power of the human will to change. The evolution of languages, he believed, took place in time, but not in history. The latter was the domain of caprice and chance and accidents; the former, a clockwork of necessity. Thus, the convergence of Eurasian languages' unconscious structural characteristics over time was of metaphysical importance. The 'Eurasian cultural conglomerate' included 200 different languages and ethnicities, comprising Eastern Slavs, Finns, Turks and Mongols; on the periphery, the Caucasian and Paleo-Asiatic peoples were related not by common origin, but instead by cultural and linguistic borrowings. These had taken on special teleological significance for the Eurasianists: this so-called tendency of common development was more important to them than having a common origin.

For the Eurasianists, the unconscious was superior, because it demonstrated a logical geometry in the absence of coercion, politics, chance and history. A national language could be spread by executive fiat or colonial force, for example; but the tone structure of languages could only converge due to some unconscious sympathy. Borrowing on a very minute, atomic level, such as sound changes, was indeed more important to them as a signifier of cultural closeness than cognate words were. For example, Trubetskoy believed that the tonal similarities between Russian, Finnic and Turkic languages were more important as a marker of internal cultural sympathy than are the obvious cognates in Czech, Polish and Russian, where *ryba* is the common word for fish and *ruka* means hand (*ręka* in Polish).

The unconscious substrates of language, in other words, showed a natural order of things, natural boundaries to cultures which best demonstrated the inner logic they were seeking to prove. The existence of 'language unions' rationalized in theoretical terms a spatial principle of identity rather than a temporal one, the former based on common geography, and the latter on a common historical origin. The inhabitants of these zones of converging culture should be recognized for their 'symphonic personality', as Trubetskoy put it – the various attributes of the individual converged with the environment to create natural wholes which were expressed in the total personalities of their members. Russia and Eastern Slavs were distinguished from their Western, Catholic and Protestant counterparts by the 'Turanian element', according to Trubetskoy – a fossil of the Mongol yoke.

The Eurasianists took seriously the idea that natural linguistic boundaries – isoglosses – denoted a sort of unconscious sovereignty. A cultural system that lay outside such a border could not be claimed; Poland, for example, could not ever be considered a natural part of the Eurasian conglomerate, and thus the multiple attempts to include it in the Russian Empire were inevitably doomed to failure, according to Trubetskoy, who wrote frequently about the hazards of ignoring the natural watersheds of human civilization.

The Eurasianists' structural theories distanced Russia from being considered a 'Slavic' country, as it had been in the nineteenth-century writings of a host of intellectuals who had co-opted the term as their own – the Slavophiles and the Pan-Slavists, such as Danilevsky. Due to a common tendency of development, 'Eurasia' had been decisively and scientifically proven to be a singular unit strictly divided by natural cultural boundaries from the Western Slavs and the 'Romano Germans'. 'Slavdom', however, was an outmoded product of the nineteenth century's obsession with origins and family trees. 'The question of limits and boundaries is thus posed right away as the key issue', according to linguist Patrick Seriot, who has exhaustively researched the Eurasianists' claims. 'Eurasianism is above all an enterprise aimed at reconfiguring frontiers, a deconstruction of entities declared false (the Slavs) to the profit of other supposed to be more real [e.g. Eurasia] because they are organic.'[13] However, he made the point that when it came to portraying the West, Trubetskoy had double standards. He was painstaking when it came to teasing out extremely subtle similarities and gradations in Eurasian cultures, while he tended to see 'Romano Germanic' civilization as an undifferentiated totality, and offered very little justification for this view.

These natural cultural boundaries buttressed the argument for the common political identity of Eurasia and put into practice the fundamental axiom: the cause of all geopolitical misfortune that had befallen the Russian Empire was the non-recognition of the frontiers of natural systems. The data adduced by the

Eurasianists nourished their certainty that while the Bolshevik revolution was doomed, the territory of the Russian Empire, reborn in the Soviet Union, was destined to remain whole. However, in the first collision between the Soviet state and its Eurasian alternative, a clear winner emerged very rapidly.

The deep state

Starting in February 1925, strange, out-of-context words – 'oil', 'Argentina', 'machinists', 'musicians' – began to appear in Trubetskoy's correspondence with other Eurasianists. 'I am angry', Trubetskoy declared in a July letter to Suvchinsky. 'I am angry because the brochure was sent to the manufacturers despite the fact that I specifically asked for that not to happen and for it only to be sent to Argentina.'[14]

The group had begun writing in code. 'Manufacturers' meant the Russian émigré community in Europe, while 'Argentina' meant Russia. 'Oil' stood for Eurasianism, while Trubetskoy was henceforth referred to as 'Yokhelson'. The secure communications, such as they were, signalled a departure for the previously apolitical group of scholars, who evidently had decided on the cipher as they began to dip their toes into the world of clandestine organizing. It had become obvious to the ivory tower academics that in order to become a serious political movement, they would have to engage in politics. And thus began a new phase in the Eurasianists' self-declared mission, entering the through-the-looking-glass world of émigré intrigue, watched at every turn by various Western secret services and the Soviet equivalent (the OGPU or Cheka) – the shadowy competition which provided some of the most lurid stories of espionage and intrigue of the twentieth century. It was a world in which virtually no one was who they said they were, where many made their living as informers for various secret services, and where operatives worked for multiple masters. The only way to succeed was to stay one step ahead of the fleet-footed game of betrayal and double-cross. It was to prove the Eurasianists' undoing.

It had all started sometime in 1922, soon after publication of *Exodus*, when Trubetskoy was approached by a group of White Army officers who expressed an interest in joining the movement. A number of new faces had joined that year, mostly scholars who had been taken with the arguments of *Exodus* or the reputations of its authors.

Although Father Florovsky soon left the group, from 1922 it was joined by a number of like-minded Russian intellectuals, including Vasily Nikitin, an orientalist and former Russian consul in Persia, and Lev Karsavin, a historian, Petr Bitsilli, a medieval historian from Odessa, and Count Dmitry Svyatopolk-Mirsky, a son of a former minister of internal affairs, who later taught at the

London School of Slavonic and East European Studies. Georgy Vernadsky, a historian and son of Vladimir Vernadsky, one of the most eminent natural scientists of Imperial Russia, also joined and would later go on to teach history at Yale University.

In contrast to these new participants, the officers were obviously no intellectuals, but Trubetskoy saw their interest as an opportunity to recruit a cadre of men who could take care of the political work that he believed needed to be started – to link the underground of anti-Bolshevik groups and liaise with other émigré movements, dominated by White officers, to gather even more recruits. They were just the sort of people who would become the raw material for all the political movements of the interwar period in Europe: young, rootless war veterans looking for a place to belong.

One of these men was Petr Arapov. He was a relative of General Wrangel, for whom Savitsky had worked, under Struve. In his mid-twenties, Arapov was the epitome of a Russian officer: well mannered, of 'exceptional appearance', fluent in four languages according to Savitsky, and with a commanding presence.[15] While he could not hope to compete with the academics in their theoretical pursuits, he was nonetheless worldly in ways they were not. They recognized that each needed something the other had: for Arapov, this was probably a purpose to which he could devote his talents; for the intellectuals, it was the realization that they were thinkers in search of doers. As Trubetskoy put it to Suvchinsky: 'Their goal is not self-reliance, rather they seek to put themselves under our authority. I think we should accept this offer . . . judging by everything, they see us as an authority, and sincerely wish to become proper Eurasians and help us in our work.'[16]

Arapov corresponded frequently with the leading members of the Eurasianist movement, particularly Suvchinsky and Savitsky. But he left few clues about his identity or what he had done prior to entering their lives. One of the scarce hints that remain of Arapov's dark side survives in the margin of a letter he wrote to Savitsky, who left a note saying Arapov had taken part in mass executions during his service with Wrangel's army during the civil war, and this was the reason for his deteriorating mental health. Savitsky also noted that Arapov had considerable success with women, but that he exploited them for money out of some dark cynical urge.[17]

Arapov's natural charisma and exceptional networking skills paid off almost immediately. On a trip to England he stayed at the home of Prince Vladimir Golitsyn and his wife Ekaterina (where his mother was also staying). There he was introduced to a wealthy British industrialist, Henry Norman Spalding, and managed to convince him to take an interest in Eurasianism. Spalding eventually agreed to finance the movement with a £10,000 grant.

In 1923, Arapov offered yet another introduction – a tantalizing and mysterious one. His good friend Yury Artamonov, a fellow former officer who
worked for the British embassy in Warsaw as a translator, introduced Arapov
to one Alexander Langovoy. Langovoy told Arapov that he was a member of a
shadowy underground movement inside the USSR known as the 'Trust', which
was dedicated to overthrowing the Bolshevik government. Arapov introduced
his new acquaintance to his Eurasianist colleagues, who apparently swallowed
the story hook, line and sinker. 'He is devoted to the Trust, but at the same time
he is devoted to us, demonstrates sincere worship for the [Eurasianist] founders,
and I believe that our authority is capable of replacing the authority of the Trust
in his eyes', wrote Trubetskoy to Suvchinsky in a series of letters recently
unearthed by historian Sergey Glebov.[18] 'The task at hand is to transform the
Trust into a Eurasianist organization, capable of carrying out Eurasianist goals',
he wrote to Savitsky in 1924.[19] 'In essence, the Trust is a good mechanism, but
without a spirit, and this mechanism could be a weapon in the hands of any
group . . . we have to use this situation.'

But he could not have been more wrong about Langovoy, the son of a famous
Moscow doctor. In fact, Langovoy was a Cheka agent. He had been a convinced
communist from an early age, had fought on the Bolshevik side in the civil war
and was the recipient of the Red Banner award for bravery. After the civil war he
had continued in the communist cause by becoming an officer in the OGPU (the
successor to the Cheka), which was eager to recruit men from intelligentsia back-
grounds who had foreign languages and could move easily in émigré circles. He
found it easy to convince the credulous academics that he had converted to
Eurasianism, and offered them cooperation with the Trust.

The fabled Trust was actually the complete opposite of what Langovoy said
it was. The organization was nothing but a Bolshevik ploy, intended to lure
émigré groups out into the open and to their doom. Believing the fledgling
Soviet regime to be in mortal danger of being overthrown by Western intelligence services working with Russian émigré groups, the Cheka had ambi-
tiously created an entire false-flag conspiracy, which presented itself to émigré
groups as an anti-Soviet movement in the heard of the USSR's establishment.
In reality, it was a trap.

The Trust organization had once been a real underground monarchist
organization, the Monarchist Organization of Central Russia, whose head,
Alexander Yakushev, former chief of the water transport department in the
tsar's Ministry of the Interior, had been arrested in 1921. Instead of executing
Yakushev, however, the Cheka worked on him, recruiting him as one of their
agents, and turning his organization into a false-flag group. Yakushev travelled
throughout Europe meeting monarchists and recruiting supporters. He claimed

to represent an underground conspiracy of anti-communists at the heart of the Bolshevik government. One of his former acquaintances had an entrée to General Kutepov, one of the White generals who were organizing terrorist attacks inside the USSR, and he had served alongside the charismatic former guards officer Arapov, who would ultimately be the conduit for the Trust into the Eurasianists' circle.

The intention of operations like the Trust was to convince the émigré groups in Europe not to act forcefully against the Bolsheviks, but instead to give the organization time to do its work on the inside. In reality, by cooperating with the Trust's objectives, they were giving the Bolshevik leadership time to consolidate its rule.

The Trust offered émigré forces in Europe what they believed was access to a network of operatives inside the USSR, dedicated to overthrowing the Bolsheviks. These 'operatives' would find real intelligence, recruit 'agents', run errands inside the USSR – anything to boost their credibility with the émigré groups. In 1925, for example, while on a trip to the Soviet Union, Langovoy received a panic-stricken note from Arapov telling him of the arrest of an agent named Demidov-Orsini. Langovoy told the OGPU, and Demidov-Orsini (who, it seems, was Wrangel's agent and had nothing to do with the Eurasianists) was freed. This operation seemed to prove the Trust's bona fides and improved relations with the émigrés.[20] Gradually the émigré forces – who were by no means neophytes in the provocation game – started to believe that the Trust was real, and began to let its operatives into their ranks. Then, mysteriously, their agents in the USSR – the real ones – began to get arrested. Their leaders in Europe were kidnapped. Their organizations somehow were infiltrated.

What helped the Trust immeasurably was the pervasive optimism of the émigrés, who continued to believe that the collapse of the Bolshevik regime was just around the corner, and with it, their return to the motherland. When the Trust appeared, it was as though something that had long been prophesied had finally come to pass. As Sergey Glebov, chronicler of the early movement, has written:

> First and foremost, the very fact of the appearance [of the Trust] was consistent with the ideology constructed by the Eurasianists. According to their theory of revolution, a narrow elite of people must inevitably evolve inside Russia who would seize power from inside. The main task would then be to convert them to Eurasianism.[21]

The Eurasianists had produced mountains of pamphlets predicting the imminent demise of the Bolsheviks, and the replacement of communism by a Eurasian ideocracy. Amid the eschatological prophecy and divine mystery that filled their rhetoric, there was something appropriately symmetrical about the appearance on their doorstep of just what they had predicted: a conspiracy within the Bolsheviks to overthrow the government. Now the conspirators sought ties with the Eurasianists. This seemed too good to be true – and of course it was. But the desperate hopes of the émigrés for a return to their motherland overcame common sense and would ultimately lead to their undoing as a movement.

Today, we know that Arapov was probably not an OGPU agent, but rather a credulous and unsophisticated dupe. In 1930, after returning to the Soviet Union, he was arrested by the OGPU, sentenced to ten years in prison in 1934, and shot for counter-revolutionary activities in 1938 (most of the OGPU's upper echelons responsible for the Trust were also executed in 1937 and 1938). An abridged summary of his interrogation was found by historian Kseniya Ermishina in the Lithuanian Special Archive. In it, Arapov described being tricked by Langovoy: 'It was clear to me that Langovoy did not fully understand our Eurasianist position – the reasons for this not understanding were not, of course, clear to me, but later they became clear when it was revealed that the Trust was in fact the OGPU.' With Langovoy's help, Arapov made trips to the USSR between 1924 and 1926.

The Eurasianist leadership required convincing of Langovoy's bona fides. But with Arapov's patient championing, in January 1925 Langovoy was invited to speak to the organization at a meeting in a Berlin flat. 'I lied mercilessly', Langovoy reminisced later. 'The worst horseshit passed for the plain-as-day truth. Things like "Eurasia is a synthesis of Slavic, European and Mongolian cultures. Its foundation is monarchistic." That sort of stuff . . . The Eurasianists argued among themselves. The essence of the debate was whether capitalism is better than a planned economy.'[22] In the end, Langovoy's patience and effort paid off handsomely. He was invited to Prague for another meeting later that year. He 'slipped across the border' by way of Poland. In Prague, he had to deliver another speech, at the end of which the Eurasianists agreed unanimously to attempt to convert the entire Trust to their world view. Langovoy was appointed to the seven-man council of the Eurasianism Organization and named Head of the Eurasianist Party (EAP) in the Soviet Union. This gave him access to all the Eurasianists' information on their associates in the USSR. All correspondence between the organization and its members passed through his hands. 'If every-thing goes well, we will have a great result – the formation of an independent oil [i.e. Eurasianism] organization in Argentina [i.e. Russia]', said Trubetskoy. 'Denisov [code for Langovoy] creates a very favourable, sincere impression.'

Largely due to Arapov's good-natured championing of the Trust, the Eurasianist movement was turned inside out, almost entirely in the service of the OGPU. Eurasianism was penetrated so pervasively that the only surviving veteran of the Trust, Boris Gudz, interviewed in 2004, described Eurasianists as a 'fictitious left-wing tendency created by the Trust'.[23] This version might well have been true: such was the penetration of the Eurasianist organization that from about 1925 it is increasingly unclear who was making the decisions for it – the original leaders or the OGPU. Vladimir Styrna, the deputy director of OGPU counterintelligence, reported to his superiors that penetration of the Eurasianist movement had been so successful that 'our agents are being introduced into the leading organs of the movement, while certain participants in the movement are ready to fulfil almost anything we ask of them'.[24]

Not everyone believed the Trust. One interesting source of information is provided by the interrogation records of Lev Karsavin, a philosopher and member of the Eurasianist organization who moved to Vilnius in 1940 and was arrested by the NKVD in 1949. His testimony was uncovered after the fall of communism and was published in 1992. He told his captors of the inner workings of the Eurasianist organization, and specifically about the suspicions within it that Langovoy was an OGPU agent: 'I understood that the ties to sympathizers in the USSR, sustained through Langovoy, were not serious and this was simply an operation by the organs of the Soviet Union'.[25] He added that Suvchinsky had in fact shared his belief that Langovoy was an OGPU officer. However, they believed that he 'sympathized' with the Eurasianist goals, and allowed himself to be used for the purpose of contacting Eurasianists in the USSR.

The Trust became increasingly audacious in its attempts to gain credibility and swindle its opponents. In February 1927, Langovoy made arrangements for Savitsky to travel across the Polish border to attend a secret Eurasianist 'congress' in Moscow, which Yakushev would also be attending. Savitsky went, saying he was going in the capacity of a 'warrior philosopher' and using false papers giving him the cover identity of 'Nikolay Petrov' from the town of Vitebsk. He would later describe to Suvchinsky ('writing with frostbitten hand') daring manoeuvres to evade surveillance in the USSR, travelling 100 *versts* on horseback in the dead of winter. He did not provide a detailed written account of the meeting, only telling Suvchinsky that he would brief him orally at their next meeting. 'Briefly,' wrote Savitsky in a letter of 24 February 1927, 'I have found oil [i.e. Eurasianism] which I was looking for, and which I hope will serve as support for all of us . . . They are relatively small (about 200 persons), but morally healthy oil'.[26]

The OGPU pulled out all the stops for the congress, fielding hundreds of agents, including Yakushev, who agreed to found a covert 'Eurasianist Party'. The event was followed by a real church service, at which Savitsky took communion from a real church metropolitan, who had evidently been recruited for the affair. All the 'Eurasianists' Savitsky met in Moscow were very well versed in the basic tenets of the movement: this elaborate show was designed solely to convince Savitsky (and in turn the Eurasianist leadership, to whom he enthusiastically recounted all this on his return) that the Trust organization was genuine, and that the Eurasianist movement had a growing constituency inside the USSR.

But Savitsky's victory was short-lived. In April 1927, only weeks after he returned from Moscow, a key OGPU operative, Eduard Uppelin (codenamed 'Opperput'), fled to Finland, surrendered to the Finnish secret service and wrote an exposé of the Trust organization in *Segodnya*, a Riga newspaper. Following his trip, Savitsky had strenuously promoted the Trust's bona fides to his sceptical fellow party members, and apparently could not credit that it had been a meticulously constructed fraud. He continued to believe that those he had met in Moscow were real Eurasianists, and he worried that he had compromised Yakushev.[27] He felt personal responsibility when Yakushev was imprisoned in the late 1930s during the Stalinist purges, believing he had put the man's life at risk. In the late 1960s, Savitsky's sons actually debated whether or not to tell their father about the 1967 Soviet book *Dead Ripple*. This was based on Yakushev's documents and told the full story of the Trust for the first time, with the aim of rehabilitating repressed OGPU officers like Artuzov and Langovoy. They decided against telling him, and he died a year later none the wiser.

Deceptions rely on one overwhelming human failing: the fact that people tend to believe what they want to believe. This is the notorious cognitive glitch known as 'confirmation bias'. Any new evidence to the contrary is discounted or somehow manipulated by the mind to reinforce one's existing point of view. It was this failing that kept the Trust in business. So powerful is this human tendency that even after the plot was unmasked, many refused to believe it. Arapov continued to champion the Trust, writing a note to the Eurasianist leadership that 'Opperput' was an OGPU provocateur, and that they should resume cooperation with the 'healthy' parts of the Trust which were not infiltrated. He continued to believe, for example, that while Langovoy was an OGPU agent, he was in reality a sympathizer of Eurasianism. In 1930 he returned to the USSR and never emerged again.[28]

The Trust was one of the most wildly successful operations in the history of intelligence, but very little is known about it even today. Indeed, had 'Opperput' not blown the whistle on the organization, it would likely never have become public knowledge. Artuzov, according to his biographer, received the only formal reprimand of his career over the bungled decommissioning of the Trust (though later he was executed). By the time the Trust was unmasked,

however, the Soviets did not even need to infiltrate the Eurasianist organization. Little by little, several Eurasianists, led by Suvchinsky in Paris, had begun
to display increasing sympathy towards the USSR. Suvchinsky had never been
as utterly convinced as his comrades – 'Eurasianism did not eat Suvchinsky',
said Vadim Kozovoy, a friend later in life (employing a phrase from Dostoevsky's
novel *The Possessed*, when the protagonist Stavrogin is 'eaten' by an idea).
He also increasingly found emigration intolerably dull, said Kozovoy. But
Suvchinsky was spellbound by Stalin, whose thesis, upon assuming power, was
'socialism in one country' and who aimed at promoting Russian nationalism.
Suvchinsky believed this was the first step towards the eventual rejection of
communism and an embrace of the Eurasianist ideals; according to Kozovoy,
he had to be repeatedly talked out of returning to the USSR.[29]

Suvchinsky (leading the left wing of Eurasianism) and Savitsky (who held
the right) had already begun to clash in 1925. The latter was bitterly opposed
to communism and atheism, and was distrustful of the Soviets. Savitsky insisted
that Eurasian orthodoxy could not be sacrificed for a temporary accommodation with Stalin. Meanwhile Trubetskoy, once the most enthusiastic and energetic of the group, gradually withdrew, demoralized, and pursued his academic
research, which was at last bearing fruit.

The schism took place amid a shift in the tectonic plates of Soviet ideology.
As Stalin consolidated his power as general secretary of the Communist
Party, his lieutenants were slowly realizing how little appeal the pantheon of
Marxism held as a tool for inspiring and mobilizing the population. Of the
official heroes of the Soviet Union, several were either foreign (Marx, Engels,
Marat) or unfamiliar (Frunze, Kotovsky) or both (Rosa Luxemburg, Karl
Liebknecht).[30]

Instead of national heroes, great battles and a shared history, Soviet commis-
sars taught of social forces and stages of economic development. The early
attempts to make stirring propaganda out of this mixture were laughable. The
Communist Party hierarchs, realizing they needed propaganda that would
work, quietly began looking for ideological alternatives to communist orthodoxy in order to mobilize the masses. Soviet nationalities policies also took
account of self-determination, however fictitious – ethnic groups were assigned
national or autonomous status, with parliaments and governments; national
languages were recognized and customs celebrated, all within the artificial
bubble of Communist Party rule.

Stalin gradually began to rehabilitate symbols and personalities of the
Russian national past, and combined this with the modern tools of mass
culture, particularly the cinema. The 'National Bolshevism' of Stalin began to
look very much like the political programme of Eurasianism. There is no

evidence that Stalin actually was influenced at all by Eurasianist writings; however, the fact that these émigré intellectual trends sprang up at more or less the same time as the very phenomenon they had predicted indicates that the Soviets and the émigrés were, in a sense, drinking from the same well.

Stalin's decisive swerve to the right in turn fed the arguments of Suvchinsky and several other left-leaning Eurasianists, who increasingly doubted that supporting Eurasianism was actually a meaningful alternative to embracing the new USSR, and who began making increasingly strident appeals for rapprochement with the Soviets. To them, the changes wrought by Stalin were proof of their fundamental argument, proof of the reality of the Eurasian revolution against the West. Arapov even wrote to Suvchinsky: 'Isn't it better for us to leave Stalin to do calmly what we like so much in his activities?'[31]

The correspondence of the left-wing Eurasianists during this period was full of praise for Stalin's reforms; and with each step towards National Bolshevism taken by Stalin, the resolve of the Eurasianist Party to supplant the Soviet regime weakened. In 1927, Suvchinsky even opened negotiations with the Soviet representative in France, though it was unclear with what objective. That same year, Suvchinsky contacted the author Maxim Gorky, a personal friend of Stalin's, then living in Italy, with a proposal to work for the Soviet cause, saying that his group of Eurasianists supported three-quarters of the Soviet ideology. Gorky wrote to Stalin in support of the proposal, but Stalin appears to have shown no interest.

The right wing of the party, led by Savitsky, grew increasingly impatient at what it saw as freelancing by the left-wingers in Paris (though it is not clear if they even knew of the extent of the contacts between the left Eurasianists and the Soviet government). But they began to disagree profoundly on everything from Marxian economics to aesthetics, as the Paris branch of Eurasianism swung around to take a more orthodox Marxian view. For a time, in 1927 and 1928, both sides sought to obstruct publications by the other.

With the growing polarization of Eurasianism, Trubetskoy began to lose interest in the movement, and his influence over the squabbling circle of academics, former officers and undercover OGPU agents began to wane. He realized that the collapse of Soviet power, which he foretold, was not imminent: 'We are working not in the present moment, but in the far future.' By 1927, Trubetskoy was already frustrated by the movement, as evidenced in a letter to Suvchinsky: 'When people accuse us of having no systems, only a mechanical mixture of heterogeneous, disconnected ideas, which people can pick and choose from as they like, this accusation is justified.'[32]

Trubetskoy by this point was demoralized and exhausted. He wrote to Suvchinsky in March 1928:

In my case, Eurasianism only prevents me from realizing my talent. If you just knew what a heavy burden on my consciousness is this ballast of Eurasianist obligations, if you knew how much it intervenes with my scholarly work . . . Eurasianism is a heavy cross for me, and without any compensation. Please understand that deep in my soul I hate it and I cannot avoid hating it. Eurasianism broke me, it did not allow me to be who I should have and could have been. It would be my greatest joy to drop it, to leave it, and to forget about it altogether . . .[33]

That October, he first raised in a letter to Suvchinsky the prospect of a 'divorce', leaving the Paris left wing free to pursue contacts with the Soviets, and the Prague-based right wing to continue with the orthodox Eurasianism. The conflict was further stoked by the Paris branch's efforts to put out a newspaper, *Evraziya*, which had an obvious pro-Soviet bent. In the eighth edition of the *Evraziya* newspaper, Trubetskoy published a letter in which he formally resigned.

That was to be the end of the movement. In January 1929, Savitsky met Suvchinsky and Lev Karsavin, a Suvchinsky ally, in which Savitsky described the editorial line of the newspaper as 'unacceptable and contradictory to the notion of moral principle'. Karsavin and Suvchinsky took this as a personal insult. The newspaper collapsed soon after, and the break-up was complete. Savitsky tried to re-energize the Prague-based Eurasianist movement off and on during the early 1930s, but to little avail.

'We hit the mark'

Following his 'Eurasianism broke me' tirade directed at Suvchinsky in the spring of 1928, a deflated Trubetskoy began to return his focus to linguistics and phonology, and to take up once again his scholarly collaboration with Jakobson and the Prague Circle. The Eurasianists, fragmented and defeated, went their separate ways.

In 1929, Trubetskoy and Jakobson published a series of papers which won them accolades, with Jakobson inventing the term 'linguistic structuralism' to describe their theories. Trubetskoy's attack on the late Shakhmatov, while never published, had driven him and Jakobson to some of the greatest linguistic breakthroughs of the twentieth century. Their theories would also be precursors to the great twentieth-century academic clash between history and 'structure'. This latter became the greatest scholarly fad of the latter half of the twentieth century, flourishing in European universities, and popularized by the late Claude Lévi-Strauss.[34] It sought the explanation for all manner of things

– from history to anthropology to psychoanalysis – in universal and timeless laws of unconscious structure that were first apparent to the linguists.

What Trubetskoy and Jakobson sought to do with phonology – to deduce laws which govern the relationships between acoustic impressions – Lévi-Strauss and a host of others sought to do with myths, folktales, literature, marriage customs and psychology. Rules could often be deduced that could create the fundamentals of a system out of what would otherwise be a jumble of data. Trubetskoy's phonemic theories, said Lévi-Strauss, some twenty years after the prince's death, were a monumental breakthrough: 'For the first time, a social science [was] able to formulate necessary relationships.' He predicted that Trubetskoy's and Jakobson's insights 'will certainly play the same renovating role with respect to the social sciences that nuclear physics, for example, has played with the physical sciences'.[35]

Eventually the euphoria of structuralism wore off, once it became clear that structuralism works for (some) phonemes, but not as one moves into progressively broader areas of culture, such as literature, psychology or folklore. 'The more elements there are, the harder it is for structuralism to work', as Anatoly Liberman, a specialist on Trubetskoy's phonology, put it. However the utopian enthusiasm of Russia's Silver Age to search for the universal geometry of our human natures, channelled by Trubetskoy and Jakobson into linguistics, is still present in that field: it has been the precursor to other projects (almost) as utopian as it was, for instance Noam Chomsky's generative grammar and the cognitive revolution in psychology. While many of Trubetskoy's findings have been forgotten, his fundamental project – to tease out necessary relationships from the elements of language – still intrigues linguists.

The excitement of his discoveries failed to rescue Trubetskoy from the deep depression that enveloped him following the collapse of the Eurasianist movement (which, for many of its members, had been less a political organization than a form of self-help). For Trubetskoy, the end of the movement and the consolidation of Bolshevik rule cemented the permanence of his exile.

Surveying Stalin's Russia, Trubetskoy realized with horror that the National Bolshevism being implemented was just the kind of national synthesis they had sought through their writings:

> We were excellent diagnosticians, not bad predictors, but very poor ideologues – in the sense that our predictions, hitting the mark, turned out to be nightmares. We predicted the emergence of a new Eurasian culture. Now that culture actually exists, but is completely a nightmare and we recoil from it in horror.[36]

Trubetskoy's life and scientific endeavours would end in tragedy. He wrote only rarely on Eurasianism after his split with the movement. Following the March 1938 Anschluss of Austria, he became a target of the Nazis, who were suspicious of all Russian émigrés, especially those with any demonstrable political sympathies. In May of that year, the Gestapo searched his flat and confiscated his correspondence with Jakobson, as well as the notes for his beloved *Prehistory of Slavic Languages*. It was evidently too much for the prince to bear. He died eight months later of a heart attack, which friends believe was brought on by the stress.

Jakobson managed, however, to save the draft of Trubetskoy's *Principles of Phonology*, which would become the prince's greatest legacy. Before fleeing the Nazis, first to Scandinavia and then to the US, Jakobson hid his own correspondence with Trubetskoy in Prague. He later recovered these valuable letters, which he published in 1976. Jakobson would live on until 1982, teaching at Harvard and MIT, and becoming one of the most eminent linguists of his time. But his friendship with Trubetskoy still haunted him late in life. Shortly before his death, Jakobson reminisced about the demise of Trubetskoy:

> The long period of our collaboration had come to an end. From now on I would have to work alone and verify for myself future findings and subsequent hypotheses. In addition it became more apparent that my vivid collaboration with the Linguistic Circle of Prague would soon come to an end, as would later the activities of the circle itself. For me the years of homeless wandering from one country to another had begun.[37]

By the late 1930s, Savitsky had become the last bearer of the Eurasianist flame. Following the schism with Suvchinsky and the left wing of the movement, the remaining cohort gradually melted away. Some, particularly Suvchinsky's followers, had returned to the USSR, where they (almost without exception) met a tragic fate. Trubetskoy had continued to publish occasional articles in Eurasianist journals organized by Savitsky, but following his break with the movement he never showed the same enthusiasm, and declined to stay in touch with most of his erstwhile comrades. Of the Prague-based movement, few were left or still interested by the late 1930s. Savitsky continued to publish articles about the USSR in the Prague-based *Slavische Rundschau*, and the Paris-based journal *Le Monde slave*. He had stopped participating in the Prague Linguistic Circle as well. Jakobson and Trubetskoy had begun to focus on their own efforts and had disengaged from the circle by the mid-1930s. Jakobson still lived in Prague and saw Savitsky often; but Trubetskoy went to Prague less and less. In the late 1930s, following Trubetskoy's death and Jakobson's departure from Prague ahead of the German invasion of Czechoslovakia, Savitsky was left without his old companions. These years were particularly unproductive for him.

The war had split the émigré community into two groups: those whose implacable hatred of the Bolsheviks blinded them to the nature of German aggression (they remained neutral or even supported Germany), and those whose loyalty to the motherland rallied them to the defence of 'Holy Russia', despite their reservations about Stalin's regime, and prevailed upon them to make temporary accommodation with the Soviet government. Savitsky was firmly of the latter group, and became more and more alienated from other émigré political groups who sided with the Germans.

When the Nazis occupied Prague in 1939, Savitsky stayed, but was fired from his job teaching Russian and Ukrainian at the German University of Prague due to his anti-German politics. He was then hired as director of pedagogy at the Russian Gymnasium, but was fired in 1944 over his refusal to mobilize older students from the schools for army service in special Russian units of the German army.

Aside from the loss of two jobs, the Savitsky family was little affected by the conflict. The children were too young to be drafted, their father too old. Czechoslovakia suffered comparatively little heavy fighting in the war, and Prague changed hands both times with scarcely a shot being fired. Soviet troops first entered Czechoslovakia in 1944, and in May 1945 Savitsky brought his family out to welcome the Soviet 'liberators' on 9 May, as the first units paraded through the city. His pride in the *rodina* or motherland, however, was to be severely tested in the coming days. Along with the Red Army, units of the Soviet counterintelligence service SMERSH (short for *Smert Shpionam* or 'death to spies') swept into Prague to round up White Russians and monarchists. They arrested 215, including Savitsky.[38]

The Savitskys' first brush with the Soviet 'special services' came in the middle of May, only days after Soviet troops entered Prague. A young uniformed officer appeared at their door wanting to speak to Savitsky. A soldier with a submachine gun waited on the stairs outside their building, while another took Savitsky's two sons for a ride in their military vehicle. The officer left after a long chat in Savitsky's apartment; he was 'happy to have met such a Russian patriot living abroad', according to Savitsky's son, Ivan. A few days later, a different group of soldiers returned and took the elder Savitsky away for interrogation somewhere in Prague. But he returned a week later in high spirits, having been given a letter stating that he had been investigated and nothing had been found against him. A week after that, however, a new group of soldiers came, and for the first time there were men with them wearing plain clothes.

They had a much more serious air about them, Ivan recalled. Despite Savitsky's protests that he had already been investigated, the soldiers said that was irrelevant. It gradually dawned on the family that something serious was happening, and that the visitors were not like the first two groups, who had probably visited all the Russian émigrés living in Prague and done cursory checks. This unit had come with express orders from on-high to arrest Savitsky. Savitsky's wife Vera, sensing that things were taking a turn for the worse, asked her husband if he would be needing winter clothes – even though it was still the middle of May. Savitsky, still confident, replied: 'No, of course that won't be necessary. I'll just have a chat with them here.'[39] That chat was to last a decade.

* * *

Savitsky was taken to Moscow, where he was imprisoned for a time in the Lubyanka, the imposing headquarters of the NKVD/KGB. The full extent of how badly the Eurasianist movement had been penetrated by Soviet intelligence was brought home to him there, during the interrogations, when he was shown evidence against himself which had clearly been prepared by people inside the movement – people whose identities he knew and whom he had trusted. 'He couldn't see the names, but he could recognize the handwriting', according to Ivan. Though Savitsky never divulged whose handwriting he had seen, one of the informants was very likely to have been Arapov.

After being held in the Lubyanka for some months, Savitsky was sent to a work camp in Mordovia, in central Russia. Little detail is known of his ordeal, and he would not speak of it on his return. But he was almost certainly tortured under interrogation, convicted of some bogus crime and transported in an unheated cattle car to his gulag, to spend the next ten years felling trees. Strangely, he seemed to bear little ill will towards his homeland. He was unutterably homesick and desperate for any reunion with Russia, even if that was in prison:

> Oh how my return was terrifying
> The sight of hometowns in ruin
> And Moscow during the early days of my internment
> The vanity of all attempts and words
>
> I lay down on my native land.
> Summer night, breathing earth
> And the moon, and the volume of the sublunary world,
> Flooded the fields with radiance

And I sensed the secret forces
In this beautiful breathing earth
The body came to life in a new effort
And poetry, like a river, flowed.[40]

For a while, his family was able to receive regular updates from Savitsky's sister, who lived in Moscow and was able to visit him in the gulag fairly regularly. But after 1948, such visits became impossible: she worked at the Academy of Sciences in Moscow, and after that year all academy personnel were forbidden from making contact with foreign countries or citizens, including, in this case, her brother.

From 1948 to June 1955, the family had no word of the elder Savitsky, and did not even know whether he was dead or alive. Finally, in June 1955, one General Chernavin visited the family in Prague and, hands shaking, produced a letter from Savitsky, who had been released from the camp. Following Stalin's death in 1953, his successor Nikita Khrushchev embarked on reforms and by 1955 had released most political prisoners. Savitsky was in the town of Potma, at a rest home, awaiting transport back to Prague. The letter had been written on the eve of Easter, 1955:

Christ has risen, my dear Vera, Nika and Vanya. I am writing you this letter to congratulate you on the coming great celebration, and give you some news about myself, and receive some news from you.

He wrote that he had been let out on 7 April. In further letters, he revealed that after an operation in 1953 he had been unable to do manual labour, and had been given the job of camp librarian. In what may have been the ultimate manifestation of Stockholm syndrome, he was also thinking about exchanging his Czech citizenship for Soviet. Finally, in January 1956, he was able to travel back to Prague, where he was met by his wife and two sons, who were now in their twenties. He was clean-shaven, emaciated and slightly stooped. He began working again, as a translator on the magazine *Soviet Czechoslovakia*.

Prague, which in the interwar years had sparkled with intellectual vigour, was now a communist country, with no chance of fostering open intellectual exchange. All the academics Savitsky had once enjoyed so much were now either dead or had emigrated. The one bright spot was when Jakobson visited once in 1956 to attend a linguistics conference. He was by now teaching at Harvard, and was making quite a name for himself with theories of 'markedness' and 'linguistic universals'; but politically it was very touchy for him. Jakobson had been investigated as a communist by the House Un-American

Activities Committee, the witch-hunt congressional committee set up by Senator Joseph McCarthy. The first thing Jakobson did when he visited the Savitsky household was to place a pillow over the telephone.

Savitsky was rescued from his boredom and despair by a chance letter from Matvey Gukovsky, a scholar he had met in Mordovia. Gukovsky wanted to put Savitsky in touch with someone – a fellow camp survivor with an abiding interest in steppe peoples; someone who shared his Eurasianist views; someone with an unmistakable and exalted surname, with whom he could share some of his lifetime of scholarship and some of his tragedy. This man was a historian by the name of Lev Gumilev.

PART II

PART II

CHAPTER FIVE

REQUIEM

Being the subject of one of the greatest poems of the twentieth century must be both an honour and a burden. Particularly the latter, if the subject is your own imminent death.

It was 1937 and the height of Stalin's terror when Lev Gumilev was arrested in Leningrad in his dormitory room and shipped to an arctic labour camp. For 17 months, his mother, the renowned Russian poet Anna Akhmatova, waited in lines and wrote countless letters beseeching police officials to inform her of the fate of her son. Her struggle is immortalized in the poem 'Requiem', her most famous work.

'Requiem' was written for all the mothers (and other women) whom Akhmatova met in the wintry streets outside police offices in Leningrad, wearing peasants' felt boots to keep their feet from freezing, waiting to send parcels or receive news of their loved ones who had not come back from work one day, or who had been bundled into black NKVD cars in the middle of the night and never returned. The poem, which alternates between elegy, lamentation and witness, culminates in its most famous stanzas – possibly the most famous lines written in Russia in the past century:

> For seventeen months I've been crying out,
> Calling you home.
> I flung myself at the hangman's feet,
> You are my son and my horror.
> Everything is confused forever,
> And it's not clear to me
> Who is beast now, who is man,
> And how long before the execution.
> And there are only dusty flowers,

And the chinking of the censer, and tracks
From somewhere to nowhere.
And staring me straight in the eyes,
And threatening impending death,
Is an enormous star.[1]

During the reign of Soviet ideology, which stressed selfless collectivism, public spirit and ululating, broad-chested heroes, Akhmatova's poetry – with its private loves, despair and tender-hearted longing – was subversive. This was her paradox: the unrelenting publicity she gave to her private life. And it bothered Lev, the subject of 'Requiem', who liked to point out that while it was *his* death that was being written about, the poem was basically about *her*. The tragedies of Akhmatova's life were public property; and Lev felt she treated the torments of those around her, including his own, above all as something that she was suffering.

Akhmatova was one of Russia's most influential public intellectuals of the twentieth century, the conscience of the nation throughout the suffering of the Stalinist era. And Lev had to share her with the entire country. Akhmatova was both an immense source of personal pride and the bane of his existence. Lev was fond of saying of his two seven-year stints in labour camps that 'the first was for papa, the second for mama'. The first spell was punishment for being the son of a martyr – his father, Nikolay Gumilev, was shot by the Bolsheviks in 1921; during the second, he was – he strongly believed – being held hostage to ensure his mother's good behaviour. 'If I wasn't her son, but the son of a simple woman, I would be, other things being equal, a flourishing professor', Lev wrote from prison in 1955 to Emma Gerstein.

But mother and son were each a heavy weight for the other to bear: Akhmatova knew that any transgressions by her would rebound on Lev, and so his very existence was a ball and chain on her artistic freedom. She could not help but see her son as an enormous responsibility and a yoke on her poetic gift – a gift which, for his sake, she refused to use for decades. This sense of their shared fates would emerge most expressively in 'Requiem' with the line '*ty syn i uzhas moi*' – literally 'you are my son and my horror'.

Lev's attachment to Akhmatova seemed to border on the neurotic. He would throw fits and tantrums (even in his mid-forties) if she ignored him, sometimes rebuking her or complaining about her in his letters ('Mama is not writing to me. I imagine I am once again the victim of psychological games'). He was also intensely jealous of her other husbands and lovers after the death of his father. After their first meeting, Gerstein said of Lev that he 'took no interest in girls. He adored his mother.'[2] It may have been coincidence, but Lev only married in 1967, the year after his mother died.

As the son of Akhmatova and Gumilev, Lev grew up with a sense of entitlement, but also under the pressure to live up to their expectations. As a child he was surrounded by all the names that would become synonymous with modern Russian poetry: Boris Pasternak, Osip Mandelstam, Marina Tsvetayeva, all of whom were close friends of his mother and father. Akhmatova herself discouraged Lev from being a poet, saying he lacked the talent. Though this was basically the truth, it used to plunge her son into bouts of depression and rejection.

Lev's father, Nikolay Gumilev, was one of the most talented poets of Russia's Silver Age. A tremendously charismatic artist, he was shot by the Bolsheviks when Lev was just nine years old. Like many boys who lose their fathers so young, Lev never had the chance to move on from his hero-worship, even though Nikolay had essentially abandoned the boy after he and Akhmatova divorced in 1918.

Akhmatova, too, was notable more for the empty spaces she left in Lev's life than for her presence. She was in a state of emotional collapse for most of his childhood, and lacked the strength to raise a child – a task which she left to her mother-in-law. Akhmatova's treatment of Lev is controversial, and the two did not speak for the final five years of her life – partly because Lev's personality changed for the worse after 14 years in labour camps, and partly, it seems, because (as he would later say in several interviews) she let her concern for her public persona get in the way of her commitment to him.

Akhmatova was a tremendously private person, and extremely introverted. Her biographer Amanda Haight has written that she was 'incapable of the simple acts of love which make it possible to live with another person'.[3] This could be seen in her poetry, which was overwhelmingly about one subject: herself. She wrote of her emotions, her feelings, her wants and her needs. Her friend, the poet Korney Chukovsky, described her poetry as: 'I love, but I am not loved; I am loved, but I do not love – this is her main specialty.'

Her obsession with the unrequited and dysfunctional was borne out in her failed marriage to Lev's father. Soon after Lev was born, his parents' marriage began to break down. The lifestyle of the avant-garde circles of St Petersburg had taken their toll; sexual experimentation was all the rage, and things were not well with the couple. Gumilev told his wife he would not continue to be faithful to her, but said she could have the freedom to take lovers as she pleased. Indeed, the following year he fathered a son by another woman. Even before their divorce, Akhmatova left Lev with her mother-in-law, Anna Sergeevna Gumileva, on their estate at Slepnevo.[4]

In 1921, Nikolay was arrested after an acquaintance accused him of plotting to overthrow the Bolshevik government. It was a common enough occurrence in those days: whatever the merits of an allegation, one simply deflected blame by naming, under interrogation, one's 'co-conspirators' in whatever deed the accusation concerned. Gumilev, however, did not crack. After days of interrogation, and before his friends could intervene to have him released, he was sentenced to death and shot on 25 August. The last time Lev saw his father had been that May. He reminisced much later: 'My grandmother kept weeping, and the atmosphere at home was desolate . . . She and my mother were convinced of my father's innocence, which . . . added a bitter twist to their sorrow.'

In death, Nikolay became a martyr, the many flaws in his indulgent character forgotten by his contemporaries. He became a ghost to haunt the Bolsheviks and a generation of Russia's finest poets grew up worshipping him. Lev spent the rest of his life trying to live up to the impossible ideal of this dead colossus. His own youthful memories of his father's infrequent visits took on gigantic proportions in his psyche. It seems his decision to devote his life to history was largely because of an offhand comment that his father had made on their last meeting: 'history is important', he had said, while presenting Lev with a history book as a gift.

The nine-year-old Lev was ostracized at school after his father's execution. In a practice characteristic of early Soviet experiments with breeding young communists, Lev's school was 'self-governed' by pupils. When his fellow nine-year-olds learned that young Lev's father had been shot as a traitor, they voted not to give him textbooks that year. Adding to the pain, his mother, who was in a state of total emotional collapse, did not visit until that December. Nikolay's death was devastating for Akhmatova, even though they had separated long ago. She would say later that, of all the men who were her 'husbands', she had been spiritually closest to him. After his death, she began what Haight calls her 40-year period of 'homelessness', during which time she was utterly dependent on others for survival, living with husbands, lovers, their relatives or her friends. That visit to Lev in 1921 would be the last he saw of her until 1925 – and that next visit was to last just one day.

After her second marriage fell apart, and following a series of romances with men who were either abusive or who abandoned her (or both), Akhmatova met the man who would be both a stabilizing factor in her turbulent life and a source of continual torment for her and Lev. Art historian Nikolay Punin, who at the time was married, became her lover and, in 1925, Akhmatova actually moved into Punin's flat, even though his wife Anna Ahrens and their daughter Irina were still living there.

This flat was in the Fountain House, one of the most beautiful mansions of eighteenth-century St Petersburg on the Fontanka river embankment. Before the revolution, the famed baroque palace had belonged to the Sheremetev family, one of the stalwarts of pre-revolutionary St Petersburg aristocracy. This was the geographical and cultural centre of Leningrad, in all its fading glory.

Above the arched gateway was the Sheremetev family motto: *Deus conservat omnia* – 'God preserves all'. The courtyard faced the central Liteyny Street, and just five blocks away was the headquarters of the NKVD – a 12-storey building nicknamed the 'Big House' that was to play such a towering role in the lives of both mother and son.

Like most of the houses of the aristocracy, the Fountain House had been broken up into communal flats, or *kommunalki*, shared by several families. Akhmatova and the Punins shared the kitchen and two rooms of apartment 44. It was a typical Soviet arrangement: in the years of severe housing and food shortages, divorced couples frequently had to stay in the same flat, leading separate lives. Ahrens was understandably miserable with the arrangement – she and her daughter slept in the room next to Punin and Akhmatova – and she rearranged her work schedule so that she would not have to be home at night.

Punin could be extremely warm, but he had a tyrannical streak, and Akhmatova became more and more isolated from her friends. She would say later that she had wanted to leave Punin but could not bring herself to because she was too weak, physically and spiritually. She had a roof over her head and some measure of security, and during the privations of the 1920s and 1930s Russians got used to all manner of compromise in the name of sheer survival.

In 1929, at the age of 17, Lev moved to Leningrad, which would be his spiritual home for the rest of his life. It was a world away from the town of Bezhetsk and the estate of Slepnevo where he had grown up. In the 1920s and 1930s, the city of Dostoevsky and Pushkin was still the cosmopolitan heart of the Russian/Soviet Empire, though a few more decades of purges would shift that mantle to Moscow. Akhmatova and her friends, Boris Pasternak and Osip Mandelstam, presided over the tarnished glory of the Russian Silver Age from the faded splendour of the imperial capital.

It was into this world that Lev Gumilev made his way in 1929, hoping to complete his secondary education there and enter Leningrad University. He also moved into the Fountain House. From the outset, Lev and Punin disliked one another. Punin had once denounced Lev's father Nikolay in the Bolshevik newspaper *Iskusstvo Kommuny*,[5] and indeed this may have influenced Nikolay's fate. Lev was also resentful of Akhmatova's relationship with Punin. A supreme attention-seeking egoist, Punin was likewise jealous of Akhmatova's affection for Lev.

Dysfunctional and miserable, this odd group lived together with no real choice in the matter.[6] Apartments were in chronic short supply in the USSR: 'future generations will never understand what living space meant to us', wrote Akhmatova's friend Nadezhda Mandelstam in her memoirs of the time:

Innumerable crimes have been committed for its sake and people are so tied
to it that to leave it would never occur to them . . . Husbands and wives who
loathe the sight of each other, mothers in law, sons in law, grown sons and
daughters, former domestic servants who have managed to hang on to a
cubby hole next to the kitchen – all are wedded to their living space and
would never part with it.[7]

Lev established himself in a pigeonhole on a wooden chest, near a partition
with another flat. A small window provided some light, and it was heated in
winter by a tiled stove. Despite the fact that Akhmatova was actually paying
him rent, Punin was resentful of having to feed the 17-year-old Lev. In an argument with Akhmatova, he was heard to complain: 'What do you expect, Anya,
I can't feed the whole city!' Lev also moaned that Punin favoured his daughter
Irina over him.

Meanwhile, the political situation for artists was worsening. While the early
1920s had been an era of relative tolerance towards artists, as the decade wore
on, heavy pressure was applied to all competitors to the orthodox Marxist
theory of art and literature. Akhmatova's friend, the children's poet Korney
Chukovsky, remembered meeting her in the early 1930s, after she had sold a
volume of poems to the publisher Sovetskaya Literatura, and they demanded
there be '1. No mysticism 2. No pessimism 3. No politics'. As Akhmatova joked:
'all that was left was the fornication'.

Pressure on Akhmatova had slowly been building. In 1925, the Communist
Party, in all probability motivated by Stalin, had taken a secret decision to forbid
her from publishing any further works. Though it is unclear if she even knew of
such a decision, and it appears to have been unevenly enforced. But she cannot
have failed to notice that many submissions were refused. Soon after, she lost
her pension.[8]

Emma Gerstein recalled that, soon after she began seeing Lev, her friends
warned her to stay away from 'Akhmatova's son'. She distinctly remembered
calling Lev from the apartment of a friend, who confronted her afterwards:
'You were talking to Akhmatova's son, weren't you? . . . Keep clear of him, he
may have some bad acquaintances . . . To be honest . . . from my apartment . . .
I'd prefer it if . . .' On her next visit to Leningrad, she was told much the same
thing by the relatives she was staying with: 'Whom do you go to see? Akhmatova?
Keep away from her son . . .'

I was staggered at the spectacle of his existence, which offered him no refuge
on this earth. 'Who is the fairest of them all?' the fairy queen demands, and
the mirror always replies, 'In this land, beyond all doubt you . . . but . . .' So

whenever I asked in like fashion, 'Who is the unhappiest person in the world?'
I would tell myself 'You are, but . . .' and remember the nobility with which
Lyova [as Lev was known] bore the miseries of a life in which he was buried
alive.[9]

Lev's first run-in with the security services had actually happened in 1933 as
a result of his association with poetry: he was translating Persian poetry in
the flat of an Arabic scholar, Vasily Eberman, when the latter was arrested.[10]
Akhmatova recalled being at home and receiving a call from the OGPU. She
asked about Lev: 'He's with us.' This time, though, Lev got off relatively easily:
he was released after nine days and was not subjected to any harsh treatment.
Eberman received a five-year sentence and was never seen again.

Lev's ambitions to study history at university were hamstrung by more than
his tenuous political status. History was actually not offered at Leningrad State
University (LGU) for years after the Bolshevik revolution, as it had not been
deemed sufficiently progressive. Instead, it had been replaced by a course on
the 'history of world grain prices'.[11] In 1934, however, came a break. The (ill-
fated) Leningrad Communist Party boss Sergey Kirov spoke of the 'disgraceful'
state of history teaching in schools, as part of the broad realization among
many in the party that the standard Marxist dogmas lacked appeal and needed
to be supplemented with genuine patriotism. As part of this change in attitude,
Lev's application to the university was accepted, and he was permitted to take
the entrance exams, which he passed. He was almost permanently short of
money, wore patches on his clothes and was always hungry. But for all that, Lev
was a dashing young man with irrepressible style and a provocative sense of
humour. He was quick with jokes and liked to get into arguments, according to
Gerstein, who endured this particular trait with some embarrassment.

One of Lev's most important, fateful friendships was with the famed poet
Osip Mandelstam, a close friend of Akhmatova's and, like her, a luminary of
Russia's Silver Age. He was apparently the basis for the character of the Master,
the embittered genius writer of Mikhail Bulgakov's famous novel *The Master
and Margarita*. Osip and his wife Nadezhda lived a bohemian life in Moscow,
and Lev stayed with them whenever he was in town. Osip had a strong anarchic
streak, like Lev, and loved to play practical jokes. According to Gerstein, whenever Lev arrived, Mandelstam would say: 'Let's go play some pranks!' The
consequences of Osip Mandelstam's gleefully mad nature and razor-sharp
artistic gift were to be fatal for him – and were to prove nearly as tragic for Lev.

CHAPTER SIX

THE 'BIG HOUSE'

On 1 December 1934, Sergey Kirov, the ranking Communist Party bureaucrat for Leningrad, walked out of his office in the Smolny Institute, a sprawling palace a few blocks from the Fountain House, where Lev and his mother were living. Behind him a mysterious man raised a revolver and shot Kirov in the head.

Kirov's death would usher in one of the most agonizing genocides of human history: the so-called 'Great Terror' of the 1930s. By many accounts (including that of a senior NKVD defector), Stalin himself wanted Kirov removed – his popularity and standing in the party were getting too high for the dictator's liking. But Stalin and his head of the NKVD, Nikolay Ezhov, used the killing of Kirov as an excuse to move on his opponents within the Communist Party, and the secret police set about 'discovering' numerous foreign spy networks and conspiracies to commit terrorism and assassinate high-ranking officials.

The repressions gained momentum. Leningrad was the epicentre of the great purge – the first place where Stalin unleashed his henchmen with orders to hunt down enemies of the regime mercilessly. In the wake of Kirov's death, meetings were held at the university, orators bayed for the blood of the conspirators and ovations followed blood-curdling calls for no mercy to be shown to the enemies of the people.

Over the course of the decade, some 40 million Soviet citizens were arrested, imprisoned or killed. The Great Terror was one of the great evils in a century of evil, and Akhmatova and Lev found themselves in the centre of it. The insanity multiplied, driven by paranoia and revenge. By the late 1930s, Stalin had imposed quotas for the secret police of each region to arrest and exterminate those deemed to be enemies of the state. Confessions were obtained through torture, and sentences were swiftly carried out – the basements of most NKVD office buildings had execution rooms lined with thick wooden planks to prevent bullets from ricocheting. Those who carried out the terror must have known what was happening, though many later claimed to have believed Stalin's claims that they were in fact rooting out foreign provocateurs. Stalin himself, according to close associates, believed the confessions obtained under torture to be true.

Anyone suspected of disloyalty was hunted down, and intellectuals were at the top of the list. Any document in the wrong hands could be a death sentence. Writing became dangerous, and poems were memorized rather than committed to paper. The lives of St Petersburg's artists and authors became inescapably intertwined with the party bureaucrats and the NKVD agents who monitored and interrogated them. The police and the artists crossed paths often, and knew each other by name.

Yakov Agranov, the NKVD officer responsible for executing Lev's father, was placed in charge of the investigation into Kirov's murder.[1] He never met Akhmatova or Gumilev, but he nevertheless became a malevolent presence at Fountain House. His signature appears on many of the arrest documents that remain in the family's files. Another recurring phantom was Leonid Zakovsky, head of the Leningrad NKVD, a Russified German whose real name was Genrikh Stubis. His irreverent attitude to the impossible cruelty he brought to his job was expressed in his favourite joke: 'If Karl Marx himself fell into my clutches, I could get him to admit that he was an agent of Bismarck.' This jest proved doubly ironic: Zakovsky himself confessed to being a German agent and a Trotsky sympathizer before being shot in 1938.[2]

Throughout the Great Terror, the Soviet Union's writers, artists and musicians lived in a fishbowl, monitored constantly for signs of any transgression by the NKVD. The first denunciation in Akhmatova's file is dated 1927.[3] More would soon follow, as the secret police was instructed to build cases against the prominent intelligentsia, who lived in dread of a knock on the door. Whenever the doorbell chimed in apartment 44 of Fountain House, a child would be asked to climb onto the bathtub to look out of the window onto the stairwell, in order to see who was calling. Meanwhile the adults waited anxiously in the hall.

They assumed that many of their friends were agents, informing on them; but they did not know who. In Gumilev's file there are numerous denunciations by one Arkady Borin, whom Lev had befriended during his first year at university, walking up to him and saying: 'You seem like an intelligent chap, isn't it time we became friends?' Arkady's denunciations are an unconventional source of material for a biography, and yet they provide an interesting – and seemingly accurate – portrait of Lev's college years. Lev's file contains this profile, written by Arkady at the behest of his NKVD handlers:

Among his fellow students, he [Gumilev] was a 'square peg' in his restrained mannerisms, in his taste in literature and lastly in his passive attitude towards social labour. In his opinion, the fate of Russia should not be decided by the masses of labourers, but rather by a chosen clique of aristo-crats ... On the subject of the Soviet Union he once said that there has never been a period of Russian history in which there was not the necessity to expend heroic effort to change the existing structure.[4]

It is unclear what had motivated Borin to spy for the NKVD; but it seems that after a certain period, the weight of his previous betrayals forced him to continue working for his shadowy masters, whatever his personal feelings.

Even worse than the betrayals of outsiders like Borin were the betrayals of families and friends. Under the dreadful, crippling beatings of interrogators, people would sign anything. Family members and friends would implicate themselves and each other, simply to avoid being crippled for life or killed. And soon this would be the fate of this unhappy group.

In 1934, Mandelstam composed a poem that he later called the 'Stalin Epigram'. So lethally funny and insulting was it that he decided not to put it down on paper, but instead had his wife and Gerstein commit it to memory ('we were constantly forced by the circumstances of our life to behave like members of a secret society', said Nadezhda in her memoirs). Lev was one of Mandelstam's 'first listeners', according to Nadezhda – one of those to whom the poet would recite a finished poem in order to get a first reaction. 'It so happens that all of M's [Mandelstam's] first listeners came to a tragic end', she wrote in her memoirs.[5]

The 'Epigram' was the most famous poem never to be seen by anyone in the Soviet Union. It became a legend in the writers' circles of St Petersburg – surviving for decades only in memories and shut away in police files. One version survives in published form:

His fat fingers are slimy like slugs, And his words are absolute, like grocers' weights.
　　His cockroach whiskers are laughing, And his boot tops shine.
　　And around him the rabble of narrow-necked chiefs – He plays with the services of half-men.
　　Who warble, or miaow, or moan. He alone pushes and prods.
　　Decree after decree he hammers them out like horseshoes, In the groin, in the forehead, in the brows, or in the eye.
　　When he has an execution it's a special treat, And the Ossetian chest swells.[6]

Gerstein remembers Nadezhda cautioning her after repeating the poem: 'Lyova especially should not know about it.' She apparently realized that Lev's provocative nature could get the better of him, and it would land both him and Mandelstam in trouble. However, Mandelstam, so proud of his creation, immediately began reciting it 'to anyone who would listen'. 'The poet could not restrain himself within the limits of common sense and entrusted the seditious verse to the "for ever" disgraced Akhmatova and the unformed young man.'[7] And sadly, Lev, it seems, was indeed unable to keep the verse to himself. On one occasion, he invited a student friend – 'a not entirely familiar guest' – to dinner. The poem was recited and, 'staggered by what he had heard, the young man immediately informed the "organs".'[8] Gerstein may be wrong – it is still not clear how the NKVD learned of the poem – whether it was the unfamiliar student or another of the dozens of people to whom Mandelstam had recited it. But it was clear that the NKVD investigators knew about the poem, and a copy of the 'Stalin Epigram', written out in Mandelstam's own handwriting, was to be found later in the NKVD file on the case (sitting in Lev's file is a version of the poem as well, written by Lev at the request of an interrogator in 1935).

During his interrogation – at which his NKVD investigators pretended to be executing friends of Mandelstam, including Gerstein, in the next room – the poet told them everything, including the names of those to whom he had recited the poem. And in the confession was found the following: 'Lev Gumilev approved the work with some vague and emotional expression such as "wonderful", but his view agreed with that of his mother, in whose presence the work was read aloud to him.'[9] 'I was angry he had not denied everything, as a good conspirator might have done', remembered Nadezhda. 'He was too straightforward to be capable of any kind of guile.'[10]

This testimony was to alter Gumilev's life. When he was finally rehabilitated in 1956, it became clear that a file on him had been opened in 1934, when Mandelstam was first interrogated.[11] The name Mandelstam would continuously appear in case notes, interrogations and appeal rejections up until 1956.

In October 1935, Gerstein remembered a conversation she had while out walking with Lev at Kolomenskoe, in the hills outside Moscow.

'When I return to Leningrad I will be arrested. In the summer an acquaintance of mine was interrogated. She was let go. But she told them everything.'
    'What did she say?'
    'There were some conversations in our house in front of her.'[12]

What had happened was that Borin, his university friend and NKVD informer, had come over to Punin's apartment on 25 May 1935, and had witnessed a conversation during which Punin had 'condoned terrorist acts against Stalin' (according to the denunciation he wrote the next day at NKVD headquarters and which was placed in Punin's file). Apparently, Punin had said something along the lines of 'shwak! [mimicking a bullet] No more Joseph!'[13] The 'woman' Lev had spoken of was Vera Anikeeva, an artist, who was called in and, under interrogation, confirmed that such a conversation had taken place.

As he predicted to Gerstein, that same month both Lev and Punin were suddenly arrested. Lev was charged with violating article 58, sections 8 and 10 of the criminal code, which concerned counter-revolutionary offences. He was further charged with belonging to an anti-Soviet group, having terrorist intentions and conducting anti-Soviet agitation. Mandelstam's poem, according to Gerstein, played a key role in the charges and, like Mandelstam, Lev was made to copy down a version of the poem by hand – a document which remained in the case file. Another charge related to his authorship of a poem parodying the popular reaction to the death of Sergey Kirov, which he had in fact written.[14]

'We all wound up in the "Big House"', recalled Lev, using the nickname for the NKVD headquarters on Liteyny Street.[15] According to him, the treatment was relatively decent; they were interrogated for eight days, but again no harsh methods were used. 'True, at that time no one was beaten, no one tortured, only questioned.' According to a transcript of the interrogation, Punin was forced to admit: 'At my home, on more than one occasion, there were readings of Mandelstam's creations, for example, against Stalin.'[16] He also named Lev as an 'anti-Soviet person':

> He made anti-Soviet statements constantly. The general content of his counter-revolutionary statements was on the necessity of toppling the Soviet regime and putting monarchy in its place ... He also said, for example, that Mandelstam's poems against Stalin were very appropriate and reflect the actual truth.

Lev denied everything at first. 'I always had the opinion that under the circumstances, fighting against the Soviet regime is impossible.' 'And with whom did you have this conversation?' asked the investigator, Shtukaturov. 'With Borin and Punin, and with my mother.' Shtukaturov then retrieved the transcript of Punin's statement and showed it to Lev. Lev knew the battle was lost: 'Yes, those conversations indeed took place.'[17]

That episode was fraught, but mercy was forthcoming. A distraught Akhmatova personally wrote to Stalin seeking clemency, and her friend Boris Pasternak did so as well.[18] Amazingly, their interventions seem to have worked: Akhmatova's letter was later found in an archive, with a note in Stalin's handwriting: 'Comrade Yagoda [chief of the NKVD]. Release both Punin and Gumilev and report to me on implementation. J. Stalin.'

Considering that the case file on Lev contained his transcription of Mandelstam's 'Stalin Epigram', and Stalin would have seen the file before his decision to dismiss the case (and would almost certainly have read the poem), Gerstein believes the dictator 'showed unheard of leniency in dismissing the case'.[19] The two were duly released on 3 November, ten days after their arrest. They walked home together in silence, Lev knowing that Punin had implicated him. Until then he had tolerated Punin, but now came the final split. Lev moved out of the Fountain House, moving in with a group of students who would soon become his cellmates.

Perhaps the most insidious aspect of the terror was the psychological impact it would have on ordinary citizens, anxious to make sense of the random disappearance of their neighbours and acquaintances. They coped by blaming the victims, including Akhmatova and Lev. As Gerstein tells it:

Each person thought he alone was afraid. But everyone was scared. People tried to convince themselves that their arrested comrade, relation, or acquaintance was indeed a very bad person: they had always been aware of it actually. This defensive reaction explains the voluntary spreading of malicious rumors about the latest victim.[20]

After his arrest, Lev was ostracized and expelled from university for a year. He was allowed to begin his second year of study only in 1937, after Akhmatova went to the university rector and pleaded with him.

Certain that he would be arrested again, Lev became obsessed about his next interrogation, and when it would come. He was anxious not to break and to keep his honour. Gerstein remembers him lying on a bed in the art studio of a friend, looking up at the ceiling and saying: 'I keep wondering what I'll say to the interrogator.'[21] He would soon find out. He was on course to finish his degree, when in 1938 a fit of temper ruined everything. During a lecture on Russian literature, he heard a professor belittle his father, saying that the late Gumilev 'wrote about Abyssinia while he never got beyond Algiers'. Lev shouted: 'He was in Abyssinia, not Algiers!' – referring to a trip his father had taken in 1915. The professor, Pompyansky, not knowing who the interrupter was, responded: 'Who is in a better position to know, you or me?' To this Lev responded: 'Me, of course.'

Several students on the course knew Lev's identity and parents, and began to laugh uproariously. Pompyansky, humiliated, filed a complaint. In any other year, Lev would have been sternly rebuked by the head of the department, or faced some other punishment for a minor infraction. But this was the height of Stalin's terror. Only months before, the rector of Leningrad University had been arrested and shot during interrogation. His body was thrown from a fourth-storey window of the NKVD building to make it appear like suicide. With nerves on edge, no one would speak on Lev's behalf.

A few days later, on 10 March, he and two other LGU students – Teodor Shumovsky and Nikolay Erekhovich – were arrested and charged with anti-Soviet agitation and membership of a banned political party (the 'Youth Wing of the Progressive Party').[22] Lev was always convinced that the reason for his arrest was his outburst. But what he did not know (and which is clear from his file) was that the NKVD had been steadily accumulating denunciations and gathering evidence against him since his last arrest.[23] In the end, all that pains-taking work proved a waste of time: they managed to extract a false confession from him under torture. But such was the culture of the Soviet Union: an intensely legalistic, if not legal, approach to work by government bureaucrats and police.

Five days later, the three students were interrogated separately by NKVD inspectors. It was clear that this was a great deal more serious than the previous two episodes. Lev wrote that the first NKVD detective inspector to interview him started the interrogation by beating him savagely and shouting: 'You love your father, you bastard! Get up ... against the wall!' Lev was tortured and beaten for eight days. The interrogator beat him on the neck, near the brain stem. 'You will remember me all your life!' he warned. And sure enough, the drubbing left Lev with spasms down the right side of his body for the rest of his life.

Between interrogations, the prisoners lay in their cramped cell, asking each other about their 'investigations' and what they were charged with. 'Almost everyone willingly shares the experience, looking for support in his own unequal struggle', recalled Teodor Shumovsky, one of the students arrested along with Gumilev. 'They give each other selfless advice on how to carry oneself with an investigator, how to behave.'[24] Shumovsky was told by a fellow prisoner:

> Your matter is sad, chap, but isn't that bad. Here, in the People's Commissariat of Internal Affairs, they produce spies, traitors, saboteurs, but you have nothing of that kind! Now look, you 'bourgeois progressivist', they will not pat you on the head for that, but still it's not like you were a fascist! Consider yourself getting a lucky number.[25]

As Lev feared, the torture apparently broke them. According to Shumovsky, after seeing a prisoner brought back motionless from the torture chamber, they all thought very hard about further resistance: 'It is immeasurably hard to take over the burden of non-existent guilt. But it is much harder to become a cripple and to deprive oneself of the opportunity to think and to create.'[26] Separately, the three students signed 'confessions' that they had created a terrorist organization. Lev was sentenced to ten years' hard labour, while his two 'accomplices' received eight years apiece.[27]

After confessing, the three were transferred by truck to another building, an old brick house with bars on the windows.[28] They were processed along with hundreds of other half-naked, unshaven prisoners housed in tight seven-square-metre cells. These at one time had been one-man cells, but they now housed 20 prisoners, locked up together with a bucket for their waste. 'Three persons per square metre. Do not forget the unit of measurement: prisoners, it is possible to put as many as you wish of those into the cell.'[29]

In late September, they found themselves again in a cell together. Together they were marched into a basement room, where they sat before a military court. Each had broken and named the others in signed confessions. They could not readily meet one another's gaze. But being reunited gave them renewed courage.

The judge, Bushmakov, was dressed in military uniform. He addressed each prisoner in turn, Lev first:

'Admit your guilt.'

'No.'

'How so? You signed the confession.'

'I was forced by inspectors Bakhudarin and that other one, he is indicated in the protocol. I was oppressed; unlawful methods were used . . .'

'What are you talking about? We do everything according to the law. Trying to avoid the blame, you do yourself a disservice. It is written clearly here: I, Gumilev, was a member . . . carried out systematic . . . my objective was to . . . Now it is useless to deny. Sit down.'[30]

Their sentences were upheld.

CHAPTER SEVEN

GULAG

Lev and his two 'accomplices' were transferred to another holding jail, from where prisoners were sent to all corners of the Soviet Union, to the gulag. Possibly because the fate of the prisoners had already been decided, the rules were relaxed and the three were allowed to stay in the same cell, along with other students. There they played chess on the floor, using chess pieces made from bread, and waited for news. On 17 November came a ray of hope: following a protest by the defence lawyers, the sentence imposed by the military tribunal had been revoked and the case sent for reinvestigation. According to Shumovsky:

> Suddenly the two of us who remained, Lyova and I were ordered to get ready for a big move . . . the prison was humming like an oriental bazaar. My heart beat faster . . . 'Maybe they will take us to different camps', Lyova says. 'Listen and try to memorize . . .' We get under the plank beds, far away from vanity, Lyova whispers his father's poems to me . . .'[1]

On 2 December they were packed into 'Stolypin wagons' (train carriages with bars on the windows designed for carrying convicts) and sent north. First they travelled to Medvezhegorsk, on the northern lip of the massive Lake Onega. There they joined a forced labour brigade digging the White Sea Canal. It was one of the many massive engineering projects undertaken by work brigades under Stalin, and had an ambitious aim: as part of the preparations for war, Stalin wanted a canal between the White Sea and the Baltic Sea so that the Soviet navy could sail from one to the other swiftly, without being forced to go round Scandinavia. Completed at a heavy price in terms of human life, like many other such projects it was dramatically flawed: dug too shallow, it was almost never used.

A popular joke from the time went as follows:

Who dug the White Sea Canal?
The right bank was dug by those who told jokes . . .
And the left bank?
By those who listened.

Lev had listened to Mandelstam's joke and his fate was sealed.

Shumovsky and Lev were given a loaf of black bread and two cured fish – a travel ration for three days – and then stuffed into the overcrowded, stinking hold of the river barge, 'as slave traders did to the slaves taken away from Africa in the Middle Ages', as Shumovsky put it.[2] On the third day of the journey up the Vodla river, the hatch to the deck was opened and the guards ordered everyone out. The barge was on a wide river, by its berth. Beyond that was a high, solid fence made of planks. The prisoners got out and stopped at a checkpoint. A yawning sergeant appeared from the guard house, took the documents from the guard, opened a gate and let the prisoners into the camp, or 'zone'. 'The barrack with its log walls, wet from the dampness that filled the air, was waiting for the newcomers.'[3]

Gumilev and Shumovsky were just two of the 15 million people to be sent to the USSR's *Glavnoe Upravlenie Lagerei* or Main Camp Administration – GULAG for short. Over 1 million would not survive the ordeal. Forced labour brigades had been used as far back as the seventeenth century to work in Siberia and Russia's north. But under the USSR, the administration and organization of slave labour reached a new level of sophistication. Throughout the twentieth century, labour camps such as the White Sea Canal project became an indelible part of the imagery of the USSR, especially after the publication in the West of Solzhenitsyn's *Gulag Archipelago* in 1974.

The 'Archipelago', as Solzhenitsyn described the camp system, coexisted with Soviet reality amid a sort of hidden muteness. Everyone knew it was there, but few knew the scale, and most pretended that it didn't. It was almost as if the camps were a trapdoor in reality: falling through it meant to disappear, not just physically, but to be wiped from the public memory. In most years up until the mid-1950s, when following Stalin's death it started to be slowly dismantled, between 500,000 and 1.7 million Soviet citizens were confined to such camps, completely unnoticed by the public.

The day after they arrived, Gumilev and Shumovsky were sent across the river to saw timber in the camp warehouse. Over the next four months, they worked themselves nearly to the point of death:

> By the new year of 1939 I had reached my final limit. I could hardly drag my feet from the barracks into the wood. Felling trees in the icy forest, waist-deep in snow, in torn footwear, without warm clothes, refreshing myself with gruel and small bread rations – even village *muzhiks*, who were used to hard physical labour, would melt down like snow on this work . . .[4]

Lev only found escape in cerebral musings; and he had ample material to muse on in his present circumstances, however awful they were. One thing that continued to occupy him was his amateur sociological survey of his fellow convicts and how they adapted to their new, arbitrary surroundings as they struggled to survive. Many camp survivors spoke of the camp life as 'cruel' and 'Darwinian'. Lev's friend Alexander Savchenko described the process of arriving in camp as 'being stripped naked':

> All the past was deleted from him like clothes in a dressing room. The bygone social status, career, profession disappeared like a light steam cloud off a red-hot frying pan. The prisoner's moral face began to be drawn up all anew.[5]

This sense of the camp as a descent into a pure state of nature was often expressed by former inmates in their memoirs: 'The camp was a test of our moral strength, of our everyday morality, and 99 per cent of us failed it', wrote ex-prisoner Varlam Shalamov in an account of his camp life.[6]

Gumilev was a keen and oddly academic observer of his own fate, and that of his fellow *zeks* (from the Russian for someone incarcerated, *zaklyuchenny*). Later, in a series of journal articles and interviews, he spoke with great interest and a somewhat odd detachment about watching men interacting with each other as they plummeted closer and closer to the primordial state of pure Darwinian survival. Lev was eventually to make his academic career with theories about the role of 'nature' in social relations. What types of relationships did men form in a state of pure competition to survive? Camp life was his laboratory. And what he gradually came to understand was that, while brutal and violent, life among inmates was not entirely Hobbesian – a war of all against all. There were certain 'laws' of social organization that seemed to be immutable, natural.

Gumilev noticed that the *zeks*, irrespective of background, education or cultural level, all displayed a tendency to form into small groups of 2–4 people. These groups were defined by who 'ate together':

> Groups of from two to four persons emerged on this principle; they 'eat together', that is, share their meal. These are real consortiums, the members

of which are obliged to help each other. The composition of such a group
depends on the internal sympathy of its members for each other.[7]

The members of these small groups would also make sacrifices for each other
and defend each other. These groups, he believed, were not an example of a
'social structure' that he believed to be different. This was not social; it was
nature.

This process of distinguishing order from chaos, he noticed, was universal.
For example, half the camp's inmates were 'criminals' – i.e. they had been
convicted of ordinary crimes, rather than political ones, as Gumilev and his
circle had. But even among the criminals there was a tendency to distinguish
the lawless from the law-abiding: the criminals divided themselves into
urki – criminals who obeyed the 'laws' or informal code of criminals – and
'hooligans' who did not. He wrote in 1990 about his later experience at another
camp where he was a prisoner, in Norilsk:

> Criminals made up about half of the incarcerated. But true hooligans were
> very rare. My acquaintance, a murderer, said: 'The hooligan is an enemy to
> us all, to you the friars (as politicals were known) and to us *urki* (slang for
> professional criminal). The hooligans have to be killed, because they create
> evil for evil's sake, and not for the sake of good, as thieves and robbers do.[8]

The emergence of social order from chaos that Lev witnessed evidently made a
profound impression on him, and formed a core part of the theory of history
that would make him famous. Prison taught him that man is not the master of
nature, but is subject to it; and the human virtues that we know – society,
friendship, and so on – are not a mark of human advancement, but a natural
biological impulse, the instinctual urge, common to all humans at all times, to
distinguish 'us' from 'them'.

As he continued to fell logs in the permafrost, watching fellow inmates die
daily of exhaustion and hypothermia, he slowly became fascinated by the irrational in history. One example he often referred to in later writings was the
march of Alexander the Great across Eurasia. Alexander, Lev surmised, could
not have been driven by any rational calculation – the small Greek army could
not possibly have held all the territory they conquered, and Alexander would
be unlikely ever to get back home.

In 1939 he was confined to the camp's infirmary, after he split his leg
open with an axe while felling trees. In a state of near delirium, he seems to
have been visited by an inspiration that he would carry with him throughout
his life:

A thought occurred to me on the motivation for human action in history.
Why did Alexander the Great go all the way to India and Central Asia, even
though he . . . could not return the spoils from these countries all the way to
Macedonia? Suddenly, it occurred to me that something had pushed him,
something inside himself.

According to him, he jumped out of his cot and, bad leg or no, ran around
shouting 'Eureka!' – 'It was revealed to me that the human has a special impulse,
called passionarity.' What Gumilev was seeking, as he described it, was 'the
powerful impulse which pulls the human towards obtaining some sort of
unnecessary benefit, in particular, posthumous honour. Because Alexander the
Great could not have counted on anything else but that.'[9]

Gumilev's studies of history at Leningrad University had focused on the
Middle East and the steppe tribes of Inner Asia – the Huns, the Xiongnu, the
Turks, the Mongols – who every few hundred years rose from nowhere,
conquered the known world and then vanished. The subject matter provided a
rich vein to mine for his historical theories. The tribes, societies and nations
which flourished were not the most rational, enlightened or advanced, he theorized, but rather those that contained the highest proportion of 'passionaries',
who were defined by their desire to sacrifice themselves, and the highest level
of 'complementarity', a sense of attraction of its members for each other. Society
was held together not by a civilizing humanism, historical progress and cumu-
lative reason, but by natural, unconscious instincts which had changed very
little over the last few millennia.

Lev's university studies may have played a role in his meditations on
passionarity and complementarity as forces in history – in his study of Middle
Eastern history he very likely came across the Arab medieval historian Ibn
Khaldun, who in the fourteenth century described the ceaseless cycle of
conquest, rise and decline in world history. In his classic work, the *Muqaddimah*,
he sought to explain why, despite their refinements, superior technology and
wealth, the cities of the medieval world did not survive intact for very long.
Every few generations in Ibn Khaldun's time, civilized towns got swept away by
tribal barbarians riding over the steppe and desert. Their greater civilization
did not win them battles. But the conquering barbarians, after a few generations of growing lazy and complacent on their new thrones, would themselves
be routed by new barbarians. While civilization has technology and wealth, he
said, the nomads have what he called *asabiya*, akin to social solidarity or spirit.
This peculiar, intangible quality offers a rather pessimistic view of history,
which consists not of progress or linear advancement towards a peak of
civilization, but of a cycle – the natural rhythms of migration, conquest and

genocide – endlessly repeating itself through eternity. Giambattista Vico and Niccolò Machiavelli also describe something akin to tribal solidarity or spirit, as a decisive force in the history of peoples – Machiavelli called this *virtù*.

The convicts were not the only ones to be scarred by the experience of prison. Akhmatova, like the spouses and relations of thousands of Leningraders sent to the camps, began the awful and tedious process of making the rounds of the various police offices and prisons, trying desperately to lobby the 'organs' – or the Kremlin in Moscow – to intervene. Like thousands of other Leningraders, she spent days and nights with her loved ones on her conscience, feeling the dreaded urgency that if only she could make one more plea, find the right official and deliver proof of innocence, or pay the right bribe to the right person, she could free her loved one from almost certain death. The truth is that the terror was not, as many believed, a miscarriage of the Soviet justice system which could be rectified by correcting a mistake. It was a preposterous human phenomenon beyond all comprehension: the combination of a mutated strain of cruelty and perversion of impersonal bureaucracy on a monstrous scale, paralleled only by the Holocaust. As Gumilev wrote:

> Mama, the innocent soul, like many other pure-hearted people, thought that the sentence passed on me was the result of the court's mistake, an accidental oversight. She could not at first imagine how far the court system had fallen.[10]

Lev would probably have finished his days clearing the canal bed in a forest near Medvezhegorsk, but for the miraculous *deus ex machina* which saved his life. The judge who had sentenced him and his friends was himself hanged – an all too frequent occurrence during the terror – and the cases that he had decided were reviewed. At the end of January, Shumovsky and Lev were summoned back to St Petersburg for a case review. It came none too soon for Lev, with his leg injury. As a result of the reinvestigation, they were given reduced sentences of five years apiece. This reversal was attributed to the abrupt arrest and removal of Nikolay Ezhov as chief of the NKVD in 1939. He confessed to a range of anti-Soviet activity and was executed in 1940. His successor was the 'kindly, just' Lavrenty Beria. Now, however, the three friends were sent to different camps – Lev to Norilsk, a huge ore mining complex in northern Siberia.[11]

He reached the port of Dudinka in the autumn of 1939 on a barge full of *zeks*. This was the starting point for the most northerly railway in the world, which ran eastwards along the seventieth parallel to the town of Norilsk. At the time, this 'town' consisted of four houses made of quarry stone, a small metal works with an enrichment plant (the silhouette of which looked like a medieval palace against the horizon) and two clusters of barracks, which contained about 24,000 prisoners. Located north of the Arctic Circle, in the Kolyma region, Norilsk was founded in 1935 on top of the largest known nickel deposit in the world. Prisoners dug nickel from the permafrost, built the processing plant, power stations, and finally a city for the NKVD guards to live in. It was one of the harshest camps to be sent to, alongside Vorkuta and Kolyma.[12] As Lev would recall, in Norilsk 'in autumn the tundra was wrapped in snow mist, in winter in deep blue polar night'.[13]

There was a mathematical equation which governed the fate of prisoners in the far north. To keep one prisoner healthy for a year, 800kg of supplies needed to be transported 2,000km across harsh terrain by rail and river. A new prisoner, however, weighed less than 100kg. It was more efficient, therefore, to starve the existing prisoners to death and bring in new replacements. *Zeks* were kept on meagre rations and died in their droves, to be replenished by new loads of prisoners. But Lev's education made him valuable: he passed himself off as a geologist and thus was entitled to extra rations.

The social life in Norilsk (such as it was) revolved around two groups: the geologists and the metallurgists. Lev was put in the geologists' barracks. According to an acquaintance of his, S.A. Snegov, the geologists were 'intellectual and priggish', and so Lev chose to spend most of his time in the 'more democratic' metallurgist barracks.[14] Snegov was the first, but not the last, to note Lev's temper and impatience, and his tendency to alienate his friends – a character trait that seems to have begun to manifest itself around this time, quite likely due to the stress of the camps. His friends from the pre-camp days hardly ever mentioned an intemperate side, but after the camps, many acquaintances were abruptly terminated by a quarrel.

The friendship between Lev and Snegov was one such case. The inmates of Norilsk had arranged to have a poetry contest, in which Lev came second to Snegov. As the son of two of Russia's greatest poets, Lev's pride was seriously damaged. So angry was he that he actually challenged Snegov to a duel. This was avoided only because they were unable to find pistols (which of course, were not ordinarily given to prisoners) and because Snegov insisted that he was 'not a butcher' and so they could not use knives. A week later, having determined that there was no realistic chance of fighting a duel, they decided to postpone it 'until better times'.

It was all particularly hurtful for Lev, because he was feeling increasingly rejected by his mother. Though she wrote beautiful and famous poems about his ordeal, she failed to write to him. In virtually every letter he wrote to Emma Gerstein at this time, he complained of his mother's neglect:

The men with me are two workers, and I have seen three females in a year: a doe hare, which fell into a wire trap, a doe deer, which came to a tent by accident, and a squirrel killed with a stick. There are no books and there is nothing good at all. Mum, apparently, is in good health . . . But she does not write to me, does not send cables. It is sad.[15]

Gerstein, one of Akhmatova's closest confidantes during those years, thought Lev was wrong to imagine that his mother had abandoned him. She believed there was an explanation for Akhmatova's behaviour that lay in her complex and somewhat mysterious poetic persona: 'Akhmatova's silence was a kind of charm: she believed there were superstitious omens in every word she wrote.' Indeed, she kept her silence through the most dangerous periods of Lev's internment and his time at the front during the war. When Berlin was finally captured and the danger to her son had passed, she began to write to him. 'I have received three very laconic postcards from Mama and I became even angrier. Well, when we meet we shall make our peace.'[16]

Lev continued to find solace in history and musing about philosophy. The Second World War gave him more inspiration to apply his theory of human behaviour to the subject of nations and civilizations.

Having completed his five-year sentence in 1943, he stayed on in Norilsk as a paid volunteer for a year, until the winter of 1944. The war was almost over and victory for the USSR was assured. Lev wanted to see some action. By his own account, he went to the local recruiting office, took out a razor and threatened to slit his wrists if he was not allowed to join the army. He arrived at the front in February 1945, which gave him enough time to see three months of easy victories before the capitulation of Germany in May. 'After Norilsk, the front line felt like a resort', he said of army life. Winter clothes were plentiful, as was food and vodka.

He was in one of the Red Army units that marched into Berlin in April 1945. The event left a lasting impression on him. And like all his experiences, it was one that he treated in scholarly gloss: when his flat was searched on his arrest in 1949, his notebooks were confiscated, including one with an article he had written (apparently for an army newspaper) but evidently thought better of publishing. The paper was later found in his file by his biographer, Vitaly Shentalinsky. It was probably a wise decision not to submit the article.

Musing further on the idea of 'passion' and complementarity which had inspired him in prison, he had evidently become more convinced that he had hit on something significant when he observed the victory of his own relatively backward country over the hugely superior technology of the Germans. He described what he saw in the German towns that his unit passed through.

There were 'ornate books', 'asphalted roads' and 'luxurious apartments and automobiles': 'In the midst of this "culture" – we, dirty and unshaven, stood and wondered, why are we stronger? How are we better than this immaculately groomed and shiny country?'

The Russians had arrived in Germany like barbarians at the gates of Rome. Primitive Russia's victory over one of the most technologically advanced societies in the world was yet another example of 'passionarity', Gumilev believed, in the natural disposition of man towards feats of sacrifice. He put it in the same terms he had used while laid up in the infirmary in 1939, when he had dreamt of Alexander's march across the Eurasian continent:

> Culture is not summed up in the quantity of automobiles, houses, and warm toilets. Not even in the quantity of books written and published, no matter how ornate their style. The former and the latter are the results of culture, not the same as culture itself. Culture is equivalent to the kind of relations people have with each other. Culture is there, where out of human relations arise strong and noble feelings – friendship, trust, mutual suffering, patriotism, love for one's own and respect for the other . . . Indeed it was this, true culture, which Germany did not possess in enough quantity.[17]

Lev's experiences of a war which pitted one nation against another – a true ethnic genocide on industrial proportions, which took place in a Europe bedecked with the trappings of the Enlightenment – must have inspired some of his profoundly pessimistic scholarship. The fact that in the name of progress and 'scientific history', millions of people would go to their deaths and that the most rationalistic of philosophies could give birth to the most irrational human behaviour, taught Gumilev that, whatever our intentions, human beings are still ruled by natural impulses.

Humanity was a virtue that could be both learned and taken away. The years spent in a disease-ridden swamp felling trees and mining north of the Arctic Circle apparently left their stamp on him, and he would never again be the 'boy-king' of Gerstein's romantic memories, who bore his burden with nobility. Instead, he returned irascible, easily panicked, and bore terrible grudges. As Gerstein put it:

> For many years we would continue to see someone who bore the name of Lev Nikolaevich Gumilev. But though we called him Lyova, it was not the Lyova we had known before his arrest in 1938. How Akhmatova suffered from his fateful change in personality! Not long before her death, she once fell into deep thought, re-examining every stage in her son's life from the

day he was born. At last she firmly declared: 'No! He wasn't always like that. They made my boy like that.'[18]

Leningrad, Akhmatova said when she returned in 1944 from Tashkent, was 'a spectre masquerading as a city'. The horrible famine during the 900-day blockade had destroyed the population; all the animals (and some people) had long since been eaten. The graceful canals were clogged with corpses and the city stank of death. It was to this that Lev finally returned in 1945. According to Maryana Kozyreva, the sister-in-law of Nikolay Kozyrev, a physicist whom Lev had met in Norilsk and who stayed friendly with him for the rest of his life, Gumilev 'was skinny, looked like spaghetti, almost boneless. When he sat down to table, his hands and legs twisted somehow; he bended. For those who knew him only in his last years, it was difficult to imagine.'[19]

Akhmatova had been rehabilitated during the war – temporarily, as it would later turn out. A genuine patriot, she refused to emigrate and stayed in her native Leningrad until it was surrounded by German forces. The stuff of her poems – private emotions, love, family – had been the antithesis of monochromatic Marxism, of trumpeted patriotism and loudly delivered manifestos; but suddenly this was the glue that bound the Russian people together.

In cold, pragmatic terms, Stalin was probably able to see plainly that the Marxist ideology could not mobilize the Soviet people to defend their land, and appeals to vague social forces could not exhort them to throw themselves on German bayonets. He tugged on the heartstrings of Russians' love for their land and for each other. He started to use the term 'brothers and sisters' in addition to 'comrades and citizens' in public speeches. This was a sea-change in the relationship between the regime and its citizens: the blaring, ululating public culture of ideology was replaced with appeals to the cherished and private realm of the family and – its natural extension – the nation.

As the German forces swept closer to Moscow, Stalin began rapidly to restore the idols of Russian patriotism that the Bolsheviks over the last 20 years and more had assiduously purged from the national existence. The patriarch of the Orthodox Church was summoned and told, as he stood dumbfounded, that the Church would be expanded, with new positions and new churches. Stalin famously drank a toast to the 'Russian people' and had the national anthem changed from the 'Internationale' to the Soviet 'Hymn' because, it was thought, soldiers would respond to an anthem dedicated to their motherland more readily than to a worldwide movement. One (probably apocryphal) story has it that Stalin ordered the Madonna of Kazan icon flown around Moscow in an aeroplane, evoking the ancient Russian practice of parading icons around cities on the eve of war to bring good fortune and God's blessing.

The near-dormant element of Russian art, literature and poetry that the Bolsheviks had sought so hard to crush in the 1930s – the family and private life – suddenly came to the aid of the *Rodina*, or motherland, which was under threat. Russia welled up with nationalism and patriotic fervour. In 1941, Akhmatova was accepted back into the Writers' Union (having been excluded in 1925). During the siege, her poems were read daily over the radio to inspire the defenders of Leningrad and its starving inhabitants (though she was in Tashkent at the time). In 1942, her poem 'Courage' appeared in *Pravda*. In 1943, a volume of her works was published and immediately sold out. Artists whose works had been in disfavour found themselves dealing with unaccustomed celebrity. Pasternak and Akhmatova, who had lived more or less as internal exiles since the revolution, were suddenly deluged with letters from well-wishers. Akhmatova was chosen to sit on the board of the Leningrad branch of the Writers' Union, and she attended official celebrations. She told an acquaintance, Isaiah Berlin, that she had received a huge number of letters from soldiers quoting from both her published and her unpublished works, and asking for interpretation, and even advice on their lives.

Berlin, who spent half a year in Russia as a diplomat in 1945, wrote of meeting Akhmatova that year and reported on the astonishing new celebrity status that she and her colleagues like Pasternak had gained:

> The status of the handful of poets who clearly rose far above the rest was, I found, unique. Neither painters nor composers nor prose writers, nor even the most popular actors, or eloquent, patriotic journalists, were loved and admired so deeply and so universally, especially by the kind of people I spoke to in trams and trains and in the underground.[20]

But already the chill was being felt in May 1944, when Akhmatova gave a poetry reading in the Polytechnic Museum in Moscow, the largest auditorium in the city, and received a standing ovation from the 3,000 listeners present. Stalin, learning of the event, is supposed to have asked his subordinates, 'Who organized this standing ovation?'

Unbeknownst to Akhmatova at the time (a fact that she later confided to Professor Berlin in 1965, when she received an honorary doctorate from Oxford), Stalin had been privately furious with her for meeting the English academic in 1945. 'So our nun now receives visits from foreign spies', Stalin is supposed to have said, followed by a string of obscenities. Stalin's jealousy knew no bounds, and with his sights now set on Akhmatova, he moved. Nationalism had served its purpose, and the genie had to be put back in the bottle. Patriotism had to be reigned in, and the old orthodoxies of class struggle and historical materialism had to be reasserted. The family, the nation, love and passion, with all its potential to inspire Russians to struggle and sacrifice, had to be annihilated, and this process of rolling back the zeitgeist started with Akhmatova and her native city.

Leningrad had been the most heroic of the Soviet cities, withstanding assault by German forces for just under three years, blockaded and starving. But in the glow of victory following the war and the 900-day siege, the leaders of Leningrad pushed their luck a bit too far. They continued Stalin's nod to Russian nationalism with enthusiasm: streets in Leningrad were renamed and 25 October Street returned to its pre-revolution name of Nevsky Prospekt. Having stuck their necks out too far, the Leningrad party bosses needed to demonstrate their loyalty. Akhmatova, who continued with other writers to write poetry for the local journal *Zvezda*, became a scapegoat.

No sooner had Lev returned to the city and resumed his studies – finally passing his exams to receive a bachelor's degree from the University of Leningrad, a full 12 years after he had started – than his mother's dramatic fall from grace interrupted his hard-won peace yet again. In August 1946, the central committee of the Soviet Communist Party issued a decree harshly rebuking *Zvezda*. Andrey Zhdanov, the party's top ideologue and himself a Leningrad native, delivered a blistering speech to Leningrad party bosses in which he publicly attacked Akhmatova's work as 'individualistic', using the now famous phrase 'half nun, half harlot' to describe her. She was expelled from the Writers' Union, and the ban on her work was reimposed. Gerstein recalls Akhmatova's 'proud condition of disgrace', to which by now she was thoroughly resigned.[21] The Fountain House was handed over to the Arctic Institute, and though she continued to live there, all who entered to see her had to show their passports and be recorded. Needless to say, this meant Lev and Akhmatova were alone for most of the time: 'People stopped greeting me in the streets. They would cross to the other side of Nevsky Prospekt to avoid me', Lev told Kozyreva's sister-in-law Maryana.

Akhmatova's ration card was taken away, and they were on the verge of starvation most of the time, surviving on a diet almost exclusively of black bread and sugarless tea. They lived on Lev's ration card – he had enrolled in graduate school, at the Institute of Oriental Studies at the University of Leningrad, and began working on his candidate's dissertation,[22] on the subject of the first Turkic khanate. Soon, however, a pretext was found and he, too, was expelled from the university.

Lev found work on several archaeological digs – 'to feed myself', he wrote. He travelled for this work, but whenever he was in Leningrad he continued to study. He found a group of like-minded bohemian friends. According to

Maryana Kozyreva, it was a 'rather cheerful diverse group, from which, every so often, somebody would utterly disappear without a trace. But they lived by a principle, "Milady death, we are asking you to wait outside the door." '[23]

The terror of the late 1930s was over, but the intelligentsia still felt the watchful eye of the secret police on them. People now covered their telephones with cushions because it was rumoured that they were equipped with listening devices. 'We all felt as if we were constantly exposed to X-rays and the principal means of control over us was mutual surveillance', wrote Nadezhda Mandelstam of the postwar period.[24]

Lev finally had what seems to have been his first adult relationship with a woman: in May 1947 he met and fell in love with Natalya Varbanets, who worked in a library. She was hauntingly beautiful, described by Kozyreva as 'a real Nastasiya Filipovna' (after the *femme fatale* of Dostoevsky's novel *The Idiot*). She was carrying on an affair with her married boss, however, and would not commit to Lev.

Lev would spend evenings describing his theory of passionarity. 'Like all the brilliant ideas . . . it came to my mind in a loo, of course', he told friends. Kozyreva described him as 'mesmerizing with his erudition'.[25] He was given a break in 1948, thanks to the influence of the Leningrad University rector, Alexander Voznesensky. 'So, your father is Nikolay Gumilev, and your mother is Akhmatova? I see you were dismissed from the postgraduate course after the Resolution on *Zvezda* magazine. Everything is clear!' said the rector. He could not offer Lev a job at the university, but he did allow him to (successfully) defend his candidate's thesis, 'The Detailed Political History of the First Turkic Khanate (546–659 AD)'.[26] At the time, this permission meant a lot to Lev.[27] Later on, one of the historians who sat on his dissertation defence found out that before the rector made his decision, the matter had gone all the way up the Soviet chain of command to Vyacheslav Molotov, at the time the USSR's foreign minister.[28]

Despite the success, Lev still impatiently sought a chance to get a doctoral degree and teach. In 1949, he began to work as a research fellow at the State Museum of Ethnography. But just as things started to turn a corner, in August Punin was rearrested and charged with the same offences as in 1935 and 1938. According to Akhmatova, as he was hustled out the door of their flat, his final words were 'Never give up despairing!'

Lev knew he was next. He packed clothes and books and kept them in a suitcase by the door of the Fountain House flat. Sure enough, one day in November 1949 Lev was expected at the home of his girlfriend Natalya Varbanets to help tape up the windows in preparation for winter. He never showed up. Three days later, Akhmatova knocked on the door of Maryana's flat. Lev had been arrested again.

'Maryana, do you have my poems?' asked Akhmatova. She did. 'Throw them in the oven.' She then explained: 'Lev was arrested on the sixth. And yesterday my flat was searched for a second time. Throw them out without any further talk.'[29]

There and back again

The charges against Gumilev were essentially the same as those pronounced against him in 1935, dusted off for the third time: the feared article 58. Added to this was a pile of denunciations from his academic colleagues, who accused him of anti-Marxism. His acerbic and arrogant style would come back to haunt him: he aimed jokes at the expense of his detractors, and these slights were not easily forgotten.

In defending his thesis, he had been criticized by one academic, Bernstam, who accused him of not knowing Marxism and eastern languages. Lev answered in Persian and then Turkish, which Bernstam did not know. Bernstam was humiliated, and soon after made a formal denunciation. Back in January 1947, another academic named Saltanov had also written a denunciation: 'Gumilev's behaviour is intolerable, and I request your [the NKVD's] assistance in working this matter out.'

These denunciations, past and present, comprised the formal case against Gumilev, though the immediate reason for his incarceration seems to have been to hold him as surety to guarantee Akhmatova's good behaviour following the decree against *Zvezda* in 1946. Lev's oft-repeated line about his stints in camp – that he served one sentence 'for papa, the other for mama' – seems to confirm this. So does the paperwork: a note in his file from a police official, Colonel Minchiv, asked the Interior Ministry for Gumilev's detailed dossier in January 1947.

Lev spent a full ten months at Lefortovo prison pending the end of the investigation, and he was only sentenced in September 1950 to ten years' corrective labour. It was back into the Stolypin wagons, this time bound for Karaganda, a rich coal basin in the midst of the endless steppe of Kazakhstan. There Gumilev was once again issued with the ragged white prison uniform with black numbers stitched onto the back, the chest, the left leg above the knee, and the cap.

In Churbay Nura, near Karaganda, he chanced to meet Lev Voznesensky, son of the Leningrad University rector who had allowed him to defend his thesis. The rector had been executed for an unrelated matter, and Lev Voznesensky was to become one of Lev's close acquaintances in Karaganda. 'It was nice to hear someone say something nice about my father', recalled Voznesensky.

Voznesensky's first impression of Gumilev in 1950 shows how the physical hardship of Lev's life had worn him down:

Just imagine a parade ground covered with snow, bound by severe frost, surrounded by barracks. In one of them, almost right after I was brought to the special camp the previous night in the Kazakhstan steppe, I saw a stooping figure of an old bearded old man keeping the fire in the oven. It was Lev Nikolaevich Gumilev. The 'old man' was 38 years old that year.[30]

The job tending the oven was a stroke of good fortune, otherwise Lev might have been sent down the mines – gruelling work in unsafe conditions.

Previous rank was nothing in the camp, and could not save one from the heaviest work, from dreadful hunger, from complete lawlessness. For Lev Nikolaevich, his post at the oven saved him at least from cold . . . They were trying to deprive prisoners of their personal origin in every possible way, to turn them, as Beria said, into 'camp dust', and even so, Lev Nikolaevich remained himself inside.[31]

Several of Lev's friends from this second camp period, like Voznesensky, remember a stooping walk. This is something that he seems to have acquired there, as previously no one described it. Another friend, Alexander Savchenko, remembers Gumilev as of medium height: 'Constitution not nearly athletic. Fingers long and thin. Aquiline nose. Stooping walk.'

The regime in the camps had improved since the dark days of the 1930s, and after returning from work and having dinner the convicts usually had some free time for relaxation. Another major improvement from the 1930s was that the criminals and the politicals were separated, so that the politicals did not have to fear for their valuables or their lives. 'Thanks to this, life in the camps became relatively bearable', recalled Savchenko. 'It would have been impossible for Lev to have made the kind of academic progress he did in the previous environment [with the criminals]. In this small way, the Lubyanka bosses helped science.'[32]

In fact, the improved conditions and the concentration of intellectuals actually lent the camp environment a vibrant intellectual atmosphere. 'The camps at that time were full of interesting people, and every evening in different corners of the barracks in the dimly lit spaces where the top tier of plank beds blocked out the light of an electric bulb, groups of convicts gathered and held debates.' The largest groups, Savchenko noticed, gathered around Gumilev:

Professors of history or philosophy from the universities of Warsaw, Riga and Sofia would come from other barracks, and furious dispute would flare up. In such cases Lev Nikolaevich simply obliterated them with reasons, proofs, historical facts, quotations from written sources or statements of great people. In most cases the opponent gave up.[33]

Having finished his candidate's degree, Lev was busy working on what would be his doctoral dissertation – a complete history of the ancient steppe peoples up to the tenth century. The immense complication was that all books had been forbidden to the prisoners: 'one should remember that in conditions of the camp regime not a single line could be committed to paper. During frequent shakedowns, any handwritten materials were confiscated by guards, and in that case their author was put in the dungeon.' Lev was forced to save all his material in his prodigious memory, or 'safe', as he called it, so that he could use it later for his book. According to Savchenko, Lev could cite whole pages from some books on a wide range of subjects.

Lev seems actually to have been able to acquire two books, which he would use as his main sources to write his first book *Xiongnu*. One was by the nineteenth-century scholar-monk Iakinf (Bichurin), who headed a Russian spiritual mission to China. He had translated medieval Chinese manuscripts and other historical documents into Russian.[34] The other was a Soviet anthology of translated ancient Chinese documents.

* * *

Then, one snowy day in March 1953, something occurred that would change their lives – and the lives of everyone in the USSR. According to Georgy Von Zigern Korn, a fellow prisoner of Lev's, the day began oddly. The camp commandant was nowhere to be seen, and other officers were hiding as well. The camp supervisors who were present 'looked subdued, lost, and suddenly were polite and gentle as willow tree buds'.[35] Later in the day they received the stunning news as it spread through the camp, whispered from prisoner to prisoner: Stalin had died.

It would be years before the changes brought about by the death of Stalin finally worked their way through the Soviet system, and it would take Lev three years to get a pardon. But the regime in the camps was finally relaxed enough to allow convicts to have books and to write.

The most precious thing for Lev, however, was free time – and, if he could get them, writing materials. 'I even started visiting a hospital barrack more often', he wrote. 'And the doctors finally took pity on me and assigned me a physical disability. Now, I was appointed to rather easy work ... So there appeared free time to think. Now I had to do the most difficult thing, to receive permission to write.'[36]

Lev and Von Korn worked together in the boot-drying shop of the prison camp. According to Von Korn, Lev had a heart ailment and was generally in frail health, so the lighter work probably saved his life. And it gave Lev what he needed most: free time.

Feeling that he was ready to write his masterpiece, and sensing that the camp authorities had grown more flexible, Lev went to one of the prison officers to request permission to write his book.

'What does this mean, to write?' The officer of the criminal investigation department knitted his brow.

'To translate poems, to write a book about Huns.'[37]

'Why do you need this?' the officer asked.

'To avoid being engaged in various gossip, to feel calm, to fill my time and to give trouble neither to myself nor to you.'

The officer looked at Lev suspiciously and said, 'I'll think about it.' In a few days, Lev had his answer: 'Huns are permitted, but not the poems.'[38]

Other prisoners helped him obtain writing paper in the form of food sacks shipped to the prison, and he was finally able to begin his first book: an account of the history of the Xiongnu, an obscure tribe of Eurasian steppe nomads first mentioned in Chinese sources in the third century BC.

The importance of the Xiongnu could not have been less obvious. But it was with them that Lev chose to start his long-delayed intellectual mission to record the history of the Eurasian steppe peoples. The only connection of the Xiongnu to the thread of greater world history was that they were the reason Emperor Qin Shi Huang began construction of what is today called the Great Wall of China to defend against nomad incursions. It was first mentioned in the third century BC by Chinese sources, which told of a tribe of northern nomads raiding Chinese settlements. They were the only tribe to stay out of the control of the Qin dynasty, the first imperial dynasty to unify the Chinese mainland.

Lev drew on a series of historical sources to argue that the reason that the Chinese never conquered the Xiongnu, or vice versa, was more fundamental than simply the vagaries of history, the outcome of battles and migrations. He cited the works of Sima Qian. According to Gumilev, the importance of Sima's work was that:

he posed the question: why were the victorious arms of the Chinese unable to vanquish these nomadic barbarians? For this he gave an answer very intelligent for his times: the geographical situation, climate, and terrain of China and Central Asia are different enough that Chinese could not live on the steppes, and the nomads could not live in China, and the conquering of another landscape and people, possessing a different way of life, is impractical.[39]

While Lev sought to establish a permanent and natural separation between the Xiongnu and the Chinese, he tried to tease out a lineage between them and the Huns, the more illustrious tribe, who under Attila invaded the Roman Empire. By establishing chronological ancestry between two great steppe tribes, he apparently sought to prove that all steppe tribes had something in common, which simultaneously set them apart from other civilizations on the Eurasian periphery, whether it was the Chinese or Europeans.

The complicated part of Lev's argument was in the timing. Maenchen-Helfen, an Austrian historian who had recently argued that the Huns and Xiongnu were separate and distinct, had made the point that the last time anyone saw the Xiongnu – the northern branch, which allegedly become the Huns – was in 155 AD in Tarbatai, in what is today Kazakhstan, when they were defeated by the khan of the Xianbei nomads, Tanshihuai, while the first mention of the Huns was five years later, in 160 AD in eastern Europe, by the ancient Greek geographer Dionysius Periegeta.

The two sightings by fairly reliable historical sources imply that, for the Huns and the Xiongnu to be the same people, the Xiongnu would have had to travel 2,600km in about five years. This would seem unlikely. But Gumilev never wasted an opportunity to add drama to the narrative, often forsaking good scholarly sense to do so. History for him was about passion and drive, after all.

Gumilev proposed that the Xiongnu had accomplished their mammoth trek across Eurasia probably by abandoning their women and children and fleeing from the victorious Chinese forces. Then he suggested that they encountered a group of Scythian women and took up with them to form a new chapter in their peoples' history. He even fished out an actual account of such an event, and found a contemporary source which recorded that the Huns had been formed from the meeting of Scythian widows, exiled by King Filimer of the Goths, and a group of 'unclean spirits', which Gumilev asserted could easily have meant desert nomads:

To put it another way, the Huns were of the same relation to Xiongnu as Americans are to the British, or perhaps more appropriately, the

Mexicans – a Creole Indian people – were to the Spaniards. The fact of such a migration is undoubtable, and moreover, it explains these deep differences which formed between the Asian-cultured Huns, and their degraded European branch, and so there is no place for the doubts expressed by Maenchen-Helfen.[40]

Fearing that the work might be confiscated, or that he might not live long enough to see its publication, Lev wrote to the prison authorities in 1954:

> I have written the *History of the Huns* for my own pleasure and the soul's consolation. There is nothing anti-Soviet in it. It is written in the same way as one would write a book for the Stalin Prize, only in a more lively style and, I hope, with more talent than would have been the case with my colleagues the historians. That is why, in the case of my demise, I request that the manuscript should not be destroyed but forwarded to the Manuscripts Department of the Oriental Institute at the Academy of Science in Leningrad.

With typically grandiose self-image, Lev completed the letter by stating that, if published, his authorship of the book could be omitted: 'The gothic cathedrals were built by nameless masters; I am content to be a nameless master of science.' It would take a further six years before the first of the books on which he began work during his gulag years saw publication, in 1960, titled *Xiongnu*; the second was published as *Ancient Turks* in 1967.

Lev's impulse to write seems to have been driven partly by the realization, clear from his letters, that his prospects of a normal life had been ruined by his camp experiences, and that he was doomed to live alone with only the solace of his books and writings: 'My future is dicey, but, apparently, I have to count on a single life, and that does not really distress me, because it is too late for me to marry, I am too lazy for courtship, and I am not at all in the mood to worry about mutual feelings.'[41]

Varbanets had not written to him for five years. It was one of the undignified truths that the women of convicted men often abandoned them to their fate after arrest, so as not to incriminate themselves and their loved ones. She only wrote to him, finally, in December 1954. They carried on a correspondence which gave Lev hope of reuniting with her – falsely, it turned out, as she was carrying on her affair with her boss the whole time. Lev learned of this only after his return. In the margin of one of her surviving letters to him he had scrawled, apparently after his release: 'Why did you have to lie so much?'

Spurred by his sufferings in camp, Lev seems to have been increasingly tormented by anger, which he directed not at his immediate oppressors and not at the dictatorial regime, but rather at all those close to him, including Akhmatova. Resentful of both real and imagined slights, he began severing contact with many of his acquaintances from his pre-camp days. Finally, his mother became the target of his wrath. Lev felt that Akhmatova was neglecting him, was not doing enough to get him released, and not writing enough to him. His accumulated resentment over his childhood abandonment, along with her unintentional complicity in his fate, seems to have crystallized into a picture of a mother's neglect – a picture which Lev nurtured.

As he wrote to Gerstein, 'I consider that one parcel a month does not fulfill all a mother's duty to her perishing son and that does not mean that I want two parcels.'[42] In another letter, Lev complains to Gerstein: 'I know what the problem is. Her poetic nature makes her frightfully lazy and egotistic, in spite of her extravagance . . . for her, my death will be a pretext for some graveside poem: how poor she is, she has lost her son. Nothing more.'[43] Gerstein, who was extremely close to both of them throughout this time and afterwards, comes down solidly on Akhmatova's side: 'Whom did he feel hurt by? The military prosecutor's office? The KGB? Or perhaps the central committee of the communist party? No, he blamed his mother for everything.'[44]

In her defence, Akhmatova does appear to have made a number of gestures intended to help Lev. In 1950, she published a poem entitled 'In Praise of Peace (and Stalin)', designed, it appears, to flatter the dictator: 'Legend speaks of a wise man who saved each of us from a terrible death.' It was a deliberate, if humiliating, act for her; later in the 1950s, she made an effort to erase all trace of the poem, by pasting new ones over it when she gave her published books to friends as gifts. However calculated, the gesture does not seem to have worked, though it possibly prevented the situation from getting worse. The poem in praise of Stalin 'would torment Akhmatova as an unhealed wound for the rest of her days', according to Gerstein.[45]

The problem was that Akhmatova, who was under 24-hour surveillance and whose correspondence with Lev was opened and read, could not communicate what she was doing in a clear way. She could not say, for instance, that she had written a poem about Stalin simply to flatter his ego. She also could not tell Lev that in 1954 she had written privately to Kliment Voroshilov, chairman of the Supreme Soviet and nominal head of state of the USSR, in an effort to convince him to get the sentence overturned; and she could not explain to him the circumstances under which her appeal had been rejected by the USSR prosecutor general. Akhmatova realized that as long as the central committee decree about *Zvezda* remained in force, Voroshilov would not take the responsibility for deciding the fate of her son, 'especially when Lev bore the name of his father, Nikolay Gumilev who had been shot by the Cheka in 1921. Voroshilov must have consulted the party presidium or Khrushchev himself, and decided to offer Akhmatova no favors.'[46]

She knew that anything of substance had to be written in code, and apparently thought that Lev recognized that he had to read between the lines of her letters, which were written in perfunctory 'telegraph style', according to him; but he seems not to have understood this – or else wilfully to have ignored it. Her letters to Lev are littered with vague non sequiturs that seem to be efforts to communicate hidden meanings:

> Your non-Confucian letters made me very sad. Believe me, I write to you absolutely everything about me, about my lifestyle and life. You forget that I am 66 years old, that I carry three fatal illnesses inside me, that all my friends and contemporaries have died. My life is dark and lonely – all this does not contribute to the flourishing of an epistolary genre.

This is immediately followed by: 'Spring has come at last – today I will go on a visit in a new summer dress – it will be my first outing.'[47]

Lev's resentment came to a head following the death of Stalin, when he saw those fellow prisoners who managed to take advantage of the political thaw under Khrushchev have their sentences reversed. In a further sign of the thaw, in 1954, Akhmatova was appointed a delegate to the USSR Writer's Congress, where she was given access to some of the most powerful people in the central committee, and a unique public forum. Lev believed she would use the forum to draw attention to his plight, and he was disappointed:

> Lev Nikolaevich and his friends in the camp imagined that Akhmatova would scream there for everyone to hear, 'Help! My son was convicted falsely!' Lev Nikolaevich did not want to understand, that Akhmatova's smallest wrong step would immediately reflect fatally on his own destiny.[48]

In a letter to Gerstein, Lev seems to be unaware of the overtures made by Akhmatova to Voroshilov:

> you write that Mama is not the culprit of my fate. Who else then? Were I not her son, but the son of some ordinary woman I would be, whatever else might happen, a flourishing Soviet professor, a non-party specialist as many have become. Mama herself knows everything about my life and that the sole reason for my difficulties was my kinship with her . . . You write that

she was powerless. I don't believe that. As a delegate to the congress she could approach a member of the central committee and explain that her son had been unjustly convicted.[49]

But it was clear to Gerstein that Lev did not know or appreciate the extent of what Akhmatova had done, and clung irrationally to his heartfelt version of being abandoned. Throwing away most of his mother's letters, Lev began keeping selected ones from her which he felt showed the extent of her neglect and abandonment. These he saved until his death when they were published by his friend Alexander Panchenko. 'The ten letters from Akhmatova preserved by Gumilev became a selective compilation intended to immortalize the image of a bad mother, which Lyova created and cherished in his tormented soul.'[50]

Akhmatova herself was not immune to the emotional maelstrom that had infected Lev. She repeatedly suggested to Lev that Varbanets, his lover, was one of those who had informed on him, and encouraged him not to see her. Lev's file (which became available following the collapse of the Soviet Union) reveals no evidence that she in fact had done so, and Akhmatova was likely driven by the same senseless, claustrophobic jealousy that sent her son into spasms of pure hate.

The miserable triangle of correspondence between mother, son and some-time lover would have continued indefinitely but for a stunning historical twist. In February 1956, Nikita Khrushchev, who had consolidated his power as Stalin's successor, felt secure enough in his position as general secretary to denounce the excesses of Stalin's reign, in an incendiary speech to the Twentieth Communist Party Congress. It was an unimaginable step, which left delegates and the world gasping in disbelief. A few words had utterly and forever changed the lives of millions of Soviet citizens, including Lev's.

On 30 July, a few months after Khrushchev's speech, the prosecutor ruled: 'it is established that there were no grounds for the conviction of Gumilev L.N.' He remained only partially rehabilitated. Full rehabilitation would only come 20 years later in 1975. But at least he was free.

A room of one's own

The 'secret speech' to delegates of the Twentieth Communist Party Congress did not stay secret for long. The delegates were shocked by what they heard: a list of accusations against Stalin, who, according to Khrushchev, had elevated himself so high that he took on 'supernatural characteristics akin to those of a god'. He denounced the cult of personality and listed Stalin's crimes, including the Great Terror, the gulag and the totalitarian society.

Following the speech, most remaining gulag camps were emptied. A mountain of repressed intellectual energy sought an outlet. As Akhmatova put it: 'Two Russias now look each other in the eye: those who did the arresting and those who were put away.' Khrushchev, still skirmishing with Stalinist hardliners, courted the intellectuals with lax censorship; this led to a flowering of intellectual culture and art on a scale not seen in three decades, and the late 1950s and early 1960s became a largely forgotten era of (relative) experimentation in all fields of art, and even in academia.

It was in this context that Lev Gumilev suddenly found himself back in St Petersburg, released from the gulag for the second (and last) time on 11 May 1956, partly rehabilitated by order of the Supreme Soviet. He arrived back in his home city clutching a plywood box tied up with string. The box was full of manuscripts, drafts and books that he had been allowed to accumulate in the camp since 1953. Among them, written on dried food sacks, were the final drafts of his two books, *Xiongnu* and *Ancient Turks*. The former he would publish in 1961 and the latter would become his doctoral dissertation, to be published in 1967.

His return from the gulag was marked by a number of minor and major breakthroughs. At 43, he had never had a room to himself since early childhood; but as a rehabilitee, he was eligible for housing and was put on a list. After a little over a year of sleeping on sofas at friends' houses, he was finally allotted a room in a *kommunalka* in a building on Bolshaya Moskovskaya Street, opposite the city administration building. Outside was a semi-legal market, where in those days black marketeers peddled garden vegetables and meat. The room itself was a mere 12 square metres – long and narrow.[51] There was one bathroom and one kitchen for three families and their children, plus Lev and an alcoholic poet named Pavel, who allowed Lev some space on his bookshelves.

For Lev, the allocation of private space, however cramped, was a gift. Suddenly he could have a writing table. He hung up a family photo of him as a child with his mother and father, and a photo of his father in military uniform. Lev's terrible grudge against his mother did not ease, and relations between them went from bad to worse after he returned to Leningrad. Akhmatova would tell her friends that Lev had 'stopped being a human being'. She spoke in one letter to her brother, Viktor Gorenko, of not having seen Lev for two years. Lev's own disappointment with his mother is clear from his memoirs.

Whether Lev had impossibly high expectations of his mother, or whether Akhmatova's self-obsession and poetic temperament had blinded her to her worldly responsibilities, is still debated in specialized literary journals to this day. But as a result of Akhmatova's neglect, whether real or imagined, Lev's relations with his mother were severely strained, and in 1961 were severed for the last five years of her life.

Lev seems to have taken out his frustrations on his friends and family, but he redoubled his efforts to prove himself as a scholar. In 1957, he got a job in the library of the Hermitage, the famous art museum perched on Leningrad's Palace Embankment and the shore of the River Neva. Every day he would take the trolley bus down the bustling Nevsky Prospekt, cross Palace Square to the library, work an 8–9 hour day, and return. That year, Lev received some positive news: articles based on the books he had worked on in prison were to be published in respected academic journals, which almost certainly meant that the books themselves would soon follow, if the articles were well received.[52]

He spent the next four years polishing *Xiongnu*, doing additional research, forging connections in Leningrad, and working on archaeological digs to make ends meet. Most importantly, a chance encounter with an old acquaintance from a labour camp, Matvey Gukovsky, led him to get in touch with a man who was to be both a kindred spirit and a mentor, who would greatly inspire Gumilev. He was one of the last survivors of the original Eurasianist movement: Petr Savitsky.

Savitsky, it turned out, had read an article by Lev published in 1949, was impressed and had told Gukovsky so. Lev had heard of Savitsky, who had written the introduction to the book *Scythians and Huns* by N.P. Tollya, which had been one of two books by the Eurasianists that were available in the Leningrad University library; but he had no idea that the elderly philosopher was still alive (or where). Lev wrote to Savitsky immediately: 'I was overjoyed on the day when Matvey Alexandrovich Gukovsky – my friend – showed me a page from your letter about my work.'

It is clear that his correspondence with Savitsky made a considerable difference to Lev's life, extricating him from his post-traumatic depression and giving him a renewed sense of mission. Lev found in Savitsky an echo of the type of man he had wanted to be, and desperately hoped he had not lost the opportunity to one day become; and, sensing his mentor's greater erudition, he eagerly adopted virtually all of the old Eurasianist's views.

Both men were passionately interested in the history and geography of Inner Asia, and were self-righteously pedantic on the subject of the steppe nomads: 'I would like', wrote Gumilev, 'to elevate the history of nomads and their culture like the humanists in the fifteenth century elevated the long-forgotten culture of Hellas, and then archaeologists raised Babylon and Sumer from the dead.'[53]

It seems to have been under Savitsky's tutelage that Gumilev's studies of Central Asian nomads began to take on a distinctly anti-Western slant – characteristic of the Eurasianist movement. While *Xiongnu* and *Ancient Turks* were politically neutral books, Lev's further histories of Russia, written over the remaining three decades of his life, not only emphasize the positive role of the steppe tribes (particularly the Mongols) in Russian history, but also make the rather tendentious case that the real enemies of Russia lay in the West: Teutonic knights, Genoan bankers and Crusaders. They, he argued (on the basis of some largely fanciful historical rationale), were fanning the flames of Russian–Mongol conflict behind the scenes.

Both Gumilev and Savitsky seem to have suffered from a kind of Stockholm syndrome following their gulag experiences. Given Lev's own suffering at the hands of Stalin's Russia, it is also interesting that he identified as positive the elements of Russia's past that were the most faithful antecedents to a brutal, arbitrary and cruel dictatorship, while rejecting as pernicious all European influences. Indeed, given his scholarly interest in the irrational, personalistic elements which guide history, it is certainly odd that the word 'Stalin' never appears in any of his writings, and in only two of over a hundred interviews – and then only when he is directly asked about the dictator. This cannot have been solely due to fear of censorship, for this blank spot in Lev's work continued through perestroika, glasnost and the end of the USSR.

Damaged but undaunted, the two men began a correspondence that lasted until 1961, when Savitsky was arrested for a second time. This time it was at the Czech government's behest: he had published the poetry he had written in the gulag with a Paris publisher. Savitsky was sentenced to 30 months in prison (shortened to a year after an international letter-writing campaign organized by friends abroad). He fell ill soon after his return, however, and never fully recovered. In 1966, Gumilev visited Savitsky in Prague, his first and only trip outside the USSR, two years before Savitsky died of cirrhosis of the liver, in April 1968.

Lev's later works owed much to the Eurasianist conception of history which poured forth in Savitsky's letters. Through Savitsky, Lev was also able to write to Vernadsky in the USA; writing direct to America was too dangerous, but writing to Czechoslovakia did not raise eyebrows. His letters to Vernadsky were enclosed in letters to Savitsky, who posted them on to New Haven and sent Vernadsky's replies back to Lev.

Vernadsky, who had built his academic career on rehabilitating the Mongols and reinterpreting their relationship with Russia, taught Lev a great deal. His patronage was also invaluable. In 1960, when *Xiongnu* finally appeared, Vernadsky helped to raise its profile by praising it as 'penetrative and well-organized' in the respected journal *American Historical Review*.[54]

Gumilev was flattered. But thaw or no thaw, one still had to be very careful: history as taught in the Soviet Union was very much hostage to the prevailing ideological winds. This time, Lev had pursued an even more un-Marxist approach, arguing that history was driven not by classes, but by peoples, tribes and nations, whose complex interrelationship with the natural environment shaped their unique cultural identity. Instead of economic forces and the evolution of the means of production, the glue that held history together, so Lev argued, was the unconscious 'complementarity' of peoples (a word which camp life had inspired him to invent) and geographical and environmental factors.

Lev had already had a taste of the politics of Soviet history when, defending his candidate's thesis in the presence of his nemesis Bernstam, the latter had accused him of anti-Marxism – a charge which Lev felt had contributed to his arrest later that year.

Academic disputes in Russia are notoriously prone to getting out of control. Scholars have always been very passionate about their subject and take disagreements very personally, tending to emotional and no-holds-barred polemics. Colleagues tend to pursue each other not just in the pages of specialist journals and in conference papers: before duelling was outlawed, many a scientific disagreement was settled at the ten-pace barrier with a pistol shot; and in the Soviet period, disagreements between academics could still be a matter of life and death. Most famously, in 1940, Trofim Lysenko, a prominent geneticist who had the ear of Stalin, denounced his scholarly rival Nikolay Vavilov after the two disagreed over theories of genetics. Vavilov was sent to a labour camp where he starved to death in 1943.

No topic – the Huns, the Turkic khanate or the Mongols – was too esoteric or obscure to attract unwelcome attention and accusations of ideological waywardness. For instance, it just so happened that the last person to publish a major book on the steppe tribes (in this case, the Huns) had been Bernstam himself. His book *History of the Xiongnu* (1951) had been savaged: a year after publication a review was published charging the unfortunate Bernstam with 'following in the footsteps of bourgeois historiography' for suggesting that the Huns had played a progressive role in history.[55] Bernstam was condemned by the board of the Institute of the History of Material Culture, which at the time oversaw academic work. It offered him the chance to write a self-criticism with analysis and the reasons for his mistakes.[56]

When Lev learned of Bernstam's fate, feelings of schadenfreude and vengeance evidently overcame empathy and a feeling of shared injustice: 'I am glad that the bastard got his comeuppance', he wrote to his mother. But Bernstam's fate showed just how precarious an existence Soviet scholars led, no matter their subject. Like Bernstam, Gumilev would be subjected to withering criticism from his colleagues in history departments. The arguments Lev was making were rather radical and most unorthodox (and quite possibly wrong), and a few months after *Xiongnu* was published in 1961, a devastating review appeared in the academic journal *Bulletin of Ancient History* by one K. Vasilyev, accusing Lev of 'ignorance of original versions of the sources used, ignorance of modern research literature in Chinese and Japanese, noncritical perception of some outdated concepts representing the past of the Oriental science'.[57] Then Lev's book provoked a row with the Mongolian Communist Party, which was anxious to toe the line of Soviet historiography even at the expense of their ancestors' reputation. The third plenum of the central committee of the Mongol People's Revolutionary Party 'strongly criticized pseudoscientific theories about the progressiveness of the Tatar–Mongol conquests of the countries of Asia and Europe'.[58]

For a short while it appeared that Lev had seriously overestimated the change in the political climate, gone too far out on a limb, and would be forced into an embarrassing retraction or self-criticism (or worse). But perhaps even more surprising than the strident criticism he received was the praise he got from unexpected quarters. The director of the Hermitage museum, Professor M.I. Artamonov, defended him, saying that 'Certainly, Gumilev had the right to work with such translations, the more so that he was creating a summarizing work, and not a specific research establishing a certain fact or amendment to its interpretation.'[59] Far from finishing his career, the controversy surrounding *Xiongnu* confirmed Lev's academic reputation. After publication, the rector of Leningrad University offered him a post as senior researcher at the university's Geographical Economic Institute, and the same year he started lecturing in the historical department of Leningrad State University as a freelance lecturer, and presented open lectures at the USSR Geographical Society. His works gained a steady following. Sergey Lavrov, Lev's biographer and boss at the institute, said that his lectures became so popular that not everyone could be accommodated in the hall (which could only hold 100 people). 'A whole team of young scientists formed around Gumilev.'[60]

Anatoly Anokhin was one such scientist. He joined the geography department in the 1960s and still teaches there. I found him in his office one day and asked him about Gumilev:

> First of all, a lot of people went to the lectures simply to look at Lev Nikolaevich. He was a unique figure, the son of two famous poets, even more so because his father's poetry was forbidden. Secondly, he allowed himself the liberty to criticize the official positions which the historical sciences at the time had stuck to. He stuck pins in it, and people liked that.[61]

The storm in a teacup over Lev's book *Xiongnu* was just one of a number of similar episodes in the wide-ranging debate over the history and direction of the USSR – often expressed in oblique metaphorical terms in the pages of the official 'thick journals'. These came to dominate the life of the intelligentsia, and figured prominently in lectures and debates in which Gumilev enthusiastically took part.

'Politics by culture'

Khrushchev's effervescent thaw was short-lived. In the early 1960s, even before he was ousted from power, life began to freeze over again. When Brezhnev succeeded him in a 'soft coup' in 1964 he immediately began to reverse Khrushchev's policy of tolerance, and in 1966, the trials of Yury Daniel and Andrey Sinyavsky, two Russian writers whose satires of the Soviet system were published abroad, became the targets of the first high-profile repression of literary figures since Stalin's day. It was a signal that the rest of the intelligentsia did not fail to register.

But while democracy and reform-minded members of the elite were put back in their boxes by a series of show trials and firings, the nationalists were not. The attitude towards nationalism that emerged under Brezhnev was of grudging acceptance of the lesser of two evils. With the nationalist intelligentsia increasingly in conflict with the liberals, the Communist Party came down in favour of the former, who were given greater latitude than the liberals to publish unorthodox views and faced less severe punishment for transgressions. It was the beginning of a new era in the Soviet Union, the introduction of nationalism into the mainstream – an era described by historian Yitzhak Brudny as 'politics by culture'.

The first concession of the regime to the nationalists came in 1965 when a number of prominent nationalists petitioned the Kremlin to allow them to create a new organization, the All Russian Society for the Preservation of Historical Monuments and Culture (the clunky VOOPIK in Russian). It was tightly controlled by the Communist Party, and ostensibly devoted only to the preservation and restoration of historical monuments, mainly Orthodox churches. But VOOPIK quickly grew into a quasi-political organization, a bauble awarded to nationalists by the central committee. It gave them a legal forum in which to meet every month, in the Vysokopetroskii monastery in central Moscow. This was the first in a series of signals that the Communist Party, which throughout its existence had claimed to have broken with Russia's past, would now embrace it.

Brezhnev was a simple man. He was not a good speaker and had a stammer due to wartime concussion. 'He was not polished, but he was a wise man in a simple way', according to Sergey Semanov, a radical nationalist intellectual who was an active combatant in the culture wars of the 1960s and 1970s between conservative nationalists and liberal reformists within the elite. 'He knew what had to be done, and it had to be done very carefully.' VOOPIK became the centre of a growing movement both inside and outside the Communist Party – known today as the 'Russian Party' – which united nationalist-minded intellectuals, party apparatchiks and even dissidents in a mutual web of influence, promoting Russian nationalism.

One regular attendee at VOOPIK sessions in the monastery was Gumilev, though, according to Semanov, he was not formally a member. Semanov remembered Lev's temper and argumentative nature:

> He was a real *enfant terrible* . . . We knew him quite well, we all loved him, but he was a bit of a hooligan, arguing all the time and picking fights . . . He unconditionally influenced the formation of Russian patriotism . . . but not in the sense that we all agreed with him. It was the arguments – they inspired us, gave us new ideas, challenged us to new formulations . . . In intellectual life it is more important if there is a living idea, something with some passion in it . . . Gumilev smashed up everything. He said two times two equals five. And it was true. Two times two equals four was simply boring.[62]

Lev's writings on Central Asian nomads were controversial among the Russian nationalists, most of whom could not accept a history which argued that Russia and the steppe nomads shared a common heritage. The Mongols had been the historical bugbears of Russian nationalists for three centuries, and the liberation from the Mongol 'yoke' at the battle of Kulikovo in 1380 was seen as the beginning of the independent Russian nation by Nikolay Karamzin, the nineteenth-century father of modern Russian historiography, who wrote in his twelve-volume *History of the Russian State*: 'The Russians went to the Kulikovo Field as citizens of various principalities and returned as a united Russian nation.' But despite these important differences, Lev fitted in among the dissident nationalists at VOOPIK; in broad historiographical terms, they agreed that Russia was a profoundly unique civilization and a natural empire.

Lev's histories were often fanciful and, strictly speaking, not very scholarly; he invented people, he invented documents, or transported things magically through time so that they would fit his narrative. 'His attitude was like Hegel, who said if the facts do not fit my theory, then so much for the facts', wrote a close acquaintance, the right-wing literary critic Vadim Kozhinov.

Following *Xiongnu*, Lev had published two further works on the steppe nomads – *Ancient Turks* and *Searches for the Imaginary Kingdom*, about the Mongols. *Ancient Turks* was devoted to a series of Turkic kings and warlords who unified the chunks of steppe land between Korea and Byzantium in the second half of the first millennium. It covered four centuries of history, until the demise of the Uighur khanate in the ninth century. This is a period about which historians know virtually nothing, and this gave Gumilev a kind of unlimited licence. As we have already seen from his first book, *Xiongnu*, he was always one to prefer the dramatic and the colourful explanation, even when a more sensible interpretation would fit the available evidence; but when the available evidence was virtually nil, it was easier to be creative. 'I love the Turks the most because in the sixth to the eighth centuries I can represent persons and events in a much livelier way', he wrote to Savitsky in 1961.

In *Ancient Turks*, Gumilev pioneered a historical methodology that would make him famous: 'historical reconstruction', which was applicable when there was little actual history to choose from. With very little in the way of supporting evidence, for example, he portrayed the demise of the Uighur khanate as a kind of Shakespearean tragedy: the degeneration of the Uighur aristocracy and the collapse of family values caused by their adoption of Manichaeism as a religion. 'Here, reconstruction appears to have been replaced by author fantasy', says even Gumilev's largely sympathetic biographer, Sergey Belyakov.[63]

Lev's imagination was a product of the prison camps. *Ancient Turks* had started out as Gumilev's candidate's dissertation at Leningrad University and had stayed with him through nearly seven years of felling trees and near-starvation. The theoretical musings on the fate of the anonymous khans and kings of ancient history appear to have been largely a coping mechanism – stories he told and retold himself and his fellow inmates to keep himself sane. In letters to friends he often spoke of the subject matter of his histories in vaguely paternal terms. As he wrote to Natalya Varbanets: 'Out of the contours and shadows, the Xiongnu, Uighurs, the Kara Kipchaks transform themselves into figures, sometimes filled with flesh and blood. I look upon them almost as my children – I have summoned them from oblivion.'[64]

In 1970, he published the third in his so-called 'steppe trilogy', focusing on the Mongols. *Searches for the Imaginary Kingdom* recounts the strange tale of a rumour that swept medieval Europe in 1145 of an unknown Christian kingdom that had been founded in Central Asia by a man named Prester John. Gumilev argued that the tale was not a hoax, as was generally believed, but actually referred to a tribe of Mongols that had converted to Nestorian Christianity. Gumilev makes a fairly controversial assertion that Nestorianism was strong among the steppe peoples around 1200, though he provided little evidence to back this up. The book, however, is a fantastic read: an engaging, ambitious and eccentric tale proposing that a Christian Mongol army in Iraq tried to unite with a Crusader army at Acre in the twelfth century, but was rebuffed by the

French. Left to their fate, the Mongols converted to Islam – a historical mistake of mega proportions, which Gumilev attributes to 'the arrogance of the civilized European, for whom everything east of the Vistula is savagery and mediocrity'. The book showcases Gumilev's first major treatment of the Mongols. He would become perhaps Russia's most famous apologist for their brutal conquests. 'Mongolia', he wrote, 'was drawn into the subsequent wars not of its own free will, but by the logic of events in world history and a policy in which it could no longer fail to take part'.

The book marked the beginning of Gumilev's complex (and not strictly scholarly) theories about the role the steppe tribes played in Russian history. In this and subsequent books he made many controversial claims about how the Golden Horde's invasions of Russian lands in the thirteenth century were actually something far more complex than simple conquest by a foreign people. The Mongols and the Russians did not consider each other to be 'foreigners', he wrote. And while the Mongols destroyed the capital city of Kiev, they left other Russian cities alone. Indeed, Russian princes and Mongol emperors frequently fought on the same side. The dual facts that the Mongols were able to hold onto the lands of Rus for two centuries and that the Russians were then able to hold onto the Mongol khanates that they conquered in the fifteenth century, indicated to Gumilev that there was a natural affinity between the Russians and the steppe tribes, which did not exist between Russians and Europeans – neither of whom had been able to hold the other's territory for long.

His opponents accused him of total disregard for the evidence. In one instance, he took on the epic poem *The Tale of the Host of Igor*, supposedly about an 1186 battle between Rus and the Cumans (a pre-Mongol nomadic people), and reinterpreted it as a thirteenth-century work about the Mongols. According to his friend Kozhinov:

> Gumilev was, if you wish, both a historian and a poet equally. Fantasy and even direct 'fiction' play a paramount role in L.N. Gumilev's works. This allows him not only to masterfully grasp the consciousness of readers, but also quite often to remarkably 'guess' secret, discreet movements of history. But at the same time, these same features cause dissatisfaction (or even indignation) in people who consider strict documenting obligatory, and do not accept any 'intuitive' conclusions in historical studies.[65]

However, it is equally clear that the official Romanov-era historiography of the Mongol invasions was just as flawed, if not more so. Gumilev was partly right on a number of accounts. Historians agree that while any talk of 'integration' between the Russians and the Mongols is hugely exaggerated, nonetheless relations between the Russians and the Mongols were slightly more complicated than Russian and Soviet historiography had held since Nikolay Karamzin's time: the actual term 'yoke', for example, in fact dates from the seventeenth century, a full 200 years after the Mongols were defeated. Also, no contemporary sources use words such as 'conquer' to describe the Mongol invasion of 1237–40, but instead prefer 'plunder' or 'capture' without implying any change in political sovereignty. It is just as clear that Russia's boyars and princes collaborated with the Mongols, and that Moscow even formed an alliance with the Mongols against the rival city state of Tver. It seemed that neither the Russian city states nor the Mongols were monolithic entities, and their histories were intertwined far more than historians chose to let on.

Kozhinov and other nationalist intellectuals were fast noticing Gumilev's works and his rising public profile. Kozhinov readily admits adopting many of Gumilev's views, and he popularized a concept very similar to Gumilev's ideas in a mass-circulation newspaper, *Literaturnaya Gazeta*, in 1969.[66] There Kozhinov questioned the veracity of Marxist historiography, and argued that Marxism was based on flawed assumptions; world history was not a story of class struggle, but the rise and fall of national civilizations. That the article appeared at all in such a top-flight publication was a milestone for the nationalist ideologues.

In *Searches for the Imaginary Kingdom*, published the following year, Gumilev reflected Kozhinov's argument. 'Here it is impossible to talk of a single [historical] process', he wrote, criticizing dialectical materialism. 'On the contrary, the interweaving of different processes with their own momentum of development is to be seen: a rapid rise, a brief stabilization at its zenith, and a gradual decline.'[67]

Lev's fortunes rose with those of the nationalists. According to his close friend, the late Savva Yamshchikov, a member of VOOPIK's presidium: 'Lev did his own thing. He wasn't into politics.' He generally did not publish in the wide-distribution journals, preferring academic articles. But his real forte was lecturing. His personal history was legendary, with such illustrious parents, and his oratorical skills were magnificent. Yamshchikov remembers organizing a lecture for him in Moscow which an astonishing 800 people attended, filling the auditorium and spilling into the halls. He found there was a nearly unquenchable thirst in Soviet society for alternative history, for summoning the lost roots of the nation – something that the Communist Party had done its best to stamp out.

Dancing on bones

Today, most think the vanished USSR was a drab, grey place of ideological conformism and rigidity; and for the most part, it was. But in the 1960s there was a heady, vibrant cultural scene lurking just below the otherwise placid, dull surface. Literary experimentation, jazz, alternative politics – all could be found if only one knew where to look. Around the corner from Lev's flat, in the vegetable market at Leningrad's Vladimirskoe metro station, black marketeers sold jazz records made from discarded X-ray plates – the records were artfully dubbed 'dancing on bones'.

The mid-1960s was a time of great personal change for Gumilev. In 1966, Akhmatova died. They had not spoken during her final five years, and guilt on this score seems to have plagued him intermittently. Nevertheless, his mother's passing removed a strong presence from his life, and it says something about Lev's attachment to his mother – which Gerstein described as an 'obsession' – that he only married after she died. He had met his wife, Natalya Simonovskaya, in 1965 at a party at a friend's apartment. She remembered that he looked like 'an overgrown child': 'Trousers a bit too short, his cuffs stick out of his sleeves.' But nonetheless he was 'gallant'. They married in 1966. She was an artist. On 15 June 1967, she moved into Gumilev's one-room *kommunalka* in Leningrad, having received a note in typical Gumilev style: '[I am] finishing the proofreading of *Ancient Turks*, and waiting for you on the appointed date. Have already washed the floor.'[68] The two never had children, however. 'Lev believed that his books were his children', recalled Natalya.[69]

Since his experience in the White Sea Canal prison camp in 1939, his epiphany about 'passionarity' had never left him. For decades, he had never tired of telling people about his breakthrough, the biological impulse that drives men to irrational deeds; or about the feature of complementarity which he had hit upon, meaning the compulsion of prisoners to band together in tight groups. Teaching in Leningrad in the 1960s he pursued this idea, inspired by the 1908 account of a Russian biologist who documented a curious episode: a massive swarm of locusts which flew across the Red Sea, from Abyssinia towards the Arabian Peninsula, and drowned entirely. Gumilev believed this mass locust suicide was analogous to Alexander's death march: 'Who could have lifted up this mass of locusts and transferred it across the sea. And not according to Darwin's rules, not for the continuation of the species, not for multiplication, but to meet death.'

His theories were at best unorthodox, and at worst quite eccentric. 'Passionarity' in Gumilev's work is a quantifiable measure of the mental and ideological energy at the disposal of a given nation at a given time. He believed one could actually calculate it with impressive equations and plot it on graphs. He even assigned it a symbol as a mathematical variable: Pik.

In 1965, he read the *Chemical Composition of the Earth's Biosphere* by the great Russian biologist Vladimir Vernadsky (father of Georgy), who described for the first time in 1908 his theory of 'bioenergy'. Energy from the sun that makes plants grow and causes photosynthesis is transferred to human beings via the digestive system. Vernadsky believed that energy from the cosmos is decisive in the behaviour of animals, as well as plants; and it even affects human beings. Gumilev, in the maximalist tradition of Russian nineteenth-century philosophy, began to try to prove Vernadsky's thesis: that episodes of intense human activity are in some way connected to solar and cosmic radiation. He became so fascinated with the idea that during the summers of 1967 and 1968 he went every Saturday to the Institute of Radiation in Obninsk to meet Nikolay Timofeev-Ressovsky, one of the USSR's most celebrated geneticists. The two men were in discussion about a joint article on passionarity.

Predictably, the potential collaboration ended when Timofeev-Resovsky learned of the truly ambitious and not entirely scientific arguments that Lev planned to make. According to Gumilev's wife Natalya: 'In the opinion of the geneticist, nation should be defined according to social relations, and Timofeev-Resovsky could not in the end agree with the conception of passionarity and the characterization of this phenomenon as natural.'[70] The two men fell out, with the elder geneticist calling Lev a 'crazy paranoiac'.

Lev published the article on his own, in 1970, in the journal *Priroda* (*Nature*), in which he laid out the idea of the 'ethnos' – something similar to a nation or ethnic group – which he described as the most basic element of world history, the national or ethnic self-identification that is 'a phenomenon so universal as to indicate its deep underlying foundation'. All *homo sapiens*, as he put it, are members of an ethnos, 'so that it is possible to distinguish those close to us from the rest of the world'.[71] With that, Lev launched a meme that was to define the rest of his career: the theory of 'Ethnogenesis'.

The term 'ethnos' had entered Soviet ethnography sometime in the late 1960s, with many claims and counterclaims as to who (re-)introduced it. It was a Greek term rediscovered by Russian émigré anthropologist Sergey Shirokogorov in the early twentieth century; but it did not penetrate the orthodox Marxist academy of his native Russia until 1966, when it was popularized by Yulian Bromley, who that year had taken over the chair of the Soviet Academy of Sciences Institute of Ethnography.

Gumilev would later accuse Bromley of plagiarizing his theory. Certainly, he had used the term 'Ethnos' before Bromley – there are 117 mentions of it in Gumilev's *Discovery of Khazaria*, published in 1965, a year before Bromley began to popularize the term. Bromley's first major theoretical take on the theory was published after Lev's article in *Priroda*, as a criticism of Lev's work.[72]

Bromley's appointment as head of the Institute of Ethnography would mark the beginning of a two-decade-long scholarly feud that would define Gumilev's further academic career. It was an argument about the nature of ethnicity and nationalism which tracked the steadily rising tide of the USSR's ethnic problems, which a quarter of a century later would tear the Union apart. In retrospect, neither man could convincingly lay claim to have correctly predicted the calamity or to have offered a solution to avert it. However, Lev's theories, focusing on nationalism as something primordial and permanent, are widely judged today to have been closer to the mark than those of Bromley, who reflected the orthodox Soviet view that nationalism was a 'socio-economic' phenomenon and would eventually melt away with progress. It didn't.

Bromley was appointed head of the Institute of Ethnography in 1966 as a relative outsider. Like most academics he had to justify his promotion by throwing out old dogmas and ushering in something new and proprietary. The theory of Ethnos fit the bill, and the term symbolized the new seriousness with which ethnic and national identity was being taken by the USSR's academic establishment – a recognition of the fact that, 50 years after class differences were officially abolished (which in theory would erase national contradictions), nations had stubbornly failed to disappear.

While the original Bolsheviks were profoundly conscious of the ethnic diversity of the Soviet Union, cataloguing and recognizing more than 200 languages of native Soviet peoples, they nevertheless remained confident that ethnicity and nationalism constituted just a stage in the progression of mankind through history; it was a fossil of tribal and feudal development, and an expression of class distinction and economic relationships. The recognition of nations and ethnic groups by the Soviets was actually meant to hasten the wheel of history; the sooner the nation was brought forth, the sooner it could be dispensed with in the inexorable rise of humanity towards true socialism. Under Stalin's constitution of 1936, ethnic groups had been classified according to their perceived level of historical consciousness, their numbers, language and territory. The first stage was the tribe, the second was the *narod* or people, while the third stage was the nation. The fifteen titular peoples of the USSR that had given their names to the Soviet republics – such as the Uzbeks, Kazakhs and Ukrainians – were given the status of nations, with a formal right of independence; while those that had autonomous status within a republic – like the Tatars, the Chechens and the Ingush – were given the lesser status of *narod*, and the eventual promise of nationhood.

It was a singularly odd policy, aimed at artificially hastening and buttressing the very thing they were trying to overcome, and the collapse of the Soviet Union would show just how badly Stalin had miscalculated. Already in the 1960s the Soviet social sciences for the first time were confronting the frustrating fact that nations were not fading away. The culture wars within the

Soviet intelligentsia between nationalists and liberals were but one symptom of this wider problem.

As Anatoly Anokhin recalls:

> The official ideology was oriented towards the achievement of social homo-geneity – a single Soviet society according to Marxist Leninist ideals formed by the ideological department of the central committee. These differences were supposed to melt away over time. But they didn't. And this became one of the main reasons for the collapse of the Soviet Union.[73]

The very use of the term ethnos – by both Bromley and Gumilev – took the field of ethnography a step back from socialist orthodoxy. Instead of the terms 'class' and 'nation', which were solidly based in the official metaphysics, ethnos implied the need for a new vocabulary and was an admission that the subject at hand – the study of ethnic differences – was something that had not been adequately addressed by orthodox Marxism. Ethnos was something old, but also something new.

Ethnography under Bromley became the study not of the ethnic features of society, but of societies conceived as *ethnoi* – a subtle but distinct shift indicating more permanence than Marxist theory had originally credited them with. However, Bromley never pushed his theory to its logical conclusion: he stressed the importance of ethnic groups, but he never addressed the possibility that there might be problems with nationalism in the USSR. Quite the opposite, in fact. In 1982 he wrote in a characteristic (and with hindsight, rather unfortunate) passage:

> As the experience of the multinational Soviet Union and other countries joining the socialist confederation shows: socialism, liquidating the socio-class basis for the exploitation of one nation by another, avoids the bases for inter-ethnic antagonisms, and stimulates the narrowing of national differences.[74]

While Bromley argued that nations are more permanent than socialist theory had predicted, he took a middle position, arguing that *ethnoi* were 'ethnosocial units', as he termed them.[75] They could change, and be assimilated away over time, with the disappearance of class antagonisms that nurture ethnic hatreds. But it would not happen as quickly as Stalinist dogma had first taught.

Gumilev, meanwhile, took the maximal position, arguing that *ethnoi* were real bounded wholes, akin to organisms with their own independent existence and life cycles. It was completely counter to orthodox Marxism, and the fact that Gumilev was permitted to teach at all is evidence of a certain degree of pluralism in the Soviet establishment.

Gumilev was not arguing that nations are permanent: the historical record was full of cases of nations being born and dying; but the death of a nation was not a case of national bonds withering away under social progress and steady enlightenment, as was the view of Marxist orthodoxy. Gumilev believed that the creation and extinction of *ethnoi* were part and parcel of the life cycle of peoples, the instinct to thrive, spread, wither and die.

Drawing on his labour camp-era theories, Gumilev argued that the existence of *ethnoi* was not a social phenomenon, but rather the result of a biological instinct – involuntary, unconscious and irreducible, which could be cured or which melted away. He believed that this universal tendency to distinguish ethnicity was associated with a biological capacity in human beings to acquire a 'stereotype of behaviour' early in life. 'There is not a single person on Earth outside of an ethnos', he was fond of saying. 'Everybody will answer the question "What are you?" with "Russian", "French", "Persian", "Maasai", etc. without a moment's hesitation.'[76]

However, he was coming close to saying that nationality was biologically determined or hereditary – a red rag to a bull in the USSR (and everywhere else, for that matter) on account of its association with Nazism. This criticism was unfair: he argued that the predisposition to distinguish one's ethnic identity was indeed a biological endowment, but the identity itself was in fact learned through interaction with the environment, mainly the parents, at a very early age. Elsewhere in the social sciences, the cognitive revolution was making many of the same arguments that Gumilev was starting in the 1970s – that human behaviour is more innate, more unconscious, less rational and less free than had been previously thought.

While Gumilev was not a highly ranked academic at the time, his social standing within intelligentsia circles gave his work wide visibility. The academic establishment of the USSR could not let such dissent go unanswered. The Institute of Ethnography took notice of Gumilev's revolt, and Bromley wrote a rebuttal in the next issue of *Priroda*. He criticized Lev's concept of stereotypes, arguing that these were not as ingrained as Lev believed. Culture was a product of the environment, and could change: 'Stable mental stereotypes are not an immanent product of the human brain, they are a product of certain external conditions, first of all socio-historical. Ethnos is not nuclear. It is made up of social as well as natural factors.'[77]

Sergey Cheshko, an ethnographer and colleague of Bromley in the former Soviet Academy of Sciences, summed up both approaches when I sought him out at the Academy of Sciences in Moscow: 'According to Bromley, ethnos was a collection of characteristics. It was not an essence. The characteristics may change . . . Gumilev believed that humanity is made up of a number of "species" and this gives each ethnos its own particular essence.' Lev was soon subjected to a number of scholarly attacks and was forbidden from publishing in major academic journals as a result of the run-in with Bromley.

There was another, darker reason for Lev's ostracism by mainstream academia, however. His association with the dissident nationalists of VOOPIK brought him into contact with a lively community of intellectuals, but also nurtured the wraiths of anti-Semitism and racism that had haunted Russia since the time of the pogroms. In addition to debating the finer points of historiography, the nationalist milieu became an echo chamber for all manner of conspiracy theories and racial demagoguery, and these became the glue which held together a rather disparate movement of iconoclasts.

The 'Russian Party' within the Soviet elite was getting stronger and bolder. VOOPIK had begun to attract not just intellectuals, but also high-ranking party sympathizers on the one hand, and serious dissidents on the other. Nationalists were being given high-ranking posts in the media and propaganda realm; in 1969 radical nationalist writer Valery Ganichev was appointed to head the Molodaya Gvardiya publishing house, and he appointed Semanov to run their most prestigious book series.[78] The nationalists were united in a loose-knit and ideologically driven group that came to be increasingly in conflict with Western-oriented reform-minded liberals within the intelligentsia and the regime. The nationalists played on traditional prejudices to demonize their opponents in culture wars that had become brutal and total.

Lev, battle-scarred after his academic conflicts, found an odd association with the serious anti-Semitic fringe of the nationalist movement. His antipathy towards Jews appears to have grown over time; while he had always been known to make the odd anti-Semitic remark, many of his childhood friends, such as Gerstein and the Mandelstams, were Jewish and had found it (mostly) harmless. It seems likely that, driven by the trauma of the camps (which nurtured his already horrible temper), his conflict with his mother's entourage, and his regular association with voluble anti-Semites, Lev's prejudices grew. In her memoirs, Gerstein calls the older Gumilev an 'anti-Semite'. Many also regarded a book he published in 1965 on the Khazars (a tribe living in the Caspian region between the seventh and the tenth centuries that had converted to Judaism) as a thinly veiled piece of anti-Jewish propaganda: Khazars were described in the work as a 'chimera' or a parasitic ethnos. Meanwhile, the reputation of his associates rubbed off on him, colouring his reputation in scholarly circles.

In 1971, he met Sergey Melnik, who was a regular at the VOOPIK gatherings in Moscow. He introduced Lev to the underground journal *Veche*, which published fringe articles with anti-Semitic overtones. It was the brainchild of dissident Vladimir Osipov, who had just returned from seven years in a labour camp in Mordovia, and who had begun to publish his journal in the town of Alexandrov using borrowed typewriters and mimeo sheets.[79] Known as the 'city without friars' – in criminal jargon, a friar was someone who had no connection to the criminal underworld – Alexandrov was a popular place for released camp inmates to settle, as it was located just outside Moscow's 101-kilometre limit: as close to the capital as former political prisoners were allowed to live.

An article in the first issue of *Veche* was devoted to the familiar nationalist bugbear: the ruin of historical monuments in Moscow. Entitled 'The Fate of the Russian Capital', it highlighted the destruction wrought by the building of new Soviet monstrosities, such as the New Arbat Street, which cut through a historical neighbourhood in the mid-sixties and raised a row of ugly high-rise buildings in its place. The culprits in the destruction of Russia's historical patrimony were not hard to find; the article listed the architects of the new buildings, almost all of whom had Jewish surnames. It is true that architecture was one profession in which Jews were not prohibited from working by a quota on nationalities, and so they were overrepresented in its ranks. But it was pure nonsense to suggest that the architects had anything to do with the decisions on which buildings to demolish: those were all made by the party at the level of the provincial committee and above – and those people were almost exclusively Russian.

Lev hosted Osipov often at his wife's apartment in Moscow, and published one article in *Veche* about his theory of passionarity. Their meetings continued until 1974, according to Osipov, when suddenly a very public spat engulfed *Veche*. In February of that year, Osipov issued an announcement, picked up on Radio Free Europe, the Munich-based US government-funded radio station, that Melnik was a KGB agent. Melnik, however, stood his ground and made a blunt denial. If the KGB paid no attention to *Veche* before, suddenly it had no choice but to intervene. In April of that year, Yury Andropov, head of the KGB, ordered a criminal case to be prepared against *Veche* – calling it an 'anti-Soviet' publication. A few months later the journal was shut; and a year after that, Osipov went to prison again for eight years. Lev's association with Melnik and Osipov may well have been one of the factors – in addition to his arguments with the academic establishment – that closed off his access to the 'thick journals' and wider public forums.

A line of ascent

As Lev's feud with Bromley (and his friendship with Osipov) was developing, the struggle within the Soviet elite over nationalism was getting fiercer. By 1970,

Brezhnev and his ideological chief Mikhail Suslov seem to have decided that the independent political activities on both sides of the ideological divide had gone far enough. Two 'thick journals' on either flank of the nationalist-liberal ideological schism were shorn of their editors; Alexander Tvardovsky, the chief editor of *Novy Mir*, resigned in February 1970, and Anatoly Nikonov, chief editor of its ideological antipode, the nationalist Komsomol journal *Molodaya Gvardiya*, was sacked in November.[80] The orthodox Communist Party was clearly anxious to put nationalism back in the box, and Brezhnev, at a meeting of the central committee, complained of 'too much church bell ringing on television' – referring to religion.[81]

One of those who had survived the purge of 1970 was Alexander Yakovlev, a young central committee bureaucrat, who at that time was acting head of the committee's department of propaganda. Eager to prove his loyalty in the wake of the shake-ups (as well as to eradicate the word 'acting' from his title), Yakovlev authored the article 'Against Anti-Historicism', published in the relatively liberal *Literaturnaya Gazeta* in November 1972. It offered a sweeping criticism of the nationalists' approach to history: that is, as a heterogeneous process composed of peoples, rather than a homogeneous one composed of a single mankind on a single ascending path up the ladder rungs of dialectical materialism. Nonsense, said Yakovlev: the half-century since the October revolution was 'brilliant proof of the fact that the history of humanity develops in a line of ascent, in full accordance with the objective laws of public life discovered by the great scholars, Karl Marx and Friedrich Engels'.[82] The article named 16 historians by name, accusing them of propagating historical errors, of romanticizing Russia's autocratic past, and of promoting a non-class approach to history.

The nationalists went berserk, writing letters and calling for Yakovlev's head. Brezhnev was apparently angered, saying: 'Well, if this guy published this kind of article without being asked to, and picks a fight with our intelligentsia, then we should send him away.'[83] It speaks volumes for the power lobby of the 'Russian Party' within the communist elite that Yakovlev, spouting nothing but pure Marxist orthodoxy and zeal, dramatically miscalculated and lost his gambit. He was sent to Canada as ambassador – a political exile, but an important one, which slightly mitigated his humiliation.

With Yakovlev's exile, 'we considered that we had won', recalled Valery Ganichev, who remained in his post at *Molodaya Gvardiya* until 1980. 'The Russian patriotic trend began to show up at the highest levels of the central committee.' By this point, the 'Russian Party' within the Communist Party had reached the very summit of the regime: 'They stood against a cosmopolitan wing in the Politburo and against dogmatic supporters of Marxism who denied any national beginning in the life of a society.' Ganichev's colleague Semanov put it another way. Talking to me in 2010, he made this comment, which says more about the nationalists than it does about their adversaries: 'In reality there were two parties: the Russian party and the Jewish party.'[84] His autobiography, published posthumously in 2011, is entitled *Russian Party: Why the Jews Will Never Win.*

The perception was that the nationalists had protection, and the illusion of favouritism encouraged those 'Russia Party' sympathizers lower down in the state hierarchy in thinking that formerly taboo interpretations of history were acceptable. Gradually, the nationalist approach to teaching and writing history was being vindicated – if not on a scholarly level, then at least on a political level. This was reflected in the curious support that Lev was suddenly receiving from within the party's Olympian central committee, where officials increasingly stepped up to back him. Lev, as we have seen, was a frequenter of nationalist gatherings and a contributor to nationalist journals. While many of his friends in high places were nationalists, several were not – they were people he had met along the way who had ties to him, or else were entranced by his parents' mystique.

One of these was Lev Voznesensky, son of the deceased rector of Leningrad University, who had kept in contact with Lev after their time together in the Karaganda labour camp. He had since joined the central committee, where he was in a position to aid Lev. 'I would only say that much of his work would not have seen the light of day without help from friends of friends.'[85] But the most powerful friend Lev made, one who would time and again intervene on his behalf in his frequent brutal fights with rival academics, was Anatoly Lukyanov, who held a high-ranking post in the presidium of the Supreme Soviet. He would eventually become chairman of the central committee and then chairman of the Supreme Soviet. Gumilev had met Lukyanov through Voznesensky.[86] Lukyanov, an avid fan of Akhmatova, offered to help Gumilev with an ugly court fight surrounding the disposal of her archive (it so happened that one of the judges deciding the case was an old friend of Lukyanov's). From that time on, Lukyanov and Gumilev maintained close contact, with Lukyanov becoming an oddly recurring fixture in Lev's life. Lukyanov almost single-handedly marshalled support for Gumilev's second PhD dissertation defence in the mid-1970s, as well as for other publications.

The presence in Lev's life of a clique of high-ranking Communist Party officials was an intriguing puzzle given Lev's politically chequered past. Indeed, he was still seen as politically unreliable in many corners of the party: he ignored communist holidays, but celebrated Christmas and Easter. Unlike other academics with whom he worked, he appears to have been forbidden to travel to capitalist countries, though he was permitted trips to Poland, Hungary and Czechoslovakia. Nevertheless, his writings were gaining converts at high levels of the state, despite being blocked by his academic peers.

I sought out Lukyanov in 2009. Over tea and cakes in Moscow at the downtown Pushkin restaurant, he reminisced about his friendship with Gumilev and the paradox that this appeared to present. In the 1970s, Lukyanov was an up-and-coming Soviet bureaucrat, whose progressively hardline views would eventually see him play a major role in the 1991 coup attempt against Mikhail Gorbachev, which destroyed his political career and sent him to jail. But he was a complex man. Though a hardline Marxist, he idolized Akhmatova – for many a symbol of private revolt against totalitarianism – and called her poetry 'the most beautiful thing in the modern Russian language'. He even made an audio recording of Lev reciting her 'Requiem', of all things.

In addition to the connection to Akhmatova, Lukyanov seems to have seen something to like in Lev's theories:

> I could always call the Leningrad officials who were putting the clamps on [Gumilev's work] and they listened to me . . . It wasn't some great feat on my part; it was just that I had an understanding of Lev Gumilev's importance and his work.[87]

For the next two decades, Lukyanov became Lev's protector – his fights with the academic establishment were sometimes solved by a phone call from the presidium of the Supreme Soviet or the central committee. Such political interference in academic life was routine: many a dissertation or journal article was published with the help of party connections. But the case of Lukyanov's interventions on Gumilev's behalf were curious – not a case of the party intervening to protect some reigning orthodoxy, but instead to support an insurgency against the carefully crafted establishment consensus.

For Lukyanov, Lev's theories represented something utterly original: not nationalism, not Marxism, but rather a third way – a synthesis of nationalism and internationalism, a way out of the brutal and total culture wars which were leading to a dangerous calamity. His histories, while profoundly un-Marxist, emphasized the unconscious sympathy of the people of the Soviet Union, the millennia-old unity of inner Eurasia, and a lurking distrust of the West. Party conservatives may not even have realized the propaganda value of Lev's theories, if used in the right way; but he nonetheless may have appeared useful. 'If one were to describe him in party terms', said Lukyanov, 'Gumilev was an internationalist. He considered that all the influences on the Russian people – from the Polovtsians, the Chinese and the Mongols – only enriched us . . . Among real communists, the ones who knew Marxism at first hand, Lev Gumilev did not have enemies.'[88]

Lukyanov also, perhaps inadvertently, explained the source of Lev's progressively anti-Western and reactionary views. Following his mother's death, he said, the ugly court fight over her estate, the feuding between Lev and some members of Akhmatova's entourage reached a crescendo of public acrimony:

> As [Gumilev] told me, in Anna Andreevna Akhmatova's circle there was [Viktor] Ardov, [Ilya] Zilbershtein, several other such people. As he said: 'Not a single one is Russian.' That's what he said . . . Akhmatova's circle were always pro-Western. Akhmatova herself was not that at all. She always blessed the Russian language, the Russian nation and so on. Why she went with such people I don't know . . . maybe it was connected to the difficulty of her existence.[89]

Lukyanov's view must be taken with a pinch of salt. The fight over Akhmatova pitted her ex-husband Punin's family against the rest of Akhmatova's entourage. Most of her Jewish friends sided with Lev, including Nadezhda Mandelstam, Joseph Brodsky, Emma Gerstein and Viktor Ardov. However, it is quite likely that Lukyanov's comments may well have reflected Lev's own descent into anti-Semitism. His biographer Sergey Belyakov reports the same observation that Lukyanov made: 'By the 1980s, Gumilev would forget about the help Akhmatova's Jewish friends had given him. Instead, he blamed them for his conflicts with his mother.'

Lev would need Lukyanov's help soon enough, when he pushed his luck and tried for a second doctorate. Given the reception of his first round of articles, and the increasing politicization of the debate about Russian history, Lev would need all the highly placed friends he could find. He was teaching at the Institute of Economic Geography, and – quite sensibly – felt that he should gain the credentials in that discipline in addition to his history doctorate. He presented his dissertation for a doctorate in geography – 'Ethnogenesis and the Biosphere of Earth' – to the geographical board.

'Ethnogenesis' was a lengthier version of his 1970 article – a detailed joust at official Marxism, espousing exactly the historical theories that Yakovlev had panned the previous November, and a lengthier attack on Bromley's more nuanced take on the concept of ethnos. In it, Gumilev tackled the question of why certain peoples become 'great'. Eurasia was a place uniquely suited to examining this idea: over two millennia, the expanses of the steppe had been dominated by tribes that had grown rapidly from nothing and had conquered vast regions of inner Eurasia, starting with the Huns under Attila, the Mongols under Genghis Khan, the Turks under Tamerlane, and finally the Russians under a succession of tsars. Part of his explanation for why such small groups of nomads became so dominant in such a short time was, of course, superior military technology and fighting spirit; but that could not explain the whole phenomenon. The peoples of Eurasia, he asserted, shared a cultural affinity, which made the spread of language and culture much more rapid than mere conquest could explain, and cemented political cohesion.

Perhaps, he theorized, it was not so much the characteristics of the peoples that created this unique cohesion, as the characteristics of the geography of Inner Asia, its network of rivers and steppe and forests and arable black soil, which favoured travel and economic integration. 'Eurasia', he suggested, formed a unique geographical zone in which all inhabitants are naturally subject to the same 'rhythms', as he called them, and display a tendency to converge on one another, to grow more similar with time, and to diverge from those outside this zone.

Russians – members of this zone for centuries – have become Eurasians, Gumilev suggested, descended not from European culture but from the ancient steppe tribes. The thrust of the dissertation was to explain how *ethnoi* are born. The quibble with the reigning orthodoxy he highlighted was similar to one commonly aired with reference to biological evolution, which is good at explaining the gradual change (i.e. evolution) of species, but runs into difficulty over how new species come into being relatively suddenly. So, too, with modern ethnography, which focuses on the 'social' aspects of culture: it is good at explaining how existing cultures change, but its weakness lies in providing a theoretical basis for the birth of completely new *ethnoi*.

Lev believed this to be the weakest point of his opponents' theory, and he hammered away at it. He believed that the strength of his theory lay in explaining 'ethnogenesis', the creation of new cultures.

For Gumilev, the birth and death of *ethnoi* are an exercise in human creativity – the result of 'passionarity' – the instinct to self-sacrifice and self-abnegation. What distinguishes an ethnos from a jumble of languages, religions and common historical experiences is a common purpose or goal, and the willingness of members to sacrifice themselves for it. *Ethnoi*, he theorized, always start with the actions of a small group of 'passionaries', and the birth of new *ethnoi* is always associated with a high intensity of passionarity, which then begins to dissipate over the lifespan of a nation.[90] It was a theory that was evocative of the romantic theories of Herder or Fichte, seeing an ethnos as akin to an organism.

And it was already getting a bit weird. But then Gumilev took the organism metaphor further, arguing that passionarity has predictable 'phases', with a typical lifespan of 1,200 years. And then he descended from a confidently argued theory into the realms of science fiction, when he tested the waters for the theory that he had bounced off Nikolay Timofeev-Resovsky at the Institute of Radiation in Obninsk a few years before: he argued that passionarity was generated by cosmic radiation from outer space.

'The biogenic migration of atoms of chemical elements in the biosphere always tends to its maximum manifestation', wrote Gumilev in chapter six of the dissertation, giving his critics their main justification for marginalizing him.

> Because the development of free energy capable of doing work is created by the action of living matter. Consequently our planet received more energy from outer space than is needed to maintain equilibrium of the biosphere, which leads to excesses that give rise to phenomena among animals like those described above, and among people impulses of drive or explosions of ethnogenesis.[91]

In hindsight, it is amazing that the doctoral project went as well as it did. Even adherents of Lev's views looked askance at the theory of bioenergy – the notion that human actions are explicable by cosmic rays: 'It's an interesting concept', said Kozhinov in an interview published long after Gumilev's death, 'but I don't think it has any objective significance. He thinks that it's all about cosmic rays or something. This looks a bit comic even.'[92]

It says something about Lev's credentials as a feared debater and public figure with powerful friends that he was even allowed to present the thesis in the first place, let alone get it past the dissertation committee with only one abstention and one 'no' vote out of 23. Much of this was due to interference by Lukyanov on his behalf. '[Lukyanov] asked the Leningrad and Moscow leadership of different ranks to present no obstacles to Gumilev in his scientific and pedagogical activity, in his presentation of his doctoral thesis', wrote Voznesensky in a memoir.[93]

Gumilev's dissertation defence was a public event; hundreds of people went to the Smolny Institute to hear it, including Western journalists. But the major obstacle lay in Moscow: all dissertations had to go through the Higher Attestation Commission (VAK) which vetted all advanced degrees. The dissertation came back with a huge number of remarks from a 'black opponent', who, according to the Soviet degree system, had the right to challenge anonymously and eventually to veto candidacies. Lev had to defend the dissertation again, but this time in a less friendly environment in Moscow. He went, promising his boss Lavrov that he would keep his temper and be deferential, and would not pick any fights that the institute would have to settle. 'Our fears came true – he lost his temper!' recalled Lavrov. 'Our protégé said too many unnecessary things and was failed. He returned to Leningrad confused and a bit guilty; not so much because of the sad result, but because of the fact that he failed to keep the promise to "stay within limits".'[94]

Months of fraught negotiations followed, but Gumilev was ultimately denied his dream of another doctorate, which was put on hold indefinitely. Nevertheless, in 1979 the dissertation was finally placed on file at the All Union Institute for Scientific and Technical Information in Moscow, an institute affiliated to the Soviet Academy of Sciences. In this way, many books which did not meet with the approval of the official censors could eventually see the light of day. It just had to be ordered and printed on request. Word got around, and *Ethnogenesis and the Human Biosphere* became one of the most requested monographs of all time in the USSR. 'They had so many orders that the paper ran out several times', said Yamshchikov.

In December 1974 came another blow. The eminent ethnographer Viktor Kozlov wrote a blistering attack on Gumilev's work in the top-flight Soviet journal *Voprosy Istorii* (*Historical Issues*): 'On the Biological–Geographical Conception of Ethnic History'.[95] Accusing Gumilev of being a racist, Kozlov spent 13 pages citing Gumilev's work and charging him with 'biologism', 'geographical determinism' and a host of other errors, and essentially saying that what he wrote was unprovable rubbish. The only reason no one had bothered to debunk it before, he said, was that 'his conceptions have largely bypassed the attention of the majority of historians and philosophers, and thereby avoided criticism'. Marina Kozyreva – the niece of Nikolay Kozyrev – remembers that the article stung: 'It was to all intents and purposes a denunciation.'[96] From that point on, until the mid-1980s, Lev was virtually unable to publish anything, and he was only permitted to teach thanks to Lukyanov's interventions.

Lavrov, Lev's boss at the Institute of Economic Geography, said that he frequently received instructions to suspend Gumilev's lectures:

> Everybody understood that it was nonsense . . . But every so often I had to ask L.N.: 'Have a rest for a couple of weeks; let Kostya lecture these times.' L.N. understood everything, he wasn't even sour with me when we met, and three or four weeks later everything was forgotten 'at the top' as well, and L.N. appeared in front of students again.[97]

At one point, the Communist Party's inspector for sciences came for a visit. Anokhin remembers the man was told by Lavrov: 'Do you want to make another dissident out of Gumilev? We can prohibit him from lecturing, and then the next day you'll be hearing it on the BBC.'

Gumilev's personal popularity and his relationship with the Communist Party were not to be underestimated, and his opponents found him intimidating. Bromley considered Lev's theories to be prominent enough for him to debunk them straightaway in his 1982 ethnology textbook *Theoretical Sketches*.[98] 'Recently there has appeared in our literature an opinion that *ethnoi* represent a biological unit – a population or a system arising as a result of some sort of mutation', wrote Bromley, footnoting Gumilev (which suggests that, despite being forbidden from publishing, Lev's concepts were very much part of mainstream thought among the intelligentsia). Cheshko remembered the 20-year Gumilev–Bromley polemic:

> In a word, Gumilev's whole conception was basically poetry. Maybe he inherited this talent from his father, but it was very effective. The simpler and more elegant, the easier it is for people, dilettantes in this case, to grasp. Gumilev was very popular among the technical intelligentsia, the creative intelligentsia. Bromley was boring to read, very boring, as with any normal scholarly book. Gumilev was fun. It was utter, unprovable nonsense, but it was good to read. Like a novel.[99]

The khan's steel sabre

In 1980, the 600th anniversary of the battle of Kulikovo Field, turned into a year-long celebration of Russian arms and valour. It was to be a milestone in Lev Gumilev's academic career. All censorship of Russia's nationalist intellectuals was suspended for the duration. In 1980 alone, Soviet publishing houses printed roughly 150 titles that directly or indirectly referenced the battle.[100]

The Kulikovo anniversary celebration seems to have been designed by the Communist Party central committee to whip up nationalist spirit and mobilize the public. This may have been inspired by two increasingly difficult challenges it faced abroad: the Polish Solidarity movement and the deepening war in Afghanistan.[101] Just as in the late 1960s, when the last upsurge in Russian nationalism coincided with a border war with China and the Prague Spring, the Kulikovo celebrations seem to have had a political purpose as well. Nationalism was allowed to flourish within carefully prescribed limits. But celebration of the origins of the Russian nation let the nationalist genie out of the bottle for good, and it would now be impossible to put back. For the rest of the decade, nationalism would provide a centre of gravity in the politics of the USSR – both the Russian and the non-Russian parts – with fateful consequences.

While Gumilev's books stayed safely in the All Union Institute for Scientific and Technical Information, he was given an exceptional opportunity to step into the limelight, publishing a number of articles (including one in the popular national magazine *Ogonek*). 'Russian ethnos was born on Kulikovo Field', wrote Lev in one article.[102] Of course, if this were true (and it surely isn't), his hypothesis that the average ethnos had a 1,200-year lifespan was convenient, because being 600 years old would place Russia at the summit of its historical existence.

His interpretation of the battle was controversial, and also convenient for his theory that Russia and the steppe peoples formed an unconscious super ethnos, a natural empire or civilization. He argued that the battle was not actually between Russians and Mongols, but was a civil war between two branches of the Mongol Empire, with the Russians fighting on one side. Mamay, leader of the Mongol forces at Kulikovo, was warring with Tokhtamysh, a rival. Russian forces led by Dmitry Donskoy at Kulikovo were allied to Tokhtamysh, while Mamay was in the pay of Catholic Europe, a clique of shadowy Genoan princes. The battle of Kulikovo Field was 'not with the Golden Horde at all', wrote Gumilev, but with the horde of Mamay, 'which was absolutely different from the former'. He pointed out that there is a record of Dmitry sending joyful news about the victory at Kulikovo Field to Tokhtamysh Khan.[103] Thus, the battle of Kulikovo was in fact, in the imagination of Gumilev, a fight not against Mongol invaders, but against the representatives of an international evil cartel in the pay of the West. The argument turned Russian history on its head. Traditionally the 'ungrateful Europe' argument had held sway in Russian historiography since the time of the Romanovs: it argues that Europe owes Russia a debt of gratitude for stopping the Golden Horde from sweeping further westward. Gumilev instead reverses this, saying that thanks to the Mongols, Russia was saved from falling under the sway of Europeans who 'wanted to turn Russia into a Genoan trading colony'.

As far as serious historians are concerned, this was based on non-existent evidence and was almost certainly the product of Lev's vivid imagination.[104] It is generally agreed by scholars that Mamay, who was not a Chingizid, was warring with Tokhtamysh, who was. Dmitry Donskoy was allied to Tokhtamysh, and after the battle of Kulikovo, in which Donskoy defeated Mamay, he continued to pay tribute to Tokhtamysh. Gumilev's assertion that Mamay was backed by Genoan princes is not substantiated by any research. But his histories were popular – more popular than other, more properly sourced history. 'It was basically like reading a novel. Unlike most history books, you read until the last page', according to contemporary author Dmitry Bykov.

Lev's friends in high places continued to support him. And even if they could not get his more controversial works (like 'Biosphere') published, there did seem to be a consensus that Eurasianist historiography pioneered by Lev was in vogue among a narrow but steadily widening section of the elite.

The deaths of both Brezhnev and Suslov in 1982 were a blow to the nationalists, and brought an end to official support for the 'Russian Party' from the Soviet Politburo. Whether Suslov had indeed been a closet nationalist, or had simply been using the nationalists as a counterweight to the liberals, is still hotly debated. But the balance which had favoured the nationalists under Brezhnev and Suslov began to be righted under Andropov and Chernenko, both orthodox internationalists. Neither had any interest in antagonizing the West, and realized that Russian chauvinism would strengthen the minority nationalist movements that threatened the USSR.

The Kremlin was increasingly preoccupied with nationalist tensions roiling underneath the seemingly placid surface of the USSR. In 1982, according to Cheshko, Bromley spoke at the presidium of the Soviet Academy of Sciences and said, for the first time, that dangerous ethnic and separatist problems existed in the USSR. 'It sounds silly, but this was stunning to hear at the time', recalls Cheshko. 'There was no discussion, everyone was in shock. It was the first time anyone had heard this.' A special ethnographic commission was created in the academy.

It became clear that neither dogmatic Stalinism nor Bromley's groundbreaking 'ethnosocial' theory was able to cope with the reality of national self-determination movements within the Soviet Union. Bromley had recognized the importance of ethnos as a field of study; but, like everything in Soviet academia, any use of his insights was stifled by the suffocating climate of orthodoxy. The fundamental problem in the field, as elsewhere in Soviet academia, was a hermetic, conservative, helpless elite governed by 'the requirement that everyone subscribe to a single universal or eternal methodology', which 'doesn't change except with the death of its principal exponent', according to Valery Tishkov, Bromley's successor as chairman of the Institute of Ethnography. However, it is doubtful whether Gumilev's theory would have saved the day, either – in fact, his valorization of the steppe tribes and micro-ethnicities of the Caspian and Caucasus region, his reverence for Cossack hetmans and Kievan princes gave evidence and inspiration to nationalist authors and self-determination movements throughout the USSR. Gumilev seems to have done more than anyone to inspire non-Russian nationalism in Central Asia and the Caucasus, with fateful consequences.

Authors like Olzhas Suleymenov and Chingiz Aytmatov, Kazakh and Kyrgyz respectively, read Gumilev for his stubborn defence of the forgotten and often maligned minority peoples. 'I was introduced to Turkology by reading Gumilev', admits Suleymenov. Gumilev's contribution to Kazakhstan's independence is so revered, for example, that the country's post-independence president, Nursultan Nazarbaev, named a university after him. His publications raised his profile to a national level for the first time. Letters poured in from all over the USSR. But this exposed him to criticism: patriotic Russian historians saw his defence of the Mongols and the way he equated Russia with steppe nomads as heresy. He was labelled a 'Russophobe' in the august bastion of nationalism, *Molodaya Gvardiya*. The attacks worsened Gumilev's already severe paranoia, and it remains somewhat tragic that he sank deeper into anti-Semitism as a result. According to his biographer Belyakov, he believed Jews to be behind the attacks on him – odd, given that the list of academics who were gunning for him was entirely composed of ethnic Russians (with the exception of Bromley, who was ethnically English).

Soon he was caught up in another scandal, which again tinged him with anti-Semitism. Gumilev's arguments were used by philosopher Yury Boroday, who wrote in *Priroda* that Western civilization was the heir to the tradition of Jewish Manichaeism.[105] It was a twisted, racist use of claims that Gumilev had made, and indeed this particular point does not seem to have been present in Gumilev's work; however, Gumilev never publicly repudiated Boroday's article. Following the essay's publication in *Priroda*, the USSR Academy of Sciences convened a special session to condemn it and, by extension, Gumilev's theories. The editorial board of *Priroda* was purged and several articles by Gumilev were rejected without explanation by scientific journals. Thus Gumilev became increasingly controversial – not only among nationalists, for whom he was too much of an internationalist, but also among liberals, who saw him as an anti-Semite and nationalist. Each camp saw him with one foot in the other.

Gumilev's histories were not generally chauvinistic; indeed he devoted most of his talent to raising the profile and histories of the USSR's minority nationalities; but they did smack of imperialism, emphasizing the 'unity' of the Soviet peoples under a benevolent Russian hand. The anti-Western slant of his histories was also very likely considered politically useful.[106] And it is probably no accident that he was given considerable latitude to publish during the Kulikovo anniversary, against the backdrop of Soviet confrontation with the West over Afghanistan and Poland.

Interest in Gumilev and his theories in the upper reaches of the party seems to have grown in direct proportion to the waning appeal of communism. By the mid-1980s, senior officials had no doubt noticed that the official metaphysics was exhausted and Leninist dogma was a joke even in top party circles. The Politburo was a 'gerontocracy' that was expiring at a furious rate – Brezhnev's death was closely followed by that of his two successors as general secretary, Yury Andropov and Konstantin Chernenko. Russia's economy was crumbling and needed reform; its dogmas needed rejuvenation; its politics needed fresh faces.

Fresh faces

Chernenko was followed by a relatively sprightly 54-year-old, Mikhail Gorbachev, who would shortly implement the political thaw known as glasnost, and economic reforms known as perestroika, which liberalized private property and paved the way for the end of communism.

Glasnost, the relaxation of censorship, was first implemented in 1988, and it rescued Lev's fate as a scholar. By 1987 he was being sought out for interviews in major publications and on television. In 1988 he was even invited to deliver a series of lectures on nationalism at the Ministry of Foreign Affairs, according to Alexander Zotov, later Russia's ambassador to Syria, who helped organize them. Lev's scholarship was, however, still under censorship. In 1987 he wrote to the central committee:

> Owing to some unclear circumstances, the publication of my works for the past ten years has been blocked. I can only explain this as the reflection of troubles which pursued me in the first half of my life. All accusations against me were revoked in 1956. Between 1959 and 1975 my work was printed, and since 1976 it has stopped, with a few exceptions.[107]

Unlike in the 1960s, it was not Lev's gulag past that was his primary difficulty in publishing. Instead, it was his colleagues in academia, who (somewhat justifiably) continued to criticize his work as science fiction. The Academy of Sciences went on blocking publication of his 'Ethnogenesis', yet eventually Lev's powerful friend Lukyanov, by then chairman of the Supreme Soviet, intervened to get the book published. That happened in 1989 – the same year that Solzhenitsyn's *Gulag Archipelago* was finally serialized, despite a counterattack by hardliners:

> I know that the Academy of Sciences blocked the publication – this was the main book, the subject of most of the confrontations. They appealed to the Leningrad party organs, who interfered in the publication. I had to tell the party organs myself in very tough language 'Let's help get this book published.'[108]

Lev was summoned that year to the Moscow provincial committee of the Communist Party to hear its verdict on the book. In a panic, he called Anatoly Chistobaev, director of the Geography Institute at LGU. Chistobaev recalls him saying: 'Something has happened. I have been asked to appear before the obkom [provincial committee] of the party. I don't know whether to bring a spoon and a plate.'[109] Gumilev thought he was going to be arrested again – he would need the utensils in prison. 'His voice was full of fear', recalls Chistobaev. Instead, he was told the book would be published. It was a sensation. Its first print run of 50,000 copies sold out almost immediately.

Exhibit A

In the final two or three years of his life, Lev Gumilev gave over a hundred press interviews in top national newspapers, and a series of his lectures was broadcast on local television in Leningrad.

Gumilev had lived to see his books published, but he was already in very poor health. In 1990 he had his first stroke, after which one of his hands was left paralysed. He became increasingly bitter about what he saw as the incompetence of the Soviet authorities and their inability to stop the break-up of the USSR, as economic catastrophe worsened. In a May 1990 interview published in *Moskovskaya Pravda*, he went so far as to hold Bromley responsible for the apparent failure of the USSR nationalities policy:

> It was he who advanced the thesis that ethnos is a social phenomenon, that is, belonged to the realm of class. And as a result, there are no ethnic groups in the Soviet Union, because we have no class distinctions, right? It is completely absurd, but he still exercises harmful influence on the theoretical side of our ethnographic sciences . . . If the inhabitants of Pompeii had known in advance about the eruption of Vesuvius, they would not have simply waited for death, but fled.[110]

The attack, according to Bromley's biographer, S.I. Vainshtein, 'worsened the condition of the already seriously ill scientist', who was in hospital. A week later, Bromley died. Lev's two-decade feud had come to a particularly inauspicious end.[111]

In fact, the coming demise of the Soviet Union would vindicate not only 'primordialist' theories of nationalism, like Gumilev's, which saw nationalism as immanent, natural and essential, a fundamental, unchanging and practically genetic identity; the constructivists – those who believed that nationalism was a 'construct' created for social reasons or out of political expediency – also proclaimed victory, and with some justification: the Soviet Union fell apart not along true national lines, but along those of largely artificial nations identified by Soviet ethnographers and cartographers in the 1920s.[112]

In other words, according to political scientists such as Rogers Brubaker, Kazakhstan, Ukraine and other republics sought independence from the USSR not due to some strong primordial ethnic unity, but rather due to the simple fact that they had been given artificial statehood. In the right circumstances (wide-ranging economic crisis, combined with a real fear of the rise of Russian nationalism) this was simple to translate into real statehood. Not a single ethnic group that was not given national status by Soviet ethnographers bothered to revolt against authority in 1991 (though later, Chechnya would).

Rather than vindicating Gumilev's theory that nations had been buried alive by the USSR, the break-up of the Soviet Union may just as well have vindicated the view of nationalism as a social force that was capable of being manipulated. The Soviet Union's nationalities policy, in other words, manipulated nations into existence instead of recognizing existing ones. However, in the mind of the reading public, Gumilev's reputation as a scholar was assured by the demise of the Soviet Union. That convincingly proved his theories of nationalism as an immanent and primordial force that could not be erased.

The combination of Gumilev's personal charisma, the mystique of his parents, and his suffering at the hands of the regime all combined to make him one of the heroes of perestroika. That aura brought his works on Eurasianism massive popularity at a time when there was a hunger for dissident literature, and when any suppressed works automatically gained a reputation for authenticity and truth. He became a formidable opponent of the liberal reformers, an ally of nationalist groups and communist hardliners.

With the withering away of the Communist Party as a moral force in Soviet society, Russians looked for anything that could take its place and offer them a solid foundation in the new agoraphobic universe, shorn of its official metaphysics, in which they lived. That was especially true of the elite, who found in Gumilev's theories a synthesis of nationalism and internationalism which could justify, in theoretical terms, the continued existence of the multinational USSR as a singular political unit, even as it was about to be torn apart by elemental nationalism.

Lukyanov's numerous interventions on Gumilev's behalf were motivated by an instinct to preserve the union, he said. In Lev's Eurasianism he saw the continuation of the USSR. In a 2009 interview, this is what he said:

> You know, it coincides with my beliefs. The fact is that Eurasianism, Eurasia and the Soviet Union are a completely different world. With all due respect, the West does not understand it . . . This is a huge territory, people settled here along the rivers, and created a conglomerate of nations and nationalities, who had to live together. The climate is very severe, so the individual, the Western individualist, would find it impossible to live here. So there was a collectivism – a special relationship.[113]

Gumilev's political beliefs legitimized, in theoretical terms, the nationalism (in all its forms and permutations) that would burst out of the collapse of communism in the late 1980s and early 1990s, creating the scientific (or pseudo-scientific) basis for many nationalist writers. His vocabulary of 'passionarity', 'complementarity', 'super ethnos' and so on has been absorbed into the political mainstream, and his theories stand today at the nexus of scholarship and power. He has been championed both by Russian hardliners such as Lukyanov and by breakaway nationalists such as Kazakhstan's President Nazarbaev. Georgian, Kyrgyz and Azeri nationalists have all claimed his inheritance.

As Sergey Cheshko put it to me: 'Marxism is gone, was thrown out, there was only an empty space left, so what took its place was either nationalism, or this supra-nationalism – Eurasianism.' The fashion for Gumilev's ideas grew out of 'firstly, mysticism, secondly, xenophobia, and thirdly, the search for some kind of universal idea to take the place of the previous one.'[114]

In 1990, Gumilev befriended Leningrad's upstart TV star Alexander Nevzorov, a young, charismatic but rather mysterious man who hosted the city's most popular television talk show of the day, *600 Seconds*. Nevzorov had begun his television career tackling corruption in high places in the Leningrad city administration, earning plaudits from reformers; but he gradually showed himself to be a nationalist zealot who was militantly in favour of preserving the Soviet Union. When nearby Lithuania declared independence from the USSR in March 1990, Nevzorov appeared in a special broadcast holding a rifle during the storming of the TV tower in Vilnius by Special Forces soldiers sent to crush the protest. Nevzorov formed a youth brigade, Nashi (literally 'Ours'), which had a strong presence on the streets of Leningrad. Its shoulder patches showed an outline of the USSR with the word 'Nashi' stencilled across it.

The friendship stunned many of Gumilev's acquaintances, who saw Nevzorov as nothing better than a demagogue. 'How often he was criticized in his last months for this turn towards "Nashi"', recalled Lavrov. Rather implausibly, he went on: 'I think L.N. understood the word "Nashi" much more broadly than any political movement, group, bloc; everyone who supported the united country and opposed its further break-up was "Nashi" to him.'

Gumilev's friends were dumbfounded when with incredible energy he plunged into the existential debates that accompanied the collapse of the USSR, defending the union with a zealotry that left many of them scratching their heads. He actively campaigned to save the USSR in a flood of broadcast and print interviews, which Emma Gerstein, one of Lev's closest friends, described in her memoirs as 'dreadful'.[115]

In 1990 he recorded an interview with Nevzorov at the latter's country house. Asked by the TV presenter if he supported democracy, he become furious:

> Not at all! . . . How could I be a democrat. I am an old soldier. My father was a soldier, and my grandfather was a soldier, and thus back to the fourteenth century. My ancestors died on the Kulikovo battlefield. We were soldiers, but we were educated people, at least starting with my grandfather. We studied . . .

He then took a jab at the nascent pro-democracy movement spreading through the streets of the USSR: 'These so-called intelligentsia are not living up to their name. The intelligentsia just talk . . .' 'Democracy', he wrote in one characteristic criticism, 'unfortunately dictates not choosing the best, but rather the promotion of the similar. Access to the control bridge, to the steering wheel, is given to casual people.'[116]

In 1991, in advance of the March referendum on the continued existence of the Soviet Union, Gumilev authored a piece entitled 'Unite, or You Will Disappear'.[117] In another interview, he ventured a prediction: 'If Russia is saved, it will only be as a Eurasian state.'

* * *

In August 1991, at the end of his life, Gumilev was given a chance offered to few people who have suffered at the hands of a cruel dictatorship: the opportunity to see his tormentors flung down in humiliation and despair. A few days after the failure of a coup d'état by hardline generals in Moscow, and the ascendancy of Boris Yeltsin, the end of the USSR was all but inevitable. The totalitarian state that had destroyed Lev's family and made his life a misery was to be expunged from the face of the earth.

But oddly enough, he was in a foul mood. Vyacheslav Ermolaev, one of Gumilev's graduate students, remembers going to visit his former teacher to congratulate him on the end of the USSR, believing the old sage would be ecstatic at the news.

'Lev Nikolaevich, I congratulate you – Soviet Power is dead!'

Gumilev was silent. 'Lev Nikolaevich, something has happened? Why are you so gloomy?' Gumilev suddenly replied: 'Yes, it seems that you are right – Soviet Power is indeed dead. Only there is no reason to be happy – the country is falling apart before our very eyes.'

Ermolaev tried to make a joke, but Gumilev cut him off. 'How can you joke about this – it is our country – our forebears fought for it, many generations of people fought so that Kazakhstan would be ours, that Fergana would be ours, that we would live with the Kazakhs and the Uzbeks in the same country. And now? What will happen to that country?'[118]

Gumilev seems to have felt an odd sense of attachment to the state that had oppressed him. Such feelings, however, were not at all unusual among many of Lev's contemporaries, even those who, like him, had been victims of Stalin's terrible labour camps. Over tea and raisin cakes at his Moscow flat, Lev Voznesensky told me:

> Lev really took it very hard when the Soviet Union disintegrated. He considered it to be his country . . . Today, this seems strange, but when we sat in the camps, we often thought: 'If we had a chance to escape, it would be great. But first of all where would we go?' And secondly, for us it was like this: 'We are Russians, let us die, but let us die in our country.'

Interestingly, Voznesensky himself, who spent ten years in a labour camp after Stalin had his father executed, dedicated his 2004 autobiography to 'The Soviet People'.

Gumilev had spent his career studying the irrational bonds that tie nations and peoples together – and here he was, Exhibit A, fighting neurotically to save his beloved, repressive Soviet state. And as the Soviet Union crumbled, so did he. Gumilev had another stroke in June 1992. Leningrad newspapers followed his progress for the next week: 'The surgery lasted for about two hours . . . Night has passed easily. However, Gumilev has still not regained consciousness.' Then came 11 June: 'Doctors continue to carry out a complex of vital procedures.' Then 13 June: 'Worsening again.' On 15 June, Gumilev died.

The death of any famous figure in St Petersburg usually begets controversy: the city's famous cemeteries host the likes of Pushkin and Dostoevsky, and when a major luminary dies, the competition to bury him is fierce. Lev did not want to be buried in Komarovo cemetery with his mother. The mayor's office suggested Volkovo cemetery, with the likes of Mendeleev. But Gumilev had made it clear to his wife that he wanted to be buried in the Alexander Nevsky cemetery, named after his historical idol, the thirteenth-century prince of Novgorod, whose alliance with the Mongols thwarted a Western invasion by the Teutonic knights. The mayor's office relented.

Gumilev's funeral was a public event. In addition to his intelligentsia friends, nationalists of every stripe turned out. The great and the good of Russia's far right wing came: Cossacks arrived attired in battle dress; dour generals emerged from black Zil limousines; bearded writers paid tribute. In charge of security, at the decision of Gumilev's wife Natalya, was Nevzorov's nationalist youth brigade, Nashi.

In life, Gumilev had been a complex figure, resisting all facile ideological pigeonholing. But in death, his legacy was transferred to the side of those who would use his wonderful and fanciful history books for demagoguery. With his reputation as a scholar assured by the demise of the USSR, Gumilev's words would soon be reconstituted into the textbooks for putting it back together.

PART III

PART III

CHAPTER EIGHT

A SOVIET VIRGIL

The two-storey wooden barracks on Yuzhinsky Pereulok, near Moscow's Patriarch's Ponds, had a single, well-worn doorbell and six flats. Each occupant had a specific number of rings designated: to get hold of the last flat – up the stairs and at the end of the hall on the right – visitors had to ring six times. This was particularly unfortunate for the neighbours, because it had visitors coming and going all day, every day, and well into the night.

The man who lived there, Yury Mamleev, was an underground author and poet, whose residence just happened to be conveniently located equidistant from two landmarks of the Moscow intelligentsia: a few blocks from a statue erected to Vladimir Mayakovsky in Triumph Square on Moscow's ring road, which had become a gathering point for poets and dissidents; and down the so-called Garden Ring from the Lenin Library, one of the few places in Moscow with a special section where foreign newspapers and books were plentiful and accessible to the general public. Mainly due to its location, Mamleev's flat became a meeting place to discuss philosophy, poetry and literature.

Yury Mamleev was one of the leading lights of the 1960s generation, achieving a cult following as the author of what on the surface resembled horror novels, but which plumbed the depths of the Soviet psyche in a vaguely subversive way; the genre came to be called 'metaphysical realism'. His flat and the people who gathered there regularly became known as the Yuzhinsky circle. (Yuzhinsky Pereulok has since returned to its pre-revolutionary name of Bolshoy Palashevsky.) A salon of sorts, the gatherings started as motley all-male assemblages of authors, artists, drunkards and hangers-on who referred to themselves collectively as the 'mystical underground'.

Mamleev was an enthusiast of the occult, and specialized in taking the Soviet reality of official spangled mythology and pinpointing the black holes and dark matter at the edge of the bright lights of the socialist future.

Mamleev's characters were zombies, mass murderers, demented primitives who lived outside the city centres, in a countryside still stricken by shortages and alcoholism – dark-thinking, isolated provincials who inhabited a metaphysical universe of their own making. Normal Soviet life was transformed into a dark fantasy world, with just enough of the everyday detritus for the reader to find a connection; Mamleev's characters rode Moscow's suburban electric trains, lived in anonymous satellite towns with ill-stocked state stores that smelled of stale milk and lamb fat. The everyday realism was a carefully served ingredient of the fantasy and occult. Mamleev's literary creations were all characterized by their neurotic rejection of the physical reality surrounding them, the conviction that the outer world either simply did not exist or must be subordinated to the inner one. 'The surrounding world for them was one of the embodiments of the Inferno', he said. One literary critic referred to Mamleev as 'our Virgil, leading the way through the Soviet hell'.[1]

'Mamleev was the describer of a Russian world that has sunk to the depths of the Inferno', wrote Arkady Rovner, a Moscow-based mystic who joined the circle in the 1960s and became one of its many chroniclers.[2] Followers would gather at his home, or occasionally in a cemetery, where Mamleev would recount stories of horror and the occult by candlelight, 'introducing a secret and grotesque atmosphere into the apartments of the intelligentsia from which nervous and impressionable women not rarely fainted', according to Rovner.[3] The Yuzhinsky circle gained a reputation for Satanism, for séances, a devotion to all things esoteric – mysticism, hypnotism, Ouija boards, Sufism, trances, pentagrams and so forth – united by heavy use of alcohol in order to achieve enlightenment, among other things. 'The rules of the circle were thus: first there was heavy drinking, followed by conversation', recalled Rovner, who described the desired state of mind as *marazm* or 'dementia', which 'was a kind of unique ski jump without which the exit to the higher state and spheres was considered impossible'.[4] Mamleev's circle was disparaged on all sides. Official culture tried to pretend that it did not exist. Even the liberal westernized liberal *nomenklatura* looked askance at the group's fascination with the occult, fascism and mysticism, while nationalists and religious believers (another fast-growing side of the intelligentsia) considered Mamleev's group to be Satanists.

The Yuzhinsky brand of unofficial culture was referred to as 'schizoid' by both its purveyors and its detractors. The schizoids adopted the pejorative term as their own, finding madness a form of gnosis, a saner alternative to a reality that was utterly hostile to them. The creators of the underground culture 'revelled in the unshakable sense of self-chosenness and self-apostasy', according to Natalya Tamruchin, a historian of the movement. They despised property, money and status, and, according to Tamruchin, focused on 'the one area which was out of reach of the eye of the state censors – the area of purely mental experience.'[5]

By 1980 the group had gone through many changes. The core remained, while Mamleev had departed for the United States where he taught at Cornell University, before moving to Paris, where he was finally published. (Publishers in the United States, like those in the USSR, rejected his books.) The circle no longer met in the Yuzhinsky Pereulok barracks, which had been demolished, but rather in the flats and dachas of its members. They camped out on each other's sofas, slept on floors, performed bizarre initiation rituals, engaged in alchemy and the transmutation of metals, pored over magic texts, created secret numerological codes, wrote in streams of consciousness, drank heavily, experimented with sex, drugs and occasionally fascism.

The accent on mysticism and the occult – and alcohol – was mainly inspired by the group's new leader, Evgeny Golovin, who had been Mamleev's chief disciple. Nicknamed 'Admiral', Golovin had a reputation as a master 'alchemist', though it was not entirely clear what this qualification was based on or indeed how he practised alchemy. 'He basically liked to drink a lot', recalled Igor Dudinsky, a frequent visitor to the circle. In 2012 I visited him in his single-room Moscow flat, hung with avant-garde paintings and the paraphernalia of the Moscow beatnik underground. Golovin was defined, as far as acquaintances could tell, by two main characteristics: alcoholism and a certain Russian-style literary genius. According to Rovner's colourful reminiscences, Golovin was 'a natural Russian phenomenon – a classical combination of aesthetic snobbishness, esoteric misanthropy, alcoholic inspiration, plus a hot peppering of black fantasy and American horror movies'.[6]

Golovin was also completely obsessed with the Third Reich, seeing in it a monstrous and mystical yin to humanity's yang. After the group of about half a dozen hardcore followers had moved into a flat on Ushakova Street, he began to refer to himself as the Führer. He named his followers 'the Black Order of the SS' and told them all to wear Nazi paraphernalia. He hung a picture of Hitler on the wall. 'There was nothing anti-Semitic about it', said Dudinsky, a bit tendentiously, as our conversation veered in this direction. 'There were lots of Jews at these gatherings. We would all shout "Sieg Heil" and "Heil Hitler" and all we meant was "down with Soviet power!"', said Dudinsky, a merry soul, who is still fond of flinging the odd 'Roman salute' just to prove a point. The police, he says, finally made them take down the Hitler poster.

In 1980, in preparation for the Olympic Games in Moscow, police cleared the riff-raff from the streets, and it was strongly suggested that the group should move out of the capital. They found new beatnik digs at a dacha in the suburb of Klyazma. It was owned by Sergey Zhigalkin, a wiry and energetic man who made a name for himself translating Heidegger and publishing Golovin's poetry.

While writing this book, I met Zhigalkin. He offered to help recreate a typical (albeit much tamer) evening get-together of the mystical underground, taking me to the Klyazma dacha, which he still owns. We sat around a bonfire and drank cognac all night long, while he explained to me the magnetic, dark charisma of Golovin, who emerges from the tales of his followers much like the leader of a cult. 'In Golovin's presence, the limits of the natural world fell away, the earth became a bigger place, a limitless place. It was like being flung out of a centrifuge. We used alcohol to start the energy, but Golovin could manipulate this energy. He could destroy your perception of the world.' The mystical underground, he said, existed in odd counterpoint to the Soviet regime: 'The two needed each other. Without the regime, there could be no underground. But they needed us too. They needed heretics.'

One evening, a young man appeared at the Klyazma dacha, brought by an acquaintance. He looked no more than 18. His head was shaved, but he had an aristocratic bearing and a quick wit. He was immediately charismatic, and came carrying a guitar. Strumming away around a bonfire in the evening sunset, he belted out a song: 'Fuck the Damned Sovdep'.[7] Even by the extreme tastes of the mystical underground this was borderline stuff, calling for the mass murder of the Soviet leadership and conquest of the globe by Russian 'legions':

> The fucking end of the Sovdep
> Is just around the corner
> Two million in the river
> Two million in the oven
> Our revolvers will not misfire.

'We all just fell down and worshipped him', said Dudinsky. 'What a great song! He was like the messiah.' His name was Alexander Dugin, and he was the newest recruit to the Moscow mystical underground. A brilliant if unformed teenager, he soon learned to idolize his guru, Golovin.

Few people from those years have forgotten their first encounter with Dugin, who had a gift for making an entrance. Konstantin Serebrov, a follower and chronicler of the mystical underground, says Dugin 'looked like a true representative of a higher race, with his strict and formal appearance. He belonged to the gilded youth of Moscow who had to satisfy great expectations.' In a memoir of the times, Serebrov recalls meeting Dugin at Moscow's Kievskaya metro station:

A look of rapture came over Alexander's face. He pulled a bottle of port wine out of his bag and threw it on the platform. 'Sieg Heil! I make this sacrifice to the god Dionysus.' The bottle shattered into a million pieces, spreading a wave of port across the platform.[8]

The subjects of Dugin's art and his fascination with Nazism were all part and parcel of his total devotion to Golovin, who had a penchant for 'zombifying' his followers and teaching them to 'zombify' others. Serebrov records that Dugin himself had an 'attendant' named Alex, whom he would order around.

Dugin is very forthright about his early Nazi antics, which he says were more about his total rebellion against a stifling Soviet upbringing than any real sympathy for Hitler. Still, virtually everyone who remembers Dugin from his early years brings it up. Serbebrov, for example, recalls Dugin reprising his famous song 'Fuck the Damned Sovdep': '20 million in the river, 20 million in the ovens, our machine guns will not misfire', after which 'Alexander threw his head back and closed his eyes as if he were in ecstasy.'[9]

In 2005, Dugin agreed to sit down with me for the first in a series of interviews about his life. Over coffee in a Mayakovsky Square café in central Moscow he unburdened himself about the (as he put it) 'shamanistic crisis of self-actualization' that characterised his early life. 'I was completely normal in every sense: morally, rationally, psychologically. But the system around me was completely hostile to me.'

Born in 1962, Dugin and his generation were the first to grow up with the accoutrements of a normal middle-class lifestyle. But Soviet life in the 1970s was like America in the 1950s: ideologically rigid, materialistic, one-dimensional and dull. The drama of everyday life in previous decades had gradually given way to a dreary, monochrome existence, in which living standards improved just enough to promote the myth of progress – the myth that Soviet society would one day overtake the West.

The Soviet middle class had moved out of communal flats in the early 1960s and now lived in two-room Khrushchev-era apartment blocks, mainly on the outskirts of cities, with identical fake wood-panelled elevators and blue-and-white tiled kitchens. They rode the *elektrichka*, or commuter train, to work in offices of government ministries or state corporations. Soviet consumer one-upmanship existed in the USSR, just as it did everywhere in the world. Most people had an Oka refrigerator, but some fortunates had a Minsk; the plebeians bought Gorizont television sets, but a select few had a colour Rubin. One could tell the status of a host by which factory had manufactured their wine glasses or crystal dessert set. One of the most popular movies of the period, *The Irony of Fate*, satirized this blank uniformity. A man from Moscow accidentally finds himself in Leningrad after a night of drinking. Believing himself still to be in Moscow, he orders a taxi driver to take him to his home address. It turns out to be an identical apartment block, in an identical street in an identical suburb. Even his key works in the door.

For Dugin's parents' generation, who grew up amid the privations of the war and the Stalin years, it was prosperity. Medical care, such as it was, was free; a pension bought enough sausage for a month. Life, for those who were not very ambitious and not very curious, was carefree. The 'bright future' portrayed on the cheerful faces of workers in countless propaganda posters and films seemed just around the corner. But many of Dugin's contemporaries found their tidy existences intolerable and dull, and Dugin hated this world – a boring, stultifying existence for a young intellectual. 'We were truly petit bourgeois.' He and his peers ridiculed his parents' generation, their credulous acceptance of orthodoxy, their passive willingness to accept the arbitrary diktat of a malfunctioning system, in exchange for the knick-knacks of a barely comfortable life.

Dugin's troubled teenage years and his hostility to convention are traceable to a personal hostility to authority in the form of his absentee father. Little is known about Geli Dugin, who left Alexander's mother when his son was three. While Dugin had very little contact with the man after that, it does appear that his father loomed large in his life. Dugin has been vague in various interviews about his father's profession. He told me and others that Geli was a general in military intelligence (the GRU). But when pressed, he admitted he didn't actually know for a fact what he did. 'At the end of his life he worked for the customs police, but where he worked before that – he did not tell me. That I do not really know.' Dugin's friends, however, are adamant that his father must have been someone of rank within the Soviet system. For starters, the family had the accoutrements of prestige – a nice dacha, relatives with nice dachas, and access to opportunities. According to Dugin's close friend and collaborator Gaidar Dzhemal, Geli Dugin had, on more than one occasion, intervened from a high-ranking position in the Soviet state to get his son out of trouble. Dzhemal said that Geli was Dugin's 'get out of jail free' card, which allowed his son to regularly violate the orthodoxies of Soviet life and get away with it. Undoubtedly this fuelled complicated feelings of both entitlement and further resentment at the unfair privilege. Dugin, however, disagrees. 'He never supported me', he told me flatly in a 2010 interview. 'At least, I never felt such support.'

Dugin failed to heed his father's request for him to enrol at the Institute for Military Translators, and instead decided on the less prestigious Civil Aviation Academy. From then on their relations were strained to breaking point by Dugin's political antics, which had repercussions on the elder Dugin's career. According to Alexander, Geli was transferred to the customs service after his son's detention in 1983 by the KGB. According to Dugin's second wife Natalya, the two men had not spoken for years when the elder Dugin died in 1998. 'I never heard him talk about his father', said Dudinsky, who recalled that Dugin appeared to live at a dacha belonging to his uncle in the Higher Party School dacha compound. Generational conflict in Russia has often assumed an epochal, millennial significance – ever since Ivan Turgenev's *Fathers and Sons* explored the subject in 1862 – and separating the personal rebellion from the political one is impossible. In many ways, Dugin's hostility to Soviet authority may have been inseparable from his anger at his own father: Geli was – professionally and paternally – the embodiment of Soviet authority.

Tellingly, the new generation of Moscow's underground was overwhelmingly drawn from the children of the privileged. Dudinsky, who joined in 1961 when he was just 15, was the son of Ilya Dudinsky, the *Pravda* Geneva correspondent and later founder of the World Systems of Socialism Institute. Dugin, meanwhile appears to have found a fatherlike figure in the shape of Gaidar Dzhemal, 12 years his senior, a thick-set man with a goatee and a severe, heavy-lidded gaze. The two apparently met at Zhigalkin's dacha, after which Dzhemal took the younger man as an 'apprentice' (in Dzhemal's words) and instructed his charge to learn French.

Dzhemal's father was from Azerbaijan, though his mother was Russian. Like Dugin he would be a fixture of the Moscow bohemian scene for decades. He was Dean Moriarty to Dugin's Jack Kerouac; John the Baptist to Dugin's Jesus. He took the unformed young man and plunged with him into Moscow's 'schizoid' underground: kitchens overflowing with poetry and cognac, underground gallery shows, and dacha debauchery at the weekend.

The underground meetings, according to Dugin, involved a sort of improvisational theatre, in which all participated in vignettes invented by Golovin. 'Golovin was always the commander', said Dudinsky.

> Maybe he was the ship's captain and we were the cabin boys or sailors. Or we were all poets of the nineteenth century, or members of Adolf Hitler's bunker, the knights of the Round Table, the entourage of the Emperor Barbarossa, the conquistadors in search of El Dorado.
>
> It is difficult now to describe this game, this aesthetic, poetic play. It was not a performance. It was played without spectators and was always moving – from one apartment or dacha to another. It was a pastime, a real bohemia.

Dugin cut a striking figure in the libertine era of 'nonconformism'. His peers remember a brilliant charismatic, who immediately drew attention to himself and who was extremely confident for his years.

Dugin's artistic outlet was his guitar, which he carried with him everywhere. Later he began to develop his stage persona, which mixed effortlessly with the more eccentric spirit of the schizoid movement, spicing his image with a dash of fascist imagery and a repertoire of occult songs. He sported a well-trimmed goatee beard and a simple pudding-bowl haircut with a straight fringe – an affectation popular in Russian intellectual circles of the time and known as a *skobka* or 'parenthesis' haircut. It evoked the simple and austere style of the medieval peasant, much like the nineteenth-century Slavophiles gathered in their St Petersburg mansions wearing peasant *murmolka* caps. He had an erect bearing and a habit of trilling his '*rs*' a little too heavily in a sign of aristocratic affectation; he sometimes accented this pose by speaking French. Most impressively, he often wore 'galife' trousers – the jodhpur-like breeches of a cavalry officer of a century before. He adopted the *nom de plume* 'Hans Sievers', which added a hint of Teutonic severity to an already colourful and fairly camp militaristic–folklore style. The impression he created was, as his later collaborator Eduard Limonov described it, a 'picture of Oscar Wildean ambiguity'.

Sievers was not just a stage name: it was a complete persona and alter ego. This was painstakingly composed of as many antisocial elements as its creator could find – a total and malevolent rebellion not just against the Soviet Union, but against convention and public taste as a whole: his namesake, Wolfram Sievers, had been the *Reichsgeschäftsführer*, or director, of the Ahnenerbe, a Nazi organization set up by Heinrich Himmler to study esoteric and paranormal phenomena. The real Sievers was hanged in 1947 by the Nuremburg court, charged with experimenting on concentration camp victims.

The lyrics composed by Dugin/Sievers were both clever and intended to achieve maximum shock value. They were mainly inspired by nineteenth-century author Isidore-Lucien Ducasse, aka the Comte de Lautréamont, whose 'Maldoror verses' were taken up by twentieth-century surrealists. *Maldoror* was the chronicle of an eponymous outcast monster who embarks on a surreal binge of torture, cannibalism and general malevolence – a vicious being in total revolt against every form of moral authority and every convention.

Dugin recounted later that his interest in Lautréamont was a product of his implacable hatred for the stultifying conformity of the Soviet existence: 'It is so out of tune with the traditional gold-plated lie of our culture that it seems there is no more anti-Soviet and non-conformist reading, no more unacceptable author, no more inappropriate discourse', he said in a radio interview a decade later.

While Dugin was exploring the surreal and the spiritual, Russia's intellectual class was dabbling in the same currents en masse, though in a less extreme manner. Evgeny Nikiforov, a friend of Dugin's in the 1980s, reminisced in an interview with me about the creative journey of the intelligentsia: 'First, we all learnt yoga, then we studied Sanskrit, then we read the New Testament. It was all the same to us at the time. Only later did we become spiritually mature. No one had the first clue. The KGB even thought karate was a religion.'

The Yuzhinsky circle was fascinated by anything esoteric, occult, mystical: from meditation to theosophy to black magic. One major focus of its spiritual studies was a philosophy known as 'traditionalism', founded in the first half of the twentieth century by French Sufi mystic René Guénon. He taught that all world religions were the outward expression of a single esoteric core – a single metaphysics that came to mankind via divine revelation. Traditionalists believed that the modern world was a profane creation, and sought to rediscover the divine centre, the content of the initial revelation, which, they believed, continues to echo through the teaching of mystical religions the world over, principally eastern ones, such as Islamic Sufism and Zen Buddhism. They did so through the study of eastern mystical religions, through meditation and by studying traditional thought, such as pagan myths and occult numerology.

Traditionalism and other esoteric studies have always had a reputation for fascism, and vice versa: the Nazi party grew out of the occultist Thule Society, launched in 1918. Guénon's most illustrious disciple, Baron Julius Evola, a monocled Italian aristocrat, eventually joined the Italian fascist movement and worked briefly for the SS, later becoming a major inspiration for postwar right-wing terror groups in Italy. Due to an apparent oversight by a librarian at the Lenin Library, the Yuzhinsky circle had discovered the books of Evola in the general reading section sometime after the Cuban missile crisis.[10] 'They clearly belonged in the restricted section', joked Dugin, who was so profoundly intrigued by Evola that he learned Italian just so that he could translate his 1961 book *Ride the Tiger* into Russian *samizdat*.

For traditionalists, separation from the profane world is prized, and everything bourgeois is anathematized. Evola believed that mankind is living in the Kali Yuga, a dark age of unleashed materialistic appetites, spiritual oblivion and organized deviancy. To counter this and summon a primordial rebirth, Evola presented his world of the spiritual and the divine. He was a proponent of rigidly hierarchical political life, and he divided humanity into 'castes' which determined one's essential function in society. His approach to 'spiritual racism' was endorsed by none other than Mussolini in 1941, and he believed that war was a form of therapy, leading mankind into a higher form of spiritual existence. According to Franco Ferraresi, a top Italian scholar of the extreme right, 'Evola's thought can be considered one of the most radically and consistently antiegalitarian, antiliberal, antidemocratic, and antipopular systems in the twentieth century.'[11]

The Yuzhinsky group, at least what was left of it under Golovin's tutelage, also dabbled in fascist kitsch: in addition to the posters of Hitler and the odd 'Roman salute', they sang songs lionizing the SS. Dudinsky committed some of these to memory, and he allowed me to record them in his Moscow flat one day, over honeyed tea and surrounded by his avant-garde paintings. One goes:

> Forward men, violent and rude
> We are inspired by the swastika in the night
> We see how your dead bodies dance the tango in the gas oven
> How nice and fresh the roses
> As happy and cheerful as the Russian forest
> On the last journey on the Via Dolorosa
> Goes the SS division.

Others wrote overtly fascistic books, such as Dzhemal's *Orientation to the North*, published in *samizdat* form in 1979. They copied and translated what they could find of writings by Europe's extreme right. Like other groups of dissidents, they learned what they could of like-minded movements abroad, treating the Western writings on their chosen field with special reverence. Terrorism by Europe's extreme right – including some of Evola's followers – was reaching fever pitch in 1980. That summer and autumn, a series of bombings and massacres in a Bologna train station, a Parisian synagogue and Munich's Oktoberfest heralded the rebirth of the extreme right as a lethal political power on the continent.

Dugin, whose youthful rebellion seemed to be leading him further and further towards nakedly fascistic politics, was also by this stage clearly the most capable intellectual of the entire group. His interest in Evola evolved naturally from his dabbling in the occult, from his comrades' interest in Guénon and mysticism. It is hard to overstate the hunger for new ideas in the stultifying atmosphere of official censorship. Anything which had the hint of the banned, the forbidden, automatically had cachet. Even if the ban was for perfectly sensible reasons – as in the case of Evola – the label only increased the hunger to read it. Evola was the channel for Dugin, Dzhemal and others to follow their occult musings and youthful rebellions into politics.

Dugin's membership of these dissident societies meant – at that time at least – that he would never get a real job on a respectable newspaper or be published in one of the wide distribution 'thick journals'. He began to come to the attention of the KGB and the police for his regular attendance at sessions. To make ends meet, he made do with a variety of odd jobs, like washing windows, cleaning streets and doing construction work on country houses outside

Moscow. In the evenings he read voraciously, learned to speak Italian, German, French and English, played the guitar and wrote songs.

It was only a matter of time before the group would attract serious attention from the KGB. It happened to Dugin first. In 1983 a friend of Dudinsky's entrusted Dugin with an archive of writings by Yury Mamleev. That December, as Hans Sievers, he gave a guitar concert for about 30 people in the Moscow art studio of Gennady Dobrov. At it he sang his most famous hit, 'Fuck the Damned Sovdep'. Not long afterwards, as Dugin recalls, a group of plainclothes KGB officers appeared at the door of his family's flat. His mother woke him up and he was taken away, while another group searched the flat and confiscated the archive. Both Dudinsky and Zhigalkin say that they suspect Dugin's father was behind the denunciation and the search. 'He probably thought things had gone far enough', said Zhigalkin, whose wife, an artist, had also been interrogated by the KGB. Such encounters were not as terrifying as they had been in the 1930s, when death or imprisonment was almost certain. But even so, said Zhigalkin, 'It took all day, they shine a light in your face and they say they'll send you to Siberia. It really was quite unpleasant.'

The KGB men hustled Dugin out of a car and up a short flight of stairs at the back entrance to the Lubyanka, the feared headquarters of the KGB. Inside, the lights were on, offices were buzzing and it was a normal workday – for an organization that worked mainly at night. Dugin, with his goatee beard and hipster clothes, was led to a small interrogation room with a table, three chairs and a lamp. On the table was a folder – the largely handwritten archive of Mamleev's work.

The interrogator's tired, practised voice bade him sit, and the lamp was shone in Dugin's face: as in the movies, the interrogator's face hovered just on the periphery of the blinding light, bobbing and weaving, disorienting him. 'What are you, some sort of idiot?' the interrogator asked him. 'For what are you singing about the "end of the Sovdep"? The USSR will stand forever, it's an eternal reality. Look at our faces. And who are you, with your guitar and your hippy appearance.'[12] During the interrogation, Dugin gave away the identity of the man who had entrusted the Mamleev archive to him. The man was fired from his job in the Ministry of Information and went on to become a lift operator, though Dudinsky says that he was 'very grateful' that he was forced to give up his 'false life'. The KGB also interviewed Dugin's mother, and sometime thereafter his father was transferred from the GRU to the customs service – according to Dugin, a severe demotion of status for the family. Dugin's father was furious, and the two men never spoke after that.

Following the incident, Dugin was reduced to menial jobs in order to make a living. With such a stain on his record he had virtually no chance of a normal life in the USSR. He swept streets, washed windows, and all the while translated, learned foreign languages, read and plunged through the looking glass deeper into the Moscow bohemia.

Many members of the mystical underground never recovered. Some committed suicide, while others 'just sort of went insane. Their heads were full of porridge', according to Dudinsky. For some it was inevitable that the flirtation with fascist symbols, songs and Nazi paraphernalia would become more than just a harmless prank, a teen rebellion. Together with Dzhemal, Dugin began to dabble more and more in the politics of the perestroika era. 'Those two, they wanted power. They were looking for any sort of elevator to the top, and they found it in fascism', said Dudinsky.

Their nineteenth-century dilettante forebears had dipped into the well of European philosophy with disastrous consequences: Pan-Slavism, the so-called 'Black Hundreds' movements of Russian fascism, and finally Bolshevism. Now, a generation's search for truth would have similarly dire consequences: the glasnost generation created not just democracy and a liberal dream, but raised some of the same monsters as before.

* * *

In 1986, Evgeny Nikiforov, a friend of Dugin's and Golovin's who also dabbled in the esoteric, introduced Dugin and Dzhemal to Dmitry Vasilyev, leader of an organization known as Pamyat.

Pamyat had actually begun in 1979 as an offshoot of VOOPIK. It was devoted to architectural restoration and had attracted a harmless intelligentsia following. But Vasilyev effectively took control of the movement during a panel debate held at a Moscow cultural centre in October 1985.[13] The evening was dedicated to the restoration of monuments in Moscow, and Vasilyev rattled off a long list of those he blamed for the destruction of so much prominent architecture. Among them were 'Zionists'. He proceeded to name several prominent Jewish communists, whom he charged to be part of a plot to destroy Russia's patrimony.

The speech caused a ruckus in the audience, with one prominent poet calling Vasilyev a 'fascist' (which probably wasn't far off the mark). But he emerged from the evening the dominant personality within Pamyat, and consolidated his control over the movement, becoming its secretary later that year. Under Vasilyev's uneven leadership and demagogic style, Pamyat mutated from a gaggle of intelligentsia curiosities into a crypto-fascist street gang – an agglomeration of football hooligans and middle-class aesthetes like Dugin and Dzhemal. It would also be a sort of boot camp for a new generation of nationalist extremists. 'It was Pamyat that gave birth to all the other patriotic movements', said Dugin.

Joining the movement in 1987, Dugin's erudition was noticed. Though he was only 24, no one else in Pamyat had read the massive amounts about fascism that he had, and his and Dzhemal's talents were spotted by Vasilyev, who elevated them to the movement's central board. They wore a uniform of sorts: a black shirt with a leather belt and shoulder strap evoking the feared 'Black Hundreds' of the tsarist times.

In turn, Dugin noticed (but was not particularly shocked by) one thing: 'There were KGB people around all the time.' Vasilyev was often summoned to the KGB. In itself that is hardly surprising for the leader of an illegal political movement in the Soviet Union. But Dugin believes that Vasilyev's contacts with the KGB may have amounted to more than simply answering questions; more than the KGB merely monitoring the organization:

> I think that somebody in the totalitarian system was responsible for Pamyat's existence. This is 100 per cent certain. In the central committee of the Communist Party. Who? How? For what purpose? I don't know. Maybe they were testing the situation. But I am sure that this could not have happened spontaneously. That is, I am sure that people in Pamyat were agents working for the KGB. They just could not have been anything else. Who would have let them exist otherwise?

Zhigalkin expressed similar doubts:

> No one had heard of Vasilyev or any of these guys before. We were in the underground, and there, everyone knew each other, or at least knew of each other. Suddenly, these guys appear on the scene out of nowhere, and everything is possible for them. They get a huge profile just like that. It doesn't just happen by accident. Their newspaper had a circulation of 100,000. How do you do that in the Soviet Union? If we wanted to start a newspaper, we'd have to sell a flat just to finance the first two issues. But they somehow can fund a newspaper with no visible effort.

The ubiquity of the KGB in the underground was something to which even Zhigalkin could testify: the first edition of Dzhemal's *Orientation to the North* was published using a KGB Xerox machine. 'Every Xerox machine in Moscow was monitored', he said blithely. 'They simply did it for money.'

The mid-1980s marked the beginning of the end of the USSR, but the KGB still did not know this. The relaxation of political life under Gorbachev's glasnost policies had not happened yet. Attending a banned meeting could still land you on a list of undesirables; it could still cost you your job. No group like Pamyat – where the most heretical ideas were openly discussed in broad daylight, which organized a pseudo-political movement around racism and nationalism – could have existed without some degree of official protection for it: a *krysha*, or 'roof', as Russians put it. As for who was covering for them, Dugin says he was never sure: 'Vasilyev said that there was a *krysha* in the central committee. But I don't know whether it is true because he did not make me privy to that.'

Vasilyev, who spoke in a barely coherent stream of consciousness, was 'an actor and a schizophrenic', according to Dugin, and easy to dismiss as a shrill fascist. He called the Bolshevik revolution a Jewish conspiracy and designed the Pamyat banner as a Romanov double-headed eagle with jagged lightning bolts evoking the Nazi swastika. He was profoundly anti-Semitic and would frequently rail against Zionist plots, which he blamed for the death of Tsar Nicholas II and for a campaign to 'alcoholize' Russia. On one occasion he said that Adolf Eichmann was a 'representative of the Jewish people'; on another he announced that if one played rock 'n' roll records backwards one could hear oaths to Satan. He read the *Protocols of the Elders of Zion*[14] at meetings, and campaigned to legalize the book.

But Pamyat was simultaneously more sophisticated and more establishment-oriented than many observers gave it credit for. The political programme is interesting to examine in hindsight: the leaders spoke in favour of the canoni-zation of Nicholas II, the rebuilding of Christ the Saviour cathedral in Moscow, a ban on communist ideology, and an end to the propagation of atheism. Each of these demands would be implemented in the coming decade by the post-communist government.

Pamyat's activities seem to have revolved around the increasingly dema-gogic speeches of Vasilyev. When he wasn't giving them, his disciples distrib-uted tapes of meetings and lectures. But Vasilyev was also paranoid: he would show up for meetings wearing a false beard, saying the disguise was necessary to evade Zionist assassins who were on his trail. He found it chronically diffi-cult to get along with anyone else in his organization.

Dugin insists that he himself is not, and never was, an anti-Semite, and that at no time did he participate in anti-Semitic activity or violence: 'There was no violence. There has never been one established fact of violence against Jews, of pogroms. It was all just talk. I am not defending it, but would say that it was acceptable then, though not now.'

Pamyat was the first independent political movement in the USSR (aside from the Communist Party) that was allowed to operate with any degree of freedom, and the question of why this was remains unanswered. Unlike its later liberal rival, the Democratic Union, Pamyat's activities seemed to have some official sanction, and it was allowed to organize public demonstrations. In fact, it held the very first unsanctioned public demonstration in the history of the USSR, when 500 rallied on Manezh Square in front of the Kremlin in May 1987.

There are two schools of thought as to why Pamyat was accorded special treatment. The first is that the 'Russian Party' within the higher echelons of the Communist Party and the KGB were sympathetic to nationalism, and so turned a blind eye to Vasilyev, seeing in him a potential ally who was worthy of support. This version is backed up somewhat by the fact that Pamyat mercilessly criticized and harassed the hardliners' opponents, such as Alexander Yakovlev, Gorbachev's right-hand man and chief liberal reformer.

In a newspaper interview published in 1997, Yakovlev said he was certain that Pamyat was a KGB front organization:

> In the beginning it was an organization with basically good intentions, made up of restorers and historians who concerned themselves with saving historical monuments and architecture . . . Then the KGB infiltrated their own guy in there, the photographer Dmitry Vasilyev, together with his cohort. The organization started to take up 'politics' – the fight against Zionism. The restorers left the organization, and the KGB gave Vasilyev a huge new apartment as a headquarters.[15]

The KGB's goal, according to Yakovlev, was to allow the dissident movement to 'let off steam', but it quickly lost control of Pamyat. 'From Pamyat there grew a new generation of more extreme Nazi movements. In this way the KGB gave birth to Russian fascism.'

A Communist Party archive opened in 1991 has shed some light on the KGB connection to Pamyat. In fact, it appears that Vasilyev himself had a KGB codename, 'Vandal', which indicated that his relationship with the organization was indeed more than a casual one. However, a KGB report file describes the activity of the KGB aimed at neutralizing Vasilyev as the leader of Pamyat and at splitting the movement: 'Measures have been carried out to deepen the split within the National Patriotic Front "Pamyat" and compromise Vasilyev (Vandal)', reads one sentence.

* * *

Pamyat may have been an impotent bunch of crazies, but it was the first manifestation of nationalism in a public movement. Until then, nationalists had stuck to their kitchens and gatherings, crossing swords with their ideological opponents only in the thick journals and newspapers. Pamyat showed how nationalism could be transformed into a mass movement.

Thanks to Pamyat, others started noticing the public appeal of nationalism, the politics of 'us' vs 'them'. One of the first people inside the system to notice street nationalism and seek to harness it for political purposes – with much better results – was a silver-haired, bear-like party official from Sverdlovsk. Boris Yeltsin had been spotted by Gorbachev and brought to Moscow as first secretary of the Moscow Communist Party city committee in 1985 – to all intents and purposes, the mayor of the capital. He was burning with ambition, however, and quickly began to challenge Gorbachev's authority and to promote himself as a successor. It was precisely while Yeltsin was head of the Moscow city party apparatus, and casting about for allies in his duel with Gorbachev, that Pamyat was able to hold its unsanctioned demonstration in Manezh Square. Yeltsin met them afterwards. He promised at the meeting to reduce the number of *limitchiki* (migrant workers) in Moscow, and to look into registering Pamyat as a society. And it may not be a coincidence that after Yeltsin was forced out by Gorbachev in 1987, Pamyat began to disintegrate, and Vasilyev's deputy Kim Andreev was excluded from the Communist Party a year later.

It was dawning on Russian political forces that the end was nigh for the monopoly of the Communist Party. There was a need to find popular support, and Pamyat's ability to generate crowds, publicity and (presumably) voters was being noticed. Yeltsin would one day prove to be the champion of Russia's liberal dream; but back in 1987 he was in the midst of an all-out political battle with Gorbachev for position within the party, and seeking allies anywhere he could. He saw the opposition – *any* opposition – as a source of potential recruits to his movement (whatever that would later turn out to be). At this stage, many around him would describe him as something of an empty vessel waiting to be filled: a man of white-hot ambition who had his finger on the national pulse and was willing to follow wherever that led. Things could have turned out very differently for Russia if Yeltsin's circle had been ultra-nationalists rather than liberal westernizers like Anatoly Chubais and Egor Gaidar, who attached themselves to his rising star a few years later.

Other nationalists were shocked by Pamyat and were harshly critical of it. Many nationalist intellectuals thought that they were going to give the whole movement a bad name. Vadim Kozhinov wrote in 1987 in the journal *Nash Sovremennik* that Pamyat was 'infantile' and its programmes contained 'ignorance'; but he refused to condemn it, saying that it was necessary to tolerate the extreme in order for nationalism to make the transition into a mass movement.

As much as they loathed Vasilyev, top nationalist intellectuals were starting to grasp the point that the movement, which had been born in the kitchens of dissidents and the pages of *samizdat*, now had to go public. For decades a small clique of intellectuals had written clever critiques and metaphors for a largely intellectual audience of sympathizers; now they had to think in terms of public slogans and personalities designed to woo the average Soviet citizen. Perhaps, one day, even voters.

Vasilyev, clearly a damaged individual, nonetheless fitted the bill. He was not afraid of the limelight, liked nothing better than public political battles, and was a tireless campaigner. Dugin says that he did not try to delve too deeply into the details of the movement – these were things that in any case were off limits, and Vasilyev discouraged members who were too curious. According to Dugin, 'I was not interested in power. I was interested in them because I was interested in people who were in tune with my ideas.' But he was also discovering in himself an ambition for leadership and for power.

Dugin's term in Pamyat was brief. His and Dzhemal's rise in the organization was seen as a threat by a group of hardline ethnic nationalists led by Alexander Barkashov, a wiry ex-welder and martial arts enthusiast, who also held a seat on Pamyat's central committee and would eventually lead his own party – Russian National Unity – in the 1990s. Jealous of the access Dugin and Dzhemal had to Vasilyev, and seeing their 'traditionalist' orientation as an ideological competitor to Russian nationalism, Barkashov set a trap.

Inviting Dugin and Dzhemal into his Moscow office, he began to discuss Vasilyev's erratic leadership, leading them to agree with him that Vasilyev was 'unacceptable' and that they must all move against him. Secretly, however, Barkashov was taping the conversation and later he played the recording back to Vasilyev. This led to the expulsion of Dugin and Dzhemal from the movement that same year, 1988. And soon after, the organization itself disintegrated in a flurry of departures.

Whatever Pamyat was – a party, a provocation, a success, a failure – it was also a watershed, helping a generation of Soviet intelligentsia to imagine a future in which the monolith of the Communist Party ceded space to competitors on the political playing field. The opening of the USSR was happening faster than anyone had thought possible. The process was accelerated by the glaring inefficiencies of the communist system: the potholed roads and shoddy consumer goods could no longer be papered over by promises of a brighter socialist future. Economic reforms and limited price liberalization coincided with even greater shortages and more discontent than at any time since the 1940s.

Yeltsin, meanwhile, channelled the growing anti-establishment mood into an astonishing political ascent. He was a political blank slate, with a genius for coalition-building, a talent for stealing his opponent's best ideas and a knack of espousing blatantly contradictory positions. For a time he managed to embody the hopes of human rights campaigners and liberal dissidents, as well as of nationalists and hardliners who saw him as the antidote to the corrupt gerontocracy of the Politburo. He managed to be a reformer and a hardliner at the same time – a nationalist and a democrat, a provincial party boss who had made common cause with both the 'lumpen youth' of the provinces and the silver-tongued Moscow intelligentsia. He staked out a position as the effective leader of the Soviet opposition.

Amid the economic chaos, the Communist Party was dealt its worst setback in over 70 years: in March 1989 elections to the Congress of People's Deputies, 38 province-level party secretaries were defeated. Lenin, faced with the same sort of revolt in 1917–18, had overturned the elections. Gorbachev did not, signalling to those who lost that they should step down.

The Soviet establishment by this point was virtually unanimous in agreement that the official metaphysics of the Communist Party was a dead end. Some saw a future in democratic reform and the Soviet Union's gradual transformation into a Western-style nation state, with a market economy and democratic political system. Others saw reform as undesirable but inevitable – a process that must, as far as possible, be channelled into a predictable and stable, and ultimately authoritarian, state.

Still others believed that reform was a dangerously fissile slippery slope to a social explosion, and that the clock must be rolled back to Stalin's time, with a new period of repressions combined with a return to an ideology of Stalin-style National Bolshevism.

But even the hardliners were in agreement that communism had zero appeal to a cynical, jaded population, and that if the regime was to survive, it needed new sources of legitimacy. This meant ideological change.

* * *

Around the same time, a joke was making the rounds of Soviet kitchens: it was simply a line from the Woody Allen film *Bananas* about CIA subversion of a Latin American country:

Question: 'Is the CIA for or against the revolutionaries?'
Answer: 'The CIA cannot take risks. Some are for, some are against.'[16]

The meaning was obvious: simply replace the words CIA with KGB, and the reality of the late 1980s reveals itself. The KGB and the upper echelons of the party did their best to straddle all three camps: nationalists, democratic reformers and die-hard communists.

As the vortex gained momentum there began a series of closed-door discussions high up in the Communist Party hierarchy. Just two decades before, speaking such heresies aloud would have been tantamount to a crime, leading to expulsion from the party, possible imprisonment, or worse. But starting in the late 1980s, a number of elite groups in the central committee or the KGB appear to have engaged in projects to create independent political organizations and ideological projects, which, taken at face value, were naked alternatives to communism. Some of these were probably intended as fifth columns, false flags and provocations designed to discredit reformers; others were more akin to side bets, aimed at keeping ahead of the political reform process via deniable but manageable pawns.

But other projects appeared to be sincere attempts to create alternatives to communism, which had lost once and for all its ability to legitimate the regime and mobilize the population. These were attempts to recreate communism along nationalist lines, or simply replace communism wholesale with something vaguely imperial and Russian-sounding, while never relinquishing ultimate control of the political process.

In detailed after-the-fact examination of these projects, one name keeps popping up in documents, in conversations with those involved, and in anecdotes: that of Vladimir Kryuchkov, chairman of the Soviet KGB.

According to Alexander Yakovlev, who had many dealings with Kryuchkov, he was a 'grey mouse' of the party apparat. As Yakovlev wrote in his 2005 memoirs:

He was polite to everyone, ingratiating, and grey, like an autumn twilight. And grey people are inclined to take themselves seriously, which is both comical and dangerous. Kryuchkov took seriously the laurels that were placed on his head, even though they were too big for his head.[17]

Kryuchkov, for his part, accused Yakovlev in his own 2003 memoirs of being an agent of the Western intelligence services.[18]

Yakovlev said that Kryuchkov oversaw the rearguard action by hardliners aimed at averting the collapse of the system. It was around this time that a number of oddly named and conceived political projects were started, helped by what Yakovlev called 'the "yesterday forever" forces grouped around Kryuchkov and a group of military and party fundamentalists frantically trying to stop the collapse of the regime, to save their regime . . . They managed to do some things, but by far not everything they tried worked.'[19]

Some would say that Pamyat was in fact the first such project, originally designed to control the democratic process. Had it not been led so erratically by an obvious sociopath, Pamyat could ultimately have been registered as an independent political party. Instead, this honour went to its successor, another obvious creation of the central committee with just as nationalist a bent. Known as the Liberal Democratic Party of Russia (LDPR), it was neither liberal nor democratic.

Vladimir Zhirinovsky, leader of the LDPR, was Vasilyev's political heir apparent. He has become one of Russia's most successful opposition politicians, although the LDPR has a suspicious track record of voting with the Kremlin on major issues. Zhirinovsky's political persona is arguably copied from none other than Vasilyev: Dugin, an associate of both men, insists that Zhirinovsky used to listen to tapes of Vasilyev's speeches and learned his trademark demagogic style from him. The *enfant terrible* of Russian politics, Zhirinovsky routinely gets into fist-fights with political opponents. He has at various times exhorted Russian soldiers to 'wash their boots in the Indian Ocean'; has demanded the return of Alaska from the United States; and has threatened to spread nuclear waste to the newly independent Baltic states using gigantic fans.

But whereas Vasilyev appears to have been truly crazy, Zhirinovsky is a talented impersonator whose insanity is purely for public consumption. In private conversations he is composed, analytical and thoroughly sober. He first came to national attention in 1991 by taking third place in the Russian Federation's presidential elections. Running against Yeltsin, he amassed 6.2 million votes – an astounding number given his lack of name recognition. At one point in the 1990s, the LDPR controlled a quarter of parliament.

Zhirinovsky's success was testament to his skill as a politician, but also to the fact that the fortunes of the nationalist hardliners were attributable to help from unseen hands (a phenomenon first witnessed in the case of Pamyat). Zhirinovsky, for example, is widely rumoured to have been be a KGB officer – in fact, he was expelled from Turkey for espionage in 1970. Though he strenuously denies any hidden help from the KGB, he was nonetheless always the subject of rumours about the real source of his success.

Registered with suspicious haste in 1991, the LDPR was the first political party to be created following the legalization of political parties, and benefited from numerous interventions by senior bureaucrats: Vitaly Koroticha, at the time editor of the popular weekly magazine *Ogonek*, tells the story of how one day in 1990, following the creation of the LDPR, Vladimir Sevruk, deputy chief of the propaganda department of the central committee, 'bombarded' him to run an interview with Zhirinovsky: 'You don't like it that we don't have a multi-party system. Why don't you raise him on your shield?'

More evidence of Communist Party help for Zhirinovsky came when Yakovlev published his memoirs in 2005. In them, he publicly accused the LDPR of being a creation of the Communist Party central committee, and specifically of Vladimir Kryuchkov, chairman of the KGB. Yakovlev included a direct quote from a document providing the initial LDPR funding, an interest-free loan of 3 million roubles of Communist Party money to a firm managed by Zhirinovsky's deputy at the time, Andrey Zavidiya, who would run as Zhirinovsky's vice-president in 1991.

The LDPR was probably the most successful of several joint Communist Party–KGB political projects to anticipate and attempt to control political reform. Some of these, like the LDPR, were designed to win elections; others were designed to avoid them.

Yet another clique of top Communist Party officials who also appear to have had the blessing of Kryuchkov attempted to salvage the legitimacy of the Communist Party by refurbishing the actual ideology of communism. This was begun in 1987 by Moscow Communist Party boss (and later Politburo member) Yury Prokofyev, who patronized the creation of something known as the Experimental Creative Centre, headed by a moon-faced former rocket scientist and theatre director named Sergey Kurginyan. Under Prokofyev's patronage, Kurginyan says that he hired hundreds of specialists, armed with computers and the latest technology, aimed at dreaming up a new Soviet ideology. 'We became the main think tank of the government', Kurginyan told me, with only mild exaggeration. After Prokofyev succeeded to the Politburo, the project was championed by Valentin Pavlov, one of the ringleaders of the doomed 1991 coup attempt. The 93-page product of the Centre was a pamphlet entitled 'Post-Perestroika' and was a blueprint for rolling back liberal reforms and replacing communist orthodoxy with something a great deal weirder.

'Post-perestroika' was a programme for ideological and spiritual renewal following the period of upheaval brought on by Gorbachev's reforms. It imbued secular communism with a theological meaning: Kurginyan proposed a 'Cosmic philosophical religious social idea' based on a 'red religion'. The Soviet economy would be transformed from ministries into state corporations, pushing the boundaries of progress, while Soviet managers were to become 'knights and priests of the Red faith'.[20] It was a bald attempt by conservatives within the party to transform communist ideology into something resembling a fusion of communism, nationalism and Orthodox Christianity, with a dash of something known as 'Cosmism'.

It was as though Kurginyan had turned the clock back to an earlier period, to the late nineteenth and early twentieth century – the maximalist era of Russian philosophy, when science merged with Christian theology and the mystical occult. In his study *Post-Perestroika* Kurginyan riffed on the mystical theology of Vladimir Solovyev, who taught that humanity strove for 'Godmanhood', a semi-divine state. He alluded to Vladimir Vernadsky, the biologist who had inspired Lev Gumilev and had proposed the unification of all knowledge in the 'noosphere'. But Kurginyan found most of his inspiration in the theories of Nikolay Fedorov, a nineteenth-century librarian whose only known work, published posthumously and called *Philosophy of the Common Task*, was devoted to the idea that mankind should devote all its resources to the resurrection of dead ancestors from particles of cosmic dust, after which, lacking space on earth, mankind would have to develop space travel in order to colonize other planets.

While Fedorov is not mentioned by name in *Post-Perestroika*, Kurginyan uses the title of his programme – 'Common Task' – capitalized four times in the pamphlet. His aim, as he described it, was: 'Accepting a communist ideology and melding it into the metaphysics of the Common Task.'

Kurginyan, who has in the past decade reinvented himself as a successful TV talk-show debater, admits that Fedorov was the main inspiration for the project of 'post-perestroika'. Fedorov, he says, symbolized a return to a more expansive era of philosophy, rooted in the nineteenth century: 'I had to demonstrate the Russian tradition, to explain that communism in Russia was not accidental, and had deep metaphysical roots in this country.'

Communism, in other words, was a profoundly Russian idea, whose philosophical roots went deep in Russian soil. Kurginyan's project, while it grabbed the imagination of some of the ruling elite, nonetheless failed because they could not hold onto power. A copy of *Post-Perestroika* was discovered on Kryuchkov's desk on 22 August 1991, the day he was arrested following the abortive three-day coup attempt by hardliners. In fact, Kurginyan's connection to the KGB may have been more than casual; in 2014, while filming a webcast with the governor of Donetsk People's Republic, Pavel Gubarev, he referred to himself an 'officer': 'You say to me, an officer, that you know better than I what the situation is?' he retorted, giving Gubarev a dressing-down. It may have been an inadvertent slip of the tongue, but, given Kurginyan's association with the senior KGB leadership, it would surprise no one if that referred to an actual military rank.

The pamphlet's real influence is debatable – Kurginyan says that Kryuchkov assured him after his arrest that he had not put the copy of *Post-Perestroika* on his desk where it was photographed following his arrest. It was a set-up, according to Kurginyan, 'to discredit me. To take me out of the equation.'

Given the enthusiasm of the KGB and an element of the central committee for programmes of ideological renewal and authoritarian alternatives to communism, Dugin's projects following his departure from Pamyat deserve some scrutiny. It was the era in which, as we have seen, Gumilev's histories were achieving monumental popularity, and the idea of 'Eurasia' was in the air, helped by the interventions of senior figures in the Communist Party such as Gumilev's patron Anatoly Lukyanov, the chairman of the Supreme Soviet.

Eurasianism, as has been discussed, was one of several authoritarian ideological projects. In the chaos enveloping the elite, it was regarded by some hardliners in the regime as an alternative both to an exhausted official metaphysics of socialism, and to the rapidly encroaching ideas of liberal democracy.

In 1990, the central committee agreed to fund a journal known as *Continent Russia*. Dugin put this together in partnership with his comrade Igor Dudinsky, who had since joined *Znamya*, the central committee's in-house journal, and who fronted the endeavour. A lacklustre project devoted to Russian civilization and Eurasia, it never achieved much success – just a few issues appear to have been produced. According to Dudinsky:

> They were in so much agony, the Central Committee. They were looking for any sort of alternative, any idea. They knew they were finished. They were willing to work with anyone, cooperate with anyone. Anything was okay, so long as it allowed them to stay in power . . . They wanted to stay in power at any price, but they were too conservative. Any initiative just drowned in their general backwardness, in the bureaucracy. They couldn't do anything. These issues of *Continent Russia* just sat on the shelf and got dusty.

More interesting were two books published by Dugin the previous year, with curiously large print runs – 100,000 each, according to him. The first was a series of essays entitled *The Way of the Absolute*. It was devoted to the traditionalist theories of Julius Evola, who taught that the authoritarian state should be based on a 'spiritual aristocracy', whose fitness to lead was based on the values of elitism and spiritual authority. The second, *The Metaphysics of the Gospel*, was based around placing the traditionalism of Guénon and Evola in the context of the Orthodox Christian faith. Dugin called for the restoration of a medieval Byzantine social hierarchy, served by elite priest and warrior castes, in a Church–state 'symphony', a 'synthesis and acme of the adequate combination of priestly and warrior principles'. Russia, wrote Dugin, is the heir to the Byzantine Empire, which provided a 'unique synthesis of the kingdom of god and the earthly kingdom, having become that providential thousand year kingdom'.[21] Both books were full of esotericism, occult numerology and very tendentious scholarship. And both books – like Kurginyan's project – harked back to the turn-of-the-century era of Russian philosophy, when theology and philosophy, the occult, aesthetics and poetry blended seamlessly in the work of Russia's greatest thinkers.

As Dugin himself put it in a history of the period: 'The model of Soviet self-knowledge had broken ... The society had lost its orientation. Everyone understood the necessity of change, but this feeling was vague and no one knew what direction it would come from.'[22] Occult movements, spiritualism, new metaphysics, conspiracy theories, anti-Semitism, nationalism, theosophy – all found their feet in the new zeitgeist. Russia had already in the twentieth century shown itself uniquely susceptible to being carried away by ideology. Now the door was once again thrown wide open.

These two books are important for another reason. According to Dugin, the huge print runs and sales of the books (which he has trouble explaining) provided enough revenue to fund several very curious trips to Western Europe from 1990 to 1992, when he met far-right activists and thinkers whose ideas he eagerly imported to Russia. He thus became, in the words of Eduard Limonov, 'the St Cyril and Methodius of fascism'. At the time, travelling to Europe was still prohibitively expensive, even disregarding the issue of Dugin's dissident status and the difficulty of getting a foreign travel passport.

Whether Dugin acted on his own, as a lone intellectual entrepreneur, or whether he had help from unseen hands is an interesting, though ultimately futile mystery. Either way, the ideas he brought back from Europe – of geopolitics and other far-right ideas – would revolutionize Russian politics over the next two decades. Perhaps it was the project of a solitary romantic. But probably more likely it was done with help from elements of the state that had an established track record, at precisely this time, of sponsoring right-wing ideological experiments.

Acquaintances are cautious about corroborating Dugin's version of his travels. Sergey Zhigalkin, for example, who published most of Evgeny Golovin's books and who has detailed knowledge of that segment of the publishing market (esoteric mysticism), doubts that Dugin made much money from his books.

However, Dugin's recollection, voiced in a 2005 interview with me, is that:

Back then, books that are now published in 1,000 or 2,000 copies, we issued in 100,000 copies. There was a boom. Some workers were buying, though it is not clear why they needed these books. We issued several editions, earned some money and went off to Paris.

1 'The question of "to where" has become more important than "from where"': Roman Jakobson (left) and Nikolay Trubetskoy (right) in Brno, 1933.

2 'Russia in search and struggle, in a bid for a city not of this world': Petr Savitsky.

3 'You are my son and my horror': Russian poets Nikolay Gumilev and Anna Akhmatova with their son Lev, 1916.

4 'It was basically like reading a novel. Unlike most history books, you read until the last page': Lev Gumilev in 1983.

5 A Soviet Virgil: Yury Mamleev.

6 'The St Cyril and
Methodius of fascism':
Alexander Dugin.

7 Neal Cassady to Dugin's
Kerouac: Gaidar Dzhemal.

8 Alain de Benoist in his Paris office.

9 The nightingale of the General Staff: Alexander Prokhanov in 1992.

10 Boris Yeltsin addresses the crowd in front of the White House, 1991.

11 It's Me, Eddie: Eduard Limonov in 1986.

12 Inside the besieged White House, October 1993.

13 'Operation Crematorium': a truck rams the entrance to Ostankino in October 1993.

14 'I was in a very radical mood': Valery Korovin on how he came to find Dugin.

15 'The Kremlin needed people who were free of intellectual complexes': spin doctor Gleb Pavlovsky in 2012.

16 'We are a victorious people! It is in our genes, in our genetic code': Vladimir Putin in front of a map of Russia and the Commonwealth of Independent States, 2006.

17 'From the pitch-black darkness of nothingness, a new Russia burst forth in front of our eyes':
Pavel Zarifullin, 2012.

18 'In 1996, we beat the Communists, but in so doing, we gave the regime a tool for staying in power
until the end of time': Marat Guelman.

19 Kremlin demiurge Vladislav Surkov, 2006. He operated an 'ideological centrifuge' which 'scattered all ideological discourses to the periphery'.

20 'You can believe those rumours if you want': Putin's confessor, Father Tikhon, in 2014.

21 The Moscow apartment bombings, September 1999.

22 People sheltering during the Kiev sniper massacre, February 2014.

23 The 'polite people': unmarked Russian troops occupy Crimea, patrolling Simferopol International Airport, 2014.

24 A 'Novorossiya' military badge worn throughout the war in Donbass.

CHAPTER NINE

PARIS 1990

Before being introduced to Alexander Dugin in June 1990, the French writer Alain de Benoist had never really gone out of his way to meet Russians, and they had never really gone out of their way to meet him. With the exception of the occasional long-time émigré, he had never really socialized with anyone from Eastern Europe, and had only once set foot in the Eastern bloc when attending a book fair in Leipzig a few years previously. It wasn't that de Benoist didn't like Russians; it just sort of went with his job. De Benoist's aristocratic countenance, scraggly beard and wire-rimmed glasses had for two decades been the leading intellectual inspiration for one of the most right-wing movements on the continent, the French Nouvelle Droite. Until that year, hanging out with Russians was not what European radical conservatives did.

But 1990 was a big year for political philosophers like him who were busy pronouncing dramatically on the fall of the Berlin Wall and the dissolution of the Warsaw Pact only a few months before. Now that 'right' and 'left', the reliable geostationary indicators of public life on the continent, had lost their traditional significance, many other barriers were coming down as well.

De Benoist had agreed to meet Dugin after hearing rave reviews of the man from a mutual acquaintance. And so, sporting a Lenin-style goatee, the 28-year-old Russian appeared one day in de Benoist's office in Paris, which overflowed with the paraphernalia of France's uniquely intellectual public life – including over 20,000 books. Dugin, de Benoist said, reminded him of 'a young Solzhenitsyn'.

Just off the plane from Moscow for his first ever trip abroad, Dugin surprised de Benoist with his erudition and his fluent French. His higher education had consisted of two years at the Moscow Civil Aviation Academy, which de Benoist could not at first believe. He recalls being struck by how remarkably well informed the Russian was about what was being published in the West. He liked the same authors as de Benoist, held similar views on the big political questions of the day, and seemed to have read almost everything de Benoist had ever written.

Dugin was a dissident, and like many others he had developed a network of contacts in the West over the years, smuggling out books and letters to those with sympathetic views. But now, after years of democratic reforms under Mikhail Gorbachev, the Communist Party general secretary, the restrictions had eased. Dugin, like many other Russians previously forbidden to go abroad, now had a *zagran* passport allowing him to travel to an outside world that until then he had only read about. But Dugin was no ordinary dissident. He had been hounded by the KGB and persecuted for his political views, had repeatedly been fired from jobs, and had been reduced to sweeping streets to earn a living. But he was no Western-oriented liberal who had cheered the collapse of the Berlin Wall and the march of democracy across Europe. From de Benoist and other New Right intellectuals he met on his European travels, Dugin would learn a new set of principles and vocabulary.

De Benoist is a figure who resists easy categorization: he himself admits to having belonged to extreme right-wing political circles in his youth. Following the political upheavals in 1968 he helped found a grouping of intellectuals known as the Nouvelle Droite – distinguishing it from the 'old' right, which was tinged by association with mid-century European fascism. 'The old right is dead and well deserves to be', he wrote in a characteristic 1979 essay.[1] The traditional Catholic, monarchist and nationalist European conservatives were increasingly challenged by a movement which sometimes espoused pagan or traditionalist beliefs, did not recognize the distinction between the political left and right, and believed that nationalism was a dead end which was to be gradually replaced by a heterogeneity of identities and political models. As de Benoist wrote in 1986:

> Already on the international level the major contradiction is no longer between right and left, liberalism and socialism, fascism and communism, 'totalitarianism' and 'democracy', it is between those who want the world to be one dimensional and those who support a plural world grounded in the diversity of cultures.[2]

The New Right never managed to shake its reputation for extremism, however. It 'let its hair grow long and hid its tyre irons in the attic', according to French historian Henry Rousso, giving intellectual lustre and respectability to right-wing views which a few decades before had been anathema to the public.[3]

The New Right has been described by some scholars as a movement devoted to 'conserving the fascist vision in the interregnum'.[4] But it has been defended by other scholars as a genuinely original and complex philosophy which combined right- and left-wing views in an anti-liberal, anti-capitalist ideology that is hard to pigeonhole. De Benoist, for his part, insists that he is not a member of the extreme right, has argued strongly against any form of racism, and calls himself 'an anti-capitalist communitarian socialist'.

While the old right was anti-Soviet, the New Right felt an equal – if not greater – antipathy for Atlantic domination by the United States. While the old right saw European integration as a threat to traditional national identities, the New Right saw 'Jacobin' nationalism as a passing, 200-year fad driven by the industrial revolution and the global market. 'What characterizes the national realm is its irresistible tendency to centralization and homogenization', wrote de Benoist in 1993 in the journal *Telos*. They believed mankind would eventually find its feet again in the millennia-old form of human organization – the empire.

> In such conditions, how can the idea of empire be ignored? Today it is the only model Europe has produced as an alternative to the nation-state. Nations are both threatened and exhausted. They must go beyond themselves if they do not want to end up as dominions of the American superpower. They can only do so by attempting to reconcile the one and the many, seeking a unity that does not lead to their impoverishment . . . Europe can only create itself in terms of a federal model, but a federal model which is the vehicle for an idea, a project, a principle, i.e. in the final analysis, an imperial model.[5]

De Benoist's soul-searching echoed that of Dugin and the rest of the Russian right wing at the time, and the two men found an easy consensus around something that Dugin described as the 'radical centre': while both men had once been profoundly anti-Soviet, the New Right ideas of both men were more anti-American. Dugin's unformed thinking eagerly devoured many of his older counterpart's views, and de Benoist remains the thinker most footnoted and most referenced by Dugin; he would serve as a kind of intellectual model for the young Russian thinker.

Both men have been identified with nationalism throughout their careers and been linked to far-right groups; but both were highly original thinkers who argued extensively against narrow ethnic definitions of nationalism and cultural imperialism. The Frenchman, however, insists that he is not responsible for some liberties that Dugin may have taken in interpreting his works.

Dugin has accentuated the similarities of his thought with that of de Benoist by ascribing many of his own views to his mentor. However, de Benoist makes it clear that this is something he is profoundly uncomfortable with, pointing out that he cannot take responsibility for the representation of his work in a language that he cannot read. As Argentine surrealist Jorge Luis Borges put it, 'all writers invent their precursors', and in practice it is difficult to separate de Benoist's real ideas from Dugin's interpretation of them. For example, in Dugin's most influential work, *The Foundations of Geopolitics*, published in 1997, he attributes to de Benoist the central argument of the book – that 'the nation state is exhausted and the future only belonged to large spaces . . . strategically unified and ethnically differentiated'; however, 'this strategic unity must be supported by the unity of the original culture'. Indeed, the European unity would be based, according to Dugin's version of de Benoist, 'on a common Indo-European origin'.[6] De Benoist, however, insists that he has never formulated any theory of large spaces, and disagrees with any attribution of these ideas to him.[7] De Benoist is a highly original thinker who has melded the right and the left, celebrating Europe's diversity on the one hand, but also defending the need to protect European civilization from foreign influences.

The Frenchman has spent much of his life defending himself against accusations that he is a closet fascist, which may have much to do with his previous 1968-era political activities. His opponents point to his cultural theories, arguing that contact between cultures must always be limited, otherwise the very integrity of a culture is undermined,[8] as evidence that he has simply retooled 1930s-era arguments for new times, substituting culture for race: 'A "high culture" version of fascist arguments', according to French scholar Brigitte Beauzamy.[9] De Benoist, however, calls this interpretation 'ridiculous', noting that he has argued extensively against racism.

It is noteworthy, though, that among the thinkers most quoted by the New Right are quite a few ex-Nazis: philosopher Martin Heidegger, legal theorist Carl Schmitt, esoteric author Julius Evola and scholar of 'geopolitics' Karl Haushofer. The movement also kept the flame alive for a German movement known during interwar politics as the 'conservative revolution' theorists: influential intellectuals radically opposed to liberalism and parliamentary democracy in general, and to the Weimar Republic in particular, and dedicated to the creation of a new post-liberal nationalistic order. They included Ernst Jünger, Arthur Moeller van den Bruck, Edgar Julius Jung, Oswald Spengler, Othmar Spann and Ernst Niekisch. Some of these went on to become Nazis, but most remained largely outside everyday politics.[10]

The popularity of these authors among the New Right continues to cast the movement as an echo, however distant, of the rise of interwar fascism, which drank from the same ideological well. Meanwhile, not all of the present-day New Right thinkers are as nuanced as de Benoist, and many of those whom

Dugin met preached almost unadulterated versions of fascism, racism and militarism. These more radical thinkers included Robert Steuckers, head of the Belgian Nouvelle Droite and publisher of the magazine *Vouloir*, which was popular in far-right circles in the early 1990s. Steuckers met Dugin by accident in a Parisian bookshop. 'It was still a time when you almost never met Russian people in Western Europe', he would write later.

> You also could recognize Soviet citizens by their clothes . . . When I heard a Russian man and his wife talking with the usual charming Russian accent, I got immediately the impression that the person in front of the bookshop's desk was Dugin himself. He had already written a couple of letters to me and . . . I knew already quite a lot about him. I went straight to him and asked: 'You are Alexander Dugin, I presume . . .?' He looked very afraid, as if I had been a policeman in plain clothes.[11]

Steuckers' journal *Vouloir* was an example of extreme-right polemics, full of interviews with pro-apartheid figures, maps of 'greater Serbia' and, in one issue, a graph showing immigration to Germany on the rise, with the caption 'Wohin zieht die Ausländer?' – 'Where are the foreigners drawn to?'

Another radical Dugin courted was Jean-François Thiriart, an eccentric Belgian optician, who was a proponent of National Bolshevism and a European empire stretching from Vladivostok to Dublin. He had advanced the view that the USSR was the 'descendant' of the Third Reich, in the sense that it was a land power surrounded by sea powers.[12] Claudio Mutti, an Italian disciple of Evola who is linked to right-wing terror groups in Italy, published Dugin's manifesto 'Russian Continent', which had appeared first in *Znamya*. Dugin also met Yves Lacoste, publisher of *Hérodote*, a journal devoted to geopolitics, who appears to have been an adviser to various French political figures.

German political philosophy from the interwar period had a distinctive historical echo for Russia at the end of the Cold War, a period not coincidentally dubbed Russia's 'Weimar era' by a number of commentators: a continental power, impoverished in defeat, whose diminished place in the international system does not suit its ambitions. The militaristic theories of geopolitics emphasizing Russia/Germany's isolated 'central position' amid adversaries in particular rationalized in theoretical terms a Russia reborn from the ashes of defeat in the Cold War, the way Germany rose from the humiliation of Versailles.

In fact, Dugin's version of Eurasianism, which would infiltrate the Kremlin, seemed to owe more to the New Right's theories of multinational empires, geopolitics and communitarianism, than it did to the writings of the original

Russian Eurasianists, whom Dugin seems to have ingested only much later in his career.[13] Dugin's later theories of geopolitics, for which he would achieve his greatest fame, came by way of Carl Schmitt and Karl Haushofer, both of whom made their appearances in Dugin's writings on his return from his maiden voyage to Europe. De Benoist readily admits that he introduced Dugin to Schmitt, but not to Haushofer.

Schmitt was the brilliant legal philosopher of the Third Reich between 1933 and 1936. His writings on questions of legal sovereignty and political philosophy are still regarded as groundbreaking by academics today. In 1945 he was forbidden to teach for the rest of his life, having written legal justifications of Hitler's dictatorship. In Schmitt's view, a legal system could not be effective without the simultaneous and paradoxical element of a power external to it acting to preserve its integrity. Schmitt believed that no system can exist without a guarantor – a sovereign – who is outside it, and who decides on what he called 'the state of exception', in which the law is suspended. His postwar work includes the magisterial *Nomos of the Earth*, which was a rebuttal of liberal notions of universal rights and moral values. It argued that the wellspring of any legal order is not universal principles, but rather local notions of how land is divided – 'the occupation of land, the foundation of cities as well as the foundation of colonies' – which in turn becomes the formative element in the unique character of each state. In this way, the law of the land is quite literally the law of the land, and is unique to each civilization, creating a unique local character for each political order, which is incommensurate with foreign legal notions and impervious to universal judgements. Schmitt's book *Land and Sea* was another clear inspiration for Dugin's work – a discussion of fundamental antagonism between maritime and continental societies. Schmitt even ascribed the tension between Catholics and Protestants to this element. While Schmitt was speaking about 'continental' Germany, the same concepts could easily be applied to 'continental' Russia after the Cold War.

Meanwhile, Haushofer became a magnet for Dugin, and possibly his main influence. Haushofer was influential mainly through his friendship with Hitler's secretary Rudolph Hess, though he was never a member of the Nazi Party and his real influence is debated by historians. But Haushofer's prescriptions for German strategy were briefly realized by the short-lived Molotov–Ribbentrop Pact of 1939, which Haushofer celebrated as a blow against the 'anaconda policy' of the 'Western Jewish plutocracy'. He praised Hitler's 'Eurasian policy' in his book *Der Kontinentalblock Mitteleuropa–Eurasien–Japan*.[14]

The terminology of geopolitics – words like 'Heartland', 'Rimland', 'Grossraum', 'Atlanticism' and the like – shows up in Dugin's writings only after his trips to Europe. In his later bestseller, *Foundations of Geopolitics*, Dugin credits the New Right, and specifically de Benoist, with providing most of his knowledge of the subject. 'One of the few European schools of geopolitical thought, retaining unbroken ties to the ideas of the pre-war German geopoliticians and continentalists, is the New Right.' He adds that de Benoist's philosophy of geopolitics 'is in full conformity with the school of Haushofer'. However, de Benoist continues to insist that he had nothing to do with teaching Dugin about Haushofer, and does not know who did.

Dugin travelled extensively in Europe. He spoke at a colloquium organized by de Benoist, and appeared on Spanish TV and at various conferences. In 1992 he would ultimately invite his new cohort of European far-rightists to Moscow, where they met some of Dugin's new patrons, who – they were surprised to realize – included quite a few military men. As Dugin told me in a 2005 interview:

> I absorbed this New Right model that resonated with Eurasianism very clearly. And it was enriching, with new names, new authors, new ideas. This was a fundamental upgrade, of conceptions, ideas, an update of the concept that had been forming in me. I was searching for parallels for this in Russian history and for resonances in Russian political philosophy of what I liked.

He referred to this as 'a kind of backwards translation'.

By his own account, after seven or eight trips Dugin grew disenchanted with Europe: 'It's not that I disliked it. I just gradually understood that there is nothing interesting there, that everything interesting exists in Russia. That in Europe the history is closed. And in Russia history is open.'

'The Nightingale'

During his first trip to Paris, Dugin had paid a call on a man who would provide a fateful introduction that would change his career.[15] Yury Mamleev, founder of the Yuzhinsky literary circle and Dugin's literary idol, had moved to France following an unsuccessful sojourn at Cornell University in the US, where he had had no better luck finding a publisher than he had in the USSR. The French, however, with more of a taste for the intellectual and metaphysical, gave him the welcome he felt he deserved, and he stayed on in France, writing, until the collapse of the Soviet Union.

In exile, Mamleev had become something of an absentee mentor for Dugin, and the two had exchanged the occasional letter during the 1980s. Dugin arranged to meet Mamleev on his first trip to Paris, and soon after that Mamleev made his first trip to Moscow in 15 years. 'He was crossing himself at each lamp post, looked glowingly on each Russian face like it was a bright Easter egg', joked Dugin later.

Mamleev now had a proposal for Dugin. The author had a good friend, a famed Soviet writer, whose close links to the Red Army high command were legendary. The two shared a counterculture background, coming of age in the 'men of the sixties' generation, though they had taken diverging paths, with Mamleev's friend having succumbed to the temptations of the establishment to become a proselytizer and propagandizer of the Soviet military. His name was Alexander Prokhanov.

Throughout emigration, Mamleev had maintained his improbable contact with Prokhanov, whose nickname was 'The Nightingale of the General Staff' on account of his close friendship with top Red Army generals. Upon Mamleev's return, the two renewed their friendship, and Prokhanov shared the details of an interesting project: he had been tasked by Vladimir Karpov, chairman of the USSR Writers' Union, with organizing a newspaper. The Writers' Union leadership had lost control of its in-house paper *Literaturnaya Gazeta*, which was seen by hardliners as being overly liberal and favouring reformist elements. Prokhanov's newspaper would be a conservative counterweight to *Literaturnaya Gazeta*, and he needed talented young writers with a nationalist bent. Did Mamleev know of anyone?

Mamleev immediately thought of the young Dugin, and set about recruiting him. 'You know, Sasha, Prokhanov is one of us', Mamleev told the sceptical dissident. 'How so?' Dugin looked surprised. He believed Prokhanov to be 'on the other side of the fence', as he put it – a 'cadre man' who served the Soviet system. 'Sasha, you are mistaken. He's secretly with us. He is undercover, autonomous.'

Dugin became interested. He was intrigued by Prokhanov's relationship with the army and the special services, seeing them immediately as a natural constituency for the radical ideas that he was exploring with his new contacts abroad in the European New Right. He went to see Prokhanov, who, it turned out, had the wild hair and spoke in the riffing style of a beatnik poet – not at all what Dugin had been expecting from a mythologizer of state power.

Born in 1938, Prokhanov had trained as a rocket scientist. But like many of his fellow 'children of the sixties' had been bitten by the Romantic bug and had left a comfortable position at his institute to work as a forester, observing nature and 'the pagan cycle of life', as he put it. He had come to nationalism by way of the quaint nostalgia of the village prose movement. But gradually Prokhanov began to be entranced with Soviet power. He himself says his epiphany came when he, a rookie journalist on *Literaturnaya Gazeta*, was sent in 1969 to cover the Sino-Soviet war. Following the March Soviet offensive on Damansky Island, he witnessed the grieving mothers of the dead Soviet soldiers, and wrote movingly about the scene, weaving elements of folklore and his knowledge of village tradition and slang into his writing. It was a sensation at the paper and catapulted Prokhanov immediately to its top ranks.

'The feeling that the country stood on the verge of war with China, the sight of the dead, the sight of these war machines which groaned and rumbled, made me understand that the state is the highest of values. Thus began my transformation into a statist', he told TV interviewer Vladimir Pozner in 2013.[16]

It also got him noticed by the Red Army who saw the makings of a gifted propagandist. Over the next two decades, Prokhanov was taken under the Red Army's General Staff, and made his name reporting on the Cold War from a front-row seat. He made over a dozen trips to Afghanistan, covering the bloody decade-long Soviet campaign there. He went several times to the front lines of confrontation between the USSR and the West: Nicaragua, Mozambique, Cambodia, Angola.

By the 1980s, he had already acquired his nickname of 'Nightingale' on account of his links to top Soviet generals and his gift of extolling their virtues. He spent much of the 1980s attached to the 40th Army fighting in Afghanistan, and in 1982 wrote *The Tree in the Centre of Kabul*, which is to this day perhaps his best recognized and most praised work. The same year, largely with the backing of the Red Army, Prokhanov won the Komsomol Literature Prize, one of the most important literary prizes in the Soviet Union, and in 1985 he was made a secretary of the Russian Writers' Union.

In 1987, Prokhanov emerged as one of the leading figures in the conservative counterattack on the Gorbachevite reformers. At a speech to the Eighth Congress of the USSR Writers' Union in April of that year, he delivered a blistering rebuttal to the proponents of political liberalization, accusing them of copying the West: 'such copying deprives us of our sovereign path and gives birth to an inferiority complex'.[17]

Prokhanov catered to the needs of his patrons in the military and security forces, and as they were drawn into the perestroika debates over reform, so was he. He became a central figure in an alliance between the military and nationalist intellectuals which began in the mid-1970s but became more active as the USSR's ideological wheels began to wobble in the late 1980s.

While the army had always been the most ideologized of the Soviet institutions, tension between the army and the political masters in the Kremlin was building through the late 1980s and early 1990s due to a string of fundamental disagreements, miscommunications, tragic mistakes and attempts to dodge responsibility, which led to greater and greater disillusionment in the officer corps. The Soviet withdrawal from Afghanistan had brought the Red Army's prestige to an all-time low, while feeding a sense among the top brass that they were being made to carry the can for a bankrupt and rudderless Kremlin. This frustration was fed by two horrific atrocities which were covered up and blamed on the field commanders. In 1989, Red Army paratroopers doing crowd control in Tbilisi lost control of a demonstration, 'kettling' demonstrators aggressively and attacking some with batons and shovels. This resulted in 21 deaths. In January 1991, 15 died when KGB commandos stormed the Lithuanian parliament and TV centre, which had been taken over by protesters. After both of these atrocities, when responsibility had to be assigned for the civilian death toll, the politicians disavowed all responsibility, pinning the blame solely on the army commanders, who insisted they had been given verbal orders. But without anything in writing, these objections were ignored.

The lesson learned by the army was that they could not trust their political masters. And all the while, the military and the KGB looked with increasing concern at the ascendancy of democratic forces, which saw no need for continued military confrontation with the West. The military's hard power, its tanks and bayonets, could not maintain its authority against the new enemy: irrelevance.

Soviet officers now disillusioned with the Kremlin were also emboldened by the new intellectual climate to seek their own ideological alliances. When the wheels of communist ideology began to wobble, the army lost no time in searching for an alternative – a very natural alliance with nationalists, who saw the army as a great source of patriotic pride. Prokhanov was a key broker of the military's overtures to the conservatives. Many military men were already closet nationalists: army officers had always felt themselves to be the heirs of great generals such as Suvorov and Kutuzov, the great defenders of the motherland, rather than the vanguard of the international proletariat.

Just as the military were casting about for ideological allies, the nationalists were in similar disarray. A series of disastrous election showings revealed them to be utterly unprepared for the new political era that was dawning. Instead, the lesson the nationalists drew was that, faced with inevitable democratic political reforms, the only way they could hope to triumph was through non-democratic means.[18]

Free elections were a wake-up call for the nationalists, who had no organization comparable to the democrats' Moscow Popular Front and Democratic Union. Only Pamyat, by this time a lame and ridiculed caricature of itself, competed on a national level in the 1989 and 1990 elections. And it was thoroughly trounced.

The nationalists realized too late that they had little public support and no national organizations. They had not made the transition from the *samizdat* press and the 'thick journals' to electoral politics. Even candidates endorsed by Pamyat in 1989 had tried to distance themselves from the group, and in every district where they had gone head to head with the democratic opposition, they had lost. Yeltsin stole his opponents' best arguments, including nationalism, and won.

As an unofficial spokesman and ideologist for the General Staff, Prokhanov had cultivated intellectual exchanges between nationalist intellectuals and top military and KGB officials – who, he believed, had common cause against the increasingly hegemonic liberals. Marshal Dmitry Yazov, the gruff, owl-like Soviet minister of defence, and Vladimir Kryuchkov, the runty, imperious head of the Soviet KGB, whose inscrutability was accentuated by his bottle-glass spectacle lenses, were increasingly ready to countenance any allies they could find, no matter how marginal.

On 24 March 1990, the military made the first of many overtures to the nationalists. Yazov and Alexey Lizichev, head of the army's main political administration, met a group of nationalist intellectuals headed by Prokhanov. This begat a number of other seminars during this period, where right-wing intellectuals traded ideas with Russia's top generals.[19]

It was around this time that the Soviet Writers' Union decreed that funding should be allocated for an additional newspaper, to be published in parallel with the liberal beacon *Literaturnaya Gazeta*. It was to be housed in the same premises and Prokhanov was to run it. Prokhanov, still writing his memoirs from Afghanistan, set up the new paper, known as *Den* or *The Day*. It was intended to be a Petri dish where the new experimental nationalism could be mixed with hardline communism and imperial nostalgia. Its pages spouted conspiracy theories of Western subversion, anti-Semitism, xenophobia, nationalism and Stalinist National Bolshevism. Its offices on Tsvetnoy Boulevard became a gathering place for generals, deputies, Cossacks, hardline communists and Orthodox priests – but also physicists, mathematicians and high-ranking Communist Party bureaucrats.

The Day was mercilessly attacked by the liberal press, and particularly by its nemesis *Literaturnaya Gazeta*. The two newspapers flanked the political spectrum – one democratic and the other nationalist – both vying to fill the vacuum soon to be left by the demise of communism. It was later described by Gorbachev's reformist-wing man Yakovlev as 'the incubator' of the August 1991 coup by hardline generals. It was, indeed, a test tube for a new ideology born of the frustration and clear failure of official Marxism-Leninism.

As one of Prokhanov's first recruits to the newspaper, Dugin now put his talents as a pamphleteer and propagandist at the service of the praetorian guardians of the USSR. The author of the song 'Fuck the Damned Sovdep' – which had earned him an interrogation by the KGB in 1983 – had evidently undergone some recent personal transformation. Prokhanov saw in Dugin something that was lacking, almost by definition, in Russia's conservative movement – hipness. Still fond of his trademark jodhpurs, his *skobka* haircut and goatee, Dugin 'was energized and young, had fresh ideas. He was like a prophet', according to Prokhanov.

It was not entirely clear what Dugin's job description was. Judging by his articles, he was hired as a professional conspiracy theorist, whose scholarly interest in the esoteric and the occult spiced up an otherwise mundane collection of standard tropes about unseen hands and malevolent forces at work behind the scenes, plotting chaos. 'One of the most pressing themes in our press and political life has become the problem of the conspiracy', wrote Dugin in the very first issue of *The Day*. Penned under the pseudonym 'L. Okhotin' and published in December 1990 under the title 'The Threat of Mondialism', it concerned nascent attempts by a conspiracy of the global elite to create a world government.

Like any competent pamphleteer, Dugin stole most of his material from other pamphleteers. Easily recognizable bugbears appeared in his texts: the Council on Foreign Relations, the Trilateral Commission, the Federal Reserve Board, the Bilderberg Group. These well-worn clichés from fringe American survivalists or bearded European radical leftists suddenly found their way to Russia through Dugin's typewriter. He was a prolific aggregator of conspiracy theories. His first article led off with a famous remark by Kaiser Wilhelm's adviser Walther Rathenau in 1909: 'Three hundred men, all of whom know one another, guide the economic destinies of the Continent and seek their successors from within their own environment.' It was a time-worn conspiracy trope, but one which nevertheless had not been widely circulated in Russian. It and other conspiracy theories were greeted by a public for whom cynicism had become a way of life.

In fact, Russia has always had the somewhat dubious distinction of being the conspiracy capital of the world: the idea of some sort of international secret sect pursuing the same revolutionary aims for decades or centuries, overthrowing the established order and ruling from behind the scenes, is pretty much the textbook definition of the Communist Party of the Soviet Union, which presented the spectacle of government by conspiracy. In fact, no leadership change occurred in 70 years of Soviet history *without* a conspiracy, and the undeniable enthusiasm of the Russian elite for secret plots stretched back into the nineteenth century, when tsarist secret police played a cat-and-mouse game with revolutionaries, each infiltrating the other until it was impossible to tell who was who. In 1904, the tsarist minister of the interior, Vyacheslav von

Plehve, was killed by a bomb thrown under his carriage in St Petersburg. It turned out that the plot had been masterminded by his own agent, Evno Azef, who continued collecting his salary from the police for informing on his revolutionary brethren for four years after the attack.[20] At around the same time, the Okhrana secret police seem to have concocted one of the most infamous conspiracy theories of all time, *The Protocols of the Elders of Zion*, written, according to the most authoritative accounts, at the behest of Petr Rachkovsky, the Okhrana's resident in Paris.

Dugin appears to have had a direct political objective similar to Rachovsky's: to discredit revolutionary elements in Russia which were on the rise, portraying them as some world-spanning, sinister threat. To be fair to Dugin, he has (albeit later) strongly condemned theories of a Jewish plot, rejected revisionism and has denied the authenticity of *The Protocols of the Elders of Zion*. He has not succumbed to the temptation to fit conspiracies around ethnic or confessional prejudices, which would have created the basis for violence. In fact, none of Dugin's conspiracies have any identifiable Leon Trotskys, Baron de Rothschilds or Emmanuel Goldsteins – no physical figures that would serve as targets. While spinning wild fantasies, he kept a studied distance from his theories and took evident care to make sure that his writings would not translate into real hatred or violence directed at actual people. He seems to have combined a commitment to responsible demagoguery with the realization that physical 'targets' were not strictly necessary, and even detracted from the strength of the argument. Evil was at its most evil when it was hidden and amorphous.

'Great War of the Continents', an article written by Dugin in February 1991, was characteristic of this effort – the closest thing to a sensation that ran in *The Day*. Drawn clearly from his readings of geopolitics and his intellectual dalliances with European extreme rightists, Dugin interpreted the esoteric meaning of the Cold War not as a struggle between communism and capitalism, but as a hidden conflict between two concealed elites – the sea people and the land people: 'A planetary conspiracy of two "occult" forces, whose secret confrontation and unwitnessed battle has determined the course of history.'

Out of Dugin's great intellect, random facts were dissolved into laws, and coincidence into consistency. The political turmoil in the former Soviet Union, he argued, was in reality a behind-the-scenes struggle between the shadowy minions of Atlantic power and the agents of Eurasia. He even went so far as to accuse the entire KGB of being a front for the Atlantic conspiracy, while patriotic Eurasians, he said, were their military intelligence rivals in the GRU, which had often had a combative relationship with the KGB – and which remained loyal to the motherland.

Later in life, after he enthusiastically applauded the ascendance of Vladimir Putin, a former KGB colonel, to the presidency, Dugin admitted that he might have been mistaken about the KGB. In a 2005 introduction to an anthology of his conspiracy theories, he alluded to a number of 'inconsistencies, inaccuracies and exaggerations and absurdities' in the original text of 'Great War of the Continents'. His wife Natasha today says categorically of his work from that period: 'Give him a break, he was 28 years old!'

Conspiracy theories were always easy to sell in Russia, where people were accustomed to read the back pages of *Pravda* first, to figure out what stories the government was seeking to suppress. And conspiracy theories in the Soviet Union were prevalent precisely because they were so often true, but also because they were a staple of regime propaganda. Such theories, according to Hannah Arendt, 'are more adequate to the needs of the human mind than reality itself'. The major advantage of conspiracy theories over reality is that reality is not logical, consistent and organized the way a conspiracy theory is. It is worth noting that Europe's twentieth-century totalitarian regimes found that conspiracy theories were always the easiest way of explaining ideology to an otherwise uninterested public. Few Germans understood the racial theories of the Third Reich, and nor did most Russians grasp the fundamentals of dialectical materialism. However, the public eagerly read and believed the *Protocols*, or the Wall Street conspiracy and the Trotskyist conspiracy. In the same way, the conspiracy theory filled the ideological void left by the collapse of communism.

In an effort to explain the incidence of conspiracy theories, some scholars have ascribed their prevalence in some societies either to a form of delusional paranoia, or to a cognitive disorder, in which people are prone to see a pattern or purpose in events where none actually exists. Others regard conspiracy theories as a vestige of religious life, the unseen battle of cosmic good against evil, a secularized fossil of the Judeo-Christian consciousness clothed in modern garb and which can proliferate against the backdrop of social crises.

Dugin adopted a clever stance in this regard, taking turns as both purveyor and ironic deconstructor of his arguments, equating conspiracy theories with myth and religious demonology. He followed 'Great War of the Continents' with 'Introduction to Conspirology' in 1990, in which he analysed his own work: 'The actual existence or non-existence of the conspiracy in question changes nothing. When one analyses religion, one is not concerned with the fact of the existence of god, but with the fact of belief.'[21, 22]

The conspiracy theory was thereby spared any need to prove itself. Rather than setting about proving that the theories were true, Dugin set about proving that they were facts: 'In our case we can say that a "conspiracy", in the most

direct sense of the word, exists insofar as there exists historically and socio-
logically established belief in it.'[23] People who believe in UFOs, grassy-knoll
sceptics and Templar Knights enthusiasts were thereby placed on the same
level as Protestants, Buddhists and Bahais, whose belief is in some sense
protected by a scholarly methodology. When one studies Islam, one's task is
generally not to try to prove or disprove the Qur'an and the Hadith, but to
study the belief as it is incarnated in the world.

The pervasiveness of conspiracy theories, according to Dugin, has a religious,
irrational element: the persistence of 'stable unconscious archetypes that would
ascribe concrete facts and events to mythological paradigms.' 'In conspirology,
there are no rules and laws. Anything can happen.'[24] This was an ironic stance to
take, with Dugin spouting fantastical conspiracy theories and simultaneously
explaining that conspiracy theories are manipulations, fakes, the products of
mental illness, psychiatric fossils of a pre-modern era which, at other times, might
have taken the form of witch-burning. Irony, in other words, was a constant
companion to Dugin's otherwise rather dire-sounding manifestos.

Dugin was simultaneously a critic, a theoretician and a practitioner of an
art in which the three roles are (or should be) mutually exclusive. Such posing
was to be a constant theme running through Dugin's work for two decades.
Two slightly unresolved parallel tracks run through his essays and his books: in
one instance he is a Machiavellian manipulator, mobilizing the gullible in a
propaganda exercise; simultaneously he deconstructs his own work, injecting
doubt and analytical distance.

Indeed, Dugin went to great lengths to let the reader in on his manipulations, and even flagrantly stated them to be such. In 2005, when 'Great War of
the Continents' was republished in an anthology *Conspirology*, Dugin wrote
proudly in the introduction that it represented the era's 'first conscious and
structured attempt at conspirology' – a vague definition but one that quite
clearly indicates a deliberate attempt to mystify and manipulate. But while this
might seemingly defeat the purpose of the conspiracy theory, which is to
convince people that it is actually true, Dugin was in fact employing a clever
rhetorical tool, which was no less effective on a cynical, jaded post-Soviet
public. By giving the reader a peek behind his magician's curtain, he was
building rapport, simultaneously offering his advice with the seductive voice of
a mandarin counsellor who whispered in the ears of princes. It was a pose that
would become his calling card as a skilled propagandist exploiting the reader's
cynicism, rather than his gullibility.

Conspiracy theories, everything from the UFO craze to the Kennedy assassination, are a product of modern times. A growing body of scholarly research
on the prevalence of conspiracy theories has focused mainly on explaining

the irrational element – psychological factors which support such beliefs, for example. However, a minority view argues that the presence of conspiracy theories can at least sometimes be explained by the presence of actual conspiracies.[25]

For the rest of the 1990s, conspiracy theories engulfed Russian society, due to almost all the factors listed above. The collapse of the Soviet Union and the rampant economic crisis that accompanied it were so sudden that they seemed artificial. How to explain, for example, that one of the most powerful states in the world had voluntarily surrendered its hard-won imperial dominions and finally ceased to exist? Surely malevolent forces were at work behind the scenes . . . But the prevalence of conspiracy theories did also appear to track a rise in actual conspiracies. Starting with the August 1991 coup and continuing through the 1990s and 2000s, Russia was ruled by little other than plots, cabals and manipulations. The events of October 1993 were a textbook conspiracy, and the re-election of Boris Yeltsin in 1996 by a group of oligarch bankers, the ascent of Vladimir Putin and the launching of the second Chechen War in 1999 all continue to be hotly debated. The exact nature of the conspiracy that led to them is still a subject of much disagreement, but the fact that each was, fundamentally, a conspiracy is beyond doubt.

And so, it is worth pointing out that while Dugin was producing most of his conspiracy theories, he was actually doing so on behalf of a conspiracy – the group of generals and security men who sought unsuccessfully to sweep to power in the August 1991 coup. Dugin's own position as writer and publicist to a cabal of military men only added to his mystique, and it is an impression that he has always sought to play up. His credibility as a conspiracy theorist was strengthened, in other words, by the impression he created that he was part of a conspiracy. And this, it turns out, was basically accurate.

On 23 July 1991, a long article appeared in the newspaper *Sovetskaya Rossiya*, penned by Prokhanov and signed by several army generals, prominent public intellectuals and government figures who would shortly become famous as the plotters in the doomed coup. (*Sovetskaya Rossiya*, rather than *The Day*, was chosen for the appeal because of its comparatively high circulation of 4.5 million.) The piece was called 'Word to the People'.

> An enormous unprecedented misfortune has occurred. The Motherland, our country, the great state entrusted to us by history, by nature and by our glorious forebears is perishing, is being broken up, is being plunged into darkness and oblivion . . . What has befallen us, Brothers? Why have we allowed evil, pompous rulers, clever and cunning apostates, greedy and wealthy money grabbers, to mock us, jeering at our beliefs, to take advantage

of our naïveté, to seize power, steal our wealth, rob people of their homes, factories and land, cut the country into pieces, turn us against each other and pull the wool over our eyes?

The piece bore the hallmark of the experimental nationalism that was being crafted by Prokhanov in the editorial offices of *The Day*, presumably in cooperation with the military. It was signed by three members of the soon-to-be-infamous State Emergency Committee (GKChP). This was the closest thing to an official statement of ideology that would emerge from the coup plotters: a thumbnail sketch of the ideas they sought to bring with them to power. It was something breathtakingly new: scant reference was made to the Communist Party, and then only as a treasonous Trojan horse 'which is being destroyed by its own leaders, and running into the arms of the enemy'.

Prokhanov referred to the October revolution, but in exclusively negative terms, in the context of significant catastrophes that had befallen the motherland: 'Can we really allow, for the second time in this century, civil strife and war, once again throwing ourselves under the cruel millstone which grinds the bones of the people and breaks the backbone of Russia?' Instead, he emphasized patriotism and statehood, and drew on religious imagery. He even referred to Yeltsin's reformers as 'the new Pharisees'.

> We appeal to the Orthodox Church, emerging from its crucifixion, which is slowly rising from the grave. The Church, whose spiritual light shone in Russian history, even in times of darkness, today ... finds itself worthy of support in a strong sovereign power. Let its clear voice be heard, calling out to save the voice of the people ... We appeal to Muslims, Buddhists, Protestants, believers of all faiths, for whom belief is synonymous with goodness, beauty and truth; they are now being attacked by cruelty, ugliness and lies, the wreck of living creatures.

A new ideal of patriotism was apparent in the article – one that was multiconfessional, linking Russians to their past, to spiritual bonds, and not to an ideological commitment to mankind. The enemy was no longer capitalism, but the hidden penetration by scurrilous foreign saboteurs, democratic reformers 'grovelling before overseas patrons from across the ocean, in search of advice and blessings'.

It was to be the clearest statement of purpose for the clumsily styled GKChP, which would shortly try in vain to reverse the tide of history. Soon, Dugin's Eurasian and Atlanticist conspiracies would leap off the pages of his cranky manifestos and spring, fully formed, to life on the streets of Moscow.

The 'Dawn Object'

Just before 5 o'clock on 18 August 1991, a sweltering Sunday afternoon, five black Volga cars arrived at the gates of Foros, Gorbachev's holiday residence (known as the 'Dawn Object') on the Black Sea coast of Crimea.

Gorbachev told Soviet prosecutors months later that he had not been expecting the visitors – five high-ranking KGB, army and party officials, plus bodyguards – and picked up the phone to call his KGB chief, Vladimir Kryuchkov, to ask what the visit was about. But the line had been cut. He called for the head of his bodyguards, General Vladimir Medvedev, whose black-humoured take on the situation, in the style of KGB generals who had seen it all before, was that this was a 'Khrushchev variant': former Soviet leader Nikita Khrushchev had been removed by a plot while staying at his dacha in Pitsunda in 1964.

The next 73 hours would see a desperate struggle between two rival conspiracies within the Soviet hierarchy to wrest control of history. The delegation, it turned out, had been sent by Kryuchkov himself to recruit Gorbachev to the side of eight party bosses and generals who had agreed to form the State Emergency Committee, the GKChP. The precipitating factor was that two days later, on 20 August, Gorbachev was due to sign a new Union Treaty aimed at transforming the USSR into a confederation, which many feared would precipitate the domino-like break-up of the 70-year-old Soviet Empire into independent states. The GKChP's objective was to secure Gorbachev's agreement to declare a state of emergency, and put off the signing of the treaty.

The coup, of course, achieved the opposite of its intended effect. Not only did it not prevent the break-up of the USSR, but it cemented Boris Yeltsin, president of the Russian Soviet Republic, as the dominant leader of the land and stripped the hardliners of their legitimacy. This drove a stake through the heart of the Union, leading directly to its demise four months later. But exactly what happened during the three tense days after Gorbachev realized that his phone lines had been cut is still hotly disputed by experts, despite thousands of pages of testimony, three separate investigations, nine trials and at least a dozen published personal accounts of the events.

To many, the defeat of the GKChP represented victory for the public politics of the democratic over the reactionary, the totalitarian, the rule of conspiracy and the gun. 'One century ended, the century of fear, and another began', as Boris Yeltsin, who vaulted to power in the coup's aftermath, put it. The enduring image of the ordeal was of Yeltsin standing on a tank in a flak jacket, facing the gun barrels of the regime. But the more one delves into the details, this convenient reading of the stand-off – as a clash between public democracy and totalitarian conspiracy – does not quite fit the facts. Rather than public choice and transparency, what was vindicated in August 1991 was quite likely the superior ability of one side to mystify, mislead and manipulate. In other words, the best conspiracy won.

The following day, 19 August, the morning sun rose on a column of tanks rumbling down Kutuzovsky Prospekt, a broad avenue that leads from the western suburbs towards Moscow's city centre. Dugin remembers being woken by his wife Natasha, and hearing the radio broadcast announcing that, for reasons of ill health, Gorbachev was handing over power to his deputy, Gennady Yanaev. 'It's our coup!' exclaimed Natasha. 'It's our people. They are coming to power!' They were ecstatic.

The radio message went on to say that Russia's democratic reforms were destroying the state, and that it was necessary to prevent the collapse of the USSR. As the GKChP said in its 'Address to the Soviet People':

> In place of the initial enthusiasm and hope came lack of faith, apathy and despair. The government at all levels has lost the trust of the population . . . The country has in essence become ungovernable . . . To remain inactive at this moment, which is critical for the fate of the fatherland, is to assume the weighty responsibility for tragic, unpredictable consequences.

The coup's unwitting propagandists had little inkling of what was to come. Even Prokhanov admits being 'completely surprised' by the rapid sequence of events, and despite having authored the manifesto of the coup, 'Word to the People', he denies any knowledge of the article's role in the unfolding events: 'I was like Pushkin, the Decembrists didn't take him either', he quipped, referencing the poet who acted as a promoter of the 1825 coup attempt by progressive army officers, but was ultimately excluded from participating in it.

The chairman of the Supreme Soviet, Anatoly Lukyanov – Lev Gumilev's great champion – came on the radio, aiding the coup plotters by announcing that the legislatures would not meet for a week, thus giving the plotters time to consolidate their power. 'Lukyanov's speech was like an angel's chorus', Dugin wrote later, 'heralding the new order of respect, honouring the commitment of past statesmen to defend a great power in the face of gathering cosmopolitan crowds that wanted to surrender to Coca-colonialists.'[26]

But from the very first day, the coup was a shambles. The first mistake was obvious: as soon as Lukyanov's address was finished, state television and radio began to play a continuous loop of *Swan Lake*, Tchaikovsky's tragic opera of the triumph of evil over good. But not using the radio and TV to buttress their case with citizens was only the first of many mistakes the plotters made. As Prokhanov says today: 'They could have made a real effort with information, with propaganda, but they had absolutely no idea how to do this. Instead we had *Swan Lake*.'

The rank amateurishness of the coup surprised many of the seasoned veterans of the cut-throat power games at the summit of the Communist Party hierarchy. As Gorbachev's bodyguard General Medvedev wrote in his autobiography:

> It's not as though we don't have experience of coups and bloody mutinies. In fact, unfortunately, we are probably ahead of the rest of the planet on this score . . . They killed Leon Trotsky in a different hemisphere [Stalin's political opponent was assassinated in Mexico in 1940]. So why couldn't they arrest Yeltsin, who was their neighbour?

Another unanswered question is whether Gorbachev, as he has always insisted, was actually under house arrest at Foros with his communications cut off, or, as a number of participants in the events allege, whether his isolation was self-imposed, allowing him to wait to find out the outcome before denouncing the coup, which he did on 21 August. 'If we had won', claims Vasily Starodubtsev, one of the 11 plotters, 'Gorbachev would simply have come back and sat on his throne, as the legitimate president.'

Today, Gorbachev is remembered as the reformer who broke the back of communism and then voluntarily bowed out of history with the fall of the USSR in December 1991. But back in August of that year, his main political opponents were not the hardliners (whom he cultivated, along with reformers, in an effort to secure political survival), but Yeltsin, who in June of that year had been elected president of the Russian Soviet Republic, giving him a broad political mandate alongside the popular charisma of a reformer. Gorbachev's attitude towards the new Union Treaty he was supposed to sign on 20 August was difficult to read; if the Soviet Union collapsed, he, as its president, was out of a job. He may have been looking for reasons not to go ahead, and the GKChP was a too-convenient outcome. 'We were the arms and hands of Gorbachev, who knew everything', the elderly Starodubtsev told me in 2011 shortly before his death, a crease of certainty on his face.[27]

The whispered questions are not limited to disgruntled ex-hardliners. Yeltsin himself, after years of backing Gorbachev's version publicly, told a television interviewer from the Russian channel Rossiya in 2006 that, in the days before the putsch, he and other reformers had tried to convince Gorbachev to fire Kryuchkov, but that Gorbachev had refused: 'He [Gorbachev] knew about this before the putsch began, this is documented, and during the putsch he was informed about everything and all the while was waiting to see who would win, us or them. In either case he would have joined the victors.' The Gorbachev Foundation in Moscow answered this charge in a press release: 'In blackening Gorbachev's name, Yeltsin is trying to rid himself of the guilt for the Belovezh Agreement [which abolished the USSR in December 1991] and other actions which led to the fall of the Union.' Soon after the piece was aired, Yeltsin died, closing the book on the spat forever.

According to Valery Boldin, Gorbachev's chief of staff, who was among the delegation sent to recruit him, the Soviet leader wanted to get rid of Yeltsin at any price. 'Gorbachev did not want to be present during the fight that was inevitably going to take place', Boldin told the *Kommersant* newspaper in 2001. 'He knew (and maybe even gave the command) that what happened during his holiday was going to happen.' Gorbachev insists that he was under house arrest and believed that his and his family's lives were in danger. After the delegation flew back to Moscow, both Gorbachev and his wife Raisa (who died in 1999) described the fear they felt during the three days at Foros. According to Leonid Proshkin, an investigator at the Soviet prosecutor's office who interviewed her after the events, Raisa Gorbacheva said she had even suffered a minor heart attack. 'They were really living in distress', he said, adding that they had refused to eat much during their three-day ordeal for fear of being poisoned. But the question remains open as to whether, had he wanted to, Gorbachev could have communicated to prove that he was not ill, as his vice-president (and coup plotter) Gennady Yanaev told a press conference the following day, after assuming Gorbachev's functions:

Mikhail Sergeevich [Gorbachev] is now on vacation. He is undergoing treatment in the south of our country. He is very tired after so many years and will need some time to recover, but it is our hope – it is our hope – that as soon as Mikhail Gorbachev feels better, he will take up his office again.

It is clear that Gorbachev never tried to leave Foros. Nor, it seems, did he try very hard to communicate with anyone outside in an effort to clear up the mystery of his absence during the coup. While his battery of government phones was indeed cut off on Kryuchkov's orders, the radio phone in his car was still operational, as were the phones in his guard house. 'He could have called from his car, or from the inter-city phones', said Oleg Baklanov, another member of the delegation, who hotly denies that Gorbachev was held prisoner.

Historian John Dunlop, whose 2003 article on the coup is considered the best academic work on the events in the West, says that during a visit to Stanford University in 1996, he was told by Alexander Yakovlev, Gorbachev's chief reformer: 'What I don't understand is why Gorbachev didn't just get up and leave. The guards would never have attempted to stop him.'[28] So long as he remained plausibly incommunicado, he was in a perfect position. If the coup failed, he could say (as he did) that he had been held against his will. If the coup succeeded, he was in a perfect position to endorse it later on. 'It appears that Gorbachev permitted the coup to go forward while declining to associate himself with it openly', concludes Dunlop.[29]

But without Gorbachev's explicit endorsement to give it legitimacy, the coup could only rely on military force, which was its undoing. Field Marshal Dmitry Yazov, the defence minister, who ordered tanks into the centre of Moscow, has since admitted several mistakes in execution. As he told an interviewer in 1997:

> The GKChP was complete improvisation. There were no plans, no one planned to arrest Yeltsin or storm the White House [the Supreme Soviet building]. We thought the people would understand us and support us. But they all hurled abuse at us for sending tanks into downtown Moscow.[30]

For starters, the military's loyalties had been badly frayed by a series of botched and bloody operations against civilian protesters in the previous two years. These left the military men with little appetite for politics, especially in the centre of Moscow. It also left the door open for Yeltsin to befriend disgruntled commanders. The only unit the putschists felt they could rely on was the KGB's Alpha Group, the elite counterterrorism team. But in this, the plotters also miscalculated. The Alpha Group demanded written orders to storm the White House, and when these were not forthcoming, they sat the crisis out.

On the afternoon of 19 August, Yeltsin drove into Moscow from his dacha, apparently passing unawares the KGB team that had been deployed in the forest with orders to arrest him. In Moscow, he walked out of the White House, mounted a tank that had defected to his side, and made his famous television address: 'I call on all Russians to give a dignified answer to the putschists and demand that the country be returned to normal constitutional order.' Protests held that day were not broken up, and foreign television crews moved around Moscow unhindered. Tens of thousands of protesters gathered to defend the White House, amid TV images of tanks with the tricolour flag of Democratic Russia waving from their turrets.

It was clear from the first day that the coup was doomed. Dugin knew it the moment he went out onto the streets and saw a throng of people on Arbat Street heading towards the Supreme Soviet building to demonstrate in favour of Yeltsin. 'I understood as I was watching this crowd, that these are like pigs walking over the cliff, like in the Bible. I understood that for the first time I am for the Soviet Union, just as it was about to die, I loved it.'

The coup plotters had not entertained the possibility that they would encounter spirited and brave resistance, and were unwilling to shoot on crowds. Three protesters were killed on the night of 20/21 August, but it was apparently an accident, after they had tried to 'blind' an armoured personnel carrier by pulling a tarp over the view slit, and it ran over them.

To be fair to the conspiracy theorists like Dugin, to this day it remains unclear how much assistance the US rendered to Yeltsin, who seemed to have been informed in real time of all the communications the GKChP plotters had passed between one another. According to Yakovlev in his 2005 memoirs, US intelligence warned Gorbachev of the impending coup – warnings that Gorbachev ignored (indeed, as we have seen, he may actually have been in on it). US journalist Seymour Hersh wrote in the *Atlantic Monthly* in 1994 that (much against the wishes of the National Security Agency), US President George H.W. Bush had ordered that Yeltsin should be provided with sensitive communications intelligence about what Kryuchkov and Yazov were telling the ground commanders. 'We told Yeltsin in real time what the communications were', wrote Hersh, quoting a US official.[31] Meanwhile Yeltsin himself readily admitted in his autobiography to having been in contact with the US embassy, and said that US diplomats had visited him during the siege of the White House. He even considered an escape plan that would have smuggled him into the US embassy, a few steps from the White House, though he declined because 'people in our country don't like it when foreigners take too active a role in our affairs'.

The night of 20 August presents a few more questions. According to Yeltsin, 'all sources were reporting that the GKChP had decided to go ahead with the storming of the White House'. However, according to his press secretary Pavel Voshchanov, Yeltsin spent that night drinking and feasting in the basement. It is possible that US communications intercepts of the deteriorating morale among the plotters were what was buttressing Yeltsin's confidence. General Medvedev writes in his autobiography that 'Yeltsin knew that there would be no storming [of the White House]' – though he is coy about where the information came from.

Around that time, it does appear that the commander of the KGB's Alpha commandos tried to order his men to storm the White House at 3 a.m., but his subordinates again refused, saying they were being 'set up for the nth time', according to an interview by airborne forces commander Pavel Grachev in the newspaper *Izvestiya* a few weeks later.

It was clear that by not moving decisively in the early hours, the coup plotters had given up the advantage and allowed the military to split. When the storming of the White House failed to take place, Defence Minister Dmitry

Yazov ordered military units out of the city, setting the stage for the denoue-ment the following day, when Gorbachev came back on line, publicly upbraiding the plotters who had flown to Foros for unclear reasons. Following their return to Moscow, they were arrested.

Kryuchkov has repeatedly said that the plotters' main mistake was not to use the airwaves to make a public call for support. As he said in 2001: 'We should have made the case to the people and opened their eyes to the danger which the country faced.'[32] And in 2006 he mused: 'I cannot say whether the people actively supported us or not, but if we had made the call, the people would have come out onto the streets.'[33] But Yazov gave the most convincing analysis of the coup's failure, when he admitted that he could not himself answer the question of why the coup was needed: 'People always ask me: why did you never give the command to fire? And I ask: and who to shoot at? In the name of what? So that Gorbachev could stay in power?'[34]

The hardliners had placed their faith in the power of tanks and soldiers, but realized too late that without an answer to the question 'Why?' they could not use them. They had spurned the public politics of democracy, but found that even if they wanted power at the point of a gun, they still needed a message, an idea, a reason for being. They still needed to explain themselves, and they could not. 'They seriously thought that history could be operated by telephone', says Dugin today.

The totally surreal death of their beloved Soviet Union astounded and capti-vated the Soviet hardliners. The coup and its aftermath did not feel like a momen-tous historical turning point: it had none of the weight, none of the consequences that would normally accompany events of this magnitude. This, they had been led to believe, was an earthquake in world history, comparable to 1789 and 1917. But it was nonsense: history demands sacrifices in blood; it advances across the bones of those it supersedes and confines to oblivion. The dawning of a new paradigm, the surrender of one totality and its replacement by a new one, should at least have been accompanied by drama and a large body count.

Yet in the three days that sounded the death knell of the Soviet Union, a total of three people lost their lives (in an accident – see above), and 11 went to prison for a matter of months. The highest drama was Yeltsin's made-for-TV spectacle of mounting a tank in front of the White House and addressing the public – yet this was CNN footage and was not even seen inside the USSR. Prokhanov felt he had just witnessed 'a giant simulation, a piece of theatre'. In the space of three days, without a shot being fired, the greatest superstate the world had ever seen was destroyed.

With the end of the coup on 21 August and Gorbachev's return to Moscow on 22 August, the USSR was dead. *The Day*, as the incubator of the coup, was closed temporarily, and its arch rival *Literaturnaya Gazeta*, across the hall at the USSR Writers' Union, published an exposé of its funding via Yazov's Ministry of Defence.

Dugin returned to work, but the country was falling apart around him. Gorbachev was finished as a politician, and everyone knew that the USSR could not survive. Slowly the negotiations got under way to manage the collapse as peacefully as possible.

Yeltsin, the president of the Russian Soviet Republic, who before the coup had already been working on plans for a Russian secession from the Soviet Union, now redoubled his efforts. In December of that year he met the chairman of the Ukrainian Communist Party, Leonid Kravchuk, and Stanislav Shushkevich, chairman of the Belarusian Supreme Soviet, in the Belovezh forest resort near Minsk, and dissolved the Union, presenting Gorbachev with a fait accompli.

In his quest to be rid of his rival, Yeltsin destroyed the Soviet Union, putting Gorbachev, its head, out of a job. One-quarter of the territory of the Soviet Union seceded over the next few months, and on 25 December the Soviet flag was lowered from the flagpole of the Kremlin forever, to be replaced with the tricolour of Democratic Russia. That was the day, says Dugin, that he became a 'Soviet man' for ever.[35] As he wrote later:

> I realized that I had become, totally, irreversibly a Soviet man. Fatally, triumphally Soviet. This after so many tortured years of implacable hatred for my surroundings, for the 'Sovdep', and following my radical, uncompromising national nonconfomism. Of course I always hated the West as well ... But in that August, (despite much conscious effort) all the internal logic of my soul was on the side of the Emergency Committee.[36]

* * *

The GKChP had delivered a victory for Yeltsin, but not a decisive one. He still had to contend with a profoundly divided society, as well as with a bureaucratic apparatus and security services that were overwhelmingly loyal to the old order, which had secured their privileges.

Soviet hardliners and patriots made their peace with the new era, but for many, these 'last soldiers of empire' did little to hide their antipathy towards Yeltsin, and clung to their belief that they had been defeated by a new, postmodern enemy (rather than simply being on the wrong side of history). Behind the scenes, old hardliners confronted a new generation of liberals in bureaucratic battles over reform across the state apparatus. This was especially noticeable in the military and special services, where loyalty to Yeltsin was so low that his bodyguard, Alexander Korzhakov, said that he was forced to create a 'mini KGB' – inside the KGB – of Kremlin loyalists.[37]

The shadowy confrontation between new-order loyalists and old-era hard-liners went largely unwitnessed by the public. However, there is evidence that Dugin and Prokhanov's fantastical stories about rival conspiracies battling at the heart of the Russian state were not so far off the mark. We have already seen evidence of one major conspiracy by Russia's security services in the post-Soviet era – that organized by Kryuchkov and Yazov (and quite possibly Gorbachev) in 1991. This is hardly an example of omnipotent behind-the-scenes manipulators – it was an obvious failure. But the existence of this plot does make clear the undeniable enthusiasm of Russia's elite for conspiracies. And the fact that the recent GKChP conspiracy failed does not mean that other, more successful ones do not exist – particularly since the definition of success in this is instance precisely that we do not know about them.

'Deep states' – conspiracies by military and security men to rule from behind the scenes – are a regular feature of new and unstable democracies. A small elite, well represented in the military or security services, will, almost without exception, feel it too risky to cede full control to a civilian constitutional govern-ment. This is both on account of concern for its own privileges and because of a well-justified fear that politically immature societies are easily seduced by populism and demagoguery. It is a fact that such 'deep state' plots are actually known to have existed in several modern states in the post-war era. One of the best known (thanks to several court cases beginning in 2008) is the *derin devlet*, 'deep state' in Turkish, in which the military and security services of Turkey sought to guide successive civilian governments from behind the scenes, through decades of turmoil.

Other well-known examples have been a number of anti-communist conspiracies in southern European states during the Cold War – such as the P2 Masonic lodge in Italy, which is so legendary that it is hard to separate myth from reality. But several respected researchers have come to the conclusion that it is not a myth: they argue that it did in fact sponsor right-wing terror and had links to the CIA, with serving generals, bankers and admirals as members. Meanwhile, successive military dictatorships in Spain, Portugal, Brazil, Argentina and Chile in the post-war era, through the 1970s and 1980s, all follow this model of a military–security 'deep state', which periodically inter-vened when the politicians lost their way, and then stepped back into the shadows during periods of civilian rule. There is no guarantee, however, that the self-appointed guardians of the 'deep state' will not themselves be seduced by the same trappings of power.

That Russia had a 'deep state' around August 1991 is very clear; but it is not so clear what became of it following the failure of the coup. Dugin's further career is evidence of a continuation of such a subterranean organization, a conspiracy of sorts. However, any 'deep state' in Russia circa 1992 would have had very little consensus about what it sought to achieve. Communism enjoyed zero prestige as an idea, while Russian nationalism, the other competitor in the field of opposition ideologies, had just led to the dissolution of the USSR. Any attempt to recreate the Soviet Empire would have stumbled at the first hurdle – thus the question posed by Yazov: Why, and in whose name?

This ideological vacuum was what created work for public intellectuals like Dugin and Prokhanov, both of whom had numerous connections to the national security bureaucracy. Prokhanov secured Dugin a rather interesting teaching credential – a lectureship at what was formerly the Soviet (now Russian) Academy of the General Staff. This was led by a good friend of Prokhanov's, General Igor Rodionov, who from 1985 to 1986 had led the Soviet 40th Army in Afghanistan, where indeed the two had met.

With Rodionov's permission, Dugin joined the Academy as an adjunct professor, and began as a guest lecturer in the department of strategy, under General Nikolay Klokotov. 'This was all new', Rodionov told me when I invited him over to the *Financial Times* offices in Moscow to talk about his days at the Academy. Over the space of an hour and a half, the tale unfolded:

> In the Soviet Union hardly anyone studied geopolitics. This type of analysis was done only in the central committee. Under the [Communist Party] everything else was forbidden, prohibited. You could only talk about it whispering in the kitchen with a glass of vodka with friends a little bit. And if the special services found out they would take measures. Then, suddenly, we had this freedom to say what we wanted.

The Academy was the premier officer-training establishment for the Soviet (now Russian) army, but for Rodionov it had been a humiliating demotion. At the height of his career he had been commander of the 40th Army in Afghanistan, and then commander of the entire Transcaucasian military district. But in April 1989 came his professional downfall. On his orders, Soviet paratroopers attacked a pro-democracy demonstration in Tbilisi, Georgia. Twenty-one people were killed in a stampede. Most died of suffocation, though some were killed by shovels and baton blows from the soldiers. The incident was hung around Rodionov's neck: 'No one wanted to take responsibility that they gave me the order, they needed a scapegoat, and it was me.'[38]

Rodionov had little respect for politicians during his career, and even less now that he had, in his prime years, been assigned to command the Academy, a traditional dumping ground for those who had fallen out of favour. He had commanded entire armies in the field as a general; now he was a teacher, a professor. It was a humiliation. His bitterness at this betrayal by the politicians was combined with the existential crisis that the fall of the Soviet Union created for him and his fellow officers.

The Academy thus became a hive of opposition to the government of Boris Yeltsin and liberal reformers – a bastion of hardcore reactionary zeal that supported Dugin's work and nourished him with strategic insights, while he fed the generals with the new thinking of the European extreme right. That said, Rodionov never totally burned his bridges with the establishment and was appointed defence minister by Yeltsin in 1996–97. It was in the Academy that the first ideological experimentation began between hardcore right-wing fanatics and the Russian establishment. Dugin and Prokhanov began a project to construct a hybrid ideology from the mutually contradictory elements of the two losing ideologies, nationalism and communism. They replaced the outdated vocabulary of monarchism and orthodoxy with new terms and phrases taken straight from the pages of Dugin's primers on geopolitics. 'Eurasia' began to take shape – a mix of Gumilev's theories and Golovin's alcohol-fuelled beatnikism with a dash of Russian fascism thrown in for good measure.

'Prokhanov opened the road for me', said Dugin in a 2005 interview. Within the space of a vertiginous three years he had gone from being a maladjusted fringe radical and member of a banned political organization to lecturing at the heart of the former USSR's security establishment, with (presumably) security clearance. His was a position that, just months previously, a dissident such as himself could never have hoped to obtain, and the notion of which would have been preposterous: 'I had no social status, it was incredible to think that they saw me as an equal, or could learn something from me.' Dugin's discussions with the generals opened up vistas for him. With the collapse of communism and official ideology, 'They were utterly lost, they had no concept of the enemy; they needed to know who the enemy was.'

* * *

It would have been hard to find more fitting evidence of the end of politics as he knew it, thought de Benoist at the time. Here he was, the leading ideologue of one of Europe's most right-wing political organizations, walking in to meet the commanders of the Red Army.

It was the end of March 1992. A few weeks earlier he had received an invitation from his acquaintance Dugin: come to Moscow and meet some people. There might be something to talk about. A few weeks after the invitation, de Benoist received a paid air ticket in the mail, then a visa.

When he arrived in Moscow he was met at the airport by an official government car, a black Volga sedan with curtains over the windows. It drove him into the city and on to the Hotel Ukraine, a spired cathedral of a building overlooking the river and what was then the new Russian parliament building on the other side – the White House.

The next morning, the black Volga picked him up at the hotel and sped through downtown Moscow, past the brooding spires of the Kremlin, and zipping down the centre lane of the broad Vernadsky Prospekt, out to the western outskirts of the city and to a palatial white-painted complex: the Frunze Academy of the General Staff. Dugin met de Benoist as he emerged from the car. He explained that he was a lecturer at the Academy, whose purpose it was to train Soviet officers ranked colonel and above in strategy and to prepare them for command of entire divisions or for staff positions in the high command (or *Genstab*) itself. Inside the Academy, the halls were dimly lit. Dugin stopped by the generals' offices, one by one. And each general joined the procession heading for a conference room. There were seven generals in all, led by Lieutenant General Nikolay Klokotov, head of the department of strategy.

It dawned on de Benoist that in order to lecture at the academy, security clearance, background checks and high-level connections were all required. If Dugin were a simple dilettante, he would not even be permitted in the Academy's car park. His association with the generals had to be more than just a casual one.

As they filed into a conference room for tea and cakes and a chat, it occurred to de Benoist that the generals looked 'like orphans'. The state they had spent their lives defending had disappeared overnight, without a shot being fired, and was mourned by no one. Fifteen former republics – lands which these men's ancestors, generals of the Russian Empire, had added to Russia and paid for in blood – had declared themselves independent. Prices had gone through the roof; starvation was imminent and the economy was in a state of total collapse.

Less than a year previously, army tanks had roared into downtown Moscow to intervene in the midst of the coup attempt. Maybe they sensed that in another year, in October 1993, they would be drawn into the midst of another constitutional crisis. The skeletal hand of civil war beckoned.

The nation's mighty officer corps had defeated Hitler and Napoleon. But it now succumbed to a new enemy which no amount of battlefield prowess or hard power could defeat. The enemy it faced, in other words, was the *lack* of an enemy – a problem adeptly diagnosed by de Benoist. 'All strategic conceptions are based on the understanding of a main enemy. Today, who is your enemy?' asked de Benoist, according to a transcript published by Dugin in the first issue of *Elements* magazine. 'One must answer indirectly, without, so to speak, naming names', responded Klokotov. 'If a state pretends to a certain role in world affairs, it must define itself in terms of military policy. And this policy must be based on who it will likely meet on the battlefield. Any state intending a leadership role must orient itself against the strongest element.'

Dugin sat quietly, translating the entire exchange from and into French. Communism had disappeared. Other empires had crumbled – the British, the Ottoman, the Austro-Hungarian – but Russia, they believed, would not succumb to this logic. Russia had not been defeated by history, but was rather temporarily indisposed. It simply needed some time and space to reassert itself. General Klokotov went on:

> Historical experience gives us hope. The entire history of Russia is made up
> of profound crises, marked by the dispersal of peoples and territories which
> it has traditionally federalized. However, the centralizing forces have always
> proven to be the strongest . . . the imperial constants always reappear.

The meeting was the beginning of a channel for New Right ideas to find their way into Russia's mainstream. Just as in Germany in the 1930s, the turmoil and economic chaos of Russia's 'Weimar Era' provided fertile ground for narratives of cultural humiliation and victimization by a global elite, as well as of identity, national purity, anti-liberalism and geopolitics – all standard tropes of Europe's extreme right.[39]

De Benoist and several other New Right figures, such as Robert Steuckers and Jean-François Thiriart, came on various trips arranged by Dugin and Prokhanov to meet army generals and politicians representing the vanquished nationalist and communist political extremes. Dugin's geopolitics, borrowed from the New Right, would simply supplement and mould the already highly developed nationalist consciousness of the army.

From 1992 until 1995, Dugin held fortnightly lectures at the General Staff Academy under Rodionov's auspices. 'We had a lot of such meetings at the Academy', said Rodionov, who added that he was often called into the office of Defence Minister Evgeny Shaposhnikov to account for why he had invited hardline ultra-nationalists, such as Vladimir Zhirinovsky and Dugin. However, there was little anyone could do about it. The state was in chaos, and random lectures on political philosophy were not the greatest threat facing the Russian army, which had to pay salaries, secure nuclear stockpiles and vacate entire countries.

Rodionov said that the idea of teaching political theory was frowned upon, but his own collision with big politics had taught him that his soldiers should have a grounding in the subject: 'I had already commanded a military district, I felt it was my responsibility to teach the officers not just to understand strategy, but also to understand what is going on in the state, and what awaits us in the future.'

Dugin says he wasn't paid a salary – or given an ID badge, as he recalls. Instead, he was picked up for his lectures and dropped off home again in military cars. After the lectures they would all go out to eat and drink, staying up late into the night discussing matters. These meetings would plant the seed of European extreme-right theory in the fertile ground of Russia's military *nomenklatura*, shorn of its status and privilege, and there it began to germinate.

Slowly, Dugin's teaching materials and notes, along with the suggestions of his audience, took shape as a textbook. It was assigned during the 1993/94 academic year, and would later be published as the blockbuster *Foundations of Geopolitics* in 1997. 'Geopolitics, it filled the vacuum of their strategic thinking', Dugin told me.

> It was a kind of psychotherapy for them . . . Imagine the shock they were feeling: they had always been told the US is our enemy. Suddenly some democrats come to power, and they say, no, the US is our friend. Because there is no ideology. They were all confused. Their job is to aim missiles and they need to be clear . . . This was once an elite caste, responsible for huge institutes, thousands and thousands of warheads. And suddenly, these democrats come and take away everything from this hugely respected caste. And nobody offers them anything. I come to them and say, 'America is our enemy, we must aim our missiles at them', and they say 'Yes that is correct.' And I explained why.

It is today not entirely clear who financed the trips by the European Nouvelle Droite to Russia, or with what goal. Dugin, asked about this in 2005, said some associates of Prokhanov's (whom he described as 'bandits' and declined to name) put up the money. Their idea, he said, was to 'upgrade their previous, paradigmatical strategic thinking . . . This is something they needed absolutely, and that is why they were willing to disregard the total absence of social status in my case.'

It was out of these meetings that the first use of the term 'Eurasianism', along with the pervasive terminology of geopolitics, began to creep into the

Russian mainstream. Twenty years before they were adopted by the Kremlin under Putin as a more or less official ideology, they began life in a series of discussions with the European right.

According to transcripts published in *The Day*, *Elements* and Steuckers' own *Vouloir* (based on *The Day* transcript), during a later meeting with Russian parliamentarians de Benoist repeatedly called for a Eurasian alliance 'on the level of culture, economy, and possibly military strategic as both necessary and desirable'.[40] Steuckers, who had also journeyed to Moscow for some of the meetings, said, according to the same transcript: 'We are condemned to continental alliance, just as we are condemned, in the geopolitical sense, to see in the United States a common enemy.' It is striking the way in which the vocabulary and concepts that were current in the New Right began to seep into the Russian political opposition.

De Benoist also once met Gennady Zyuganov, at the time a rising star within the reformed Communist Party of the Russian Federation (KPRF), the provincial rump of the banned Communist Party of the Soviet Union (CPSU), which was to become the perennially second most powerful party in national politics, after a succession of official Kremlin-backed parties. When Zyuganov succeeded as chairman of the KPRF, he proceeded to retool the party with new nationalist messages that had little in common with an orthodox socialist message, and were strikingly similar to the 'radical centre' theories that Dugin says he imbibed from the European New Right (but which de Benoist insists he is not responsible for).

As we have seen, the Frenchman is dismissive about the influence his theories had – channelled via Dugin and Prokhanov – on Russian politics. 'I cannot take responsibility for the representation of my writings in a language I don't understand', he has said. He is seemingly suspicious that some of his words have been translated inaccurately or invented – something that seems obvious in light of Dugin's version, compared to his own.

In a 1993 interview, de Benoist described a number of ideological divergences with Dugin. After that the two ceased communication for a number of years. 'I have a lot of reservations about a "Eurasian" construction, which seems to me to be mainly phantasmagorical', de Benoist told philosopher Pierre-André Taguieff.[41] But de Benoist remained one of Dugin's chief inspirations. And in the words of some mutual acquaintances, the European theories filtered through Dugin were decisive in the ideology of the post-Soviet Communist Party, which was to go on to be the largest and most influential opposition political group in Russia for the next two decades.

Those close to both Zyuganov and Dugin, for example, said that many of Zyuganov's ideas were originally Dugin's, and the latter happily takes credit for

the ideologically Eurasianist line of the Communist Party, writing: 'At the critical moment of ideological choice, Zyuganov placed a bet on neo-Eurasianist
populism, the main contours of which were described and formulated by
myself and my colleagues at *The Day* newspaper'.[42] Dugin's view is supported
by Alexey Poberezkin, chairman of the Spiritual Heritage think tank, which
published most of Zyuganov's books and helped to finance the party.[43] Gennady
Seleznev, former Duma speaker and Zyuganov's perpetual rival for power until
he was forced out of the party in 2002, says the same.

Thus began the first experiment with what Dugin referred to as 'National
Bolshevism' (and what came to be known as 'Red Brown' ideology in the
Russian press): the marriage of communist ideology with hardline nationalism
and geopolitics.

CHAPTER TEN

SATAN'S BALL

Moscow's Central House of Writers is, for both good and bad reasons, one of the most written-about buildings in Russian literature of the twentieth century. Built on leafy Herzen Street (now Bolshaya Nikitskaya) in 1934 by Stalin to house the USSR's Writers' Union, membership was a bauble awarded to the loyal, denoting membership of the elite club of the purveyors of official culture.

One of the few proper functioning restaurants in Moscow in hard times, the Central House of Writers (Tsentralny Dom Literatov – TsDL) was endlessly hagiographed by favour-seeking hacks who spun its rather bland official atmosphere as an incubator of literary genius. But it was just as large a bull's eye for dissident writers and satirists such as Mikhail Bulgakov, who featured it as the 'House of Griboedov' in *The Master and Margarita* (from which the reputation of the building never recovered). The TsDL was the slightly adjusted 'old, two-storeyed, cream-coloured house' with an asphalt veranda into which the novel's poet Ivan Bezdomny bursts, half-crazed having witnessed Satan and a giant pistol-toting housecat decapitate the head of the Writers' Union, carrying a wedding candle and wearing only his underwear (and causing a major ruckus).

There was a certain symmetrical and slightly demonic surrealism in the air in December 1992 when Prokhanov, chairman of the Russian Writers' Union, threw a gala dinner there for opposition nationalists. One of these happened to be Eduard Limonov, a wiry, goateed dissident, recently arrived back from exile in France, having decided, according to his own account, 'that it was time to interfere in history as it was unfolding in Russia'. Another attendee happened to be Dugin, sporting his pudding-bowl *skobka* haircut ('*à la* a young Alexey Tolstoy', as Limonov recollected). He had clearly been drinking before he arrived.

There, at tables festooned with fine food and endless bottles of liquor, were assembled the *beau monde* of hardline nationalism in Russia. At one table was

Prokhanov. *The Day* was the nerve centre of the patriotic opposition, the 'ship of dignity in the midst of an ocean of shamelessness and hyper conformism', according to Dugin, who called Prokhanov the 'Russian Don Quixote' for his continued idealistic loyalty to the lost cause. Across the room sat Zyuganov, the potato-faced chairman of the rejuvenated Communist Party, with whom Dugin was currently feuding, accusing him (justifiably) of stealing his ideas.

By 1992, the 'Red Brown' opposition was a pastiche of contradictions: Orthodox monks carrying portraits of Stalin and retired Soviet Army political officers alongside atamans of refounded Cossack troops; appeals to proletarian internationalism vying with the darkest anti-Semitism in the same speeches. New opposition organizations sprang up like mushrooms, mostly on the model of the old ultra-nationalist gang Pamyat. These mainly consisted of a rabid, polyphonic leader, some armbands and a bit of money from who knew where.

The evening featured a host of other nationalist political and cultural figures, such as deputy speaker of the Duma, Sergey Baburin; Stanislav Kunyayev, chief editor of the nationalist 'thick journal' *Nash Sovremennik*; Valentin Rasputin, the acclaimed nationalist author; and the mathematician Igor Shafarevich, author of famous *samizdat* essays.

Limonov himself was a recent convert to the nationalist cause. A former dissident writer, like Solzhenitsyn he was exiled in the early 1970s. (Or, as he put it: 'I was detained by the KGB in 1973 and they suggested I emigrate.') He had lived for years in the US and France before returning to Russia following the collapse of communism. Unlike other exiles who came back to a life of slippers, tea and occasional quotes in the newspaper decrying the state of the country for an audience that barely remembered them, Limonov was determined to make his mark once again.

He had not had the average dissident's life in the US. He was no Joseph Brodsky or Alexander Solzhenitsyn, retiring to the rural perfection of Vermont. Nor did he stay in the nostalgic lap of the Russian émigré community in Brighton Beach. Instead Limonov took to 1970s America like a fish to water: sex, drugs, rock 'n' roll. Limonov's world revolved around Manhattan's Lower East Side – the drugs, the punk scene of the CBGB music club, the Ramones and plenty of heroin. His first and most famous book, *It's Me, Eddie*, was completed in New York in 1976 and managed to shock the jaded US literary establishment with the tale of 'Eddie', a Russian émigré writer, who (one only hopes) was not based entirely on Limonov himself. Solzhenitsyn famously called it 'pornographic'. 'I am on welfare. I live at your expense, you pay taxes and I don't do a fucking thing', wrote Limonov in one of the most oft-quoted portions of the book. 'I consider myself to be scum, the dregs of society, I have no shame or conscience.' The book was an account of the disintegration of

Limonov's first marriage soon after he emigrated to New York with his wife Elena Shapova, a stunning Russian beauty who left him for an Italian aristocrat. It records his feelings of betrayal by both his native Soviet Union and the ugly American capitalism that confronted him. In agony over his divorce, Eddie turns to homosexuality, while Elena overdoses on sex and drugs – exploits recorded by Limonov in several rather graphic passages. She is 'typically Russian, throwing herself into the very thick of life without reflection'.[1]

Limonov managed to catch the American zeitgeist at just the right time. An edgy beatnik, he was more a personality than a writer, trading on his mysterious, unhinged Russianness, which still had scarcity value on the New York literary scene. He played to the crowd, with stereotypical Russian temper and drunken exploits, dating a succession of models after Shapova. He also married another striking model, Natalya Medvedeva, who posed for *Playboy* and whose face adorns the cover of The Cars' first album.

Limonov collided with the typical immigrant's emotional response to living in the United States, with its vast wealth, its impersonal and arm's-length social culture, and its intolerance of emotion. 'I scorn you because you lead dull lives, sell yourselves into the slavery of work', he addresses US readers in a characteristic passage. Limonov's feelings of provincial inadequacy, nostalgia for the vanished motherland and unvanquished resurgent pride in his nation show through in his writings. He loved and hated his boring, hidebound country, his cobwebbed and creaking Russian culture living on the achievements of a century ago:

> I think vicious thoughts about the whole of my loathsome native Russian literature, which has been largely responsible for my life. Dull green bastards, Chekhov languishing in boredom, his eternal students, people who don't know how to get themselves going, who vegetate through this life, they lurk in these pages like diaphanous husks . . . I hate the past, as I always have, the name of the present.[2]

In the United States, Limonov confronted the inferiority complex that is often the wellspring of radicalism, driven inwards by the agoraphobia of modern America. He became a nationalist who had no real use for the nation, a loose cannon looking for a cause. Nation for him wasn't a value, it was a purpose. As he put it in *Eddie*:

> Whom shall I meet, what lies ahead, none can guess. I may happen upon a group of armed extremists, renegades like myself, and perish in an airplane hijacking or a bank robbery. I may not, and I'll go away somewhere, to the

Palestinians, if they survive, or to Colonel Qaddafi in Libya, or someplace else – to lay down Eddie-baby's life for a people, for a nation.

It was in this vein that he found the perfect outlet for his intellectual energy in the cause of Serbia, where he witnessed (and some say participated in) the shelling of besieged Sarajevo in 1992.[3]

The fighting in Yugoslavia had become a magnet for many Russian nationalists, who saw in Serbia a fellow Orthodox Slavic civilization under siege, and in the break-up of Yugoslavia a microcosm of Russia's humiliation following the collapse of the USSR. Russian state television broadcast sympathetic portrayals of the Serbs, even as they proceeded to commit the worst genocide Europe had seen since 1945. Russian volunteers organized into two battalions, one Cossack-led, the other led by a former Russian general.

Limonov's pro-Serbian sympathies fit the bad-boy image he had worked so hard to cultivate in polite Parisian literary society. He has been persona non grata in Western literary circles ever since he was filmed shooting a machine gun into a besieged Sarajevo, in the company of Bosnian Serb leader Radovan Karadžić. He claims he was only shooting at a practice target range. The incident – captured by Bafta award-winning director Pawel Pawlikowski in his *Serbian Epics* documentary and shown at Karadžić's trial at The Hague – cost Limonov publishing contracts in both Europe and the US.

In Belgrade he had met Vojislav Šešelj, head of the Serbian Radical Party, who convinced Limonov that there was a political future in hardline nationalism. Back in Russia, Limonov began to hang around nationalist salons. And now, at the dinner, Limonov was seated next to Gennady Zyuganov, talking about the future of Russian patriotism. Many toasts had been drunk, first to Russia, then to the future and great endeavours, when suddenly Dugin walked up to both of them, obviously very drunk. 'Hey, Limonov, what are you doing with this shit?' he asked, slurring and wavering a bit.

Zyuganov was startled, but then his expression turned to sympathetic fatherly concern when he saw it was Dugin. He broke in and introduced the newcomer: 'This is our Alexander Dugin, a very talented young philosopher.' 'And you're shit, Gennady Andreevich, what do you know?' said Dugin, wobbling and turning back to Limonov. 'Why are you with them, these mediocre shits?'

Dugin's relationship with Zyuganov was complicated, to say the least. The two men had been close collaborators, developing an ideology for the opposition Communist Party until their recent falling out had put an end to their cooperation. Dugin was quick to anger when he felt he wasn't given credit for ideas (surely a major flaw in a ghost writer). He had broken off communication with Zyuganov for this reason. 'When he got into the Duma, he acted arrogantly. We fell out', says Dugin.

Limonov tried valiantly to defuse the situation. 'Why? Why are you with these mediocre shits?' the very drunk Dugin continued to complain. Finally, in frustration, Limonov retorted: 'Why are *you*?' This only made Dugin more belligerent. Soon Prokhanov, editor of *The Day* and patron of the evening, came over and interceded to avoid a scandal.

Limonov had never met Dugin, but this encounter was to be the start of a friendship that would see them through most of the decade as partners in an exotic political project known as the National Bolshevik Party. Limonov was struck by Dugin's imposing physical stature combined with a certain gracefulness: Dugin was a big man with heavy thighs, but when he walked he took small ballet steps, lending him a poise almost 'inappropriate for the massive figure of this young man'.

They left the party, very drunk, the two of them and Prokhanov. Crossing Tverskoy Boulevard, near the Kremlin, a car screeched to a halt: Dugin had drunkenly kicked in its taillight after the driver had turned too close to them. The driver got out, pulled a gun and pointed it at Dugin's head. In an instant the situation had grown decidedly dangerous, but Dugin seemed amused by the whole thing. The gunman looked like he knew how to handle a weapon.

Limonov looked at Dugin helplessly. Suddenly, Dugin blurted out: 'Hey, I'm Eduard Limonov!' and smiled drunkenly. The gunman looked confused, but clearly had never heard of Limonov. Limonov stepped in: 'Actually, I'm Limonov. My friend didn't want to ... just excuse us?' The driver finally lowered the gun, spat, and with a final 'Fuck you!' got in the car and drove off.

Limonov wasn't the first person to notice Dugin's drinking. The latter also had a fearsome temper – 'exaggerated emotions', as Limonov would put it. 'It was a spot on the reputation of a philosopher – that's all. Not even a speck, if you look at Dugin in the context of the Russian tradition.' And indeed, for a Russian philosopher, alcohol abuse was practically the sine qua non of the profession. Dugin and Limonov got on like a house on fire, and were practically inseparable for the next five years.

The year after they met, in May 1993, Limonov was by his own account returning from the fighting in Knin Krajina, near Sarajevo, when he decided it was time to create his own national radical party, the National Bolshevik Front, together with a group of teenage gang members from a Moscow suburb. The experiment ended farcically after his gang beat up their allies, the Communist Youth League of Zyuganov's party. 'It became clear that we had to start again, from zero', he writes in his autobiography. He remembered Dugin, got in touch and, despite the latter's bruising experience in Pamyat, after which he had forsworn politics, Dugin decided he liked Limonov enough to give it another try. The two created the National Bolshevik Front in June, just three months before the constitutional crisis between Yeltsin and the State Duma nearly led to civil war.

Each man found in the other something he lacked. Limonov sensed in Dugin a Russia that he had missed during his 20-year sojourn in the West, while Dugin envied Limonov's Western experience, writing credentials and fluency. Limonov may not have been far off the mark when he wrote in his biography about the drunken scene on Tverskoy Boulevard, when Dugin introduced himself to the gun-toting Mercedes driver as Limonov: 'The scene in the street was symbolic – Dugin sometimes mistook himself for me. I think he really genuinely wanted to be Limonov.' In Dugin, Limonov had found a cause, at least temporarily. As Dugin told me: 'Limonov as a writer was incapable of invention, and so he only wrote about what happened to him. He needed events to write about.' In Limonov, Dugin had found a publicist: 'Dugin always needed a director, he couldn't function on his own', according to Limonov.

As Limonov gradually got to know Dugin, he found he was materially better-off than he let on. He had a vaulted Stalin-era apartment in the centre of Moscow, rare books and a computer. As Limonov wrote: 'I think Dugin exaggerated his poverty because he was embarrassed. I think when I left they threw the sausages in the trash and ate meat.' Dugin's relative wealth is perhaps an indication that the writer received funding beyond what can be explained by his book sales.

Dugin, according to Limonov, was an impossible romantic, but otherwise had no real strict beliefs: 'Dugin was like a chameleon or an octopus, who can mimic the colours of whatever environment it is put in. He lived in a fascist environment, and so he assumed fascist colours.' He also brought a 'bright spirit of megalomania' to the party, and an indifference to traditional ideas of right and left. 'Unconditionally, as an intellectual, Dugin surpassed practically any other single figure in the Russian world at the time', said Limonov, even after their acrimonious break-up in 1998.

'Operation Crematorium'

In 1993, amid economic shock therapy that plunged Russia into crisis, the situations of the democrats and the patriotic opposition were reversed. Once ascendant, Yeltsin's camp very rapidly lost support to a growing opposition nationalist mood, stoked by hardliners in the system.

The economy was mostly to blame. Yeltsin had come to power on the promise that democracy would usher in an era of Western-style economic prosperity; instead, in 1992 the economy collapsed. In January of that year came the first market reforms, which saw prices rise by 245 per cent that month alone, creating widespread panic. Hyperinflation wiped out the savings of the university professors, bureaucrats and intellectuals who, just a few months before, had been the strongest bulwark of liberal reforms. The balance of opinion in the Supreme Soviet shifted fast. Hundreds of deputies who had once backed Yeltsin drifted into the opposition camp.

The nationalists, whose initial experiences at the ballot box had been farcical, began to gain popular support, becoming a political threat to Yeltsin. And it was he – the selfsame politician who, just two years before, had faced down tanks – who ultimately would be forced to rely on armed force to secure his power.

Politically, the reformers were in trouble. There were mass defections from the democratic camp to the side of the patriotic opposition. Ruslan Khasbulatov, an economist who was speaker of the Supreme Soviet, and even Yeltsin's own vice-president, former fighter pilot Alexander Rutskoy, joined the opposition against him.

Yeltsin deftly managed to shed most of the blame for the dislocation caused by economic reforms and push it onto his prime minister, the 35-year-old whiz-kid Egor Gaidar (who was in and out of power according to Yeltsin's mood), and his privatization chief, the enigmatic economist Anatoly Chubais. Yeltsin was still popular: when parliament threatened to impeach him, he held a referendum and won 59 per cent of the vote. But his influence was nonetheless waning, and Russia's political system slid towards conflict once again. Throughout the summer of 1993, Yeltsin plotted to dissolve parliament and hold fresh elections, while his opponents still planned to try again to impeach him. But neither could garner the political support to finish the other off.

The events of September–October 1993 would lead to armed conflict in the centre of Moscow, the worst fighting there since 1917, and very nearly to full-scale civil war. The motives and behaviour of both sides remain extremely puzzling to this day. After the conflict was over, US President Bill Clinton said Yeltsin had 'bent over backwards' to avoid bloodshed; however, there is accumulating evidence that bloodshed is exactly what he wanted – to do militarily what he could not do politically: destroy the opposition, suspend the constitution, and unilaterally redress the balance between executive and legislative powers to create a super-presidency. That is exactly what he got.

On 21 September, Yeltsin struck, signing 'Decree 1400' dissolving parliament. He freely admits in his memoirs that this was an unconstitutional measure, but ironically it was the only way to defend democracy in Russia, he claimed: 'Formally the president was violating the constitution, going the route of antidemocratic measures, and dispersing the parliament – all for the sake of establishing democracy and rule of law in the country.'

Again, at the centre of the stand-off was the famed White House, which was a familiar symbol of freedom to Western television viewers – the very place where Yeltsin had stood stalwart and called for resistance to the generals' coup in August 1991. This time the tables were turned: Rutskoy and Khasbulatov were ready and they barricaded themselves in the White House. The political confrontation turned increasingly ugly with each passing day, as the city of Moscow turned off the electricity and water to the building. But parliament held firm, voting to impeach Yeltsin, who was on thin legal ice in dissolving parliament. For days the confrontation hung in the balance. The army did not want to become involved in politics, as it had been in 1991 and during the various independence struggles around the Soviet Union which had preceded its break-up. However, it became clear that only the army could eventually decide the outcome.

Curiously, while electricity to parliament was cut off immediately, it took a week before the Interior Ministry put a cordon of razor wire and police around the building – a delay that allowed political leaders, ex-generals, thrill-seeking teenagers, disgruntled pensioners and everyone in between to flood in. They all milled around inside the building, meeting by candlelight, with no one visibly in charge.

Vladislav Achalov, a former tank commander who was drummed out of the army for supporting the August 1991 coup, was the acting defence minister, appointed by Rutskoy. He made the fateful decision – in retrospect a bad miscalculation – to appeal to paramilitary patriotic opposition groups to join the defenders. Thus Dugin, Prokhanov, Limonov and other nationalists joined the parliamentary defenders in the gloomy candlelit darkness. Dugin was deeply unimpressed: 'There was chaos. Everyone was wandering around, they thought they would receive new government posts, that they would rule the country. Nobody thought they would simply be shot.'

The arrival of fighters and radical extremists was welcomed by Khasbulatov and Rutskoy as an extra show of muscle. But throwing in their lot with the nationalist opposition would ultimately prove a gigantic mistake. They were out of their depth. They thought they would be fighting for control of buildings and neighbourhoods, when the real battle was for television screens and world opinion.

That was the only thing constraining Yeltsin. He did not lack muscle – he used only a handful of the 6,000 riot police during the crisis.[4] He had army Special Forces units, tough-eyed commandos under the command of the Federal Security Service (FSB – the successor to the KGB) and the Interior

Ministry; and although it remained officially neutral, he also controlled the army. The Taman Motor Rifle Division, which had roared into Moscow two years previously, was based an hour away, as was the Kantemirov Tank Division. The only thing Yeltsin lacked was the legitimacy to use the force arrayed at his disposal. Had he declared a state of emergency and fired on parliament during the first day, there would have been an outcry worldwide and probably a mutiny within the armed forces. But the appearance of gangs of communists, mercenaries, crypto-fascists and neo-Nazis may have provided the spectacle he needed to justify the use of force, and to call parliament a 'fascist communist armed rebellion', which he did on 4 October, an hour before tanks opened fire.

Ilya Konstantinov, a former boiler-room worker who was head of the opposition National Salvation Front, recalls:

> It was obvious that [the paramilitary groups] were compromising the whole parliament. I don't even think they were aware they were doing it. But by the time they were in the building, we couldn't get them out. We couldn't eject them without a fight, and no one wanted this.

International public opinion, initially wavering and unwilling to tolerate violent repression of parliament by the Yeltsin administration, gradually swung in the president's favour as Khasbulatov and Rutskoy faltered and erred.

For two weeks, the siege was static, as parliamentarians and protesters milled around the darkened White House, meeting by candlelight, going home every day to take showers and shave. Rebel leaders tried to whip up support in the streets, and gangs of opposition protesters clashed frequently with police. Yeltsin, meanwhile, used the airwaves to coax the population over to his side.

There was little bloodshed until 3 October, when the momentum seemed suddenly to shift in favour of the mutineers. A massive crowd gathered in Moscow's October Square, under a statue of Lenin, and began marching north along the ring road, towards parliament, in a bold attempt to break the police blockade of the building. They overwhelmed an outnumbered detachment of riot police on the Krymsky Bridge, capturing weapons and ten military trucks; and then, to their utter astonishment, police surrounding parliament gave way after a small scuffle, surrendering to protesters. The crowd then broke through the police lines surrounding parliament, breaking the blockade.

In the euphoria, as they massed in front of the building, the protesters waited to be told what to do next by the very confused leaders of the revolt. From the balcony of the White House, Khasbulatov said to move on the Kremlin; Rutskoy said to go to Ostankino – the needle of a tower from where the city's radio and television signals are broadcast and which houses the offices of the main national broadcasters. As the crowd decided on Ostankino, the battle appeared to hang in the balance. No loyal military units barred the way of the 700-odd protesters who set out on the ring road towards the television tower, driving in captured military trucks and school buses. Dugin, Limonov and Prokhanov were among them, hanging off the backs of trucks or crammed into buses. 'The city seemed to be ours', said Limonov. 'But it only seemed that way.'

The man leading the protesters to take the TV tower was General Albert Makashov. Riding in a jeep with a few heavily armed bodyguards, he led the motley motorcade around the ring road and towards Ostankino. As they drove, he looked out at the road and saw ten armoured personnel carriers (APCs) roaring alongside. 'Our guys', he assured his men. He appeared to believe that the APCs were carrying mutinous forces that had switched sides to join the protesters. But he was wrong. They were, in fact, transporting a unit of 80 commandos from the elite Vityaz battalion of the Interior Ministry's Dzerzhinsky Division, still under Yeltsin's control, that had been scrambled to defend the TV centre. Their vehicles drove alongside those of the protesters for most of the way.[5] One account of the day, albeit on a pro-rebel website known only as Anathema-2, deserves some attention. It (and numerous witnesses) reported, fairly plausibly, that the Moscow ring road at Mayakovsky Square was blocked by Vityaz APCs, and that, more incredibly, the column of armed demonstrators in vehicles had stopped in front of it, but was allowed to continue.[6]

The protesters and the Vityaz commandos arrived at Ostankino at roughly the same time. Sergey Lisyuk, the Vityaz commander, says he was given the order via radio to return fire if fired upon. 'I made them repeat it twice, so those riding next to me also heard it.'[7] The soldiers, arrayed in body armour and clinking with weaponry, ran through the same underpass as the protesters and entered the building. Meanwhile the protesters set up outside with megaphones and heavy trucks. Nightfall was drawing near. The protesters were jubilant, toting truncheons and riot shields captured from police. Eighteen of them had assault rifles and one had an RPG-7 rocket-propelled grenade launcher. Makashov, the former general who commanded the armed men, ordered the vehicles to turn around and ferry more demonstrators, until the crowd outside the TV centre numbered over a thousand. Journalists arrived in vans and jeeps, dragging tripods and hurriedly unwinding cables. Inside, the Vityaz men, in grey camouflage with black balaclavas, could be seen scurrying around erecting barricades and taking up firing positions.

Night fell. It was around 19:20 when General Makashov, wearing a black leather overcoat and black paratrooper beret, addressed the Vityaz defenders inside Ostankino: 'You have ten minutes to lay down your arms and surrender, or we will begin storming the building!' The Vityaz men made no public response, though negotiations between Makashov and Lisyuk were ongoing via radio, according to numerous accounts.

At 19:30 a group of protesters brought in a heavy military truck, captured that day from riot police, to try to break into the television compound. Over and over, it battered against the glass and steel entrance, trying to smash through; but it was unable to get through the concrete building supports. Near the truck squatted the man toting the grenade launcher. Details of this man, including his last name, are scant, though Alexander Barkashov told me his name was 'Kostya' and he was a veteran of the Trans-Dniester conflict of 1990. Other witnesses say that he was a civilian, and did not know how to fire the grenade launcher until a policeman who had joined the parliamentary mutiny showed him how. What happened next is still the subject of a great deal of controversy.

To this day, the specific actions that led to the carnage at the TV centre are still debated, but what can be established is that as the truck was smashing its way into the compound, snipers on the upper floors of the building opened fire. Simultaneously, an explosion reverberated on the lower floors of the TV centre, and a Vityaz private named Nikolay Sitnikov was killed. Colonel Lisyuk said he was hit by a rocket-propelled grenade fired from the crowd. He said his men opened fire in self-defence, and only after Private Sitnikov's death.

Every witness has a slightly different memory. Dugin recalls that a Vityaz soldier fired a shot which hit the leg of the man with the grenade launcher, who accidentally triggered his weapon: 'The Vityaz men started shooting people, unarmed people. At first some started shooting back, three or four machine-gun rounds, and that was it, later the shooting was only from Vityaz.' Prokhanov saw the grenade man fall. He 'suddenly began to sit, to slip along a wall. Nearby the twilight flashed and a small cloud of concrete debris was lifted into the air by a bullet strike.' That was his description of the scene, taken from *Red Brown*, his (very) semi-autobiographical novel about the events, published the following year.

Tracers flew out of the TV centre. Bullets cracked overhead and thudded into bodies. 'A wave of heavy red explosions covered us all', according to Limonov. He dropped to his belly and crawled away. At one point he looked back to where he had been standing, near the truck, and saw 20 bodies, 'some of them were groaning, most said nothing'. Tracer bullets rained down on the crowd for over an hour. At least 62 people were killed in the mêlée, mainly bystanders, but also several journalists.

Dugin wrote movingly about the tragedy, finding esoteric meaning in the events. In one account of the chaos he described how he had 'felt the breath of spirit' during the massacre, when, seeking cover, he dived behind a car and accidentally pushed someone who had already taken cover there into the open. Instead of shoving him angrily 'as a live human body should involuntarily do', the man simply embraced him, exposing himself to fire and shielding Dugin from the shots. Dugin wrote of the transcendent spiritual feeling 'above the flesh and above life' which he felt, being under fire for the first time.

'It was a day of severe defeat', he wrote seven years later, 'when it seemed that not only our brothers and sisters and our children, but also the huge structure of Russian history had fallen.'[8] He spent most of the night under the car, and finally crawled away into the nearby stand of trees after the shooting subsided, finding Oleg Bakhtiyarov, one of Makashov's bodyguards, who had been shot in the leg. Dugin flagged a car down, took Oleg to hospital, and went back to the Duma at about 3 a.m. The mood was sombre, as news of the scale of the catastrophe at Ostankino filtered back. 'That's when I understood that our leaders were bastards, that they started this war, they started this confrontation, they sent people with no weapons, no instructions, to die. They simply committed a crime.' Knowing the end was coming, Dugin left parliament in the small hours of the morning.

To this day Lisyuk defends the actions of his men: 'The firing was aimed only at those who were armed, or who tried to obtain arms', he said in a 2003 interview. However, he added:

Try yourself to figure out, in the dark, who is a journalist and who is a fighter . . . I don't have any guilt – I followed orders. Of course, I feel very sorry for the ones who died, especially the ones who were innocent. We were all victims of a political crisis. But I want to say the following: the price would be high if the military did not follow orders.[9]

However, Colonel Lisyuk's version is disputed, and a number of inconsistencies add to the mystery of exactly what, and who, caused the massacre. Leonid Proshkin, the head of a special investigative team from the Russian general prosecutor's office, spent months investigating the parliamentary uprising. He found no evidence that a rocket-propelled grenade had hit the building because there was no damage found that was consistent with such an explosion:

Such a grenade can burn through half a metre of concrete, the grenade from an RPG-7. And all that was there were marks from a large-calibre machine gun, from an APC. It all boiled down to this: if Sitnikov had been killed by an RPG, it would have looked completely different.[10]

Proshkin determined that the wounds received by Sitnikov, and the damage to his bullet-proof vest, were not consistent with an RPG-7, which is designed to penetrate tank armour. Rather, it was likely caused by a simple hand grenade:

> Sitnikov died not from the firing of the grenade launcher from the direction of Supreme Soviet supporters standing near the entrance, but as a result of the explosion of some sort of device located inside the building, that is, in the possession of the defenders.[11]

It remains possible, therefore, that Sitnikov's death was either an accidental grenade detonation or, more ominously, the result of a provocation aimed at goading the building's nervous defenders into massacring the crowd.

For Yeltsin, Ostankino was a tragedy, but a tactical success in his duel with parliament. It was portrayed on TV screens and newspapers across the world as an armed attack by protesters on the TV station, coming in the wake of the successful seizure of the mayor's office. It was possible (and partly true) for the Kremlin to say that, rather than massacring dozens of nearly defenceless demonstrators, they had repelled an armed attack.

After Ostankino, the end of the conflict was no longer in doubt. At 7 a.m. on 4 October, several T-80 tanks positioned themselves across the Moscow River from the White House. They were manned entirely by officers. Meanwhile, commandos from Alpha Group reluctantly took up positions around the building, waiting for the order to storm it.

It was during the lead-up to the operation that another mysterious tragedy occurred. As the Alpha detachment was exiting their APCs, one of the soldiers was hit by a sniper and mortally wounded. Korzhakov – Yeltsin's former KGB bodyguard, who took a leading role in managing the 1993 parliamentary crisis – writes of this incident in his biography. Seeing one of their own killed, he said, had brought Alpha's fighting spirit back: 'Suddenly their military instincts returned, and their doubts vanished.'[12] To this day, however, the mysterious shooting is debated. After his retirement, Gennady Zaytsev, the Alpha commander at the time, gave an interview saying that the shot did not come from the White House, but rather from forces loyal to President Yeltsin in the Mir Hotel.[13] He made the incendiary accusation that the shot had been a deliberate attempt to provoke his forces: 'It did not come from the White House. That's a lie. That was done with one goal in mind, to make Alpha angry, so that we rushed in there and cut everyone to pieces.'[14] If true, it might cast new light on the killing of Private Sitnikov the previous day, which had provoked the massacre at Ostankino by the Vityaz commandos.

Korzhakov disputed this account, saying in an interview that Zaytsev was 'in a bad psychological state' during the operation: 'And how anyway is he able to tell where [the soldier] was shot from? Did he do proper police work? Did he line up the body and take measurements? No. They took the guy off the battlefield alive, it was only later he died.' Zaytsev said, however, that he understood the situation immediately, and despite what he believed to be a provocation that had cost a young soldier his life, he ordered the operation to go ahead: 'I understood that, if we completely refuse the operation, Alpha would be disbanded. It would be the end.'[15] However, he is sure in retrospect that the reason Alpha was transferred to the Ministry of Security's control after the conflict was that it did not perform its duties 'using different methods' – i.e. taking the building by force and killing Rutskoy and Khasbulatov.

The identity of the sniper, the killer of the Alpha soldier, remains one of the key mysteries yet to be unravelled in the events of that October, just like the explosion at the Ostankino tower. If Alpha, the elite soldiers of Russia's intelligence service, were themselves merely rats in the maze of a broader conspiracy, it is chilling to think of who could have been higher up the food chain.

Shortly before 9 a.m., one of the T-80 tanks fired a 150mm shell at the White House, hitting the top floors. There followed several more shells, likewise aimed at the top floors in order to avoid killing the building's occupants. The shelling was mainly symbolic, to break the morale of the defenders. Nonetheless, some 70 people are believed to have been killed, including some bystanders. After the shelling, the Alpha commandos positioned around parliament moved in and led the mutineers out peacefully.

Ultimately, the snipers firing on the pro-Kremlin forces throughout the siege of the White House were never found or tried. Korzhakov suggested that they belonged to the Union of Officers and had escaped from the White House via tunnels, under the Moscow River and out of the Hotel Ukraine on the other side. Security Minister Nikolay Golushko was thought to have sealed these off but had not, according to Korzhakov.

The events of late 1993 were grist to the mill of conspiracy theorists, reflecting the overwhelming conviction of the parliamentary defenders that they had been the victims of a great deception, designed to lure them into a trap. The Red Brown protesters now believed that Ostankino had been a set-up – that the trucks they had captured from riot police (with keys still in the ignition!) were part of a grand strategy to goad them into the killing fields outside Ostankino, where they could provide their own pretext for getting massacred. They claimed to have been emboldened by specially planted disinformation concerning the supposed defection of army units to their side. They had – in the version described on Anathema – even been allowed through a roadblock on Moscow's ring road, all for the sole purpose of providing a provocation aimed at giving Yeltsin the excuse to use tanks against parliament.

Prokhanov's account of the events is encased in his surrealistic fantasy novel *Red Brown*, which described the fictional 'Operation Crematorium': a conspiracy by Yeltsin and his American puppeteers aimed at trapping the patriotic opposition in the kill-zone of Ostankino and the smoking tomb of the White House. But the use of provocateurs by the regime may not simply have been a figment of Prokhanov's vivid imagination. This became apparent when I interviewed Alexander Barkashov about his role in the 1993 confrontation.

I had to drive for three hours to his dacha outside Moscow, where he keeps fighting dogs and a collection of hunting bows. As the evening wore on, he became more and more conspiratorial, until eventually I asked him why he had taken part on the side of the parliamentary defenders. He dumbfounded me by replying that he had been acting under the orders of his commander in the 'active reserve', by which he meant the retired chain of command of the former KGB. He identified his commander as acting Defence Minister Achalov, the same man who had originally issued the call for armed nationalist gangs to come to the aid of the White House defenders: 'If Achalov had told me to shoot Khasbulatov or Rutskoy, I would have.' If his claim is true, it would explain a great deal. Barkashov played the role of a provocateur in the parliamentary siege, discrediting the defenders in the eyes of world opinion by publicly aligning them with neo-Nazis. Curiously, Barkashov's forces from Russian National Unity (RNU) did not take part in the Ostankino siege, and the party lost only two members killed in the fighting.

Achalov, whom I interviewed about Barkashov's claim, flatly denied the accusations: 'I'm just a tank soldier, nothing more. I don't know what Barkashov is talking about.' If Barkashov, in his own words, was acting not according to the convictions of an ideologue, but on the orders of a state structure, then the goals of that structure must be wondered at. The rise of nationalism in post-communist Russia may have been a far more complicated event than first meets the eye.

* * *

Dugin had left the White House in the small hours of the morning, knowing what would come. He went back to his apartment and, his belongings packed, waited to be arrested. 'I was one of the ideologists, I was sure they would arrest me, but they didn't. We were all waiting for the repressions, but they never came.' Instead, there arrived an invitation to appear on *Red Square*, at the time a popular talk show, where he was asked about his role in the attempted coup.

Clearly, the Kremlin was trying another tack. Instead of suffering repressions, which might have been expected, the rebels were by and large left untouched. Many were encouraged to return to political life. Prokhanov went into hiding in the forest for months, but it turned out that no one was actually looking for him. *The Day* was closed by the authorities, but Prokhanov was allowed almost immediately to open a successor newspaper, *Zavtra* (*Tomorrow*).

The remarkable turn of events showed how Yeltsin changed strategy: after killing a significant number of the opposition, he now moved to co-opt them, holding elections in which he allowed the Communist Party to participate, following which he allowed the rebel plotters to be amnestied. Yeltsin also pushed through a new constitution, creating in effect a super-presidency that emasculated parliament and gave the post-1993 status quo legal form. Following the October 1993 confrontation, the opposition was never again able (or inclined) to challenge Yeltsin on any matter of substance.

The terrible power of the state was reborn once again in the hands of the Kremlin. The old USSR had not been able to lift a finger to save itself in 1991, when Marshal Yazov could not think 'in whose name' to give the order to fire on demonstrators. Now that state had revealed itself only too clearly outside Ostankino and the White House. It was every bit the unblinking methodical killer that the old Soviet Union had been. But the conflict of 1993 changed the ruling equation in Russia. The shelling of parliament both strengthened Yeltsin and crippled him at the same time. His approval rating plummeted from 59 per cent to 3 per cent, and the Communists and Liberal Democrats swept the next parliamentary elections to comprise the bulk of the opposition to Yeltsin.

Zhirinovsky's Liberal Democrats were rewarded for their decision to stay neutral in the uprising, enjoying the Kremlin's good offices and favourable TV coverage. He and his deputy Alexey Mitrofanov had weathered the crisis in Germany ('like true Bolshevik revolutionaries', jokes Mitrofanov), and Zhirinovsky showed up at the White House in the aftermath with bottles of duty-free wine. 'They are Molotov cocktails!' he scolded deputies who questioned his commitment to the patriotic cause. Winning a quarter of the votes cast for party lists, the LDPR won so many seats, in comparison to its small membership, that even bodyguards found themselves on the list of deputies; when even that was not enough, they took some Communist Party deputies from Zyuganov's election list. The new Duma elections were a considerable windfall – 'a gift from the sky to the moderate-communist *nomenklatura* opposition', according to Limonov. 'In a normal, non-parliamentary context of political struggle, what awaited them were their slippers and disputes over tea.'

That appeared to most observers to be part of some grand bargain by Yeltsin, allowing some nationalist parties to run in the election, in exchange for support in passing the new constitution. The February 1994 amnesty, which freed Rutskoy, Khasbulatov and other kingpins of the 1993 crisis, also seemed to be a political trade; soon afterwards, parliament ended its investigation into the official crisis death toll of 173, principally at Ostankino and as a result of the shelling of the White House.

But the strength of the nationalist message could already be seen in Yeltsin's eagerness to co-opt it. Yeltsin was forced to embrace his opponents' ideas in order to stay in power: his team had proved its fitness to rule through its cynicism and ruthlessness, its ideology steadily adapted to the reality of the country. Yeltsin once again stole his opponents' proposals. He had stolen Gorbachev's reform agenda, and now he began to co-opt the ideology of his nationalist opponents. He put out a barrage of new initiatives designed to outflank the nationalists from the right. He reinvigorated the Commonwealth of Independent States, and negotiated a Union Treaty with Belarus, whose new president, Alexander Lukashenko, elected in 1994, publicly advocated such a step. He championed nationalist causes, throwing the Kremlin's weight behind efforts to rebuild the Christ the Saviour cathedral in the centre of Moscow, which had been demolished and turned into a swimming pool by Stalin in 1932. He also allowed the Duma a largely free hand to legislate on nationalist and religious issues, creating a commission in 1996 to come up with a Russian 'national idea'.

Dugin and many other extremists said they sensed a sharp shift in the Kremlin's attitude towards nationalism and away from the West in the wake of the events of that October. 'Yeltsin made a correction, a profound correction, after 1993', says Dugin today. 'Politically he castrated the political opposition, but also he has corrected, improved and changed his own political course.'

Yeltsin's strategy of carrots and sticks split the nationalists – the Communists and the LDPR went into parliament, where they never again challenged the authority of the Kremlin. Meanwhile, Dugin and Limonov refused to join them. 'We tried to remain radical and irreconcilable', wrote Dugin, though he admitted that, during the following six years of Yeltsin rule,

> ... we, the defeated, humiliated, crushed party, can hardly brag about anything ... But we have kept the most important thing, and no matter how dispersed, scattered, divided and separated we are we have kept precisely the Spirit that breathed then [at the massacre of Ostankino]. It doesn't

matter that it no longer burns, but it is obviously smouldering independently, it aches in us, torments us.

The shock of what he had seen, Dugin says, was profound. During his appearance on *Red Square* he was asked whether he bore responsibility for the killing that had taken place. The question shook him, but he handled matters skilfully, blurting out: 'Yes, but your Yeltsin is a bloody assassin.' The answer came in a single breath and so nothing could be edited out. The interview was not used. Nonetheless, 'It was a trauma.' Dugin withdrew temporarily from political life.

Limonov was just as demoralized, and disgusted with the nationalist movement in the wake of the 1993 disaster. He wanted to create a real opposition party, with an ideology 'based not on ethnic emotions of bleating, primeval people, not based on some outdated ideology of orthodoxy, but on the concept of national interest'.

The two men sat in Limonov's flat one day in the spring of 1994. Limonov proposed taking the National Bolshevik Front, which they had created the previous July, and turning it into a party. Dugin was none too keen on the idea. Since he had left Pamyat in 1988, he had vowed not to participate in political organizations, and the experience of October had even further decreased his appetite for politics. He said he would help in the organization of the National Bolshevik Party (NBP), but he did not want a formal post. In time, Dugin came around. The two men discussed their project in a beer tent on Old Arbat Street in Moscow. Dugin leaned over and said: 'Eduard, your task as a warrior and *kshatriya* is to lead people; and I am but a priest, magician, Merlin, I have a woman's role to explain and console.'[16]

In fact, the party was arguably Dugin's brainchild – the name was his idea, as was the flag: a black hammer and sickle in a white circle on a red background, evoking the Nazi swastika. It was not going to win them any elections, in a country that lost 20 million to Hitler's fascism; but that was not the NBP's goal. The official NBP salute was a straight arm raised with a fist, alongside a cry of '*Da, Smert!*' (Yes! Death!).[17] Inside the group's headquarters, the highest-ranking party member present was always referred to as the *Bunkerführer*. The veneer of fascism was very much calculated – it was a bohemian 'political art project', in Dugin's words. He, according to Limonov, 'seemed to have deciphered and translated the bright shock that Soviet youth experience when they pronounce the initials "SS"'.

The NBP's ironic stance towards fascism, though, was also a carefully calculated ploy. The salutes, the slogans ('Stalin, Beria, Gulag!' was one) were so odd and over the top that they verged on parody. Equating their party with fascist symbols, however, was a pose – pioneered by Dugin – that would come to define Russia's image of authoritarian rule under Putin in the coming decade. The NBP was a 'sight gag' that undercut criticism by making it seem – ever so slightly – as though it was missing the point. Calling the swastika-waving, goose-stepping NBP members 'fascists' frankly sounded so odd that no one ever did it, for fear of looking ridiculous. Both men were instinctive haters of conventional wisdom. They loved to shock. And the movement they founded was a mélange of each man's upbringing: Dugin a product of the overly intellectual Moscow bohemia of the 1980s; Limonov, the pre-AIDS Lower East Side of Manhattan in the 1970s transplanted to central Moscow.

The name of the party made no difference to Limonov, Dugin told American diplomats in 2008 (the cable was published in 2010 by Wikileaks): 'He wanted to call it "National Socialism", "National Fascism", "National Communism" – whatever. Ideology was never his thing. The scream in the wilderness – that was his goal.'

Limonov, according to Dugin (they had had a bad falling-out by this point), was like 'a clown in a little traveling circus. The better he performs, the more attention he wins, the happier he is'.[18] At around the same time, when he spoke to me in 2009, Limonov called Dugin 'a degenerate servitor of the regime, and shameful conformist'.

It would be a mistake to view the NBP as a serious political party with clear goals: the party's code of conduct includes 'the right not to listen when your girlfriend is talking to you', and members were encouraged to vandalize Russian cinemas showing Western films (though no one in the party has any memory of this actually having happened). Instead, the NBP was designed to become the germ of a new counterculture, the core of what Andreas Umland, an expert on Russian nationalist groups, refers to as 'uncivil society', whose goal is not necessarily conquest of executive and legislative power, but rather ideological subversion aimed at acquiring dominance over the cultural superstructure.[19] The NBP quickly became an icon. 'You had three choices if you were a teenager here in the 1990s', explained Andrey Karagodin, an NBP veteran. 'You could get into rave, you could become a gangster, or you could join the NBP. That was it.'

Limonov enlisted his friend Egor Letov, lead singer with the popular band Civil Defence. His NBP membership card was number 4. He would routinely interrupt concerts with long diatribes against Yeltsin and in support of the NBP. Aside from Letov, ex-NBP members have distinguished themselves in some of the most creative professions in Russia. Zakhar Prilepin, who joined the movement later on, went on to become one of Russia's most interesting young authors, after a career that, oddly, began in the elite police force, the OMON. Alexey Belyayev-Gintovt went on to win the coveted Kandinsky Art Prize. And Karagodin himself is now editor of Russia's edition of *Vogue*.

The NBP was an exploration of the limits of freedom. In this Limonov and Dugin represented diametrically opposite poles: the anarchy of the Russian spirit on the one side; on the other, the ever-present totalitarian impulses that have gripped the Russian soul over five centuries of history. It was a party which espoused fascist ideas, yet simultaneously revelled in the libertine Moscow of the 1990s. It was a living demonstration of the paradox of freedom and a simultaneous suggestion of the authoritarian alternative. As Letov put it: 'Everything which isn't anarchy is fascism, and there is no anarchy.' This dialectic of contradictory thesis and antithesis was played out in the playground of Yeltsin's Russia, and became the ruling synthesis of the next decade. The movement pioneered the creation of 'youth leagues', which sprang up everywhere in the Putin era in a bid by the Kremlin to control the streets. 'They stole all our ideas', complained Limonov to me in 2011. Limonov went on to become the shouting conscience of the Putin era – the highest-profile dissident of a new regime; while Dugin would become the ideologist of the new autocracy.

The first issue of their newspaper, created by Limonov and named *Limonka* (the nickname for a Second World War grenade), came out in 1994, with a front page denouncing the 'old opposition' in favour of the new. Dugin presented the founding idea of the party, arguing that the difference between old and new opposition was not one of political ideology, but one of psychology and style. The 'old patriots' were focused on restoring the old, while the new patriots were not reactionary 'whatever their views, from communism to monarchism to Russian fascism, they think in terms of a new society, a revolutionary process . . . their goal is to create something principally new'.

Funding was going to be difficult. 'There was basically never any money', remembers Dugin. Without money to rent an office, they decided to try and extort one – with surprising results. In mid-December they wrote to the Moscow mayor, Yury Luzhkov, vaguely threatening that unspecified disturbances would befall the city of Moscow if they were denied. Luzhkov, a rotund, proletarian former chemical industry specialist who had arrived on Yeltsin's coat-tails to govern the city, was not in the mood for trouble and seemed to think that a free flat was a small price to pay for the good behaviour of yet another radical fringe group of sociopaths. Out of the blue, a few weeks later, someone from Luzhkov's office called and made an appointment for them with the Moscow Commission of State Property. The beaming city bureaucrat who received them assured them that 'art and the state should work hand in hand'. He offered them accommodation for 17 roubles per year per square metre – 'that is basically free', Dugin assured a perplexed Limonov.

The apartment they chose was a basement on Frunzenskaya Street, not coincidentally located below a police station. The flat 'had the notable quality that every so often, due to a cracked sewer pipe located in the wall, it would become covered in shit', according to Dugin. 'The bunker', as it became known, was a focal point for the NBP. As Prilepin described it in his semi-autobiographical novel *Sankya*:

> It was similar to a boarding school for sociopathic children, the workshop of a mad artist and a military headquarters for barbarians who had decided to go to war against God knows where . . . There were a lot of young people who cut their hair in all manner of ways – either letting it vegetate, or leaving a single bang, or a Mohawk, or even weird whiskers above the ears. However, there were unexpectedly also boys with perfect hair styles in suits, and ordinary workers with simple faces.

With their new premises, they began to coalesce. But not really. Limonov was a committed revolutionary who wanted to declare war on convention in all forms, an instinctive hater of the political establishment. Dugin, still lecturing at the General Staff Academy and not wanting to burn his bridges entirely with the political order, was more restrained. Dugin and Limonov more than once clashed over Dugin's lack of extremism. Dugin readily admits that he was gently putting the brake on the more radical tendencies of the NBP. As he told me in 2010: 'During my period in the NBP, one could say under my supervision, there were no illegal acts, no criminal cases. Limonov would plan them, I would put the brakes on. I was opposed to violating the law for no reason.'

Limonka, meanwhile, was full of polemics and provocation. But the editorial line of the paper, again under Dugin's supervision, seemed to stick closely to the agenda of conservatives in the Kremlin clan led by Yeltsin's bodyguard Alexander Korzhakov, who was fighting constantly with liberal opponents in Yeltsin's entourage.

A close reading of *Limonka*, according to NBP veteran and former Dugin acolyte Arkady Maaler, was illuminating. Rather than straight opposition, Dugin's editorials (for he ran the editorial department of *Limonka*) were more nuanced, praising the line of Kremlin hardliners like Korzhakov, while criticizing the liberal lobby within the government (such as privatization chief Anatoly Chubais).[20] Maaler believes that Dugin was actually working the whole time for Kremlin hardliners, a faction led until 1996 by Korzhakov, while Limonov was not – something that Dugin categorically denies.

Yeltsin's most fateful concession to the hardliner lobby was the December 1994 invasion of Chechnya, which had effectively seceded from the Russian Federation, declaring full independence from Moscow in 1993 under the leadership of former Soviet Air Force General Dzhokhar Dudaev. Russia had supported the anti-Dudaev opposition, but attempts to wrest control of the autonomous region from separatist forces had stalled. In December 1994, Yeltsin ordered Russian forces to 'restore constitutional order' in Chechnya, and this sparked a wave of resignations among army generals. Instead of a quick, surgical strike aimed at regime change, the campaign was a botched, bloody affair, and the Russian army quickly became bogged down in the conflict, taking an estimated 5,500 dead until a ceasefire was declared in 1996. A horrific toll was inflicted on Chechen civilians.

Chechnya quickly became synonymous with Yeltsin's impotence as a leader, but it symbolized a 'correction' in the Kremlin's attitude, as Dugin put it, away from liberalism and towards nationalism in the wake of the events of October 1993. The conflict inspired some singularly ghastly headlines in *Limonka*. When Russian forces invaded, the paper's headline blared: 'Welcome, War!' And after the Chechen capital fell (and before Russian forces were routed the following year) another banner headline read: 'Hooray! Grozny is Taken!'

It is telling that the line on Chechnya changed soon after Dugin and Limonov split, when Limonov took control of the paper's editorial line: the paper began to support Chechen independence from Russia. The attitude to revolution also changed – in 2001 Limonov would be arrested for plotting terrorist attacks in Northern Kazakhstan. A cursory reading of *Limonka* headlines appears to confirm Maaler's allegation (though neither Dugin nor Limonov will admit it) that the NBP was operating within strict political limits during Dugin's time there. While cultivating a reputation for anarchy, the party never strayed far from certain boundaries, and it seems these were set by Dugin.

If the NBP had an agenda other than uncompromising nihilism and radical revolution, however, it was not obvious to the rank and file. It became the political party of choice among Russia's counterculture musicians and artists – popularizing nationalism within a stratum of society uniquely predisposed to avoiding it. *Limonka* became something of a phenomenon, both in Moscow and in boring Russian provincial towns, where it gingered up the stale atmosphere. It united disparate youth countercultures in its readership. 'They didn't join the NBP, but they read us', says Limonov. The paper was particularly strong for its cultural offerings, its reviews of avant-garde cinema, rock groups and underground poets.

For many provincial Russian youths, languishing in stultifying mining towns and crushing poverty, the NBP offered a rush of adrenaline. Valery Korovin was one such convert, joining the movement in 1995. I found him ten years later, still Dugin's disciple and one of the leaders of the Eurasian movement in the Putin years. He told me how he had arrived there.

Growing up in the far eastern city of Vladivostok in the 1980s, he was the quintessential target audience of the NBP: talented, young and bored. A self-described 'head banger', he happened to see a TV interview with Letov calling for revolution against the 'Yeltsin regime', at which point the programme suddenly cut away for a commercial break. As Korovin recalls: 'I realized I was completely out of it, I was sitting in Vladivostok out in the middle of nowhere, and meanwhile in Moscow Letov and somebody I'd never heard of, Limonov, were planning a world revolution. I had to get there and be part of it.' He took a train to Moscow, enrolled on a university course at the Moscow State Construction Institute, and sought out Limonov, finding him with about ten followers in the basement on Frunzenskaya Street. 'I was in a very radical mood, expecting I would be given a bomb or a grenade to throw somewhere. I was serious-minded. They started to calm me down, saying "Easy, we have to prepare first".' Dugin was sitting in the far room, half-naked, typing seriously, surrounded by books and beer bottles. It was Saturday, and they had to clean the place once a week. Korovin remembers Limonov called to Dugin: 'Sasha! What are all these bottles for?' 'They are required for my work', said Dugin flatly. Korovin remembers: 'They worked well together. Dugin was a philosopher, a metaphysician, works with the mind. Limonov was all in public. He was for public actions. Radical revolution.'

But gradually, the two men drifted apart. Limonov was not the first collaborator with whom Dugin quarrelled. In his autobiography, Limonov described his 'Merlin' as 'vindictive, destructive, totally jealous'.

In 1995, the NBP was thoroughly trounced in parliamentary elections, and the first serious rift appeared between Dugin and Limonov. Dugin evidently saw that Limonov was not serious about reaching the establishment, and began working with Zhirinovsky's LDPR, which made Limonov crazy with anger. 'Merlin was looking into the forest, searching for a new King Arthur', related Limonov in his autobiography. Korovin noticed the tension. It was clear to everyone in the NBP that, 'Staying with Limonov, Dugin could not reach the establishment, could not address the Duma, ministers. Limonov made the party marginal.' Limonov loved the counterculture, bohemian project, but as a permanent malcontent he was uncomfortable with any role other than die-hard opposition. Dugin had greater ambitions. 'I was holding him back', concedes Limonov today.[21]

Tensions continued in the NBP. It was divided into the intellectuals, who were with Dugin, and on Limonov's side the 'chess faction', described by Korovin as 'lumpen youths' who mainly played chess and worked out with dumbbells in the Frunzenskaya basement.

In 1997, Dugin further exacerbated the divide when he joined the Old Believer sect – a sixteenth-century schismatic version of the Orthodox Church, preferred by the original Eurasianists because it was the faith of Russia at the time of the Golden Horde. It was also soon after the publication of *Khlyst*, a book by Alexander Etkind, a professor of history at Cambridge University, on the role of Orthodox Christian sects in moulding the eschatological world-views of the Bolshevik revolutionaries. In fact, Limonov complained in his biography that Dugin had made the entire NBP buy the book and read it.

Whatever the cause of Dugin's conversion, he convinced nine members of the NBP to convert as well, and even took the unusual step of inviting monks from the Preobrazhensky Old Believers monastery in Moscow to come and sew traditional black *kosovorotki*, or peasant blouses, for the entire NBP. According to Korovin, who followed Dugin into the Old Believers and still wears a long flowing beard to prove it: 'Dugin's embrace of Old Belief irritated Limonov, even more so when most active members of the party followed this idea and started to fast, grow beards, sew shirts and go to church.' Limonov criticized Dugin openly. 'Dugin's going mad', Limonov told one meeting. 'He has zombified you and you follow him like blind moles. You have forgotten about the party, the revolution. It's necessary to give up all this crap.'

Dugin's faction started cultivating beards and dressing in black. 'I thought it was a phase, a hobby, it would pass', wrote Limonov. 'But the party was not made to serve the intellectual dalliances of our Merlin.' Dugin also stopped drinking – a step that was seen as intensely disloyal among the 'chess faction' of his party. He even gave a lecture in 1997 on the need to delay revolution, saying that before any bloodshed they must first create a new type of human being – the 'philosophical Russian'.[22] 'Only after this, sometime in the far distant future could we have a revolution', related Limonov in his memoirs, describing Dugin's speech. After Dugin left the bunker to host a radio show, Limonov immediately countermanded him: 'The party is not a circle for the study of art and literature', he told members. 'The party has political goals and self-improvement is not one of them. I am all for self-improvement, but you can do this in your own time.'[23]

The movement split along theological lines. The final straw was an argument over 248 roubles which disappeared from the party's cash box, with the two groups pointing the finger at each other. Dugin wrote a long-winded article in *Limonka* pouring bile on 'useless beer-swilling, chess-playing half dolts' in the NBP. Limonov's libelled loyalists demanded an apology. Dugin left in a huff, taking his nine followers, including Korovin. He settled in an office in a library across from the Novodevichy Convent in Moscow, hung with post-modern art nouveau posters. Weeks before the split, Dugin had already begun his journey towards the political establishment, with the publication of a new book that would change his fate – and arguably that of Russia as well. 'Dugin requalified as the guru of geopolitics in Russia', as Limonov put it.

CHAPTER ELEVEN

HEARTLAND

It would be extremely unpleasant for Sir Halford Mackinder, a bespectacled and slightly aloof Edwardian academic, to witness the use to which his life's work has been put in post-communist Russia.

Best-known for a lecture entitled 'The Geographical Pivot of History', which he delivered to the Royal Geographical Society in 1904, Mackinder argued that Russia, not Germany, was Britain's main strategic opponent. This he illustrated with a colourful theory that came to be known as 'geopolitics'. The timing of his prediction, prior to two world wars against Germany, subsequently did not do his theory any favours. However, Mackinder was finally vindicated in the last year of his life by the start of the Cold War, the epitome of his teachings. He saw the world arrayed in pretty much the shape he had foreseen in 1904: Britain and America, whose navies ruled the world's oceans, against the Soviet Union, the world's predominant land power, whose vast steppe and harsh winters had defeated Napoleon and Hitler – all but impregnable behind a land fortress, the 'Heartland' of Eurasia.

Despite the centuries of technological progress and human enlightenment, Mackinder believed that geography remained the fundamental constituent of world order, just as it had been during the Peloponnesian War, in which sea-power Athens faced off against Greece's greatest land army Sparta. Since then, geopoliticians have argued, most armed conflicts have always featured a stronger navy against a stronger army. Sea power and land power, in other words, are fated to clash. The global seat of land power – inner Eurasia, the territory of the Russian Empire – would forever be in global competition with the sea power, the mantle of which was soon to be transferred from Britain to the United States. Geography dictated that Russia would forever seek to break out of continental isolation, seize warm-water ports and build a world-beating navy, while the UK (and its successor the US) would seek to encroach land-wards into Eastern Europe and Inner Asia.

In 1919, Mackinder still clung to the notion that Russia was Britain's main adversary: he advocated 'a complete territorial buffer between Russia and Germany', which French President Georges Clemenceau later named a *cordon sanitaire* aimed at containing communism (though it ultimately failed to prevent a war). Mackinder justified the move with the most famous sentences he ever penned: 'Who rules East Europe commands the Heartland; Who rules the Heartland commands the World Island; Who rules the World Island commands the World.'

It took about 50 years for those words to get noticed in the heartland itself; but when they were, Mackinder was suddenly plucked from obscurity to fame and given the status of prophet – for all the wrong reasons. His dire warnings, issued about the latent potential of Russia for conquest and domination, were intended to coax a consensus among the interwar-era European elite to prevent this from happening; instead they became the lightning rod for a new Russian version of 'Manifest Destiny'.

Mackinder's arguments were useful to Dugin and other hardliners who contended that conflict with the West was a permanent condition for Russia, though they had trouble explaining why. The reasons for the Cold War had seemingly evaporated with the end of ideological confrontation, in a new era of universal tolerance, democracy and the 'end of history'. But, the geopoliticians argued, what if the conflict with the West was more fundamental than just a disagreement over what Hegel meant? What if the ideological conflict was part of some greater, strategic contradiction, which had not gone away and was destined to resurface? The historical schism between land and sea provided an argument for why this might be the case, casting doubt on the triumphalism surrounding the end of communism. And what better proof of the clandestine continuation of the conflict with the West than the words of one of Whitehall's secret cardinals that it is eternal?

The Englishman's elevation to the status of grand mufti of Atlantic power was assisted by Dugin, who in 1997 published *The Foundations of Geopolitics*, one of the most curious, impressive and terrifying books to come out of Russia during the entire post-Soviet era, and one that became a pole star for a broad section of Russian hardliners. The book grew out of Dugin's hobnobbing with New Right thinkers and his fortnightly lectures at the General Staff Academy under Rodionov's auspices. By 1993/94, according to Dugin, the notes from his lectures had been compiled as a set of materials, which all entrants to the Academy were supposed to use, and which were frequently amended and annotated by new insights from the generals, or following the odd lecture by a right-wing ideologue flown in from Paris or Milan.

In Dugin's capable hands, Mackinder was transformed from an obscure Edwardian curiosity who never got tenure at Oxford, into a sort of Cardinal Richelieu of Whitehall, whose whispered counsels to the great men of state provided a sure hand on the tiller of British strategic thinking for half a century, and whose ideas continue to be the strategic imperatives for a new generation of secret mandarins.

In addition to Mackinder, there were the opposing geopoliticians profiled by Dugin, mostly German, who argued from the same logic as Mackinder but in defence of continental land power rather than global sea power. These included Friedrich Ratzel, a late nineteenth-century German geographer who coined the term *Lebensraum*, or 'living space', which later was co-opted as an imperative by the Third Reich. The second generation of geopolitical writings earned the theory a lingering association with Nazism. Mackinder's contemporary Karl Haushofer was a German army general and strategic theorist who was a strong proponent of a three-way alliance between Berlin, Moscow and Tokyo.

Mainstream political scientists look slightly askance at the subset of geopolitics. They regard geopoliticians much as mainstream economists regard the so-called 'gold bugs', who persist in believing in the eternal value of gold as a medium of exchange and who place their faith in the old constants which they are sure will inevitably reappear. Similarly, the geopoliticans, an exotic subculture within the expert community, believe that despite lofty principles and progress, the mean – strategic conflict over land – will always prevail. Sometimes, they are right.

The Foundations of Geopolitics sold out in four editions, and continues to be assigned as a textbook at the General Staff Academy and other military universities in Russia. 'There has probably not been another book published in Russia during the post-communist period which has exerted a comparable influence on Russian military, police, and statist foreign policy elites', writes historian John Dunlop, a Hoover Institution specialist on the Russian right.[1]

The book fell on fertile ground. The years 1994 to 1997 had witnessed a sea-change in the Russian elite as a result of economic collapse, military defeat in Chechnya and a string of diplomatic setbacks at the hands of the US, culminating in the 1996 decision to enlarge NATO to include Poland, the Czech Republic and Hungary. This all discredited democratic reformers and put the wind in the sails of hardliners, who had been warning all along of the pitfalls of trusting a partnership with the West.

In 1996, Andrey Kozyrev, the foreign minister who was a symbol of the westernizing strain in Yeltsin's policies, was sacked, and the same year, General

Igor Rodionov, the hardliner's hardliner – and Dugin's patron at the General Staff Academy – was appointed defence minister, replacing Pavel Grachev, who, as head of the airborne forces, had sided with Yeltsin in August 1991. Also in 1996, the Duma voted to abrogate the decision of the Belovezh Agreement of 1991, and simultaneously to recognize as legally binding the results of the 1991 referendum, in which 70 per cent of Russian voters supported the preservation of the USSR.[2] It was obviously only symbolic, but a mere five years after the dissolution of the USSR, a majority of the Russian elite – if one accepts the overwhelming Duma vote as an adequate bellwether – supported the restoration of empire.

Foundations arrived at just the moment when Russia's elite was undergoing a seismic shift, though it would not be until the collapse of the rouble in August 1998 that liberalism in Russia was finally dealt a death blow. *Foundations* was helped by curiously ubiquitous product placement in Moscow's best bookstores – almost invariably next to the cash register.

Dugin's main argument in *Foundations* came straight from Haushofer's pages: the need to thwart the conspiracy of 'Atlanticism' led by the US and NATO and aimed at containing Russia within successive geographic rings of newly independent states. The plan was simple: first put the Soviet Union back together, counselled Dugin, and then use clever alliance diplomacy focused on partnerships with Japan, Iran and Germany to eject the United States and its Atlanticist minions from the continent.

The key to creating 'Eurasia' is to reject a narrow nationalistic agenda which could alienate potential allies. He quoted New Right theorist Jean-François Thiriart, who said 'the main mistake of Hitler was that he tried to make Europe German. Instead, he should have tried to make it European.' Russia, it followed, would not be making a Russian Empire, but a Eurasian one.[3] 'The Eurasian Empire will be constructed on the fundamental principle of the common enemy: the rejection of Atlanticism, the strategic control of the USA, and the refusal to allow liberal values to dominate us', wrote Dugin.

It did not seem to matter that around 1997 this idea seemed completely insane. Russia's GDP was smaller than that of the Netherlands, and the once formidable Red Army had just been defeated on the battlefield and forced into a humiliating peace by a rag-tag group of Chechen insurgents. It was a period of Russian history when analogies to Weimar Germany were plentiful, and Dugin's book was evidence that the same dark forces that had been radicalized by Germany's interwar collapse seemed to be in the ascendant in Russia. It preached that the country's humiliation was the result of foreign conspiracies. The dust jacket was emblazoned with a swastika-like runic symbol known in occult circles as the 'star of chaos',[4] and the book itself favourably profiled several Nazis and extreme rightists. If the parallels with the Third Reich were not already plentiful enough, it called for the formation of a geopolitical 'axis' which would include Germany and Japan.

Foundations was premised on the notion – an easy sell to a conspiracy-mad reading public – that real politics took place behind a veil of intrigue, according to rules that the elites and regimes of the world had internalized for centuries behind their bastions of privilege, but were loath to demonstrate publicly. It came with all the esoteric trappings of an initiation to secret wisdom: runic inscriptions, arcane maps with all manner of arrows and cross-hatching, introductions to unheard-of grey cardinals of world diplomacy. But there were just enough actual facts in support of the fantastic conclusions for the reader (I must admit, I was one) to be instantly intrigued – just as players at a Ouija board are often most impressed when the planchette lands on some fact of which they are already aware.

The reason that geopolitics is so obscure, it turns out, is not because its practitioners are crazy, hopelessly abstruse, or were prosecuted at the Nuremburg trials; but rather, because of a clever cover-up by the powers-that-be. Or, as Dugin puts it, 'because geopolitics too openly demonstrates the fundamental mechanism of international politics, which various regimes more often than not would prefer to hide behind foggy rhetoric and abstract ideological schemes'.[5]

Dugin thus set out self-consciously to write a how-to manual for conquest and political rule in the manner of Niccolò Machiavelli. Like *The Prince* (which was essentially a fawning job application written to Florentine ruler Lorenzo de' Medici after Machiavelli had been out of power and exiled for ten years), Dugin wrote his book as an ode to Russia's national security *nomenklatura* from the depths of his post-1993 wilderness, sitting in the dirty basement on Frunzenskaya Street, surrounded by chess-playing, beer-drinking head bangers.

Foundations was more sober than Dugin's previous books, better argued, and shorn of occult references, numerology, traditionalism and other eccentric metaphysics. In fact, it is quite possible that he had significant help from high-level people at the General Staff Academy, where he still lectured. Historian John Dunlop has observed that 'it may be of significance that Dugin's "Foundations of Geopolitics" was written during the time that Rodionov was serving as defense minister', though by the time the book was published Rodionov – a fierce opponent of civilian control over the military and of NATO expansion – was already out.[6]

Dugin did not try to hide his connection to the army: on the first page he credited General Klokotov, his main collaborator at the Academy of the General Staff, with being his co-author and major inspiration (though Klokotov insists he was not). But the clever association with the military gave Dugin's work some authority and a veneer of official respectability, as well as the pervasive notion that he was the front man for some putative Russian 'deep state' conspiracy of hardliners, straight off the pages of one of his pamphlets. And it is not impossible that this was actually the case.

Dugin clearly longed to walk the corridors of power, and did his best to make his case to those who abided there. Only those who understood the imperatives of geography and power, he wrote, could be considered qualified to hold the tiller of state: 'The dependence of the human being on geography is only apparent the closer one gets to the summit of power. Geopolitics is a worldview of power, a science of power, for power.'

The plan for Russia's national rebirth was as follows. In the West, Germany must be coaxed into an alliance with Russia:

> Germany today is an economic giant and a political dwarf. Russia is exactly the opposite – a political giant and an economic cripple. A 'Moscow–Berlin axis' would cure the ailments of both partners and lay the foundation for a future prosperous Great Russia and Greater Germany.[7]

Successive generations of statesmen have found that Russia–Germany alliances often end badly. For that reason, Dugin counselled, the two countries must destroy the 'sanitary cordon' or buffer zone of unstable weak states in Eastern Europe, by dividing the space into two spheres of influence, similar to the Holy Alliance of 1815 or the Molotov–Ribbentrop Pact of 1939. It will be necessary 'to dispel the illusions held by intermediate states regarding their potential independence from geopolitically powerful neighbours. We must create an immediate and clear boundary between Russia and friendly Central Europe (Germany).'[8] Russia could even give Kaliningrad back to Germany, in exchange for strategic guarantees in other areas.

A German-Russian alliance would reorient Europe away from Atlantic influence and towards Eurasia. France would be encouraged to orient towards Germany, which would cement the Eurasian vector of Europe around a 'Moscow–Berlin–Paris' axis:

> The tendency towards European unification around Germany [Dugin never uses the term 'European Union'] will have positive significance only on one fundamental condition – the creation of a firm geopolitical and strategic Moscow–Berlin axis. By itself Central Europe does not have enough political and military potential to gain independence from the Atlantic United States.[9]

In the east, Dugin oriented his hopes on nascent Japanese nationalism. The Moscow–Tokyo axis could be created by giving the Kurile Islands back to Japan, in exchange for Tokyo abolishing its mutual security treaty with the United States. China, which had undergone a 'liberal' revolution and therefore is a 'platform for Atlantic influence in Asia', needs to be either neutralized or given a sphere of influence in Southeast Asia, where it cannot harm Russian strategic interests.

Of course, it went without saying that the USSR must be put back together; Georgia must be dismembered and Ukraine annexed: 'Ukraine, as an independent state with certain territorial ambitions, represents an enormous danger for all of Eurasia.' Azerbaijan, though, could be given away to Iran in exchange for a 'Moscow–Tehran axis'. Finland could be added to the Russian province of Murmansk, while Serbia, Romania, Bulgaria and Greece would join Russia as an Orthodox 'Third Rome' or Russian South.

The other thing the book gives short shrift to, despite Dugin's erudite style and exhaustive presentation, was exactly *why* Russia needed an empire. Russian thinkers, from Alexander Herzen to Andrey Sakharov, have been adamant that the empire is the primary culprit for Russia's eternal backwardness. Few would say that modern-day Russia's dysfunction and lack of status and influence commensurate with its ambitions on the global stage are due to any deficiency in size – it is, after all, still geographically the largest country in the world, despite losing 14 post-Soviet territories. Additionally, Russia's land-based civilization was not just a strategic opponent of sea-based powers, but culturally and civilizationally anomalous, inherently more hierarchical and authoritarian than the more mercantile and democratic Atlantic world. Dugin argued that empire was the only way to stop the march of liberalism, which was antithetical to Russia's value system.

'Tellurocracy' (supremacy on the land – referring to land-based societies like Russia's) is:

> associated with the fixity of space and stability of its qualitative characteristics and orientations. On the level of civilization this is embodied in settlement, conservatism, in strict legal regulations that govern the large associations of men – of tribes, nations, states, empires. The hardness of the land is culturally embodied in the hardness and stability of social traditions.

Meanwhile, 'thalassocracy' (sea power) in Dugin's terminology, is:

> dynamic, mobile, prone to technological development. [Its] priorities are nomadism (especially sailing), trade, the spirit of individual enterprise. The individual as the most mobile part of the team is given the supreme value.[10]

While this view that culture, civilization and geography are interrelated had its roots in the Eurasianist teachings of Trubetskoy and Savitsky, Dugin reached for support instead to a former Nazi: Carl Schmitt, the brilliant legal philosopher of the Third Reich, whose concept of *Nomos* (discussed earlier) foresaw a holistic unity between the state, culture, land and environment. A society's juridical order and state institutions are expressions of the particular character of geography, argued Dugin: 'The most important conclusion [of Schmitt's *Nomos* theory] is that Schmitt came close to the global historic antagonism and confrontation between land civilization and sea civilization.'

Beyond that, Dugin's specific reasons for advocating empire and worldwide conquest are not clearly spelled out, though elsewhere in his writings he frequently views upheaval and violence less as means to an end than as spiritual values in themselves. He followed in the footsteps of totalitarian thinkers – from Hitler to Spengler to Danilevsky – promising revolution for revolution's sake. Why does Russia need its empire back? Because Russia needs an empire, said Dugin. Empire, he wrote, was the essence of a uniquely messianic nation:

> In fact, the unique characteristic of Russian nationalism is its global scope –
> it is associated not so much with blood [relations] as with space, soil, land.
> Outside of empire, Russians lose their identity and disappear as a nation.[11]

Like all manner of utopian philosophers, Dugin seemed to promise global turmoil as the harbinger of earthly beatitude; an eschatological historical apocalypse which simultaneously gives birth to a new perfect world. He claimed that in the death of communism five short years before, another destiny and mission for the Russian people had been born.

The influence of *Foundations* was profound if measured by book sales; but even more profound if measured by the true yardstick of the scribbler – plagiarism. Dugin's ideas became a 'virus', as he put it. They were reprinted in dozens of similar manuals and textbooks, all of which devoted themselves to the theories of Mackinder, Haushofer and others. Bookstores began to have a 'Geopolitics' section; the Duma formed a 'Geopolitics' committee stacked with LDPR deputies; Boris Berezovsky, influential oligarch and behind-the-scenes power broker, ended an appearance on the *Hero of the Day* television chat show in 1998 with the statement 'I just want to say one more thing: geopolitics is the destiny of Russia.'

Geopolitics was like 'open source computer software', as Dugin put it. He wrote the programme, and everyone copied it.

* * *

Foundations opened many doors for Dugin in his post-NBP phase. In 1998, following publication, he was invited to appear together with Gennady Seleznev, the speaker of the Russian Duma, on a radio talk show. Afterwards, Seleznev invited him to come and work for him as an adviser.

A rotund man, formerly chief editor of the newspaper *Pravda*, Seleznev was constantly mounting behind-the-scenes coup attempts against Zyuganov for leadership of the Communist Party, from which he was ultimately excluded in 2002. Dugin, still offended at Zyuganov for plagiarizing his ideas, found it satisfying to work for the competition: 'I supported Seleznev more to get on Zyuganov's nerves.' Seleznev also saw value in Dugin, 'mainly as a consultant for public opinion', but also as a way to outflank Zyuganov on the right – as a way of burnishing his credentials as a patriot and nationalist in the rapidly approaching post-Yeltsin era.

The connection to Seleznev opened still more doors. Alexander Tarantsev, the head of the concern Russkoe Zoloto (Russian Gold), which controlled almost all the open-air markets in Moscow, asked to finance a new edition of *Foundations*, to which Dugin was only too happy to agree. Tarantsev was[12] a real-estate mogul with a supermodel wife, a wardrobe of flashy suits and an armoured Mercedes. The reinforced door of his office was pockmarked with bullet holes from a 1997 assassination attempt. Formidable and intense, he was also leader of the notorious Orekhovskaya mafia gang, according to the 2008 testimony of three convicted murderers (something he would always deny).[13]

Another addition to Dugin's rogue's gallery of new sponsors and contacts arrived in the form of a radical Jewish nationalist named Avigdor Eskin, who had emigrated from Russia to Israel in 1988 and become an early supporter of the extremist Kach movement there. Dugin and Eskin shared an interest in Kabbalah, the ancient Jewish form of esoteric mysticism, which Dugin had come to via his study of traditionalism. Both men also belonged to the extreme right wing: Eskin became famous in 1995 when he responded to the Oslo Accords by pronouncing an ancient Kabbalistic death curse known as 'lashes of fire' (*pulsa d'nura* in Aramaic) on Prime Minister Yitzhak Rabin. The curse is believed generally to work within 30 days; 32 days later, Rabin was assassinated by Yigal Amir. In 1997, Eskin was given a four-month prison sentence for incitement.

Back in Moscow following his prison term, Eskin and Dugin struck up a friendship – an unlikely acquaintance given one was a radical Zionist and the other had just published a book advocating the construction of a world-dominating 'axis' with Germany and Japan as members. Dugin immediately invited Eskin to appear with him on numerous panels and at public events, and would eventually give him a seat on the central committee of the short-lived

Eurasia Party that he was to found in 2001. Eskin believes that Dugin needed him 'as a shield against being called anti-Semitic', which suddenly was useful to Dugin, who was trying to shed his extremist image and reinvent himself as an establishment pundit.

The main benefit to Dugin from the acquaintance, however, was one Mikhail Gagloev, a wealthy South Ossetian banker and friend of Eskin's, who came to sponsor Dugin's various political activities for much of the coming decade. Gagloev's business activities focused on Moscow's army football club, CSKA, and he was a key player in a 'business group' known informally in Moscow circles as the Luzhniki group, after the city's main football stadium where CSKA played. The business front for the group – which included a Ukrainian ex-mobster, Evgeny Giner, and the deputy speaker of Russia's parliament, Alexander Babakov – was a UK Channel Islands-registered company called Bluecastle Enterprises. Gagloev's Tempbank had the distinction of financing all Bluecastle's transactions.

And so, just as Dugin began his march towards the mainstream, he found the mainstream – such as it was – marching towards him. In fact, the very concept of 'mainstream' culture was the subject of some serious revision by the end of one of the most appallingly destructive decades Russia has yet known.

The prestige of the political establishment was at an all-time low. Birth rates plummeted and death rates soared, as economic reforms impoverished much of the population. The first war in Chechnya, which ended with a ceasefire in 1996 with the rebel government still in power, graphically demonstrated the weakness of the Russian state, while the collapse of the rouble in 1998 destroyed all faith in the liberal market model of society, just as queues and shortages had ruined communism in the 1970s and 1980s. Nothing approaching a consensus was detectable in a society that had become unstuck by the progressive calamities, and centrifugal forces appeared gradually to be taking control of the country's destiny, as they had at the end of the previous decade.

Whereas in normal times the Kremlin provided the glue for cultural and public life, during the late Yeltsin years the executive branch was increasingly marginal and ignored – just one more power centre in a growing patchwork of elite clans struggling for dominance. Individual law enforcement agencies and security services formed their own feudal fiefdoms; organized crime was rampant; provincial governors and factory directors across Russia's 11 time zones were emboldened by the widening gulf to thumb their noses at Moscow and take matters into their own hands. And after Yeltsin's re-election in 1996, the Kremlin was essentially taken over by seven hyper-wealthy individuals who had helped put him there. They had made their money from cheap property sales by the state and had become the original so-called 'oligarchs' in the process, combining executive power and economic wealth.

A consistent thread ran through much of the literature and media of the period: alienation from a rotting, navel-gazing urban establishment, and the embrace of rural, traditional and unspoiled Russian identity. Not since the 1860s and Dostoevsky's time had the meaning of Russianness became such a central focus of much popular official culture; in 1996 the Kremlin even convened a committee to examine the 'Russian idea' (though it did not get anywhere). Russians were encouraged to take pride and seek salvation in their enigmatic nation, the vast, immortal landscapes of the hinterland; while urban cosmopolitan values became synonymous with cowardice and betrayal.

Moscow in the 1990s looked like a gigantic Chekhov play in reverse: instead of the chuckleheaded urban bourgeoisie invading the idyllic country life of the Russian aristocracy, it was the provincial steel kings, West Siberian oil barons and canned food merchants from Krasnodar and Tyumen who were blundering around the capital, pricing the snobbish intelligentsia out of their own central neighbourhoods. This kitchen-dwelling class's traditional place in the Soviet pecking order was gradually being usurped by dunderheaded, but rich, provincials.

The intelligentsia – the class which, since the nineteenth century, had made it its business to criticize the established order – had been one of the primary reasons for the recent collapse of communism, which in turn had consigned its members to irrelevance. In the new world, where money was the determinant of all value, there was no room for ideas. Academics were forced to work in pitiful conditions or to emigrate; authors who used to enjoy unquestioned moral authority now found themselves selling their services to the highest bidder for not very much.

For Dugin, as for many of his fellow intellectuals, taking on a wealthy patron was a perfectly respectable ploy: as Eskin put it, 'all Russian intellectuals come with a price tag'. Many newly wealthy Russians found it useful to keep an intellectual or two on the payroll, to elevate them above the average, run-of-the-mill provincial plutocrat. Dugin, with his impeccable Moscow bohemian pedigree, had none of his patron's provincial qualms or shyness: his natural nerve cut through the Muscovites' condescension. Dugin was always polite and respectful to his new patron, though he had a marked habit of changing the subject whenever Gagloev spoke up in company.

The corruption and commercialization of the intelligentsia and their New Russian clients became a target for one of Russia's funniest satirists, Viktor Pelevin, whose 1999 breakout novel *Generation P* – which told the story of an advertising copywriter named Vladlen Tatarsky, who is recruited to work at an ad agency, adapting Western advertising to the 'Russian mentality' – best expressed this bewilderment at the transformation of the country into a consumer paradise. Indeed, in reality, for the average Muscovite the landscape of the capital had changed little in the half-decade since the end of communism – aside from the replacement of the dominating symbols of Soviet power (the statues of Lenin, Marx and Dzerzhinsky) with large billboards and neon-lit signs. The circular trisected Mercedes logo stared across the Moscow River, rising ghostily above the Kremlin from the south bank. On Pushkin Square, a statue of the great nineteenth-century author of *Evgeny Onegin* was overshadowed by a gigantic blue Nokia sign, hovering above the golden arches of a McDonalds.

A meditation on brands, which seemed to embody a new official metaphysics of the former USSR, *Generation P* was devoted to Western consumer culture and its oddly obsessive effect on post-Soviet Russia. The novel is set against the backdrop of the 1990s, when Pelevin's generation saw the 'evil empire' of their parents transformed into an 'evil banana republic which imported its bananas from Finland', while consumer society is presented as a high-tech form of totalitarian mind control. It had replaced the dysfunctional Soviet authoritarianism with something altogether more pernicious and malevolent. Just as Mikhail Bulgakov had sent up half of the 1930s Soviet literary establishment in his novel *The Master and Margarita* – in which Stalin's Moscow is terrorized by Satan and a large pistol-toting cat – Pelevin presents Moscow as a surreal simulacrum of consumer advertising, recreational drug use and Babylonian mythology, in which shamanistic significance is attributed to run-of-the-mill marketing gimmicks.

The surreal landscape of *Generation P* was populated by a number of doppelgangers for actual historical figures. One such is the magician Farsuk Seiful-Farseikin. He first appears in the novel as a lowly TV commentator, but he is later revealed to be the high priest who presides over the digitized new world order of media, spin and mind control. A clue as to Farseikin's 'true' identity is the fact that he always appears wearing his 'famous pince-nez'. For the cognoscenti of Pelevin's Moscow, that could be none other than the personage of the owl-like Kremlin spin doctor Gleb Pavlovsky. Perhaps more than any other single person, Russians owe their postmodern simulacrum of politics – lampooned by Pelevin – to this man.

Pavlovsky, by all accounts, is a uniquely talented political operative who has had a hand in virtually every election since 1996. He is even more skilled at giving the impression – whether or not it is true, though often it is – that he is behind whatever great intrigue is brewing at the time. With his ever-present pair of glasses perched on the tip of his nose (though I have never actually seen him wear a pince-nez), his reputation as the black prince of Kremlin *piar* (Russian for PR) was cemented in 1996, when he and a small group of 'political technologists' achieved the impossible by getting Boris Yeltsin re-elected as president. Soon, he would help mastermind the ascendancy of Vladimir Putin.

Pavlovsky is a former dissident, with a dark and melancholy streak. According to former acquaintances, his cynicism may have been born out of a painful and conflicted memory from his dissident days. In 1974, he and several members of his dissident circle in Odessa were hauled in by the KGB for possession of anti-Soviet literature. During interrogation, Pavlovsky testified against his colleague, Vyacheslav Igrunov, though he later retracted his testimony in court. While he walked free, Igrunov was placed in a Soviet psychiatric hospital. Igrunov today says he was never angry at Pavlovsky: 'He made a mistake, then owned up to it and tried to correct it. Yes, he put me away, but I was already going away no matter what.' According to acquaintances, however, Pavlovsky's own semi-betrayal seems to have affected him deeply, hardening his idealism into an instrument of brilliant manipulation. 'The Kremlin needed people who were free of intellectual complexes', according to the newspaper *Komsomolskaya Pravda*. In a profile from 2001, it described Pavlovsky as someone who possessed 'the combination of cynicism with a rare talent for orienting himself in the information space'.[14]

At his political consultancy, the Foundation for Effective Politics, Pavlovsky had been one of the pioneers of the use of Western-style political communications – public opinion polls, quantitative methods, television advertising, direct messaging. And in 1996, with Yeltsin lagging badly in the polls in the election race of that year, Pavlovsky was put in charge of television propaganda. He ran a 'thermonuclear' campaign, as he put it. All television channels bombarded the public with images of the Communist leader Zyuganov as a loathsome fascist who wanted to bring Russia back to the dark ages. Television stations ran documentaries about the Stalinist gulag, lines for bread in Brezhnev's time, reminders that the Soviet Union was not the cheerful place many now remembered it after a decade of market reforms. There was also the frequent and mysterious appearance on national television of neo-Nazi groups flinging Hitleresque salutes and shouting 'Heil Zyuganov!' Meanwhile, a more positive image of Yeltsin was beamed into Russian living rooms. He even danced on stage – something unheard of and unprecedented for an official of his standing. 'It was an exercise in mass hypnosis', said Kremlin pollster Alexander Oslon of the campaign. In July, Yeltsin won in a run-off, with 53 per cent of the vote.

The campaign heralded the arrival of 'political technology' – the application of Western-style political communications and instruments to a partly authoritarian Russian context. The Soviet Union had been ruled by brute force and ideology, while the new era dawning in 1996 was ruled by postmodernistic manipulations and television.

By 1997, Gleb Pavlovsky was one of the gatekeepers of the Kremlin establishment – 'a privy counsellor, a black-clad magician', according to the *Komsomolskaya Pravda* profile. He was part of a narrow group of academics, businessmen and journalists who guided public opinion and acted as an informal 'war council' for Yeltsin. In 1997 his influence was increasing, and he would soon win more fame for his role in what was arguably one of the greatest political manipulations in Russian history since 1917.

* * *

While I was based in Moscow as a journalist, I often sought Pavlovsky out for his opinions on Kremlin politics. Once, I asked him about the question of Yeltsin's succession and Putin's rise to power, in which I knew he had played a key role. 'We knew Yeltsin had to go, but how?' replied Pavlovsky. 'If Yeltsin went just like that, the state would stop existing.'

But things were heading from bad to worse, and within months of his election Yeltsin's presidency had begun to go off the rails. First came quintuple bypass surgery in 1996, after which Yeltsin's behaviour was increasingly erratic. He was visibly unsteady on his feet, and made headlines with seemingly drunken antics. He played spoons on the head of the president of Kyrgyzstan; he toasted his 'love for Italian women' in a banquet with Pope John Paul II; and visiting Sweden in 1997, he announced a one-third cut in Russia's nuclear arsenal, which his advisers were later forced to retract.

The nail in the coffin of Yeltsin's presidency, however, was Chechnya, which had become a graphic demonstration of the impotence of the Kremlin under his leadership, and of the danger to Russia's statehood caused by the country's weakness. Some 5,000 Russian soldiers had died during the two-year campaign to re-establish federal control, and Russia had still been defeated by the tiny nation: in the winter of 1996, Russia signed a peace accord with the breakaway state of Ichkeria at the border town of Khasavyurt.

Few ordinary Russians cared about losing Chechnya – quite the opposite, they were only too glad to see the end of the horrific war. But to the patriotic segments of the elite, especially the officer class, it represented a threat to the core of the nation. 'It was a huge blow, so huge that it changed our relationship to the state', according to Pavlovsky, who said that discussion of a successor to Yeltsin started almost immediately after Khasavyurt. The disaster in Chechnya was the once-and-for-all rupture between Yeltsin and much of the political class, according to Pavlovsky, particularly the military and security elite, known as the *siloviki* or 'strong guys':

> There was a very severe problem that the *siloviki* – that is, the army, the FSB, the police – had become alienated from the state, that is, fallen outside the state's control. They were criminalized. It was a very dangerous situation. We had to somehow integrate the power structures back into the state apparatus.[15]

Meanwhile, regional potentates seemed increasingly indifferent to federal authority. In 1998, the governor of the Krasnoyarsk region threatened to take control of strategic nuclear missiles located in the province, while another governor of far-eastern Primorsky Kray denounced a border demarcation agreement with China. The president of Tatarstan, Russia's largest autonomous Islamic republic, established independent diplomatic ties with both Iraq and Iran, and warned that if Russia sent troops to fight on the side of Serbs in the Balkans, they could end up facing 'volunteers' from Russia's Muslim regions.

Things were falling apart faster than they could be fixed. In August 1998, following a six-month run on the rouble after a dip in the price of oil and the Asian financial crisis, the rouble crashed, and with it the bank deposits of most of the population. The fortunes of liberalism in Russia were closely tied to whether its ideas could bring prosperity to the population. And just as the shortages of the 1980s discredited communism, so the crash of 1998 was a most spectacular demonstration that the market democracy model promoted by Yeltsin in the 1990s had failed as well. Russia's liberal dream was in tatters.

Yeltin's unsteady, flailing personality began to symbolize the waywardness of Russia. It became clear that he had to go, but his exit had to be handled carefully, said Pavlovsky:

> We had to create a certain situation, elections in such a way that the successor to Yeltsin would be chosen, who would have the legitimacy of being elected, but at the same time would be one of 'ours' belonging to the state, not disposed to liquidating it.[16]

In other words, Yeltsin could not just roll the dice in the next election and hope for the best. It was understood that whomever he handed over to had to be appointed. Yeltsin would resign and name a successor, who would run as an incumbent and would grant Yeltsin amnesty as one of his first acts. It even became known as 'Operation Successor' within the Kremlin. The mandarins around Yeltsin gradually convinced him that he would have to step down early. The last years of Yeltsin's second term saw a revolving door of prime ministers – Sergey Kirienko, Evgeny Primakov, Sergey Stepashin, and finally Vladimir Putin. 'We were looking for the successor, the way a director casts a film', recalls Pavlovsky.

There were a number of criteria they were looking for. First of all, Yeltsin's priority was loyalty: it should be someone who could guarantee that his family and their interests would be protected, and who would not succumb to public pressure to revoke his amnesty. Secondly, Pavlovsky said, they needed someone with a military or security services background to inspire loyalty in Russia's increasingly rebellious *siloviki*. But most importantly, they needed someone who could win. In its search for the perfect candidate, the Kremlin combed mountains of sociological data that its department of domestic politics used to keep track of the public mood.

At the end of 1998, at the Kremlin's behest, the agency Imidzh Kontakt (two English words: 'Image' and 'Contact') conducted a poll of 204 federal districts and 350,000 respondents. This went little-noticed at the time, but it was the clearest signal yet that they were conducting 'casting' (as Pavlovsky put it) for a new president. It was perhaps the largest poll ever carried out in Russia at the time, and it found that the electorate overwhelmingly wanted candidates in the forthcoming presidential election 'of military bearing, who say little but act decisively'.

One poll interested them the most, according to Pavlovsky. In May 1999, polling agencies Romir and VTsIOM (Russian Public Opinion Research Centre) put out multiple-choice polls which asked Russians 'Which film character would you vote for in the upcoming presidential elections?' The most popular answers were: Marshal Zhukov, commander of Soviet forces during the Second World War, who had often been portrayed in film; Gleb Zheglov, a hard-bitten detective from the 1979 crime thriller *The Meeting Place Must Not Be Changed*; and a third name – Max Stierlitz, the protagonist of a hugely successful television series called *Seventeen Moments of Spring*, broadcast on Soviet television as far back as 1973.

Stierlitz was the stoic, yet human, model for Soviet manhood. The 12-part series detailed the exploits of this fictional KGB deep-penetration agent inside the German Gestapo during the Second World War. He uncovers plans for the Americans to violate the Yalta accord with Stalin and conclude a separate peace with Hitler, shutting the Soviets out of Eastern Europe. Decisive, introspective, patriotic, but gentle, he was a clever marketing tool for the KGB (which had funded the series) and a moral compass for a generation of Russians. Now, he would become the presidential ideal.

Pavlovsky said this poll was particularly exciting because at the time the Kremlin was working on 'Operation Successor' with a shortlist of two ex-security officers – Prime Minister Sergey Stepashin, formerly of the Soviet Interior Ministry, and Vladimir Putin, a former Dresden-based colonel in the KGB, who was at the time head of the Federal Security Service. They had had a problem: how to sell someone from the security services – perhaps the least popular profession in Russia – to voters? Now things fell into place. They needed a KGB agent who had been based in Germany. That narrowed the shortlist down to one name.

It was a sign of the times: the Kremlin, in an effort to avoid actual politics, was to rule instead with political technology, with television avatars straight out of Viktor Pelevin's fiction. The Canadian philosopher Marshall McLuhan's phrase 'the medium is the message' had been transformed from harmless cocktail-party chatter into a deadly serious axiom of statecraft.

On 14 March 2000, after Vladimir Putin was elected, the weekly magazine *Kommersant Vlast* ran a banner headline, with a photo of Stierlitz in his Gestapo uniform: 'Stierlitz – Our President'.

CHAPTER TWELVE

THE CHESS PIECE

Vladimir Putin had joined the KGB right out of Leningrad law faculty in 1975, and had been stationed for several years during the Cold War in the German city of Dresden. He had gone into politics (whether he had actually left the KGB is unclear) working for the mayor of St Petersburg, Anatoly Sobchak, and, after the latter was defeated in a 1996 election, Putin was invited to Moscow to take up various mid-level jobs in the Kremlin. Finally, in 1998, he was appointed head of the FSB, the domestic secret police.

The young Putin made an instant impression as someone both smart and ruthless. And he had demonstrated unswerving loyalty to his former boss, Sobchak. This latter quality was something that Yeltsin was particularly looking for – he wanted guarantees that he and his family would be safe after he resigned from office. And Putin would indeed go on to demonstrate unswerving loyalty to Yeltsin. When Yury Skuratov, the general prosecutor, began to investigate Yeltsin's family and associates on suspicion of corrupt links to a Swiss construction company, the retribution was swift: in April 1999, a video of Skuratov cavorting with two naked women in a hotel room was broadcast on national television. The episode had reportedly been organized by Putin, at the time still the head of the FSB. Putin, at a press conference, confirmed that Skuratov was the man on the tape and accused him of having connections with known criminals.

Putin had never got very far in the KGB, rising only to the rank of lieutenant colonel. But in a sense, this made him the perfect candidate. He spoke the language of the *chekists*, or spies, but clearly owed his job to Yeltsin – and he wouldn't forget it. Yeltsin, in his memoirs, indicates that Putin was all along his top choice as a successor, and he had settled on him in 1998, even before appointing him head of the FSB. 'I will work wherever you assign me', Putin supposedly told Yeltsin, according to the latter's memoirs, after being offered the post of prime minister.

'And in the very highest post?' Yeltsin asked. Putin hesitated. 'I sensed that, for the first time, he truly realized what the conversation was about', according to Yeltsin. 'I had not thought about that. I don't know if I am prepared for that', said Putin. 'Think about it, I have faith in you', Yeltsin told him.

Getting a KGB officer elected was not going to be easy. Old memories died hard, and the KGB's popularity hovered somewhere above organized crime but below Russia's notoriously corrupt traffic cops on the scale of public approval. Putin, uncomfortable in front of a microphone, would be a tough sell.

But all the polling showed that after the disappointment of democrats, Russians wanted order, and were willing to tolerate an authoritarian figure and fewer freedoms in exchange. The stern, expressionless and teetotal Putin contrasted positively with the carousing and reckless Yeltsin. Russians wanted a strong hand. Putin was an exceptional leader, and he arrived at a unique time, when a series of still unexplained events made Russians increasingly fearful for their security.

Taking the reins as prime minister in August, Putin was confronted by his first major military crisis. Chechen militants under the leadership of warlord Shamil Basaev launched an invasion of the neighbouring province of Dagestan. For the first time since the Khasavyurt accords, it appeared that the Chechen militants were expanding their ambitions and threatening the surrounding north Caucasus region with renewed war. Russian commandos were sent into Dagestan to repel the invasion, as Putin's government once again declared war on Chechnya.

But Russia's appetite for more war in the mountain hinterland was questionable, until a set of terrible and mysterious bombings transformed the war from a minor police action into a national crusade that dominated television news around the country.

* * *

On 4 September, at 22:00, a car bomb detonated outside a five-storey building in the town of Buynaksk, in Dagestan, near the Chechen border. It housed Russian border guards and their families, and 64 people died. Five days later, another, larger bomb went off in a nine-storey building on Guryanova Street, in a Moscow suburb, killing 94 and cleaving the building down the middle like a collapsed wedding cake. Over the next week, two more buildings were bombed – one in Moscow and the other in Volgodonsk – while a number of attempted bombings were reportedly discovered in the nick of time.

Pictures of imploded apartment blocks, toilet fixtures hanging from rooms carved in two, seared themselves into the minds of Russian television viewers.

Huge amounts of hexogen explosives had been used, and nothing of this sort had been experienced in Russia's cities since the Second World War. Neighbourhood watch committees were formed and citizen patrols organized. Russians were terrified, and were ready to accept a new war in exchange for order.

Putin came into his own during the second Chechen war. Cool under fire, his tough-guy TV personality was tailor-made for a war commander, and his approval ratings skyrocketed during the autumn to over 50 per cent – at the time an unheard-of rating for any senior government official. At this level, his succession to the presidency the following spring was assured.

However, the murky events surrounding the beginning of the second Chechen war would fuel many conspiracy theories, rivalling August 1991 and October 1993 in the lore of mysterious and weird events of the decade. There are still some troubling facts about the bombings. Four bombs exploded, but several more were discovered and defused, including one that was planted in the city of Ryazan, on 22 September, that was found by vigilant residents before it could go off. Hours later, tipped off by a suspicious phone intercept, local police and security services closed in on the hideout of the suspected bombers.[1] Then something very strange happened: on 24 September, FSB chief Nikolay Patrushev announced on national television that the Ryazan 'bombing' had been an FSB drill all along, and the 'bombers' were in fact FSB operatives using three bags of sugar made up to look like real explosives. 'The incident in Ryazan was not a bombing, nor was it a foiled bombing. It was an exercise.'

It looked more than a little suspicious: the 'bombers' were about to be (or had already been) captured and revealed to be FSB operatives, so the FSB stepped in and gave them an alibi – but having waited a day and a half to do so. Things did not add up: clearly no one else had been informed of this exercise, and FSB spokesman General Alexander Zdanovich had gone on a chat show on 23 September to praise the vigilance of local residents; he had said nothing about an exercise. While the FSB insisted that the bomb was fake, the Ryazan police bomb-disposal expert who defused the device insisted it was real. Meanwhile, Patrushev's suspiciously timed announcement was followed by a string of contradictory statements. There was also a failure to explain why such a drill would have been held in the first place – why were war manoeuvres being held in the midst of a war?

Russia's State Duma has never investigated the bombings, despite there having been two motions to do so. Duma deputy and investigative journalist Yury Shchekochikhin, who filed the motions for the investigation, died in a manner consistent with radiation poisoning in 2003.

Few people in Russia believe that the full truth of the events of August and September 1999 has been told.[2] The bombings, like the invasion of Dagestan, fit a bit too neatly into Putin's rise to power, a bit too coincidentally for comfort. Putin and his team have spent years fending off allegations that he or the Kremlin was in some way involved in the bombings, as part of a 'false flag' operation designed to justify the reconquest of Chechnya. They certainly had the means and the motive to try and provoke a conflict – the future of Russia as a federal state depended on reconquering Chechnya; but it also couldn't hurt to boost the ratings of the chosen candidate for president.

However, the conspiracy theory is tempered by a few other observations. Most importantly, in retrospect the Kremlin's interest in stoking war would seem clear, given the consequences. However, it has been argued that *at the time* it was impossible to predict how association with war in Chechnya would reflect on Putin's popularity. It was a fact that, then, every politician who became identified with the war in Chechnya lost popularity, including Yeltsin and Alexander Lebed, the former general and negotiator of the Khasavyurt accord. 'When Basaev invaded Dagestan', said Pavlovsky, 'we were all telling Putin "Don't touch this. You don't want to be identified with this. You will lose points."' Associating himself with the Chechen civil war could just as easily have backfired badly for Putin if he had lost. But Russia's army won easy victories, bolstered by the timely defection of several senior Chechen figures, including Akhmad Kadyrov, rebel Chechnya's mufti and a powerful clan leader.

The truth of the 1999 events will likely never be known for certain. But on the back of the successful Chechen campaign, Putin's popularity skyrocketed. And Yeltsin, according to plan, stood down on New Year's Eve 1999 to make way for his heir, who won an easy election the following spring.

* * *

Just as Brezhnev had done with his *Dnepropetrovtsy* from his hometown of Dnepropetrovsk in Ukraine, and just as Yeltsin had with his 'Sverdlovsk mafia', so Putin staffed his government with his own people, a group known as the 'St Petersburg *chekists*'. Like him, they hailed from St Petersburg, and all had a background in the security services.

They were men such as Igor Sechin, a former military interpreter in Angola and Mozambique, who speaks fluent Portuguese but probably was not just an interpreter. He would become deputy chief of the President's Administration, essentially controlling physical access to his boss; in 2004, he became chairman of the board of state oil company Rosneft. Sergey Ivanov, a KGB officer since 1975 who knew Putin from Leningrad, became defence minister and later deputy prime minister. Viktor Ivanov, another KGB man since 1977 and Putin associate was named deputy chief of staff for personnel, and essentially vetted all senior civil service appointments in Russia; in 2008 he became the head of the Federal Narcotics Control Agency. Nikolay Patrushev, a KGB counterintelligence officer since 1975, began the Putin era as director of the FSB and then moved to chair the National Security Council. Vladimir Yakunin, who officially worked as a diplomat with the Soviet delegation in New York, was also probably a KGB man; he went on to head the federal railway company. Almost all had worked in Leningrad at various points in their careers and had become friends with Putin. Some were even Putin's neighbours, owning dachas in the same compound as Putin on Lake Komsomolskaya, near Leningrad.

The influx of *siloviki* into government was the culmination of a trend that had been gaining momentum throughout the 1990s. During the Soviet period, the military and security services – the police and KGB – had been a key pillar of the regime, but had played a very minor role in politics. For understandable reasons, the USSR had made a priority out of civilian party control over these 'power structures', as they were known. Up to 41 per cent of the posts in the upper echelons of the KGB during its last years had been occupied by civilians from the Communist Party, while only 5 per cent of government positions were occupied by military and KGB men.[3] Now the civilian–military balance under the Soviets had been reversed, with an influx of military and security men into civilian government. Since the end of the Soviet Union, the share of the military in government increased dramatically: from 5.4 per cent in 1988 to 32 per cent by the middle of Putin's first term.[4]

Many of these security men had heard of Dugin, via his popular book *Foundations*, and in 1999, after Putin had been appointed prime minister and it was clear that he would become Yeltsin's successor, Dugin made a vertiginous U-turn and began his political transformation from hardline opposition ideologue to pro-establishment pundit. That year his piece 'Dawn in Boots' appeared in Prokhanov's newspaper, *Zavtra*, on the subject of the coming revolution in Russian politics:

> People of special services have the basic preconditions to become the bulwark of the Eurasian Renaissance. They are officials, but disciplined and hierarchical. They are patriots, because patriotism was professionally instilled in them during training. Most importantly, they are constantly dealing with 'the enemy'; they, better than anyone, learn to divide everyone into 'us' and 'them'. And this division is the main condition of adequate political consciousness.

He began aggressively to court Pavlovsky, using his popularity in *siloviki* circles as a bargaining chip. 'He practically stormed the President's Administration', according to Pavlovsky. 'Dugin had always been on the periphery, and suddenly he wound up in the mainstream, not really as a result of anything that he did. He felt like his job was just to stay there.'

Dugin had got to know Pavlovsky in the 1990s, having written articles in *Russian Journal*, an internet publication founded by Pavlovsky, who had seemingly filed Dugin away in his prodigious memory as someone who might turn out to be useful later on. 'Of course I didn't support his politics', said Pavlovsky, 'but I welcomed his arrival in the establishment. At least I didn't see anything dangerous in it.'

Pavlovsky's star as a Kremlin political demiurge was at its zenith following Putin's successful election, and even though he had no formal position in the administration, two of his former deputies were chiefs of Kremlin departments in the directorate of domestic politics, and his recommendations carried much weight. He saw Dugin as potentially useful, given the direction the political winds were blowing:

> He suggested some political projects, some of which I sent forward, because I thought it was important to widen the political front so to speak, that the regime should represent a wide spectrum, that it should contain a number of different groups.

At some point in the spring, Dugin appears to have acquired a 'curator' in the Kremlin – a *kurator* is essentially a handler, a 'points person' through whom all communication with the regime passes. Virtually all political organizations of any note have a Kremlin *kurator*; it is a sign that they are seen as worth keeping track of.

Alexander Voloshin, Putin's chief of staff, has no recollection of this (which is plausible, given that the Eurasianists were but a speck on the Kremlin's windscreen at the time). The first contact with the President's Administration appears to have been made by Pavel Zarifullin, an ambitious former law student who had been entranced by the theories of Lev Gumilev ever since he had read them in high school, joined the NBP and was one of the nine acolytes who left the organization along with Dugin. Zarifullin arrived in Moscow in May after graduating from the University of Kazan. He immediately called the Kremlin, demanding to speak to Voloshin on behalf of 'the adviser to Duma Speaker Seleznev'. After numerous failures, he was finally given an appointment with Leonid Ivlev, one of Voloshin's deputies.

Ivlev was the type of grey bureaucrat prized most of all in the Kremlin. A former political officer in the paratroopers, he had studied for a doctorate in philosophy from the Lenin Military Political Academy, and with such an ideology-heavy background in the military, it was not hard to guess that he had worked in what is known euphemistically as 'cadres'. Ivlev had moved to the Kremlin in 1996. His military background clearly smoothed the way for Dugin, whose reputation among military men was high, thanks to *The Foundations of Geopolitics*.

It helped that the Kremlin had not yet evolved into the monolith of Russian politics that it would become under Putin. 'It was complete chaos', recalls Zarifullin. Putin's team were just getting their feet under their desks, and few had any explicit instructions as to how to proceed. In such situations Russian bureaucrats are used to reading signals emanating from the top to try to determine how they should be doing their jobs. Amid the martial rhetoric issuing from the Kremlin, and the revival of Soviet symbols, an overture to Dugin may have seemed like a convenient hedge. Meanwhile, this fact was enthusiastically propagandized by Dugin's group to inflate its own importance. 'The President's Administration is an amorphous structure, it's like an octopus', said Korovin. 'Not all the arms know what the other arms are doing. As soon as someone gets an ID card, suddenly a lot of people come to him.'

Sure enough, Eurasianism began to creep into mainstream discourse. A new set of foreign policy guidelines issued in 2000 decried a 'strengthening tendency towards the formation of a unipolar world under financial and military domination by the United States' and called for a 'multipolar world order'. It described Russia's most important strength as its 'geopolitical position as the largest Eurasian state'.[5]

That autumn, Dugin was introduced to Putin. Dugin refuses to discuss the meeting, but it would change his career. Soon there were sponsors, contacts and open doors.

Indeed, Putin himself seems to have taken an interest in Eurasianism, and on 13 November 2000 he issued the first ever endorsement of the movement by a Russian head of state: 'Russia has always perceived itself as a Eurasian country', he said during a state visit to Kazakhstan. It was hardly a ringing endorsement, but it was not a random off-the-cuff remark either. Dugin at the time called the speech 'an epochal, grandiose revolutionary admission, which, in general, changes everything'.[6]

In late 2000, Dugin made another fateful contact – this time with a square-jawed, barrel-chested man with a deep voice and a high tolerance for alcohol. His name was Petr Suslov and he was a 20-year veteran of the KGB. A fluent Portuguese speaker, Suslov had served in Afghanistan, Mozambique and Angola, where he had worked in a KGB special detachment known as Vympel (Pennant), which ran illegal operations, including political assassinations.

After retiring in 1995, he remained close to the service, in the 'active reserve'. Like most of Dugin's most interesting contacts, there is no consensus on how they met. Suslov says he worked with Dugin on the expert committee for the State Duma under Seleznev, the Duma speaker.[7] However, Seleznev (who died in 2015) claimed never to have heard of Suslov. Dugin's version is that the acquaintanceship was 'complete coincidence, we met through some mutual friends who were musicians'. As always, Dugin's *Foundations* was his calling card with this particular audience. Suslov told Dugin he was an avid fan of the book, and wanted to finance a new edition – an offer Dugin enthusiastically accepted. A few months later, in March 2001, they agreed to set up a political party.

A month after that, a very interesting piece about Suslov appeared in *Novaya Gazeta*, a Moscow newspaper. Yury Shchekochikhin, the paper's investigations editor, wrote an account of a splinter cell within the KGB that was working behind the scenes to bring back the USSR. He named Suslov and Vladimir Revsky (head of the Honour and Dignity KGB veterans' society) as members. Shchekochikhin had apparently recently met an informant somewhere in the French Alps whom he named only as 'Alexey', who provided evidence, in the form of multiple computer files and interviews, that since 1991 he had been working for the cell, which he described as 'Patriots of State Security'.[8] In three serialized *Novaya Gazeta* excerpts, 'Alexey' told Shchekochikhin that the conspiracy had high-ranking protectors in the Russian state, as well as business interests – oil and gas, transport, real estate, banks, arms trading and gambling. 'Alexey' said that he first heard the name Vladimir Putin from his handler in this group, along with the names of several of those in Putin's circle, members of the so-called 'St Petersburg clan'. In addition to Suslov, he named as a 'Patriots' member Suslov's friend, Vladimir Revsky.

The article offered little proof that what 'Alexey' said was true, though Shchekochikhin, a highly respected investigative journalist and parliamentarian, put his reputation on the line to vouch for him. 'Something is going on in our country that makes us believe "Alexey". When I returned I found direct proof of this', wrote Shchekochikhin in the sign-off to his third article in the 'Alexey' series. The 'proof' that Shchekochikhin wrote about in 2002 was never forthcoming. What was supposed to be a four-part series turned into a three-part series, the fourth article never appearing. The following year, Shchekochikhin died in a manner consistent with radiation poisoning (though *Novaya Gazeta* later published an article indicating there was no evidence that he had been poisoned).

Soon after the articles were published, 'Alexey' was outed in the Russian press. His real name, it turns out, was Evgeny Limarev, a Russian businessman living in Haute Savoie in the French Alps, near Geneva.[9] The publicly verifiable parts of his story added up. Indeed, like 'Alexey', Limarev had a father who was a general in the KGB. Evgeny had joined the KGB as a language tutor in 1989, but he was never inducted into the first directorate, and left the service mysteriously in 1991. All this was consistent with 'Alexey's' story that he was recruited to work in a 'stay behind' cell that was outside the organization. Other details also seemed to chime with the original account. 'Alexey' told Shchekochikhin that he had worked for a 'big politician of the left-wing tendency'; Limarev had in fact worked for Seleznev, the Duma speaker (like Dugin, and possibly Suslov) in the late 1990s. Limarev clearly had a deep association with the security services – and had clearly enjoyed a degree of political protection consistent with his story of having high-level connections.

But the claims of the story must be balanced by certain other facts: after Limarev's identity was revealed, it soon turned out that he was running a website funded by fugitive tycoon Boris Berezovsky, the confidant of the Yeltsin family, who had a key role in bringing Putin to power but who had been exiled by him that year. Berezovsky – who wielded a great deal of influence at *Novaya Gazeta* at the time of Shchekochikhin's article – had a clear interest in discrediting the Kremlin, by painting the newly arrived Putin as a product of a fascist plot by the security services to seize power.

The truth of 'Alexey's' revelations will never convincingly be established, though the articles are given credence by highly placed representatives of foreign governments. I approached Suslov about the articles, and over coffee at a central Moscow shopping mall he said it was all 'utter nonsense', echoed by his alleged collaborator Revsky. Suslov, however, is just the sort of raw material for 'deep state' conspiracies that one finds all over the world – a smart, capable and loyal operative, who still offhandedly refers to Soviet-era dissidents as *izmenniki* or 'traitors'. He simultaneously embodies the sort of contradictions and compromises that praetorian guardians of order are often forced to make – and conspiracies seem to follow him wherever he goes.

In fact, in 2002 Alexander Litvinenko, a former FSB officer who fled Russia and was famously murdered in London by radioactive polonium four years later, published a book accusing the Russian state of masterminding the 1999 apartment bombings. As evidence he brought up a similar, if less lethal, sequence of events from five years previously. Suslov, wrote Litvinenko, had run an agent known as Max Lazovsky, who sprang to infamy in the early 1990s as a gangster suspected of more than ten contract murders. Litvinenko claimed that Lazovsky was also behind a mysterious bombing campaign in Moscow, masterminded by the security services, designed to mobilize public opinion behind an invasion at the outset of the Chechen war.

There are facts to back up these assertions: in November 1994, an employee of Lazovsky's Lanako oil trading company was blown up while planting a bomb on a railway track crossing the Yauza River in Moscow. A month later, a Moscow commuter bus was blown up (thankfully it was empty, save for the driver, who was injured). The man who was eventually convicted of the crime in 1996 was another Lazovsky associate.

Lazovsky was not put on the federal wanted list until 1996, and when a Moscow police organized crime squad finally arrested him in February of that year, charging him with more than ten contract murders and other killings, they identified six members of the gang who were FSB operatives – a fact confirmed in writing in November of that year by First Deputy Interior Minister Vladimir Kolesnikov in response to an official request for information from Russia's Duma.[10]

In responding to the disclosures, the FSB only further muddied the waters. FSB director Nikolay Kovalev responded to deputies' concerns by writing in a letter to parliament that the actions of the FSB operatives in Lazovsky's gang 'involved certain deviations from the requirements of departmental regulations . . . Nonetheless, despite this regrettable misunderstanding, the main goal was achieved, since Lazovsky's gang was neutralized.' In the FSB version, Lazovsky and his men were infiltrating the gang in order to eventually liquidate it; the alternative version, believed by most journalists and deputies who followed the scandal, was that the FSB actually *was* the gang, and their actions were not a deviation from protocol in an effort to bolster their bona fides, but were in response to direct orders – the object of which can only be guessed at, but was quite possibly to create a provocation, to be blamed on Chechen militants, that would justify Russia's invasion of Chechnya in 1994.

In 1996, Lazovsky and one other gang member were given a slap on the wrist. 'He seemed to have a secret guardian angel', as the *Moskovskaya Pravda* put it. Lazovsky was eventually convicted of narcotics and weapons offences (charges of forgery had to be dropped, because it was determined that the two men had been carrying genuine security service identity documents) and sentenced to two years' imprisonment and a fine. No mention of murder, bombings or collaboration between organized crime gangs and the special services was heard in the courtroom. In 1998, Lazovsky was released.

While Suslov denies the specifics of Litvinenko's accusations against him – and the fact that he ran Lazovsky as an agent – he was clearly a part of Lazovsky's world. Lazovsky, when he emerged from prison, became Suslov's deputy at the latter's Unity Foundation, which worked in the Caucasus. He was assassinated by a sniper outside his home in 2000.[11]

This entire Suslov episode calls to mind the Umberto Eco novel *Foucault's Pendulum*, in which the protagonists, who make money by peddling phoney conspiracy theories to the gullible, suddenly have to contend with the appearance of the actual secret society they have been writing about, which is demanding to be cut in.

So, too, was Dugin, having spent the last decade peddling the Eurasia conspiracy, suddenly slightly blindsided by the overture from one of its minions. Dugin says today that Suslov had described himself as 'a sort of state envoy to the organized crime world', who was tired of the stress and wanted 'to get out of such work'. The allegations of Suslov's criminal links didn't particularly trouble Dugin, however. After falling out with Suslov in 2003, he told me in an interview, 'Who are our political leaders after all? We are ruled by no one but bandits. They all have their own Max [Lazovsky]. You think Putin and Medvedev are any different? No matter where you go, bandits here bandits there. It's that type of country'. Dugin became leader of their joint party, and Suslov chairman of the executive committee. In a 2005 interview, Korovin recalled that the party:

> was the project of Dugin in conjunction with representatives of Russian special services . . . It is no secret that the special services were given a free hand in policy and business under Putin. In time of Yeltsin they were far more restricted, while under Putin they became more free and participated in politics.[12]

Registering a new political party under Putin's Kremlin was no mean feat – but the Eurasia Party sailed through the justice ministry process, largely thanks to their uncompromising obsequiousness to the Kremlin. In one declaration Dugin wrote: 'The real victory of Eurasianist ideas has become the rule of Putin . . . we totally, radically support the president'.

The party's founding congress was held in April 2001 in the hall on New Arbat Street belonging to the Honour and Dignity Club, the organization of veterans of the special services. Vladimir Revsky (mentioned above) was the club's chairman, and he agreed to join Eurasia's board. Like Suslov, Revsky had been an officer in Vympel, the special operations unit attached to the KGB. Funding came from Gagloev's Tempbank. Dugin told the audience that the movement aimed to work behind the scenes: 'Our aim is not to reach power and not to fight for power; our aim is to fight for influence over the regime'.

The founding conference was accompanied by much buzz – partly due to the publication in the same month of Shchekochikhin's article on the 'Patriots of State Security', which gave even more oxygen to the notion of the new

Eurasia Party as a front for a 'deep state' conspiracy designed to bring back the USSR. This naturally aided their recruiting efforts, according to Zarifullin: 'Because no one knew what was going on in Putin's head, there started to circulate rumours that on the basis of this movement a new ruling party was being born. We did not deny this, of course.' In May 2001, the weekly *Obshchaya Gazeta* observed: 'Dugin is already being perceived not as the preacher of an ideological sect, but as an officially recognized specialist on geopolitical questions.'[13] In a similar vein, the weekly *Versiya* wrote the same month: 'Contacts between Pavlovsky and "Eurasia" actually do occur, but most likely on the level of personal consultations. Alexander Dugin and the head of Kremlin politico-technology enjoy good, friendly relations.'

Pavlovsky at the time was regarded as the master spin doctor of the Kremlin, on the basis of his participation in Operation Successor, though in reality his contacts with Dugin were relatively modest. However, he generally confirms the assessment in *Versiya*, though he denies that Dugin was ever his 'project', or that he ever helped Dugin:

> There was a period where we truly did work together very closely, it was a period when there was an accent on the *siloviki*. I did indeed pass his projects along to various people. I don't remember that they received a huge amount of enthusiasm, but I think he did find himself some sponsors.

Dugin, it turns out, had quite a fan club in some of the darker recesses of post-Yeltsin Russia, and Suslov now took Dugin aside with a proposal. There was a new 'client' to work with, and a lot was at stake. His name was Khoj Akhmed Nukhaev, a shadowy Chechen field commander with a mane of silver hair, aristocratic features and a well-groomed beard, who was so steeped in intrigue that he became the inspiration for the Chechen gang leader Umar Gunaev in Frederick Forsyth's 1996 spy thriller *Icon*.[14] 'Darkly handsome, urbane and polished', according to Forsyth, Gunaev was a former KGB officer who 'had risen in his new life to become the undisputed overlord of all the Chechen underworld west of the Urals'.

Despite his gentle demeanour, Nukhaev was indeed a Chechen criminal mastermind (though it would have been a stretch to say that his empire encompassed everything west of the Urals). Starting in 1987, he ran protection rackets in Moscow, based in a restaurant on Pyatnitskaya Street; and among the businesses he 'protected' was Logovaz, the car dealership owned by future oligarch Boris Berezovsky. In those days, before the first Chechen war started in 1994, Chechen gangs dominated the Moscow underworld, having forced competing ethnically Slav gangs, such as Solntsevo and Lyubertsy, into withdrawing from

prime downtown regions. But after Russian ground troops invaded his homeland in 1994, 'Khan', as he was known, joined the struggle of his brethren. Injured
in 1995 fighting in Grozny, he walked with a cane and a limp. In 1996 he became
first deputy prime minister in the breakaway Chechen republic of Ichkeria, under
acting president Zelimkhan Yandarbiyev, though after the election of field
commander Aslan Maskhadov as president, Nukhaev escaped to Turkey.

Nukhaev seemed to have a penchant for intellectual exploration, which is
what led him to Dugin. He told his biographer Paul Khlebnikov in 2000 that he
was a convinced Eurasianist: 'Eurasianism means the alliance of Orthodoxy
and Islam on the grounds of confrontation against the West.'[15] The late Anna
Politkovskaya, a journalist who covered the Chechen war extensively and was
murdered in 2006, called him a former field commander who began to represent himself 'as a philosopher, which he was not'.[16] He was also, perhaps not
uncoincidentally, identified in a press article in 1999 as an agent of the SVR,
Russia's foreign intelligence agency, run by Suslov.[17]

Suslov and Nukhaev clearly had some sort of previous relationship
according to Zarifullin, but it was unclear to him whether Nukhaev was Suslov's
agent or whether Suslov was actually working for Nukhaev: 'It was hard to tell
who was running the show.' Suslov admits that he and Nukhaev had a long
history of contacts, but he put it rather vaguely: 'Nukhaev was unrecruitable.
He was a very strong person, and his type of personality is one you have to
work with in another way.'[18] Since 2004, Nukhaev has disappeared – either
dead, in hiding or granted asylum somewhere (Suslov believes the last of these).
He remains an official suspect in the murder of his biographer Khlebnikov in
Moscow the same year.

Were Nukhaev indeed a KGB agent, this could help explain his meteoric
ascent through the ranks of organized crime and the rebel government, and the
somewhat unique role that he carved out for himself in the summer of 2001 as
the primary conduit for negotiations between the Kremlin and the Russian-
recognized Chechen interim president Akhmad Kadyrov. At that time, both
sides were trying to find enough common ground for a political settlement of
the conflict that would end the war and further split the dead-enders in the
resistance who had been pushed out of the capital of Grozny and into the
mountains in the early months of 2001.

For whatever reason, both sides in the negotiations seemed to think it
would be a good idea to have a philosopher on board as well, though it was not
clear whether bringing Dugin in was originally Suslov's idea or whether it was
a request from Nukhaev. Dugin was introduced to Nukhaev and was quickly
enraptured by the Chechen – 'a man from another era', he said. 'One finds very
few people who are prepared to act according to their principles.'

Nukhaev was an enthusiastic convert to Eurasianism and had read all Dugin's books. It was clear to Zarifullin at least that the real driver of the contacts with Dugin was the Chechen, and not Suslov, whose interest in Eurasianism was, according to Zarifullin, 'virtually nil'.

The context for the new project was an elusive solution to the second Chechen war, and the integration of Chechnya back into the Russian Federation. Nukhaev appeared to believe that Eurasianism held out the promise of some sort of cultural autonomy and political sovereignty, but under the aegis of Russian 'civilization', which would be acceptable to a majority of the elites in both countries. Russia had already recognized Akhmad Kadyrov as interim president in Chechnya, but a full political settlement to the conflict had eluded negotiators thus far, and Russian forces still faced resistance from rebels under Maskhadov. Talks with Nukhaev centred on a renunciation of separatism and the constitutional basis of Chechnya's existence within the Russian Federation.

The project was so convoluted that I asked Suslov himself to explain it to me at a Czech beer tavern on Moscow's Boulevard Ring. Suslov added further mystery, implying that he had received top-level sanction to undertake a carefully delineated mission using Eurasianism to solve the political impasse with the Chechens:

> I represented the special services. The people I worked with were interested in Eurasianism from a pragmatic point of view. They were looking for something that would work in Chechnya, something that would be a legitimate reason not to secede, an idea we could build a regime around ... We are not great idealists. We approached this from a practical perspective. We wanted to show the Chechens that national minorities could by nature be nationalists but also have an idea of what the motherland is. That is Eurasianism.[19]

Fundamentally, it seemed to be easier to allow Chechnya to save face by declaring allegiance to 'Eurasia' rather than surrender to Russia. At least that seemed to be the semantic gambit held out by Nukhaev.

The Chechen resistance at the time was divided between traditionalists like Nukhaev and radical Islamic fundamentalists – either from abroad, or locals educated in foreign madrassas – who were welcomed by the Chechen resistance during the war. Following the armistice in 1996, the two sides who had fought the Russians to a standstill began to fight between themselves. The Chechen nationalists like Nukhaev and Kadyrov valued the old north Caucasian ways of life: adherence to the *teip* or clan, a strict code of honour and vengeance, and the traditional Islamic beliefs of the Sufi *tariqats*, or sects. Many of the traditional customs – such as ubiquitous accordion music and dancing the 'Lezginka' – were anathema to the radicals, led by field commander Shamil Basaev, who had been brought in as a deputy to President Maskhadov after his election in 1997. Many of the radicals made an effort to forbid music and dancing, and held Sufism to be a form of polytheism on account of its practice of worshipping at the tombs of saints.

As its lightning-fast military drive into the heart of Chechnya piled pressure on the militants, Russia also worked to exacerbate this Chechen schism. Kadyrov finally agreed to a Kremlin demand – a public statement by the Chechens renouncing separatism and radical Islamic Wahhabism. The venue for the announcement was to be a conference in Moscow, while the 'points man' for this project was to be Suslov, with Dugin 'adding intellectual flair', according to Zarifullin.

The conference, hosted by Seleznev and the Eurasia Party, and devoted to the issue of Islamic extremism, was held at Moscow's fancy Marriott President Hotel in July 2001. Clearly the organizers had help in high places. For starters, their star guest, Nukhaev, was the subject of a police manhunt, as well as being a senior leader in an armed rebellion against the Russian Federation. Despite this, he somehow managed to fly in from Turkey, listen to a speech of welcome from Gennady Seleznev, Russia's Duma speaker, and then give the keynote speech to the audience at the glitzy hotel in downtown Moscow. He breezily flew back to Turkey from Sheremetyevo airport after the conference ended.

It is important to note that this particular venue, the Marriott President Hotel, down the street from the Bolshoy theatre, was not chosen at random. Security there was under the control of the FSO (the bodyguard service directly subordinate to Putin) and access was denied to other law enforcement agencies such as the police and the FSB. Nukhaev needed strict guarantees that he would not be arrested, and in the chaotic early Putin period, when the state was still fractured to a large extent and different agencies had different agendas, this was the only way to ensure that the deal remained intact.

The Chechens wanted one more guarantee of Nukhaev's safety: a hostage. This role fell to Korovin, Dugin's lieutenant. 'The Chechens demanded that one of us should visit as a "representative" during Nukhaev's trip', said Zarifullin. 'If the negotiations had not worked out, we understood we would get Korovin's head sent to us in the post.' Korovin denies he was a hostage, but confirmed he had undertaken a 'visit' to some of Nukhaev's representatives.

With all the arrangements in place – Nukhaev under presidential security and Korovin somewhere else – a high-level conference convened to debate Islamic extremism. It was hosted jointly by Seleznev, in whose name a statement was read, and Talgat Tadzhuddin, Russia's official mufti. The conference was a historic one: Nukhaev was the first high-ranking Chechen to begin a dialogue with Russian officials about reconciling Russian statehood with the national aspirations of the Chechens; his speech was the first time that a Chechen official had condemned radical 'Wahhabism' in public; and Nukhaev was also the first high-level Chechen politician to reject separatism and embrace cultural autonomy, in the name of common civilizational bonds with fellow 'Eurasians'.

The freedom of Eurasia's peoples can only be guaranteed, Nukhaev said, through a 'Eurasian authoritarianism', which is 'aimed at reviving spiritual relics, the religious and national self-consciousness of the Eurasian peoples':

> An application of the value and effectiveness of this ideology you can see in the fact that I, convinced supporter of Chechen independence, today appear at this conference in the capital of a state which is at war with my people. Eurasianism creates that level of dialogue between Chechens and Russians on which, for the first time in our history, we have a real basis for mutual understanding, for peace, and for union against the common enemy.

A day after the conference ended, parliamentary elections were announced in Chechnya for the following year. This turn of events sounded the death knell for the Chechen resistance movement, further splitting rebel commander Aslan Maskhadov's base of support. Weeks after Nukhaev's speech, Kadyrov issued a decree banning Islamic extremism in Chechnya, and by 2002 the war would be all but over, though ultimately the settlement reached at the President Hotel was ignored. Further negotiations focused entirely on enfranchising Kadyrov's clan as a guarantor of stability in the region, whose loyalty was ensured by massive subsidies from the federal budget. 'The Kremlin, in the end, just gave all the power to the Kadyrov clan, and that became the model for running Chechnya, not some theoretical multi-vectored nationalism', said Zarifullin.

For the next decade, Chechnya would be an anomaly in the Russian Federation: an island of near self-rule where polygamy flourished, Islamic courts made judgments, and women were forced to wear headscarves in public – all blatant violations of the Russian constitution. The Chechen elite, the so-called Kadyrovtsy, would become one of the most powerful clans in the capital, literally able to get away with murder (mainly of each other) in downtown Moscow. For Chechens, being subjects of the Russian Federation was a largely feudal relationship. It was not a tidy social contract of state and citizen; it was an imperial relationship of a people to a capital.

The Eurasianist philosophy had at last managed to be useful to the Kremlin in a practical matter. The theory had been dreamt up in the 1920s as an ideological antidote to the long-running problem of national self-determination in the multi-ethnic Imperial Russian state, and it had passed its first historical test, providing at least an ideological gloss for a solution to the intractable problem of Chechen separatism – even if it was simply a face-saving veneer of words covering a problem that had been solved with military force and massive federal subsidies.

It was also a demonstration of the way politics under Putin's Kremlin worked: rather than a strict, centrally directed symphony orchestra, the Kremlin functioned more like a jazz improvisation, adhering to the general rhythm and targeting a certain chord. Policy was practised by deniable pawns, who in turn benefited politically. The President's Administration seldom issued direct orders, but rather worked on the basis of sending opaque signals, which were read by the elite, who translated them into practical political 'projects', some of which won favour and others (which missed the overall trend) did not.

This latter fate was the destiny of the Eurasia Party, even at the apogee of its first success. Just as it was poised to reap the fruits of mainstream acceptance and establishment credentials, the world changed. Just two months after the Chechnya conference the world witnessed the 11 September attack on the United States. Putin, who had held the West at arm's length for his first year in power, suddenly went to America's aid: he was the first world leader to call President Bush in the wake of the tragedy, offering support on the UN Security Council and helping the US to secure an airbase in Kyrgyzstan (in Russia's post-Soviet sphere) to resupply troops in Afghanistan. Continuing his pro-Western policy, he also voluntarily removed Russian bases from Cuba and Vietnam.

In a blog post-dated 12 September, Dugin offered condolences to the victims of the attack; but he went on to predict a cataclysm, writing that the planes that had destroyed the Twin Towers were 'swallows of the apocalypse', like the bullets from the gun of Gavrilo Princip which killed Archduke Franz Ferdinand in Sarajevo in 1914 and led to the First World War. The 9/11 attack would forever change world politics, forcing America to respond in such a way that would ignite an apocalyptic 'war between unipolar globalism . . . and the rest of the world'. 'It cannot be excluded that we stand now on the threshold of the end of history. The fight of America against all the rest, given the present technologies of mass destruction, can hardly end, even theoretically, with something positive', wrote Dugin. Indeed, the attacks strengthened US unipolar resolve, leading to conflicts that would severely test its relationships around the world and its international credibility.

Dugin still considers Putin's pro-American policy in the wake of 9/11 to be 'the first mistake of his presidency', a view shared by other hardliners who applauded one of their own as he ascended to the Kremlin, but then felt let down by Putin's reformist, conciliatory policies in his first term as president.

In the wake of 11 September, hardliners suddenly had difficulty getting radio and television airtime and slots in major newspapers, and they were discouraged from being too vocal. Traditionally, shifts in the Kremlin's foreign policy had systemic effects throughout Russian politics, all the way down the line: who gave what speeches, which editorials were run by which newspapers, and so on. In what seemed to be a pointed renunciation of his patriotic endeavours in his first year as president, Putin announced during a January 2002 visit to Poland that 'Russia is a European country and not a Eurasian one'.

The President Hotel conference would be the last anyone heard of the Eurasia Party, which would compete unsuccessfully in the 2003 parliamentary elections and shortly thereafter would close its doors.

'After 11 September, everything was put on hold, due to pressure from the Americans', said Zarifullin. 'It was clear by then that the regime was not going to become Eurasianist, we were not going to recreate the USSR, and we were not playing at the level we thought we were going to be playing at.' He describes the next four years as 'just a bunch of small projects'. Dugin, according to Zarifullin, thought seriously about going back into the opposition, creating an analogy to the National Bolshevik Party. But he stayed with the Kremlin, which was still a reliable, if unsteady, source of patronage.

CHAPTER THIRTEEN

POLITICAL TECHNOLOGY

Putin and his circle had learned one thing from the experience of his two predecessors, Yeltsin and Gorbachev. Both had enjoyed immense popularity at the start of their rule, but soon lost it – with catastrophic consequences. Gorbachev lost control of the state he had been entrusted with; and Yeltsin nearly did, too. The lesson was that, in order to keep power, one had to win and preserve overwhelming popularity. And the failures of Gorbachev and Yeltsin taught the Kremlin that popularity above all depends on studious focus on the national mood.

Polling, focus groups and spin-doctoring became a Kremlin obsession, as 'political technology' became the new religion of power – denoting the adoption of Western-style political messaging techniques, but with an authoritarian twist: the experience of Putin's predecessors also taught his team that staying in power meant not tolerating any alternatives. An 'election', for instance, might involve massive fraud and disqualification of anyone deemed a threat to the ruling party; but it might also feature a huge number of surveys designed to register public preferences and to gather information on which themes resonate with the people, what they care most about and how to appeal to them.

Russians became consumers of politics, in the same way that they were consumers of cosmetics or electronic goods, with their opinions registered through tireless market research and sales data which filtered through opinion polls and focus groups to the Kremlin's department of domestic politics and to Putin's staff, who planned speeches, public appearances and other symbolic paraphernalia of the regime accordingly. But aside from influencing the decorative exterior of the Kremlin's machine – such as whether the national anthem should be changed and to what; which flags should fly on Victory Day; or whether a non-Russian coach would be chosen for the national football squad – there was very little left for Russia's ordinary citizens to pronounce upon. Opinion polls had largely replaced any formal way of influencing the process.

Meanwhile, slowly but surely, any competition was removed. Oligarchs were cowed after the forced expulsion in 2000 of Boris Berezovsky and Vladimir Gusinsky, the owners of the two main private federal TV stations (which were summarily nationalized), and the arrest and prosecution in 2003 of Mikhail Khodorkovsky on charges of tax evasion. Independent political parties such as the Communists, along with smaller liberal parties – the Union of Right Forces and Yabloko – were either subdued (in the former case) or excluded from parliament after the 2003 elections (in the latter two cases). The State Duma became 'a machine for passing the necessary laws', according to Pavlovsky.

Russians appeared willing to sacrifice their freedoms in exchange for rising living standards and order. The Yeltsin-era public commitment to democracy and press freedom was replaced with patriotic rhetoric and nationalist symbols of great power. Putin's Kremlin was a curious hybrid regime: deeply solicitous of the popular will, but hermetically sealed from the public all the same.

Putin started his presidency as something of a blank slate, with a gift for appearing to every potential interest group as *nash* or 'one of ours'. Despite his hardliner image, for example, liberals liked his free-market economics, such as land reform and tax reform, believing his nationalism was a bluff – symbolism and nothing more. Conservatives, meanwhile, saw his overtures to the liberals as tactical, while they believed his real sympathies lay with them. It all presented a confusing picture for observers. Putin was like a Rorschach test: he could appear to be anything an observer wanted to see. Nationalists and hardline statists – but also liberals who longed for a strong modernizer to cut through the entrenched political interests and introduce reforms – all warily embraced a man who represented an enigma.

Helped by large oil surpluses and the devaluation of the rouble in 1998, Russia's economy began to boom. The elusive middle class that Western reformers hoped would be a bulwark of democracy and civil society was instead fashioned by an authoritarian, paternalistic system. Rising incomes were supposed to lead to greater acceptance of liberal values. But the opposite was happening. The new middle class thought they owed their better fortune to Putin and to the social compact they believed they had made with him – giving away their freedoms in exchange for rising incomes. Products of the 1990s, they associated democracy with social anarchy and impoverishment.

Thus, affluence and optimism coincided with deepening nationalism. Following the first year of economic growth since the end of the Soviet Union, a study of publicly available opinion research by the Centre for Political Technology in 2001 showed fresh optimism, combined with (for the first time in a decade) a near-majority of Russians (46 per cent) believing that the coming year would be better than the previous. But simultaneously, according to one study, 'A mood which was formerly concentrated in the Soviet Communist subculture and limited to those with poor education, low income, and non-urban groups, has started to penetrate the layers of society which until recently acted as the agents of modernization'.[1] Some 79 per cent of Russians, for example, felt the end of the USSR to have been a mistake, compared with 69 per cent in 1992; 56 per cent saw NATO as a 'bloc of aggression' rather than a defensive alliance, an 18 percentage point rise since 1997. One of the largest subcategories to subscribe to this view included those with higher education (68 per cent). Increasingly, nationalism was becoming the centre of gravity in Russia's domestic politics, and the Kremlin struggled to keep pace with this mood.

The Kremlin's efforts to centralize power were mirrored in the centralization of the production of images and symbols. Pavlovsky was the public face of the Kremlin's efforts at political technology, and during Putin's first term he and his Kremlin handlers oversaw a shift in politics and the media away from the liberal parties and voices of the Yeltsin era, and towards a preponderance of more conservative and nationalist figures, to which they recruited Dugin and his Eurasianists.

Dugin was given a small role on Russia's First Channel, the great beacon of state propaganda, alongside the station's deputy director Marat Guelman. Guelman was Pavlovsky's partner in the Foundation for Effective Politics, a gallery owner with an almost endless supply of aerodynamic-looking designer spectacles which framed his chubby, cherubic face and permanent scraggly beard. His background as an art critic and collector gave him credibility when pronouncing enigmatically on the postmodernistic playground of Russian political theatre.

Guelman told me he had got to know Dugin in the 1990s as a Moscow art dealer who held weekly soirees at his gallery. The two men were very much part of the bohemian world of Moscow intelligentsia: Dugin was co-leader of the coolest fascist group in the city; Guelman was a liberal hipster who exhibited plainly subversive artwork – such as orthodox icons chopped up with an axe. Neither held against the other the fact that they came from opposite sides of the political spectrum: 'We came from the same *tusovka*', Guelman said of Dugin, using the Russian word for 'clique'.

As deputy director of First Channel, Guelman was responsible for overseeing a shift in the way the channel covered news to suit the Kremlin's needs. 'Official censorship is direct prohibition. All the rest is editorial policy', he breezily told a journalist in 2005, in an interview which seems to have combined the unburdening of a guilty conscience with the pride of a maestro who could not resist an admiring glance back at his work. Later in life, having left the channel and his political consulting business in 2004, Guelman looked back on the system he had helped to create with some misgivings. 'In 1996, we beat the Communists, but in so doing, we gave the regime a tool for staying in power until the end of time', he told me.

At First Channel, Guelman coordinated the work of a 25-man expert panel, which met once a week to advise the station director, Konstantin Ernst. Guelman invited Dugin to join it. It is a sign of the times that the committee had a preponderance of conservative hardline voices. In addition to Dugin there was Sergey Kurginyan – the author of the *Post-Perestroika* pamphlet whom we saw back in 1991 – who was fighting his way back into the mainstream and would shortly be given star billing in political debate shows. There was also Maxim Shevchenko, a fiery critic of Western hypocrisy, who would have a brilliant career as a TV host. Kurginyan told me in a 2011 interview that the swing towards conservative nationalism was a coldly calculated move: 'They brought us in not because they love our ideas, but because they are reading the public opinion polls, the sociological research.'[2]

The appearance of the conservatives heralded the end of an era for Russian television, which had been dominated by liberal, questioning voices since Yeltsin's time. Slowly, prominent anchors like Evgeny Kiselev, Leonid Parfenov and Alexey Pivovarov were driven out and replaced by pro-Kremlin voices such as Shevchenko, Kurginyan and Dugin. Arguably the first and most prominent of the First Channel patriots was Mikhail Leontyev, anchor of the TV talk show *Odnako* ('On the Other Hand'). He was a hugely influential conservative and a member of Dugin's Eurasianist movement. Leontyev is one of the most persuasive voices in Russian state television, with powerful friends in the Kremlin. He set the ideological tone for Russian TV news broadcasts. Strident, quick and brutal in his judgements, he is one of the most powerful TV anchors. His programme would appear every evening after the *Vesti* news broadcasts, and were almost invariably devoted to skewering Western hypocrisy or hinting darkly at foreign forces at work sabotaging the work of the Russian state.

Leontyev was something strange in the corridors of Russia's postmodern and irony-laden propaganda machine, which is staffed mainly by people like Guelman, who do not take it too seriously. Leontyev is a true believer. A former liberal, he became progressively disillusioned with his colleagues in the media over their critical coverage of the Chechen war, accusing them of 'shooting our soldiers in the back'. Around the time of his epiphany, he met Dugin, though he is slightly vague about how this happened: 'we met when Putin first appeared' is all he would say. But soon after, in 2001, he had joined the board of Dugin's

Eurasia Party. 'I don't see any alternative to Eurasianism in the long run', he told me in 2012.

With Leontyev's help, Dugin's profile in the media soon rose; he was invited to write op-ed pieces in major newspapers and appear on major talk shows. He became a fixture on Ekho Moskvy, an opposition-oriented radio station, which balanced its preponderance of liberal views by inviting handpicked conservatives, such as Dugin, Prokhanov and Shevchenko on air. One other fateful contact Dugin met on First Channel was Ivan Demidov, a former liberal in the perestroika era who had evolved with the times; in 2005 he became the chief editor of Russia's first Orthodox cable TV channel, Salvation, and then in February 2008 head of the directorate for ideological work on the central executive committee of Putin's United Russia political party. 'Doubtlessly, a crucial factor, a certain breaking point, in my life, was the appearance of Alexander Dugin, in the sense that his appearance was very strange, because it made me realize that me and my circle of friends were missing an ideologue', he said in a 2007 interview. Demidov announced that 'it is high time to start realizing the ideas, as formulated by Alexander Dugin, of the radical centre through projects'. In the interview, Demidov calls himself, with reference to Dugin, a 'convinced Eurasianist'.[3]

The changing landscape of journalism was mirrored in the changing political spectrum, partly engineered by the Kremlin and partly brought about by a growing conservative mood in the country. No liberal parties made it into the Duma in the December 2003 elections, largely thanks to another exercise in political technology called the United Russia Party, formed that year as a merger of Putin's Unity Party (largely the creation of Pavlovsky) and the opposition Fatherland Party (headed by Putin's former opponents Yury Luzhkov and Evgeny Primakov). Oil industry magnate Mikhail Khodorkovsky, who was an important bankroller of liberal political parties, was jailed the same year, in an unmistakable warning to other businessmen to stay out of politics.

In 2003, Guelman and Dugin worked together on a new political project/ party, intended to marginalize the Communist Party. It was known as Rodina, or 'Motherland'. Both men agree that Dugin ghost-wrote what is known in Russian as the 'carcass' of the project – a slang term for a party's position papers, platform and overall ideological bent. Rodina had been the brainchild of left-wing economist Sergey Glazyev. 'Taking votes from the Communists didn't start out as the goal', recalls Guelman, who had thought up the party with Glazyev.

It became one of the goals, simply because to create a successful party, you need to have access to TV. Access to TV is granted in one office, so you have

to go to this office, and offer them some reason to give you this access. So
you tell them that it will take votes from the Communists, and then they
give you access to TV.

However, just as Rodina was getting off the ground, Putin's circle parachuted
into its midst a new leader named Dmitry Rogozin, who undid their plans. A
flaming nationalist politician, Rogozin had been earmarked for a senior role in
United Russia; but Luzhkov, Moscow's mayor, had objected. Putin had to find
a new role for him, and he was given a soft landing in the Rodina Party. Dugin
and Rogozin had clashed previously, and as soon as Rogozin took over, the
writing was on the wall: 'We were out', as Korovin put it.

Dugin left, saying the party had been taken over by 'racists, anti-Semites
and members of the Russian National Unity' – the party of Dugin's former
nemesis, Alexander Barkashov, whose members had been drafted in by
Rogozin. Dugin 'was too exotic even for our nationalists', according to Guelman,
who is anything but a nationalist; his arthouse style and airy demeanour
contrast oddly with the black-shirted nationalists of Rodina, which he regards
as one of his 'political art projects'.

Rodina's popularity proved greater than the Kremlin expected – a testament to the power of nationalist demagoguery in Russian society. In fact, a
week before 2003 elections to the State Duma, Rogozin says he got an urgent
call from the head of the main national TV network with bad news: it had been
ordered by the Kremlin to pull all of Rodina's campaign ads and coverage. The
party was getting too popular. Despite the blackout, which was designed to
keep Rodina from stealing too many votes from United Russia, the party still
got 9 per cent of the vote – not as much as it had hoped, but still a crushing
blow to the Communists, whose 13 per cent was less than half of what they had
polled previously. The big winner was United Russia. Packed with government
bureaucrats, the faceless party resembled the old Soviet Communist Party.
Liberal, Western-style parties such as Yabloko and Union of Right Forces got
no seats at all. 'A new political era is coming', Vladislav Surkov, deputy chief of
staff to Putin, told the Interfax news agency after the vote. 'The parties that
have not got into the Duma should be calm about it and realize that their
historical mission has been completed.'

The 2003 elections showed that politics in Russia had become almost
entirely virtual – a combination of manipulation and populism that would
characterize the 'managed democracy' of the Putin era. The stars of the new era
were not the politicians (who, aside from Putin, were viewed as unthinking
marionettes acting out their lines), but rather the unseen puppet masters
behind the scenes, the political technologists such as Pavlovsky and (before he

left) Guelman. They had demonstrated their skills by getting Yeltsin re-elected in 1996. Then they had taken an unknown, relatively mid-ranking officer from the KGB – perhaps the least popular profession in the country – and made him president. As Guelman says:

> We took a guy [Putin] whose rating was on the same level as a statistical error in September, and by January he is the electoral leader. Three months later, he wins the presidency. Very impressive. But then how to keep it there? That has been the puzzle at the centre of Russian politics ever since.

Thanks to the efforts of the technologists, Putin's approval ratings steadily rose throughout much of the decade, hitting highs of 60 and 70 per cent – unheard of for any politician. 'He had the scores of a celebrity, a football star or singer', was how Pavlovsky put it. 'He ceased to be regarded as a mere politician.' Putin, he said, was viewed as a traditional tsar, who in the public imagination could do no wrong. In this centuries-old model of rule, Russians blamed the errors and injustices of the state on the bad 'boyars' or nobles surrounding the tsar, and blissfully assumed that the omnipotent tsar simply must not be aware of them.

The task of maintaining these ratings fell largely to the Kremlin's Svengali-like chief of staff, Alexander Voloshin, and his deputy Vladislav Surkov, head of the Kremlin's department of domestic politics. These two men were important exceptions to the general rule that Yeltsin-era officials were excluded from the new Putin team. They retained their influence, according to Guelman, mainly because none of the ex-KGB men around Putin really understood how the 'technology' worked: 'They [Putin's team] didn't understand how these ratings stayed so high and they were reluctant to make any drastic changes to the machinery.' After Voloshin's departure in 2004, amid the fallout from the jailing of Khodorkovsky, the informal title of Kremlin grey cardinal passed to his deputy Surkov, who became something of a cult figure in Kremlin circles.

'Surkov created the Russian political system of the 2000s, and he almost single-handedly ran it', wrote Dugin in a 2012 article, published a few months after Surkov stepped down:

> Putin seems to believe that the realm of ideas, including political ideas, is minor and inconsequential, and is only concerned about one thing – that it goes smoothly. Surkov at least created the appearance that everything went smoothly . . . But the price for the 'smoothness' was the creation of a political, social and ideological system that was understandable to only one

person in the country – Vladislav Surkov. Everyone else knew only parts of it. My guess is that even Putin doesn't understand it.[4]

The system Surkov presided over from 1999 to 2011, under three presidents, was aimed at managing dissent rather than crushing it. This emphasized his background as a successful advertising man. The postmodernistic pseudo-democracy he created ensured that every political persuasion had a voice provided by a Kremlin-backed political party or movement. Liberals, nationalists, statists, environmentalists, rightists, leftists – all were represented by a series of doppelgangers, stooges and pastiches in a Kremlin-financed simulation of politics which lasted for over a decade. 'Political life by 2004 was packed full of simulacra, doubles and pacifiers, creating the appearance of pluralism and a wide range of choice', said Dugin, clearly referring in part to his own efforts at Rodina. 'It will go into the textbooks as one of the most colossally successful social swindles of historic magnitude. It was a triumph of nonsense, bad taste and vulgarity.'

Boyish and fresh-faced, Surkov was one of the top creative minds in the Kremlin. He was also the quintessential grey man, skilled at hiding in broad daylight. 'Against the backdrop of the Kremlin camouflage, he was absolutely unnoticeable as a living person', said Elena Tregubova, a muckraking reporter for *Kommersant* newspaper: 'He blended in with office furniture and corridors and with other dark-suited officials.' His tailored $2,000 suits were appropriately chosen from among 45 shades of grey available. In spite of his unassuming public persona, Surkov did not fit the mould of the dour Kremlin bureaucrat cultivated by most of the top echelon. Half-Russian, half-Chechen, he has a poster of Che Guevara on his office wall, is a fan of Tupac Shakur, and writes rock lyrics in his spare time. Surkov, Tregubova also observed, was virtually alone among the Kremlin officials she met in that he read books.[5] He has a particular passion for collecting rare editions of Dostoevsky, especially *The Possessed* – the story of a clique of nineteenth-century revolutionaries driven mad by their obsession with philosophy.

Among other tasks, Surkov coordinated the work of the Kremlin's team of private political consultants, pollsters, provocateurs and pocket politicians. He did everything from inventing political parties and youth movements to coaxing pieces of legislation through the Duma 'by attending to the needs of the deputies', according to Tregubova.

Surkov got his start in the late 1980s, when he had the good fortune to have the same martial arts trainer as Mikhail Khodorkovsky, the owner of Bank Menatep – one of several banks that benefited from state connections – and soon to be one of the richest men in Russia. Surkov would end up running Menatep's advertizing department. His signature accomplishment was to copy the Olivetti logotype, which he saw on TV, and use it for Menatep, according to the authors of *Operation United Russia*, a book which details Surkov's career.[6] Surkov was thus in the right place at the right time. 'Putin rarely entrusted a key post to someone who was not a friend or a [KGB] comrade from St Petersburg', state the authors of *Operation United Russia*. 'Surkov was almost the only person in whose hands was placed the entire domestic politics of the country, and yet he was a representative of the old Yeltsin team.'[7]

As a former advertising man, Surkov revelled in the postmodern playground of Kremlin spin. 'Everything that was on TV was decided in one office', says Dugin, tellingly. Instead of coherent programmes, Surkovian politics were a kind of *bricolage*, as Dugin put it, using a term popularized by French stucturalist Claude Lévi-Strauss to denote an art form using whatever materials are to hand, regardless of their original purpose. Surkovian formulations were clever puns and inherently contradictory Orwellian wordplays – such as 'sovereign democracy', 'illiberal capitalism' and 'managed nationalism'. Surkov, says Dugin, operated a postmodern 'ideological centrifuge' which 'scattered all ideological discourses to the periphery'.[8]

Dugin says he met Surkov for the first time in 2002, though he would not say who introduced them. Pavlovsky says he cannot remember if it was his doing but he 'does not rule it out'; others say Leontyev made the introduction, but Leontyev says he cannot remember. As Dugin told me in an interview, 'Surkov is first and foremost an intellectual. He said "I don't share your views" but he was interested to talk – he is a collector of other intellectuals.' It was via Surkov that several of Dugin's political projects got off the ground. However, they were never permitted to get too large in scale: 'He basically kept me out of big politics', says Dugin.

Soon after the Rodina debacle ended their chances of getting into parliament, Dugin and Petr Suslov split and the Eurasia Party closed its doors. It was reborn in 2004 as the International Eurasian Movement, with a steering committee that consisted entirely of Old Believers: Korovin and Zarifullin (whom Dugin had christened), Dugin's wife Natalya (a formidable intellectual and professor of philosophy at Moscow State University) and Dmitry Furtsev (who had baptized Dugin into the sect in 1998). Tempbank chairman Gagloev, the Ossetian banker whom Dugin had baptized, was the sixth member of the steering committee. Crucially, Gagloev agreed to pay for everything, according to Zarifullin, who says he believes Gagloev was acting independently but was funding the movement in order to curry favour with the Kremlin, as a way of burnishing his credentials as a patriot. He 'financed us on his own initiative due to his interest in Eurasianism', said Zarifullin. However, he admitted that Gagloev's interest in the ideology only went so far: 'Had we been in opposition, he would not have been very interested in us because he was very focused on the Kremlin.'[9]

* * *

As Dugin's profile rose, a number of external factors taken together caused Russia to reassert its confrontational line towards the West. Oil prices were booming, allowing Russia to repay its large national debt, and economic self-sufficiency freed the Kremlin's hands from dependence on Western financial markets.

Meanwhile Putin felt increasingly betrayed by a US White House that took him for granted. In 2001 President George W. Bush renounced the Anti-Ballistic Missile Treaty and plunged ahead with a missile defence initiative, which the Kremlin feared would render Russia's own strategic nuclear deterrent useless. The Kremlin was also growing increasingly uneasy as the US made inroads into the countries of the former Soviet Union, long considered a Russian 'sphere of influence'. After the Kremlin had rushed to aid the US in the wake of the 9/11 attacks, offering assistance in acquiring for Washington a key airbase in Kyrgyzstan, the US continued to build its military presence in the Central Asia states of Uzbekistan and Kyrgyzstan, where it operated military airbases and showed no sign of gratitude to Russia. Nor did it give any indication that it regarded its presence in Russia's strategic backyard as temporary.

Then, in 2003–04, the 'Rose' and the 'Orange' revolutions in Georgia and Ukraine further inflamed opinion in Russia. These revolutions swept pro-Western reformers to power, in the form of Mikheil Saakashvili and Viktor Yushchenko, respectively. The US gave verbal backing to the Ukrainian Orange revolutionaries, who also got material help from US-backed non-governmental organizations such as the National Endowment for Democracy. This is turn spread the general impression in Moscow that they had covert help from US intelligence organizations. In March 2004, meanwhile, a second post-Cold War wave of NATO expansion to Eastern Europe included the three former Soviet Baltic States. The sum total of the White House policies amounted to total contempt for Putin's pro-US overtures, which even made US officials uneasy. According to former US ambassador to Moscow Jack Matlock, this was 'the diplomatic equivalent of swift kicks to the groin'.[10]

It was a familiar pattern: Gorbachev, Yeltsin and now Putin all began their Kremlin terms with overtures to the United States. These all elicited a pat on the head and a dismissive yawn from Washington. Now, wounded by the diplomatic slights, Putin appears to have overreacted, believing that Russia was the next target of the Orange revolution in Ukraine. Today, Pavlovsky, who at the time had been delegated the task of marshalling 'anti-Orange' propaganda for the Kremlin, admits that 'we overestimated the likelihood of an Orange revolution in Russia'. Patriotism and hysteria suddenly poured out of the airwaves as the Kremlin set about stiffening the spines of the citizenry for confrontation in the streets with Western-backed Orange revolutionaries. 'We all have to realize that the enemy is at the gates' said Surkov, in an interview with *Komsomolskaya Pravda* in 2004:

> The front line passes through every city, every street, every house. We need vigilance, solidarity, mutual assistance, joint efforts of citizens and the state. The common thread binding fake liberals and real Nazis is increasingly real. Their sponsors are of foreign origin. They share a common hatred. For Putin, and in fact, for Russia as such.[11]

Meanwhile, the Kremlin set about organizing its own street mobs to counter potential opposition protesters in Russia. 'There will be no uprisings here', Surkov told the German magazine *Der Spiegel* at the time.

Garibaldi's army

It was a cold 25 February 2005 when busloads of activists pulled up in the sixteenth-century Kremlin in the town of Alexandrov, 100 kilometres outside Moscow. Among them were Dugin, Korovin and Zarifullin, who had invited the assembled throng to a conference about the future of the Russian state, to be held in the historic residence of Ivan the Terrible.

The townspeople of Alexandrov, seeing the assortment of oddly dressed Moscow hipsters and bearded coffeehouse bohemians disembark, assumed they were foreigners. But they were soon assured by the new arrivals that nothing could be further from the truth. They were real Russians, some with actual Kremlin ID badges, founding a movement of simple people, like themselves – the real Russian folk, who would take back the country from the perversion of the liberal West.

But it would not be an easy task, and that was why they had chosen the home of Russia's feared medieval tyrant – a genuine Russian patriot who had cleansed Russia of pernicious foreign influences – to launch a movement devoted to patriotism, autocracy and empire. It was the founding convention of the Eurasian Youth Union, created in the wake of the Orange revolution in Ukraine, as the prototype for a series of pro-Kremlin urban mobs. Their extremely ambitious self-declared mission would be to guard the streets of

Russia's major cities lest home-grown Orange revolutionaries tried to spread their liberal filth.

The throng clamoured inside the chapel, which 'seemed very small, not pretending to the scale of a tsar', recalled journalist Dmitry Popov, part of the throng. First to speak at the meeting was the director of the Ivan the Terrible museum. She was 'dumbfounded at the unruly crowd of people who had taken over her museum', according to Popov. Her speech was a variation of 'Thank you, Comrade Stalin, for our happy childhood, except that she replaced Stalin with Putin'. Popov added that the proceedings 'were like a Komsomol meeting with too many speeches. Most had come just to listen to Alexander Dugin.'

Eventually, they got their wish. As Dugin, dressed in a black cassock for the occasion, got up to speak, the audience stood in rapt attention:

> Because of the shocking incompetence of the regime, we are all gathered in these vaults which once echoed with the footsteps of a man who understood that a state needs guardian structures . . . It is necessary to create a new force, a third force. Yes, it is pro-state, aimed at the Orange revolutionaries, but with its own agenda.[12]

He was announcing the creation of a youth wing of the Eurasianist movement which was to be the first, if not the most successful, of the Kremlin-organized street movements aimed at protecting Russia from real or imagined Western-backed revolutionaries. Once Dugin had finished, the audience settled down to watch the 1944 black-and-white film *Ivan the Terrible* by Sergey Eisenstein, one of Stalin's favourite movies.

The movement drew inspiration from the sixteenth-century Oprichniki, Ivan's personal secret police, who murdered and imprisoned the regime's enemies. A great deal more colourful and camp than its forbears, the Eurasian Youth Union was also, thankfully, far less murderous. Like the Oprichniki, they wore black clothing and some sported their long, Old-Believer beards; but unlike the real Oprichniki, their violence was mainly symbolic. With the exception of one July 2006 incident, in which a Union activist punched opposition leader Mikhail Kasyanov in the face, there is no record of it engaging in any organized violence (bar the odd bit of jostling).

Obviously inspired by its previous incarnation as the National Bolshevik Party, the Eurasian Youth Union was a movement of culture warriors. The terrain they fought for was intellectual rather than physical. They made war on the symbols of the West, arranging sit-ins at Western embassies, destroying the symbols of independence in Ukraine and Estonia and harassing the diplomats of countries accused of 'humiliating' Russia. These included most notably

Britain's ambassador in Moscow, Tony Brenton, whom the group trolled mercilessly, following him and disrupting his speeches after he shared a podium with Russian opposition politicians.

The group had a surfeit of creative energy and directed its aggression mainly into a series of art-house lecture projects, street theatre and 'improv' style public 'happenings'. Its standard was designed by artist Alexey Belyayev-Gintovt, who would go on to win the prestigious Kandinsky Art Prize in 2009: it was a refashioned and easily recognizable Second World War-era propaganda poster entitled 'Motherland' – the ghostly figure of an elderly woman sweeping out of the Russian steppe, exhorting her children to fight the invaders.

The group obviously enjoyed the Kremlin's favour, though according to Zarifullin, Kremlin patronage only started flowing in the months after its launch. 'We created the movement as entrepreneurs', he said impishly. Gagloev, the ever-faithful Moscow banker, paid for its headquarters in an old factory building near Avtozavodskaya metro station. Later, in 2009, Korovin told me conspiratorially: 'No one goes to the Kremlin and gets a paper bag full of money. There are always sponsors.'[13]

'There was a symmetrical logic to how Slava [Surkov] thought', Guelman told me, explaining the creation of the youth brigades in 2004–05:

> If there are people on the internet fighting against the regime, then there must be those who are for the regime. If there is an opposition demonstration, there must be a pro-regime demonstration. If the opposition has crazy people who do anything and break the law, then the regime has to have them too. Cold-hearted, ready to do anything, stamp on the portraits of their enemies.

Zarifullin says the movement was autonomous, fancifully called 'Garibaldi's Army', a reference to the rag-tag group of idealists who became the nucleus of the movement to unite Italy in the nineteenth century. Their goal, the tag implied, would be the unification of 'Eurasia' in the twenty-first.

The Eurasian Youth Union was the first of a series of Kremlin-backed unofficial street gangs tasked with controlling the streets of Moscow, confronting Russia's 'Orange revolutionaries' and working as a conduit between the Kremlin and Russia's youth. Others were arguably more successful.

Three days after the Eurasian Youth Union was founded, Vasily Yakemenko, a pro-Kremlin youth leader, announced the creation of Nashi, another Kremlin-backed youth movement (not to be confused with the 1990s-era Nashi in St Petersburg). This Nashi was a combination of the Soviet Young Pioneers and a fascist skinhead gang. Nationalist ideology was fed to teenagers at its summer camps. Other groups soon sprang up – 'Young Russia' and 'United Russia – Young Guard', for example: mobs of mainly provincial youth paid to go and wave flags at official speeches, to picket foreign embassies and arrange counter-demonstrations at opposition marches. Nashi was a much larger organization, better funded, more aggressive, and given the objective of organizing counter-demonstrations wherever they might be needed. It was made up of dozens of hardcore skinheads from the 'Gladiators' football gang – fans of Spartak Moscow football club – who sport telltale tattoos of a gladiator with a spear. The Gladiators' leader, Roman Verbitsky, was the leader of Nashi's 'volunteer youth brigade'.[14] Officially these hardcore skinheads worked as guards and security, but in practice they were provocateurs and muscle. In 2005, baseball bat-wielding Gladiators attacked a meeting of Limonov's National Bolshevik Party, severely injuring ten of its supporters. After the bloody mêlée, Verbitsky hung around to pose for photographs and answer journalists' questions. Eventually the police showed up and rounded up the Gladiators, but then let them go almost immediately after a phone call from Nikita Ivanov, a young Kremlin apparatchik who was Nashi's *kurator* and Surkov's deputy.

Even the Eurasian Youth Union seemed to have a secret guardian angel, which became apparent during the single recorded instance that the group engaged in violence – apparently by accident. Zarifullin relates in his memoirs that in July 2006 he sent an operative named Vladimir Nikitin to disrupt an opposition speech by former prime minister (turned opposition leader) Mikhail Kasyanov. He gave Nikitin no specific instructions: 'We just told him go and do something, we didn't say what, or to whom.' Zarifullin was later to regret the vagueness of the mission:

> I received a telephone call later and was told that Nikitin, in full view of an audience and dozens of television cameras, had gone up to Kasyanov and given him several sharp jabs to the mouth … I phoned some lawyers, expecting he would be in police custody. Then in walks Nikitin. I asked him: 'Why are you not in jail?'

The police, it turned out, said they could not believe he had punched Kasyanov (despite several videos of the fracas being posted online) because 'that is simply not possible'. Nikitin was released.

It would be a mistake to believe that the Eurasian Youth Union, Nashi and other youth gangs like Young Guard and Young Russia were entirely top-down projects, centrally directed from the Kremlin offices. Instead they represented something more complex – a milieu of deniable, autonomous groupings of money, executive power and ideology, the wishes of which were carried out by operatives who most often functioned without central direction and clear leadership, responding instead to ideological 'signals'. But it must be said that these groups certainly enjoyed some degree of official protection from the Kremlin – so long as they did not overdo it or violate too many laws (as the Nikitin episode shows). The imperatives were obvious and the limits were (hopefully) understood. Funding, like Gagloev's financing of the Eurasian Youth Union, was indirect, but everybody won: Gagloev, via Dugin's contacts, got the ear of the Kremlin; Dugin got the movement financed; the Kremlin got a 'patriotic' youth project which would do its bidding and was another oar in the water of politics.

These pseudo-official organizations got scholarly treatment from Korovin in a June 2008 lecture at a forum in Foros, in the Crimea (it is interesting that Crimea was to see Russia use these same 'network' or 'asymmetric' structures on a wide scale in the 2014 takeover). Korovin identified them as 'network structures' in that they functioned without clear hierarchies and explicit orders but followed a generally recognized ideology – as deniable tools of domestic and foreign policy. He called them 'the newest technology to capture terrain', and claimed, albeit without any supporting evidence, that they had been 'developed by the Pentagon'. Again, without much evidence, he attributed to such 'network structures' under US control many of the most recent popular uprisings, such as those in Yugoslavia, Georgia and Ukraine. 'The network is not controlled from a unified centre', Korovin said in his lecture, published later as part of an anthology.[15] 'Participants in the network have to understand the meaning of events. They don't receive direct commands such as "go there" or "do this", because it's not the army.' Instructions are issued indirectly, through cues given in the media, or at forums and conferences – just like the one he was attending, and giving cues to. 'Tasks for agents in network wars are not transmitted in code, but directly through the media. Anyone can listen to it, but isolating and decoding it from the general flow of information is not something everyone can do.' The key is deniability: 'If the activity is not a success, or is indeed a failure, the network centre does not carry responsibility for this.'

Dugin's and Korovin's treatment of 'networks' actually prefigured a series of policy documents on 'asymmetric warfare' by the Russian General Staff on the eve of the culmination of the strategy in eastern Ukraine. For instance, Valery Gerasimov (chief of the Russian armed forces General Staff) notably wrote in a 2013 issue of *Military Industrial Courier*: 'The role of non-military means to achieving political and strategic goals has grown, and in many cases, these means have exceeded the power of force of weapons in their effectiveness.' It would not be the first time that ideas which later received treatment in formal military strategy were first floated by Dugin and his group. According to Korovin's 2008 lecture: 'In the postmodern age, the most important weapon in conquering a state and establishing control over it has become its own society.'[16]

* * *

The ever more hysterical anti-Western tone of the state media, state-sponsored hooligan gangs, official patriotism and nationalism characterized the 'Orange fever' era of Russia in the mid-2000s.

Dugin's youth movement was satirized as the 'Duginjugend' and inspired a wicked parody by Vladimir Sorokin, one of Russia's most celebrated contemporary authors. In 2006, after his books were ritually burned by Nashi activists, Sorokin wrote *Day of the Oprichnik*, about a dystopian near-future Moscow. Set in 2028, Europe has decayed due to its liberal perversions, and is now separated from Russia by the 'Great Western Wall'. The citizenry has renounced all foreign travel, ritually burning their passports in Red Square. The 'Holy Russia' of Ivan the Terrible's time has been reborn under the watchful eye of the Oprichniki, who draw inspiration from a statue of Malyuta Skuratov, the leader of the Oprichiniki of Ivan's day, which has replaced Felix Dzerzhinsky, founder of the NKVD, in Lubyanka Square. Sorokin's novel is an account of a day in the life of a futuristic Oprichnik named Andrey Danilovich Komyaga, whose mobile phone rings with an audio recording of his torture victims' screams. He and his brethren cruise through the Moscow streets in red 'Mercedovs' with brooms and the severed heads of dogs attached to the bumpers, seeking out dissent and killing, raping and plundering with impunity. This is all described by Sorokin in a blasé workaday style reminiscent of Anthony Burgess's *A Clockwork Orange*.

The book is an ironic sidelong glance at the Putin era, where the FSB has (actually, in real life) done its best to cover itself in the mantle of the Church. Under the leadership of Putin's friend Nikolay Patrushev, for example, in 2002 the FSB erected an Orthodox chapel for its members, who in earlier incarnations had imprisoned or killed 300,000 churchmen and women. The same year that Sorokin's novel was published, the FSB switched to black dress uniform for its officers, evoking the attire of Ivan's Oprichniki.[17] In a nod to the muftiate of political technology, which had erected the simulacra of medieval Russia under Putin, Sorokin at several points parodies Pavlovsky and Dugin as two 'holy fools' with Old Church Slavonic derivations of their names. 'Pavlushka-ezh' and 'Duga-Leshi' appear throughout the novel, spouting neologistic nonsense words: *V-ast!* (a cipher of the Russia word for 'regime') and *Ev-gazia* (a neologism combining 'Eurasia' and 'gas').

The parallel visions for Russian reality put forward by Sorokin and Dugin show just how propaganda and parody raced to anticipate each other: both men equated official, pro-Kremlin patriotism with the Oprichinina of Ivan the Terrible – Sorokin in parody, but Dugin in ostensible earnestness. However, Dugin's project, undertaken with a postmodern wink to the audience, was so over the top that it was approaching subversiveness, too. Like the National Bolshevik Party, it was almost a self-conscious parody of itself.

This ironic attitude to one's own work was a constant theme in the Surkov era, described by author Peter Pomerantsev in an essay on Surkov as 'a world of masks and poses', where political expression was extraordinarily multifaceted: 'The sucking-up to the master is completely genuine, but as we're all liberated 21st-century people who enjoy Coen brothers films, we'll do our sucking up with an ironic grin.'[18] This pose is shared by Surkov himself. In 2009 he authored a book (under a pseudonym) about a publisher who runs a sideline in political public relations, working for corrupt officials and publishing their ghost-written novels as their own work. It was an oddly self-referential message, made slippery by Surkov's own denial that he wrote it – a book about the venality and corruption of the official culture industry in Russia, which is simultaneously a send-up, an apology, a self-criticism and a lie.

It was in this ironic, decentred, postmodern intellectual milieu that Dugin really came into his own – his political projects born of the same stuff as surrealist art, his books littered with references to Jean-François Lyotard and Gilles Deleuze. There was no lack of French post-structuralists bent on skewering the pretensions of liberal universalism, and Dugin cited practically all of them; buzzwords such as 'rhizome', 'splintered consciousness' and 'schizomasses' litter his later works.

The Putin-era Kremlin had no interest in creating a new metaphysics; instead they subverted an existing one by presenting all politics – particularly the pretensions of liberal universalism – as a self-conscious manipulation. As an ideologist, Dugin cast himself not as a purveyor of a single truth, but as a defender of the local and the particular from the hegemony of a new totalitarianism. Liberalism is 'an updated version and continuation of a Western universalism that has been passed from the Roman Empire, Medieval Christianity, modernity in terms of the Enlightenment, and colonization, up to the present-day', wrote Dugin in what was probably his most significant book since *The Foundations of Geopolitics*, entitled *The Fourth Political Theory*, published in 2009.[19] Drawing on his readings of the European New Right, Dugin channelled the philosophy of as many ex-Nazis as he could lay his hands on – the political theories of Carl Schmitt, the philosophy of Martin Heidegger, the geopolitical theories of Karl Haushofer, and the traditionalism of Julius Evola – into a profoundly anti-liberal metaphysical project:

> Liberalism is responsible for no fewer historic crimes than fascism (Auschwitz) and Communism (the gulag) . . . It is responsible for slavery, the destruction of the Native Americans in the United States, for Hiroshima and Nagasaki, for the aggression in Serbia, Iraq and Afghanistan, for the devastation and the economic exploitation of millions of people on the planet.

The hero of Dugin's blistering polemic was a term invented by Heidegger to denote man in organic harmony with being – *dasein*, or 'there-being'.[20] *Dasein* became in Dugin's telling a version of Nietzsche's superman, the Übermensch: 'Having left the limits of individuality, man can be crushed by the elements of life and by a dangerous chaos. He may want to establish order. And this is entirely within his right – the right of a great man – a real man of "Being and Time"'. *Dasein* was a none-too-subtle reference to Putin.[21]

The Fourth Political Theory was the first of Dugin's major books to be translated into English, and was widely read and reviewed by ultra-right-wing circles in Europe. Liberalism in all its manifestations – political correctness, tolerance, gay rights, multiculturalism – was soon to take the place that capitalism had occupied under the Soviet Union: an official bugbear of a new (if un-enunciated) ideology of far-right-wing politics.

* * *

Since Putin had come to power the accent had been on nationalism and patriotic symbols, in an effort to consolidate support around a tough, authoritarian Kremlin. Support for nationalism was growing every year along with a deep nostalgia for the vanished greatness of the USSR. The economic dislocation of the 1990s was partly to blame, but it was also a consequence of political opportunism in the Kremlin, which saw nationalism as a ready-made programme for political mobilization that simultaneously justified, in a vaguely emotional way, the strong state and authoritarian rule that Putin sought to implement.

In the right hands, nationalism could be a tool for political consolidation. But the inherent contradictions of nationalism were something that worried the Kremlin. Yeltsin, after all, had come to power as a nationalist, and his appearance on the political scene in the 1980s had coincided with (in some sense, had perhaps even precipitated) a cascade of separatist movements which led to the collapse of the USSR and the war in Chechnya.

Street nationalism had existed in Russia since Pamyat in the 1980s, and it retained a powerful populist hold on the Russian public. The mobilizational power of Russian nationalism was plain to see from recent history: in the right hands it could be the rocket fuel for gangs that could sweep the streets of Western-inspired opposition; in the wrong hands it could be a deadly virus – one that had already destroyed one incarnation of the state, the USSR, and could yet destroy the Russian Federation. Nationalist opposition groups were considered a mortal threat to the regime; but also, paradoxically, a new political force that could be tremendously useful if handled correctly.

In the first decade of Putin's rule, a new generation of nationalist leaders had emerged to rule the streets, as Dugin, Barkashov and Limonov all receded into the background – and most of these nationalists were anti-Kremlin. Arguably the most important figure was Alexander Belov (whose real name, Potkin, was distinctly Jewish), leader of the Movement Against Illegal Migration, which he started in 2002. Charismatic and fond of suede loafers, Belov/Potkin had got his start in Pamyat as a teenager, had graduated to Barkashov's blackshirts in the 1990s, and was now ready for the big time, having founded his own movement. He was an organizing genius with the air of a French intellectual; he also had an instinct for power, having worked for a number of parliamentary deputies, but he had clearly judged the opposition route to politics to be the more fruitful approach. Another underground leader was Dmitry Demushkin, the chunky, muscular leader of the Slavic Union, which grew out of his Moscow Ultimate Fighting gym and into a national umbrella movement for skinhead groups. The third in the triad of new leaders was Dmitry Rumyantsev, hawk-faced leader of the National Socialist Organization (NSO), created in 2004. Like Belov/Potkin he had got his start in Barkashov's blackshirted Russian National Unity, had worked for two Duma deputies and had real political ambitions.

All these nationalist political groups disavowed violence publicly, but were made up of hardcore 'autonomous' cells, mainly football hooligans, who were barely under the leadership's control. There was very little in practice to distinguish between them. They were made of the same raw material; the culture was violent, fascistic, with straight-armed salutes and swastikas. They wore Thor Steinar and Lonsdale clothes, fashionable among Western European skinheads and football fans. Skinhead violence was an endemic problem in some cities, where the various gangs fought migrants or each other, in more or less equal measure. Saturday night for a skinhead gang might consist of a raid on an immigrant shelter, or the videotaped beating of Tajik guest workers coming home from work on an *elektrichka* commuter train.

The nationalist milieu steadily became more and more opposition-minded, as migration from Central Asia and the Caucasus increased. Tensions ran high in cities throughout Russia as pitched battles raged between ethnic Caucasian youths and ethnic Russians. The police often refused to intervene. A brawl in the northern town of Kondopoga in August 2006 became a touchstone for the nationalists. The fight, between an Azerbaijani waiter and two Russians, spiralled out of control, and two bystanders were killed. The police, having (allegedly) been paid by Chechen gangsters, did not intervene, and the incident blew up into a full-blown pogrom against ethnic Caucasians during which many were chased out of town. Moscow-based nationalists flew to Kondopoga to organize rallies.

Alexey Navalny, a liberal member of the Yabloko Party, became what was to be one of the most recognizable of a new liberal-friendly brand of opposition nationalists. Following the events in Kondopoga he created a movement known as Narod ('People'), and began attending nationalist rallies: 'My liberal friends were in shock, they tore their shirts, "It's fascism", they said.' But he, a solid member of the Moscow intelligentsia with impeccable liberal credentials, persisted with the experimental overtures to the lumpen street brigades: 'It was clear to me that what is said at the Russian March, if you abstract from the people shouting "Sieg Heil!" reflects the real agenda and concerns of the majority,' he told his biographer, Konstantin Voronkov.[22]

Navalny was to be the pretty face of Russian nationalism, who made it acceptable to a liberal audience: he modelled himself as a European-style right-winger, opposed to immigration and multiculturalism, speaking in recogniz-able 'dog whistles' (like 'ethnic crime') but never once saying the wrong thing out loud. Nationalism, unlike appeals to liberal democracy, was capable of drawing huge crowds, but Navalny also campaigned against corruption in the regime, trying to exercise minority shareholder rights at leading state companies like Gazprom and Rosneft, and publicizing investigations into the corrupt dealings of management. It was a heady opposition cocktail, and Navalny was increasingly a force to be reckoned with.

Another face of opposition nationalism was the rump of the National Bolshevik Party, under Eduard Limonov, who had transitioned from political prankster of the 1990s to a hardened revolutionary following Dugin's exit from the NBP. He had been jailed in 2001 for plotting terror attacks in Kazakhstan, designed to create a 'second Russia' among ethnic Russians in the north. On his release, the NBP was now in full, albeit not very effective, opposition to the Kremlin. For a time Limonov even became the darling of the Western media, after he joined forces with chess champion Garry Kasparov to form an opposition movement in the mid-2000s, transforming itself into a weird hybrid combining liberal hipster chic with hardcore skinhead subculture. A few years later, that strange synthesis would become the defining trait of the middle-class opposition movement that would break out onto the streets of Moscow in the winter of 2011.

On the parliamentary level, Rodina leader Dmitry Rogozin appeared to capitalize on the new mood – also increasingly in opposition to the Kremlin. Rodina ran a series of advertisements mocking immigrants' rural customs and command of the Russian language, and promising to clean up the streets. Rogozin was soon ousted from Rodina, which was closed down; later he was sent into exile as Russia's ambassador to NATO, returning in 2011 to the fold and the role of deputy prime minister, following large-scale protests against Putin's rule.

Seeing the power of Russian nationalism in opposition hands, the Kremlin, under Surkov's direction, sought to control it and co-opt it. In Putin's Russia, Belov told me when I asked to meet him to discuss rising nationalism in 2010, there is a guiding principle for dealing with any independent political organization: 'If they cannot destroy it, they will lead it. And they cannot destroy the nationalists.' Thus began a broad-based effort to lead them. It was called 'managed nationalism' and was a broad effort spanning around five years, from 2005 to 2010, to recruit, co-opt or otherwise seduce nationalist leaders into a pro-Kremlin orbit. It ultimately proved to be a disastrous contradiction in terms – a monument to the hubris and arrogance of the Kremlin spin doctors that led directly to precisely the thing they were trying to prevent: the emergence of a virulent nationalist opposition movement that took the mainstream hostage.

This effort to forge a pro-Kremlin force out of underground nationalist and skinhead movements featured Dugin's Eurasian Youth Union in a key, but brief, role of political manipulation that went badly wrong.

* * *

Since the 1920s, Eurasianism had represented an attempt to neutralize nationalism in the service of the supranational, the imperial and the continental. The popularity of Samuel Huntington's 'clash of civilizations' hypothesis since the 11 September attacks in the United States had helped the Russian elite to think in those terms, easily seduced by the idea that the street-level power of racism and ultra-nationalism among Russia's disgruntled urban youth could yet give way to patriotic fervour, 'civilization' identity and a sort of easily managed civic anti-Westernism.

The Kremlin may well have believed that a movement like Dugin's – with all the accoutrements of a nationalist street gang, without the ethnic racism – could translate this highly theoretical goal into practice, rallying the skinhead gangs on the streets of Moscow and turning them into a pro-Kremlin force. In other words, Eurasianism was seen as something that promised to provide the mobilizational benefits of nationalism without provoking ethnic hostility and leading to separatism. That was the goal of the first major project carried out by the movement in 2005, known as the 'Russian March' – to offer Russia's street nationalists, a growing political force, a muscular version of Eurasianism and a supra-ethnic Russian civilization alternative to ethnic racism.

On 4 November of that year – the anniversary of the expulsion of Polish armies from Moscow in 1612 – the Eurasian Youth Union was granted permission to hold a large march just steps from the Kremlin, on Slavyansky Square. The location was pure gold, according to Zarifullin, who said the intention was to use it to cut a deal with other nationalist groups with larger memberships in order to hold a joint demonstration. They sought out Alexander Belov/Potkin, the goateed doyen of the skinhead movement, to join the march with his Movement Against Illegal Migration (DPNI). The decision to include Belov is still controversial – but the point of the march was to co-opt the skinheads. It was also a way for the Eurasian Youth Union to compete with the larger, better-funded movement using the DPNI's numbers. 'We could have done a real, normal march without [Belov]. But we would have had 500 and not 10,000 marchers', said Zarifullin.

But on the day of the march, the price of cooperation with the unpredictable skinhead gangs became clear: Belov's Hitleresque followers didn't stick to the agreed script. Instead, they crowded around TV cameras, gleefully throwing straight-armed salutes amid shouts of 'Sieg Heil!' Right under the podium where Zarifullin was speaking about the pernicious influence of ethnic nationalism and the common destiny of the Eurasian peoples, a group of skinheads unfurled a banner that read 'Russians On the Move'. Dmitry Demushkin managed to raise a flag with a Slavic swastika, known as a *kolovrat*, while Zarifullin was forced to give the microphone to Belov who made a five-minute speech. Despite the ostensible pro-Kremlin goal of the meeting, Belov was dressed in an orange shirt. Photographs of black-clad straight arms upraised against the blue sky, flanked by red banners with all manner of prohibited symbols, flashed around the world's news agencies, and a few days later Zarifullin and Korovin were forced to publicly disown their participation at a joint press conference. Korovin blamed provocation by competing elements in the Kremlin who did not want their project to go ahead. Today, however, Zarifullin disagrees. Interviewed in 2013 about the episode, he said that the bungled march arose out of a conscious strategy to co-opt the nationalist street movements to Eurasianism. 'It was pure voluntarism by Dugin', said Zarifullin, of the effort to invite Belov's DPNI. 'We could have easily prevented [Belov] from attending, but that was not the point.'

Surkov had blundered badly; he had underestimated nationalism, treating it as just another papier-mâché political movement that could be cleverly spoofed with a few slogans and transformed into a Kremlin doppelganger, like all the rest. Instead, 'managed nationalism' was a contradiction in terms. Holding the Russian March had let a genie out of the bottle and it would not be put back. Today, opposition nationalists see the Kremlin's move as a decisive opening for them. 'After that, nationalism became a real phenomenon in Russian politics. It was impossible to put back in the box. Really, we opened the sluice gates for them', admitted Zarifullin. Surkov, he said, was 'in a trance' after the march: 'Surkov became disappointed in the prospects for Eurasianism because he wanted something that could control the street, and the street is nationalist.'

The split between Dugin and the radical nationalists was decisive: from then on Eurasianism was not a 'nationalist' project, but rather an official ideology. Its purveyors, like Dugin, Zarifullin and Korovin, could not cover themselves in the mantle of populism as they had in the past. Instead they were accorded the careful accolades of regime henchmen. 'Dugin was given a choice – either you are with the nationalists or you are with the regime. And nationalism was the street. So we, and the regime, were forced to give up the streets', according to Zarifullin.

Seeing the strategy in tatters, the Kremlin began to move aggressively against the radical nationalist groups. This only pushed them harder into opposition. By 2009, a number of leading nationalists were in jail for murder, while the DPNI and Slavic Union had been banned. Surkov's managed nationalism was in pieces. Instead of having contained or co-opted the nationalists, it had let the horse bolt, with dire consequences that are being reckoned with still.

＊ ＊ ＊

Moscow's Prechistenka neighbourhood has a swanky, bohemian air, corniced and painted and colonnaded in the nineteenth-century manner of Paris's Left Bank. On 19 January 2009, Stanislav Markelov, a human rights lawyer, and Anastasia Baburova, a journalist for Moscow's opposition *Novaya Gazeta*, left a press conference on Prechistenka Street and walked at a slow pace through crunching snow towards Kropotkinskaya metro station. They were easily followed by a man several steps behind them.

Just before the narrow street opened out onto a busy square dominated by the golden domes of Christ the Saviour cathedral, the pursuer picked up speed.

He took out a pistol with a silencer and, from a distance of a few metres, shot Markelov in the head. Baburova, according to investigators, turned on the assailant, grabbing his arm. He fired again, then walked briskly across the intersection and into the metro, leaving the two bodies lying in a pool of rapidly freezing blood.

For nearly a year, the identity of that man remained a mystery. The killing of Markelov, one of a small group of high-profile human rights lawyers in Moscow, was the crime of the year. In a decade-and-a-half career defending opposition journalists and Chechen refugees, and prosecuting war criminals and skinheads, Markelov had made many powerful and potentially violent enemies. Friends and colleagues speculated about the involvement of security services. The killer appeared to have been well trained: police searching the crime scene found 140 cigarette butts in the snow, but no shell casings to identify the weapon, which was probably a modified air pistol.

Thus, many were surprised when, on 4 November 2009, police arrested Nikita Tikhonov, a weedy 29-year-old intellectual, for the crime. Friends described him as bookish and bright, and a fanatical nationalist, but not a killer. Initially, Tikhonov confessed to the crime, but then retracted the confession. Finally, in 2011, he was convicted of the killings and sentenced to life in prison.

It turned out that Markelov and Tikhonov had crossed paths before. In 2006 Markelov had helped prosecute Tikhonov for participating in the murder of human rights advocate Alexander Riukhin, a youth in the anti-fascist movement, who was knifed to death by a gang. Tikhonov went into hiding and was sentenced in absentia for murder. A motive in the killing of Markelov was not hard to find – 'personal hatred', said his lawyer. But Tikhonov was no psychotic; rather, he seems to have travelled the path of the true believer. Like Raskolnikov, the anti-hero of Dostoevsky's novel *Crime and Punishment*, his life is a case of idealism gone wrong. The murders of Riukhin and Markelov were the product of a twisted ideology that gradually got the better of him.

As we have seen throughout this book, fierce attachment to ideas is a tragically recurring theme throughout the history of Russia, a nation where intellectuals are noted, and have long been judged, on the basis of total commitment to their principles. Today's generation of Russian youths is every bit as ferocious and serious of purpose. They grew up amid the political agoraphobia of the 1990s, acutely conscious of Russia's humiliation as a nation following the end of the Cold War and the economic privations they had suffered as the Russian economy collapsed.

But Tikhonov also symbolized something else: the waywardness and desperation of Kremlin policy towards nationalism. It would shortly emerge that he was not only a maladjusted young man, but also the founder of a

Kremlin-backed nationalist gang, Russky Obraz ('Russian Image') – a political experiment designed to consolidate nationalist street gangs under a state umbrella, which had just gone very badly wrong.

The policy of managed nationalism, which had received its first public expression in the Russian March of 2005, appeared to extend not just to harmless and semi-official Kremlin-backed organizations like the Eurasian Youth Union and Nashi, but also to hardcore groups which engaged in violence, like Tikhonov's. The incident presented the troubling picture of the founder of a Kremlin-sponsored skinhead gang murdering ideological opponents in downtown Moscow. This raised questions about what the true objectives of the Kremlin's policy on nationalism really were.

Tikhonov had been a time bomb waiting to explode. A typical teenager, according to a newspaper interview with his sister, Evgeniya, he listened to rap and heavy metal music, but had shown a flair for the intellectual, gaining entrance to the prestigious history faculty of Moscow State University, where he earned a coveted Red Diploma for academic excellence – and evidently also came into contact with hardline nationalist ideas. Following university, his family lost contact with him. 'I don't even know where he had been living the past few years', said Evgeniya, who mentioned that he had had a falling out with their father, though she gave no details. 'I don't know what to say. We had no communication with him for a long time.'

It is clear that at university he became involved with radical student nationalist politics, writing his thesis on Chechen separatism, and gradually embracing the ideology that would give his life a meaning and a cause. At university he befriended Russian Image's eventual co-founder, Ilya Goryachev. He was studying in the same faculty, writing about the genocide against the Serbs in 1941–45. In 2004 the two men created *Russian Image* as a nationalist journal, based on a similar journal published in Serbia. 'We are not a gang, not a propaganda agency, not a political party. We are all three in one', read their manifesto, which also demanded that foreigners living in Russia be limited to prison-style facilities and their movement curtailed. The group likewise sought to deny women the vote, and agitated for Russia to become a 'racially and ethnically sovereign' state. But despite the radical political rhetoric, Russian Image – the movement, which grew out of the journal – was always believed in skinhead circles to serve a higher master. It had consistently received lenient treatment from Russia's government and law enforcement agencies; in November 2009 it was given permission to hold that year's iteration of the Russian March on Bolotnaya Square, just 800 metres from the Kremlin – a sure sign of Kremlin patronage. 'We have to hold our march [Slavic Union] way out in the middle of nowhere, and Russian Image gets prime real estate right next to the Kremlin for their march. What does that tell you?' pondered Dmitry Demushkin. 'It was a double organization, created by the Kremlin.'

Meanwhile, Russian Image was fairly candid about its source of political support. Evgeny Valyayev, a spokesman for the movement, told me in September 2010:

> I believe the President's Administration, the department of internal politics, sees in Russian Image an organization which could become a vector for the direction of nationalism, that is, legal nationalism. We do not have direct cooperation from the Kremlin, but I believe they give us a 'green light' which would allow us to take over the political field.

Later, at Tikhonov's murder trial, his girlfriend Evgeniya Khasis, who would be charged as an accessory to the murder, testified that the growth of Russian Image 'attracted the attention of the President's Administration, which was trying to influence youth politics. At that time it was under the control of Vladislav Surkov.'

The decision to move towards the establishment was evidently taken in 2007, when suddenly the organization was able to set up 20 regional branches in various Russian cities. As a profile on the online site Gazeta.ru surmised:

> The regime financed them because they saw in them the first European-style legal nationalist organization – moderate, intelligent, successful. This had never been before. Slavic Union, DPNI and NSO created much less trust because their members were members of subcultures and marginals.[23]

However, Tikhonov's violent past shows what can go wrong with such a policy, and there are even questions about exactly how and with what methods state support flowed.

In the month before they arrested him, the FSB installed listening devices in Tikhonov's flat, recording conversations between he and his girlfriend. Tikhonov frequently referred to someone he called 'Comrade Captain', which may have been in jest or could have denoted someone who had a real military or police rank. Once Tikhonov was recorded saying he wanted to obtain weapons from the man: 'I want to put in an order with Comrade Captain for pistol magazine bullets, a Parabellum and an AK [Kalashnikov]. He has to give them to "Student" and Student immediately gives them to you.'[24] It is unknown whom 'Student' refers to.

Russian Image (the movement), according to Valyayev, had long since cut its ties with Tikhonov after the latter was sought in the 2006 murder of Alexander Riukhin. But contacts between Tikhonov and members of the organization appear to have continued long after this point. Goryachev testified at the trial that in 2009 he introduced Tikhonov to Leonid Simunin, a deputy of Nikita Ivanov – the same Nikita Ivanov who worked for the President's Administration under Surkov and was the *kurator* of Nashi. Tikhonov later testified in court that Goryachev referred to the case of Roman Verbitsky (see above), leader of the Gladiators gang which had been allegedly recruited by the Kremlin to attack opposition groups: '[Goryachev] told me Roman did these things because there was a criminal case against him, and they promised to make it go away in exchange for specific services. You could do the same.'

Khasis, Tikhonov's girlfriend, identified Simunin as Goryachev's *kurator* from the President's Administration:

> Goryachev, like many others, received crumbs from the President's Administration, but he wanted more. He asked Simunin to pass his requests up the chain of command, but Simunin refused . . . That is when Goryachev decided to a create a radical organization.[25]

And that is when he brought Tikhonov back in, creating in 2008 a militant terrorist organization known as the Military Organization of Russian Nationalists (the acronym in Russian is BORN), thought to be behind at least six killings. Tikhonov actually testified that he met with Simunin three times in 2009, and the latter even offered to pay him to commit several murders and assaults, which he refused to carry out.

Before Tikhonov's sentencing, Goryachev escaped to Serbia, where he was arrested two years later and extradited to Russia on 8 November 2013. He revoked his testimony against Tikhonov in writing. However, in 2015 he was sentenced to life in prison for ordering Markelov's murder, which Tikhonov carried out. In testimony against Goryachev on June 2015, Tikhonov told the court, 'Ilya said that killing Markelov was now in the interest of the regime. They will forgive you everything.'

Russian Image, which folded in 2010, saw itself very much as producing soldiers for what it believed was a coming battle of worldviews. But the shadowy hand of the Kremlin, made visible in court testimony surrounding Tikhonov's murder trial, represents a problem. The evidence of Kremlin involvement is too great to ignore, though exactly how involved it was is an open question. At the very least the group seems to have been another oar in the water of nationalist politics, designed to steer the masses of street hooligans towards a pro-Kremlin idea. However, the events raise some troubling questions about just what that idea is. The fact that the Kremlin considered violent skinhead racists to be potential allies shows just how far the political markers had moved in Putin's Russia following the coloured revolutions in Ukraine and Georgia.

As we have seen, Russian Image was not the first attempt to co-opt street nationalism and mould it into a political force. The Kremlin helped to create the nationalist political party Rodina to accomplish certain political objectives, and supported skinhead racist gangs such as the Gladiators for different goals. Dugin's Eurasian Youth Union clearly enjoyed Kremlin patronage, and radical ideologies of all types had grown from a marginal phenomenon into the mainstream. It is important to remember that the Kremlin was not supporting these groups because it believed in their ideologies, but rather its multilayered, complex political agendas led it to consider nationalism as the least bad of several alternatives.

But these efforts also paralleled a greater openness to all types of nationalism – whether ethnic racism, Soviet-style imperialism, Eurasianist expansionism or Orthodox confessionalism – at all levels of officialdom. One thing was indisputable: nationalism of all types, allowed to flourish by the Kremlin, had become the centre of gravity in Russian politics.

* * *

Nikolay Patrushev, chairman of Russia's Security Council, had a lot on his mind in the first week of May 2009, when he arranged for Elena Ovcharenko, chief editor of the *Izvestiya* newspaper, to come over and record for posterity his thoughts on the subject of threats to Russian statehood. She was a veteran of such engagements: this was her fifth interview with Patrushev.

He was, according to a US State Department cable's account, a 'smaller, slighter man than photos and TV images led us to expect'; he projected a highly controlled 'Putinesque' persona, with occasional flashes of 'sardonic humor'. He has sharp features and a Gallic beak of a nose, his manner is quiet but firm. And his biography is rather vague – a characteristic of most of the former KGB officers who accompanied Vladimir Putin into the Kremlin in 2000. Under Putin, Patrushev served first as head of the Federal Security Service, the successor to the feared KGB. But at the end of 2008 he moved 800 metres down the hill from the brooding fortress of the Lubyanka to Old Square, where he became secretary of the National Security Council. Patrushev is as blue-blooded as they come in the Kremlin – a colleague of Putin from the St Petersburg days. No matter what his position, he remains at the centre of policy-making – one of the three or four men in whom Putin regularly confides and from whom he seeks counsel on international matters.

Patrushev has a rather uncanny ability to see foreign agents pretty much everywhere – doubtless an important trait in a counterintelligence officer. It was also at the time proving to be important for a senior bureaucrat. He had publicly accused foreign relief organizations of fomenting terrorism in the North

Caucasus, based largely on a confession by an employee of the Danish Refugee Council extracted under unclear circumstances. The FSB's one unequivocal success under Patrushev came in 2006, when the agency caught four British diplomats passing information via an electronic 'spy rock' in a Moscow park.

In fact, soon after Patrushev moved over to the National Security Council he began a project to review Russia's national security guidelines, because he felt they were badly underestimating one thing: the likelihood of subversion by a Western intelligence agency. The guidelines he drew up contained a list of top 'threats to Russian statehood'. At the very top, sure enough, there was 'intelligence gathering and other activities of foreign special services and organizations of foreign states aimed at damaging the security of the Russian Federation'. Less important priorities were terrorism, organized crime and 'frightening the population through the use of nuclear or chemical weapons, or dangerous radioactive, chemical, or biological materials'.

In the best traditions of Kremlin honchos past and present, Patrushev had reserved an entire page of *Izvestiya*. Ms Ovcharenko had arrived with a set of pre-approved questions. But towards the middle of the interview, things got a little weird. 'The history of the formation, development, unification and the collapse of European and Asian countries', replied Patrushev to a question about conflicts over natural resources, 'suggests that the political climate here is mainly determined by the interests of the world's leading nations and peoples living in these territories.' Nothing too controversial thus far. But then he took a detour:

> This idea was briefly stated and substantiated by one of the leading political scientists of the twentieth century, Halford Mackinder, who wrote:
>
> 'Who rules East Europe commands the Heartland; Who rules the Heartland commands the World Island; Who rules the World Island commands the world.'[26]

It was an odd thing for a director of national security to say. Patrushev was quoting a obscure academic named Mackinder on world domination – which, luckily for everyone, was nowhere to be found in the new national security guidelines.

Ovcharenko perhaps sensed that venturing farther down the rabbithole was not to be encouraged – or perhaps she had grown so inured to the wild conspiratorial musings of the new generation of Russian statesmen that she didn't even register the answer as newsworthy. One way or another, she quickly changed the subject to economic security, and the quote was buried in the article the next day.

But the piece caused a stir in certain circles: not because of the mention of world domination by one of the most powerful men in Russia, but because of the stray mention of the obscure British geographer Sir Halford Mackinder (unmistakably a reference to Dugin). The message was classic dog-whistle politics, communicating a message to supporters which only they could hear. 'Mackinder' and 'Heartland' were two codewords which meant very little to the uninitiated; but Patrushev's comments were the first time that the vocabulary and thinking of a new Russian empire had emerged in public at such a senior level.

* * *

Dugin himself explained in a 2007 television interview that his theories were penetrating the establishment, describing the process in his own words not as a monolithic act of handing down stone tablets but as an indirect and often frustrating effort. His ideas, he said, arrive at their destination in often hackneyed form by navigating 'circles' of authority which he himself had no contact with:

> My thought prevails, my discourse reigns. Yes, the government does not disclose its sources . . . Yes, there are whole circles that stand between me and the government . . . that add on to the concentrated idea of Eurasian geopolitics, conservative Traditionalism, and the other ideologies I am developing . . . and create a watered-down version. But in the end, this version reaches the government, which incorporates it as if it were something obvious.

It was an astonishingly arrogant thing to say. However, few would dispute that Dugin was right: his ideas, or at least ideas very much like his, *had* penetrated the establishment and appeared in 'watered-down' versions in the vocabulary of the ruling class. But this was not Dugin's doing; nor was it even Putin's doing. In fact, it was testament to a decentred and messy public life, rather than a well-organized command chain, that Dugin's writings made their appearance at the summit of the regime at all. That his *Foundations of Geopolitics* found its way onto Patrushev's desk tells us a lot about how Kremlin power works.

* * *

While Putin is unquestionably the most powerful figure in Russia, it is clear that he does not entirely lay claim to the aura either of an absolutist tsar, as projected by his supporters, or of an autocratic despot, as proposed by his detractors. Instead of an Olympian throne, it would seem that Putin sits at the nexus of modern-day boyar clans in perpetual conflict over property, policies and perks, a new version of the Soviet Politburo, in which decisions were taken by consensus and powerful interest groups balanced each other's potency.

The plethora of competing interest groups in the Kremlin often resembles a medieval court. While bickering, fighting and (literally) backstabbing, they can fall into line when their collective interests are threatened, and then go back to fighting again after seeing off the intruder. Ideology plays little role in elite battles – one frequently finds liberals and conservatives in the same political clique, and groups of hardliners on opposite sides.

The pluralism at the centre of Russian autocracy has been a common feature of the state for centuries. Indeed, Harvard historian Edward L. Keenan argued that the analogy to medieval court politics was appropriate up until the modern era in his classic article 'Muscovite Political Folkways', which showed that the notion of an omnipotent, autocratic tsar has largely been a myth throughout 500 years of Russian history. Keenan outlined instead the ways in which rule has been by a system of Kremlin court politics within which the guiding principle is consensus. Clan politics within the Kremlin, he wrote, was 'symbolically expressed in a kind of self-imposed fictional subservience to an autocratic tsar, and ensured by the awareness that the fiction was the central element of a conspiracy against political chaos that would ensue if clan were to be set against clan'.[27] Keenan's conclusions appear every bit as valid today as they did 30 years ago.

In the case of Putin, his direct authority over his most senior lieutenants has been questioned by a number of analysts who argue that, rather, the president has to tack politically between these competing interests, obeying a strict balance, in order to preserve his neutrality.[28] His political authority rests on his being primarily a problem solver and adjudicator in elite disputes. Ideology is always subservient to these more paramount considerations of elite power dynamics.

Instead of an authoritarian dictator, Putin may rather resemble the fictional Prince Petr Bagratian, heroic general of Leo Tolstoy's *War and Peace*. Bagratian never gave any orders at the battle of Austerlitz, but 'confined himself to trying to appear as though everything that was being done by necessity, by chance, and by the will of individual officers, was all done, if not by his order, at least in accordance with his intentions'.

This is the essence of the 'political technology' of the Putin era, the ability to discern where society is going, and get there faster. Putin's authority appears to rest more on the wilful suspension of disbelief of his upper-echelon elite – on their general collusion in a spectacle of awesome despotic power. The reality may be more complex: cliques and clans more or less free to challenge each other and push boundaries in a complicated and extemporaneous political theatre, with few rules and a script written by collective effort. 'The Kremlin has many towers', according to the well-worn saying.

Rather than viewing the Kremlin as a military unit with a strict top-down command and control structure, the concept of network organizations seems to provide a better metaphor. Networks are horizontal, loosely connected structures, responsive to cues and signals rather than a classic chain of command. It was a milieu within which the suppliers of ideological cues, while they might not wield any executive power whatsoever and be virtual strangers to those that do, might leave their imprint. It becomes easier to see how a small group of talented intellectuals was able to hijack a fairly lacklustre propaganda effort and use it to suit their purposes, accompanied all the while by a never-ending effort to publicize their own rather tenuous ties to Putin's inner circle.

But Moscow's hierarchs, like Patrushev, seemed to have played along. Many were not overly intellectual, and their priorities were worldly. The symbolic exterior of the regime was something that they gave little thought to. Amid the siege mentality of the mid-2000s, when Kremlin-sponsored journalists were writing and broadcasting that the enemy was at the gates, those hysterical messages were digested by the political class in a feedback loop in which the propaganda slowly became fact. In that environment, it is easier to see how fringe nationalism and empire-drumming ideas like Eurasianism managed to capture the imaginations of Russia's ruling class. Ideology was, in the Surkovian era, a game of masks and poses which encouraged ever more extreme declarations of xenophobia as proof of political loyalty. Bent on proving their bona fides, there was no penalty for going too far.

As Dugin said later in his 2007 interview:

> Therefore, in my opinion, Putin is becoming more and more like Dugin, or at least implementing the programme I have been building my entire life . . .
> It is becoming less and less of a simulacrum and more and more real, the closer he [Putin] comes to us, the more he finds himself. When he becomes 100 per cent Dugin, he will become 100 per cent Putin.[29]

Dugin's links to the hardliners in the Kremlin had by this point become the stuff of hyperbole and legend. Much of it is false, but there are kernels of truth. Dugin does indeed enjoy ties to a group of high-ranking ideological conservatives, mainly former KGB officers who have close links to the Orthodox Church and many with high positions in the state. The informal leader of the 'Orthodox Chekists', as they are known, is Vladimir Yakunin, a former diplomat. A close associate of Putin's, he was made head of the country's railway system – a virtual state within a state, with 1.3 million employees, an independent media empire, a budget of 1.3 trillion roubles, and 30,000 armed police.

Yakunin footnotes Dugin eight times in his 2006 book *The Russian School of Geopolitics*. He is also named as the editor of two anthologies of Dugin's writing published by Yakunin's Centre for Analysis of Problems and Public Governance. In a reference to Dugin's paper 'Russia and the West', prepared for that think tank, Yakunin states that: 'The value of his [Dugin's] approach is that he is the first . . . to say that the fundamental contradiction in the modern age is not the fight for energy resources, or the battle for economic pre-eminence, but a schism, a civilizational schism.'[30] The idea of civilizational divides has preoccupied Yakunin, who runs or otherwise controls at least three non-profit organizations, including the Centre for the National Glory of Russia, which helps promote Russian Orthodox values, Russian history and strong ties with the Slavic world. Every year since 2004 he has run an annual gathering of Russian conservatives, churchmen and political leaders known as the 'Dialogue of Civilizations' in an Orthodox monastery on the Greek island of Rhodes. Dugin has attended most years. 'We work on the same assembly line', said Yakunin of Dugin when I asked him about their joint activities. Stepan Sulakshin, who until 2013 ran the Centre for Analysis of Problems and Public Governance, has said that Dugin was a frequent contributor and enjoyed a high reputation in Yakunin's circle: 'Putin takes him very seriously.'

Another group of conservatives is centred around Igor Sechin, chairman of Rosneft, who – coincidentally or not – is an acquaintance of Dugin's former co-conspirator and ex-KGB man Petr Suslov. Both are Portuguese speakers, having served together in Mozambique and Angola, though Suslov is very vague about his relationship to Sechin. In 2013 Sechin hired media-man Mikahil Leontyev as a vice-president at Rosneft. This move was clearly intended to send a political message: the windfalls of Russian oil patronage are the reward for ideological steadfastness.

Leontyev himself has a long-term patron – conservative businessman Mikhail Yuryev. Like Leontyev, Yuryev is a former liberal from the Yabloko Party, who, since Putin came to power, has swerved to the right. With shale gas interests in the United States, he is estimated to be worth about $4 billion, and has authored a series of articles and books such as *Fortress Russia*, about the need for economic autarky. *Third Imperium* is his latest book, a work of fiction about a future Russia which, due to its wise policy of isolationism, manages to avoid the collapse of Western civilization and remain intact.

Yet another group of conservatives focuses on businessman Konstantin Malofeev, chairman of the private equity firm Marshall Capital Partners, which has a 10 per cent stake in Rostelekom,[31] the state fixed-line telecom monopoly. Malofeev runs the Foundation of St Vasily, a charity with a $40 million annual budget. A devout Orthodox Christian, his father confessor is particularly interesting: a senior monk in the Russian Orthodox Church by the name of Archimandrite Tikhon Shevkunov.

* * *

Father Tikhon, whom I met several times when I profiled him in the *Financial Times*, is perhaps the most important of the new generation of ideological influencers in the orbit of the Kremlin. He presides over the whitewashed walls and onion domes of Sretensky monastery, in downtown Moscow, just along from the Lubyanka. A picture of movie-star self-assurance, Father Tikhon looks a little too polished to fit the image of the Orthodox Christian monk branded into the Western imagination by Dostoevsky. His chin is a little too sculpted, his mane of shoulder-length hair too full and flowing, and his TV delivery too flawless to belong to any crazed, self-flagellating anchorite from *The Brothers Karamazov*.

He wields influence in the Church far above his modest rank of archimandrite, or abbot, due primarily to his contacts in the Kremlin. The story that travels with him, which he will neither confirm nor deny, is that he is the confessor to Vladimir Putin. The only details he gives is that Putin, sometime before he became president at the end of 1999 (most likely while he was head of Russia's FSB security service between 1998 and 1999), appeared at the doors of the monastery one day. Since then, the two men have maintained a very public association, with Tikhon accompanying Putin on foreign and domestic trips, dealing with ecclesiastical problems. But, according to persistent rumour, Tikhon ushered the former KGB colonel into the Orthodox faith and became his *dukhovnik*, or godfather.

Father Tikhon does appear to have a very intimate knowledge of Putin's religious life. In 2001 he gave an intriguing interview to a Greek newspaper saying that Putin 'really is an Orthodox Christian, and not just nominally, but a person who makes confession, takes communion and understands his responsibility before God for the high service entrusted to him and for his immortal soul'. Throughout my meetings with Father Tikhon, I pressed him on the real extent of his relationship with Putin. He would say only that he and Putin are well acquainted; he refuses to be drawn on the question of whether he is Putin's godfather: 'You can believe those rumours if you want, but they

certainly aren't spread by me.' Whatever the truth, it is something that the
Kremlin finds useful not to deny. 'It's a very private matter', says Putin's
spokesman Dmitry Peskov. 'I simply don't know.' He did confirm that Tikhon
is 'very popular' and the two men do know each other well. 'No one for sure
would know whether or not he is the *dukhovnik*. If someone knows you are the
dukhovnik, then you are not the *dukhovnik* any more.'

A former film-school student who was baptized in 1982 at the age of
24, Father Tikhon has found himself in the uniquely influential role of other
historical churchmen in close proximity to the ear of state power – though he
insists, rather credibly, 'I am no Cardinal Richelieu!' Strictly speaking, he is
right, says Evgeny Nikiforov, Dugin's friend from the Pamyat days:

> In our confessions there is not very much specific information. You just say
> 'I stole' or 'I fornicated'. Maybe you add a few specific details like how much
> and how often. But you don't need to be very specific. If Father Tikhon is
> captured by some foreign intelligence service and tortured, there would not
> be much he could tell them.

The association between Putin and Father Tikhon is odd for any number of
reasons; but the first and foremost is historical. Visitors to the Sretensky
monastery may miss the innocuous stone cross unless they are looking for it
especially. It sits in the garden, abutting one of the whitewashed walls, tended
by cassocked monks and genuflected over by kerchiefed ladies with the look of
salvation on their faces. There is a bronze plaque to one side: 'In memory of
faithful Orthodox Christians, tortured and killed here in the years of turmoil.'

Placed in its present spot in 1995, the cross seems to exist in oddly tragic
symmetry with the building just a block away, at the other end of Bolshaya
Lubyanka Street – the eponymous headquarters of the former KGB, an organization which, in various incarnations, killed or imprisoned more than
300,000 church workers in the name of official atheism since 1917. During
Soviet times, the 600-year-old monastery was closed and housed an NKVD
(precursor to the KGB) barracks. It is said the premises were even used for
executions.

Today, much has changed. The Lubyanka, which houses the KGB's successor,
the Federal Security Service, now has its own dedicated Orthodox chapel.
Sretensky monastery, reopened and renovated, has come to symbolize an
awkward alliance of the Church and its former persecutors. It has become the
centre of a spiritual revival among Russia's ruling circles, who are dispropor-
tionately drawn from among the former KGB, and who flooded into the
Kremlin 12 years ago on Putin's coat-tails.

For Father Tikhon, the ravages directed at the Church by the institution which to all intents and purposes governs Russia today are not something to dwell on – not a matter for public confrontation, but neither something to be specifically hidden away. They are, like the stone cross in his cloister garden, there to be seen only if one is looking for them.

He says he will never be reconciled with the Soviet period of Russian history, but he nonetheless does not consider the crimes of the NKVD or the KGB to be the responsibility of contemporary individuals: 'They didn't have anything to do with that. It would be like blaming some American soldier today for what happened in Vietnam.' Rather than apportioning blame, Father Tikhon seems eager to hammer the 70-year Soviet period into a single arc of historical Russian statehood. Even as they worked for the Soviet state, he says, many of those KGB officers were in fact serving Russia: 'The intelligence officers that I know did what they did on behalf of the Russian state, and so to say they were guilty of repressions would be totally false.'

This is, needless to say, something of a minority attitude within the Church, especially among the formerly dissident rank-and-file clergy. But it is a view that is nonetheless welcomed and cultivated by the Kremlin leadership, which seems keen to overcompensate for its atheist past and to take advantage of the Church's image. According to a 2010 poll, the Church is the second most trusted public institution in Russia, despite the fact that only a small minority of Russians attend regularly. Falling approval ratings and the rise of a street protest movement appear to have accelerated Putin's efforts to co-opt the Church. Sretensky is at the centre of this effort: the head of one Moscow public relations firm jokingly calls the monastery 'the Kremlin's department of ideology'. But it is not really a joke. Father Innokenty Pavlov, who retired from the Church in 1993 and is a noted liberal opponent of the Orthodox establishment, says he doubts whether there is anything aside from political expediency behind the newly religious attitude of Russia's rulers. 'It seems our leaders learnt one useful thing from their scientific atheism classes', he laughs: 'Voltaire said "if there were no God it would be necessary to invent him". They thought, what a good idea, let's implement this.'

The word 'Putin' is nowhere to be found in Tikhon's autobiography, *Everyday Saints and Other Stories*, which became a publishing sensation – the best-selling book of 2012, beating even the Russian translation of *Fifty Shades of Grey*. The book was a success at bridging the chasm between the Church and the communist period of Russia's history, at normalizing an era that was far from normal and making it possible for Russians to embrace their religious traditions. At the same time it assuaged some of the lurking discomfort Russians felt about what their own parents and grandparents might have been guilty of.

Tikhon presents the Soviet period not as a dark age, but as a time when the faithful were tested; where, instead of messiahs, there were 'everyday saints', whose ordinary heroism often went unnoticed. *Everyday Saints* is written in a mellow and forgiving spirit. It is devoted mainly to personal reminiscences of the quirks and lovable foibles of an older generation of churchmen – those 'everyday saints' Tikhon calls his teachers – who endured far more than he did at the hands of the Soviet regime. Father Tikhon's own *dukhovnik*, Father John Krestyankin, the late archimandrite of the Pskov Caves monastery, had his fingers broken during interrogation by the NKVD, shortly before being sent off to the gulag for five years in 1950. 'Thank God, I did not have the same serious conflicts which my predecessors had', says Tikhon today. 'In the 1980s, we did not have such repressions, they could ruin your professional life, ban you from studying, or from having prestigious work; but no more than that.' Critics say the book is notable for what it leaves out: that in addition to clashes with authorities, the clergy often compromised. Many level the accusation that church dignitaries worked for the KGB, which essentially controlled the levers of promotion within the Church through the end of the 1980s.

No one knows more about this painful episode in the Church's history – the cooperation between top-level clergy and the KGB – than Father Gleb Yakunin, a former priest and liberal reformer who was excommunicated in 1997, partly for his criticism of the Church. I asked Yakunin, still a noted dissident, about the Church's painful past of collaborating with the KGB. In 1992, under pressure from then President Boris Yeltsin, fighting to weaken the KGB at the time, Yakunin was granted access to the archives of the KGB's fifth directorate, fourth department, which dealt with religious groups. He spent a month going through the agent reports. While he was never given the card file with the identities of the agents, he was able to glean from the patterns of their reports who they were by comparing their codenames with information on the activities of top-level clergy. For instance, he found an intriguing travel itinerary of agent 'Mikhailov', who, according to his reports, travelled to New Zealand and Australia in February 1972 and then to Thailand in January 1973 for meetings of the World Council of Churches. Cross-checking these with news entries in the *Journal of the Moscow Patriarchate*, Yakunin found that a certain Archimandrite Kirill, who worked in the Church's department of external relations, took such trips on those dates. In 2009, after four decades of rising through the ranks, the white-bearded, portly Kirill was named patriarch of the Russian Church. The Church maintains that Kirill was never an employee or agent of the KGB. Representatives of the patriarch declined to comment further. According to Father Yakunin, the Church was so thoroughly infiltrated by the KGB that 'virtually the entire episcopate were recruited as informers'.

There is no evidence that Father Tikhon was himself compromised by association with the KGB – he would have been too young to make an attractive target for recruitment. However, people he writes about were. For example, in the mid-1980s he spent two years as assistant to Father Pitirim, head of the publications department of the Church, to whom Father Yakunin refers by his alleged KGB codename 'Abbot'.

Twenty years later, compromises made under the Soviet regime are still the subject of a painful debate within the Church. Instead of purging the former collaborators, it is those who have raised the issue, like Father Yakunin, who have been purged. Yakunin believes that as a result of the Soviet period, the Church needs 'a new protestant reformation', in which the entire episcopate would be replaced. Anything short of that would leave the Church, and its immense moral weight, in the hands of the KGB, which once infiltrated it and now (in its new incarnation) runs it as a bastion of a new version of imperial nationalism – a 'virus', as he put it – which is eating Russia from within. Russia's Christian Church, as the organization that suffered most from communism, had a chance to be the nation's conscience. With its moral weight, it could have guided Russia beyond its Soviet nightmare, by helping the country confront its past, accept it and heal itself. Instead, it has become a hive of former collaborators, who see the Orthodox Church not as a way to remember, but as a way to forget.

* * *

Once suffused with ideology at every level, Russian political life has, for centuries, been vulnerable to all-encompassing doctrines and programmes, and many see the kind of muscular, politically tinged Orthodox Christianity espoused by Father Tikhon, Yakunin, Malofeev and Dugin as starting to fill this awkward vacuum left by the disappearance of communism. These various groups in Putin's orbit – Yakunin's 'Orthodox chekists', Malofeev's 'Orthodox businessmen' and Father Tikhon's conservative circle within the Church itself – all form part of Dugin's contact network within the Russian elite.

Dugin's ill-fated 'Russian March' and the deniable but protected antics of the Eurasian Youth Union were evidence that he clearly had the ear of high-ranking people in the President's Administration, who were willing to flirt with radical ideologies in order to sort out political problems. There is evidence that a number of foreign trips by Dugin had Kremlin fingerprints on them as well. In 2004, for instance, he made a curious visit to Turkey in advance of a state visit by Putin. According to the US embassy in Ankara (in a cable revealed in 2010 by Wikileaks), a source close to Tuncer Kılınç, head of Turkey's National

Security Council, told US diplomats that 'Putin sent "Eurasia" architect Alexander Dugin to visit Kılınç preceding Putin's arrival to consolidate a Turkish "Eurasia" bloc.' This appears to have been an effort by Russia to gain traction among Turkish hardliners, but it went nowhere.[32]

Another example of deniable foreign adventure that in some way seems to have been inspired by the Kremlin came in 2007, following a trip by Dugin and Zarifullin to Crimea where they took part in protests against 'Orange' rule in Ukraine. In June of that year, both men were declared persona non grata and deported from Kiev's Borispil airport. Interestingly, the Russian government immediately retaliated by deporting Ukrainian presidential adviser Mykola Zhulynsky and his family, who had arrived in St Petersburg on a personal visit.[33] Russia's ambassador in Ukraine, explaining the deportation, said: 'What can I say? Recently our representative has not been allowed to Crimea. Then the same situation with your representative.' In October, Dugin and Zarifullin were again banned from entering Ukraine after vandalizing a statue of the national crest on top of Mount Hoverla. The following February, the Kremlin deported Ukrainian political analyst Sergey Taran. Russia's Foreign Ministry said the ban was a direct response to the blacklisting of the two Russians.[34]

It was an important signal that Dugin was not simply freelancing. But it is difficult to detect whose interests he was serving with his activities; certainly, if there was Kremlin support, it was not monolithic. Modest Kolerov, who at the time was head of President Putin's directorate for cultural and international ties with the states of the CIS, flatly denies that the Kremlin had any official role in the Ukraine trips and calls Dugin's antics 'idiocy'.[35] But it is impossible to tell whether Dugin was calling the shots or someone else was. And in the house of mirrors of Moscow power politics, it did not really matter. As Dugin put it in the 2007 interview, his theories were 'becoming less and less of a simulacrum and more and more real'. Just how real would become clear very shortly.

CHAPTER FOURTEEN

WAG THE DOG

Sitting in the Georgian town of town of Sokhs, amid the sweep of the high Caucasus mountains, Pavel Zarifullin felt he was witnessing the dawn of a new era in Russian history.

It was the morning of 8 August 2008, and Sokhs, located at the southern entrance to the Roki Tunnel, which spans the Caucasus mountain range, linking Georgia with Russia, was on the invasion route of Russia's 58th Army. Tanks, trucks, armoured personnel carriers and missile launchers burst through the tunnel's mouth 'as though it were an oven door', as Zarifullin put it, and poured south. In his memoirs he writes:

> They appeared to have been born from the depths of the sacred Ossetian mountain, as if the ancient Caucasus spat out of its fire-breathing mouth these imperial figures of the war. From the pitch-black darkness of nothing-ness, a new Russia burst forth in front of our eyes.[1]

War had been brewing for months in South Ossetia, which since 1993 had been all but independent of Georgia following a brief civil war in which Russia had backed the separatists. A ceasefire line between Georgian troops and Ossetian irregulars was monitored by United Nations troops, and though the conflict had turned hot several times in the past, both Russia and Georgia had managed to keep their sides back from the brink – until now.

That night, following an escalating series of tit-for-tat artillery and sniper exchanges over the past week, Georgian regular army forces had attacked the capital Tskhinvali with rockets and a massed invasion force. Russia, clearly expecting a war, was ready. It poured an armoured column into Georgia. It was a feat of unprecedented boldness: previously Moscow had only ventured full-scale invasions of foreign countries like Hungary and Afghanistan, which were solidly within its sphere of influence. Georgia was a key US ally, a member of NATO's Partnership for Peace programme, under a pro-US president Mikheil Saakashvili. Russia's invasion forces were fighting Georgian troops trained by NATO and using US vehicles – not very well, as it turned out. In three days, the war was over. Georgia's army had been routed, and Moscow had shown it was capable of a strategic masterstroke: Georgia got the blame, while the rest of Russia's neighbours were cowed. In the wake of the conflict, Russian President Dmitry Medvedev claimed the countries of the former Soviet Union as 'a zone of special influence' for Russia, the first time Moscow had made such an explicit claim.

But one lingering question, among many, remained unanswered: what were Zarifullin and the rest of Dugin's Eurasian Youth Union doing there?

* * *

The war in Georgia, it turns out, was not only an epic moment in Russia's post-Soviet history, but also the climax of a very surreal summer camp that Dugin and Zarifullin had organized in the alpine meadows of Ossetia, designed as a celebration of the eternal friendship between the fraternal Ossetian and Russian peoples.

Held in cooperation with the ruling Ossetian Fedebasta (Socialist) Party north of the South Ossetian capital Tskhinvali, it was a rather hurried demonstration of semi-official support for the embattled pro-Russian regime of Eduard Kokoity, the thuggish president of the enclave. The camp, as Zarifullin put it, was 'a total immersion in the Iranian unconscious' of the Ossetian people, 'according to Gestalt psychology and the search for Iranian archetypes in the subconscious of the Russian people'. The campers took part in not very serious weapons training, as well as 'Gestalt experiments' aimed at teasing out the common psychic threads that wove together the common destiny of the Russian and the Sarmatian/Iranian peoples, perhaps buttressing on some level the claim of Russia to hegemony in the region. 'We were there in the capacity of military ethnographers', joked Zarifullin in his memoirs, proudly reporting that: 'The Iranian protoplast survives in the Russian collective unconscious . . . The blood of the Sarmatians beats in our temples. The glorious title of Russian envelops us all in shining light.' The camp itself was called 'Thus Spake Zarathustra' – a vaguely fascistic analogy to Friedrich Nietzsche's writings about Zoroastrian culture of the sixth century BC, which Hitler issued to every German soldier in the Second World War.

Dugin denies that they received any official funding from the Kremlin, saying that the camp was undertaken 'to show the support of a pro-Kremlin group to Kokoity'.[2] It may have helped that the movement's principal financier,

Gagloev, hailed from South Ossetia. It also turns out that Eduard Kokoity, South Ossetia's dictatorial leader, had found his way onto the Eurasianist movement's board of directors in 2005, and Dugin had hosted him on a number of radio broadcasts. The camp followers paid their own way (or rather, Mikhail Gagloev did). But the real goals of the exercise, given the singularly odd timing, on the eve of war, have to be wondered at. 'Kokoity knew there was an armed conflict coming, and he was looking for support wherever he could get it', says Leonid Savin, a member of the Eurasian Youth Union. 'I think he knew that Dugin had contacts in the Kremlin, and was looking for any way to find support on the Russian side.'

Russia had a complicated relationship with Kokoity. Historically, Moscow had supported South Ossetia, which had a generations-old feud with Georgia and refused to be incorporated into Georgia following the collapse of the USSR. A brief civil war in 1991–92, in which Russia supported South Ossetian independence, resulted in a UN ceasefire line, monitored by Russian peace-keeping troops. In response to some tensions earlier in the decade, the Russian government had begun handing out Russian passports to South Ossetians, as a warning to Georgia not to overstep the bounds. However, Russian support only went so far, and the Kremlin had kept Kokoity at arm's length, likely for fear of provoking a conflict, but also to preserve a fig leaf of impartiality. An aide to Kokoity who welcomed the campers, for example, told them that they were the first official Russian organization to come in 17 years. The following day, Kokoity addressed the participants, telling them in no uncertain terms that his goal was 'independence and eventually to join the Russian Federation'.

Kokoity may well have been concerned that the Kremlin's façade of neutrality might prevent it from coming to his aid, and the Eurasianist campers may have given him some measure of courage that he had the ear of Moscow as South Ossetia and Georgia lurched ever closer to war that summer. However, like the Ukraine trips, Dugin's South Ossetian summer camp might have enjoyed some official support on some level, but Kolerov, the former Kremlin official, ridiculed the idea that it was anything more than 'purely Dugin's initiative': 'They drank a lot, stayed for a few days and then left. It had no political significance whatsoever. They thought the tail could wag the dog.' But clearly, on some level, it did.

* * *

The war for Georgia had been brewing for some time, and came at the apogee of anti-Orange hysteria in Russia. The catalogue of Russian grievances against the West was by this point long indeed. The United States' war in Iraq had divided NATO and portrayed Washington as an international bully, acting unilaterally and provocatively throughout the world. The Bush administration had floated the idea of an anti-ballistic missile system in Eastern Europe and had declared the US airbase in Russia's former vassal state of Kyrgyzstan to be a US 'strategic interest', from which there was no intention of pulling out.

This culminated in a speech by Putin delivered at the annual Munich Conference on Security Policy in October 2007. In it, he accused the West of seeking world domination – 'a world in which there is one master, one sovereign', as he put it. 'And at the end of the day, this is pernicious not only for all those within this system, but also for the sovereign itself, because it destroys itself from within.'[3] Observers labelled the speech the beginning of a 'new Cold War' between Russia and the West.

The focus of the East–West rift shortly became Georgia, where Tbilisi and Moscow were on opposite sides of shadowy ethnic conflicts in Abkhazia on the Black Sea and the mountainous enclave of South Ossetia. The South Ossetian conflict had turned hot several times in the past 15 years, but each time wisdom had prevailed and Russia had managed to keep a lid on the fighting and thwart any attempts to rewrite the status quo. Famed for smuggling and lawlessness under successive Russian-backed strongmen, the little enclave remained a Russian client and a thorn in the side of Georgian nationalism, a key geopolitical lever in the Caucasus conflict. It was also, crucially, located at the southern entrance to the Roki Tunnel, a key strategic objective which Moscow had an interest in securing. But the arrival in power of Georgia's hot-headed pro-US president Mikheil Saakashvili in 2004 had changed the equation.

In the spring of 2008, the US revealed that it was discussing a NATO 'Membership Action Plan' for Georgia and Ukraine, and recognized the state of Kosovo, which had broken away from Russia's ally Serbia. For Russia, any hint of NATO membership for any other former Soviet republics outside the Baltics was a red line. It appeared that the region, in particular Georgia and Ukraine, was about to become what Eastern Europe had been in 1945–47: 'the object and the prize of a new Cold War', according to Dmitri Trenin, head of the Moscow Carnegie Center.

Already that summer, fighting had broken out between Georgian militias and Ossetian forces along the demarcation line, with the Georgian army occasionally shelling inside South Ossetia. Then, in the first week in August, the shelling and sniping began again. The conflict continued to escalate. And on the night of 7/8 August, Georgian units assembled outside Gori with tanks and 122mm Grad rocket launchers.

What happened next has been the subject of much guesswork, conspiracy theories, books, at least one feature film, and even an exhaustive investigation by the European Union. Saakashvili has always claimed that he was defending Georgia from a Russian invasion when he launched a blitzkrieg against Tskhinvali, raining down Grad rockets – intended for use against tanks – and killing dozens of civilians, as well as several Russian peacekeeping troops. Russia, however, claims its invasion of South Ossetia was in response to the aforementioned assault by Saakashvili. A year after the conflict, a European Union commission that was assigned to study the conflict, and which was headed by Swiss diplomat Heidi Tagliavini, came down largely on Russia's side. The report, issued in 2009, stated categorically that 'it was Georgia which triggered off the war when it attacked Tskhinvali with heavy artillery on the night of 7/8 August 2008'.[4] However, the report also established that Russian military units had been operating in South Ossetia before the Georgian invasion: 'While the onus of having actually triggered off the war lies with the Georgian side, the Russian side, too, carries the blame for a substantial number of violations of international law.'

Within hours of the bombardment, a Russian invasion force was flooding into the Roki Tunnel and into Georgia. Russia simultaneously invaded Abkhazia in the west, another breakaway province under the control of a Russian-supported ethnic militia. Saakashvili had made a major miscalculation. President Dmitry Medvedev and Vladimir Putin sought to outdo each other in war-hysteria hyperbole.

Dugin also played a rather underappreciated propaganda role. Speaking on liberal radio station Ekho Moskvy, he was the first Russian commentator to use the word 'genocide' to describe the Georgian attack on Tskhinvali: 'Genocide is killing based on ethnic principles. This is genocide.' A few hours later, on 9 August, Putin used the word as well. On his return from the Olympic Games in Beijing, he landed in Vladikavkaz. In remarks broadcast on television about the attack on Tskhinvali, he said: 'I believe there were elements of genocide'.[5]

Russia's 58th Army easily crushed Georgia's outnumbered and outgunned military in three days of fighting. The Western reaction to the Russian invasion was shock. Many feared the war would herald a new round of Russian imperialism in the former Soviet Union, which President Dmitry Medvedev declared a 'zone of privileged interest' on 31 August.

The Eurasian summer campers played no practical part in the war. However, the presence of a semi-official Kremlin-backed organization may have emboldened Kokoity to continue to escalate a low-level conflict to an extent that forced the Georgian government of Mikheil Saakashvili to intervene with a badly planned and bloody operation – wagering (incorrectly) that Russia would not intervene militarily.

The US government sought to punish Moscow for what appeared to be a stunningly successful military adventure. But cooler-headed European leaders, noting that, technically, Georgia had started the war, talked Washington down. And once it became clear that Saakashvili had at least been one of the principal instigators of the conflict, the moral force of the movements for sanctions dissipated.

Russia had won a major military victory against a NATO-backed ally and had got away with it. Hardliners in the regime sensed that a new confrontation with the West was imminent, and that the victory would translate into a long-held goal: a new era of imperial consolidation of geopolitical control over the former Soviet Union. The US and Russia came closer to war than they had in several decades after US President Bush airlifted supplies to a beleaguered Georgian government, putting US transport aircraft on Georgian runways in the midst of a Russian aerial bombing campaign.

But then, as suddenly as the new zeitgeist of confrontation had appeared, it vanished.

* * *

Three weeks after the invasion of Georgia, Russia's central bank was hit by a run on the rouble. Investors, hearing the hardline rhetoric booming out of the Kremlin, reassessed the political risk to their investments and, following the bankruptcy of Lehman Brothers, sold *en masse*. The Kremlin was forced to spend $200 billion of its hard currency reserves bailing out its worst-hit industries and banks. That winter, the rouble fell by a third against the dollar, and Russia was to end 2009 with a 7.9 per cent fall in GDP.

Amid the fallout from the crisis, the anti-Western campaign in Russia abated. Loans need to be rolled over, trade and technology transfers needed to increase. The resource-exporting model of the Russian economy needed to be replaced by a modernized technology-focused economy.

The US was anxious to build bridges with Russia, too, and threw a lifeline to Medvedev, who, despite the war, was perceived as being more friendly to America and more liberal than Putin. Speaking in Munich in February 2009, Vice President Joe Biden announced a 'reset' of US policy toward Russia. This ushered in a period of constructive and productive relations between the two countries, symbolized by the entry into force in February 2011 of the New START Treaty (Strategic Arms Reduction Treaty).

Dugin's career by this point had become a barometer of Russia's relations with the West: the more one saw Dugin, the worse things probably were. But starting almost immediately after the Georgia war, and with the onset of the financial crisis, his profile plummeted as Russia reached out to the West. A few weeks after the war, he was fired from his talk show on Russian Radio, the popular state-run station. In 2009, the Eurasian Youth Union was rolled up, albeit temporarily, and Zarifullin quit after falling out with the rest of the organization: 'The project was closely associated with the policy of the President's Administration, and when they lost interest in it, Dugin lost interest in it, too. He did not want to go into opposition', said Zarifullin. It must be said, he did not go into the opposition either. Today, he runs a think tank for Eurasianist ideas in Moscow. 'Dugin always wanted to be part of the establishment, he considered himself a part of it.'[6] Dugin made a soft landing: a professorship in Moscow State University's department of sociology. He was back on the shelf, but not for long.

* * *

Today the global American Empire tries to establish control over all countries of the world, they invade whoever they please, not asking for permission from anyone! . . . They have already invaded Iraq, Afghanistan, Libya; they plan to invade Syria and Iran; and they have their sights on Russia!

It was a freezing cold 4 February 2012, and Dugin was yelling into a microphone, addressing a pro-Kremlin demonstration of 120,000 in Moscow's Victory Park. Steam rose from the crowd, and from the pavilion that Dugin shared with fellow hardline ideologues Kurginyan, Prokhanov and Shevchenko, who stamped their feet to keep warm as they took turns blasting the Western conspiracy to destroy Russia. Demonstrators, many bussed in for the event with the promise that they would be taken shopping at IKEA, sprawled across the pavements and frigid snowy ground. Migrant workers, high-schoolers – anyone who could be mustered for a show of numbers and force. Few showed any great interest, except a vanguard of flag-waving Nashi supporters in the front ranks.

Two months earlier, the Kremlin had been shaken by a cataclysm when tens of thousands of people – many of them wealthy, well-fed Muscovites – had taken to the streets to protest against Vladimir Putin's rule following rigged parliamentary elections. In March, Putin was supposed to return to the presidency for a third term, according to a carefully choreographed deal with Medvedev who was to take up the prime ministership. In terms of numbers, the opposition demonstrations were unprecedented; until that point, such protests had usually consisted of more grey-clad OMON riot police than protesters, who were quickly packed into police vans or 'kettled' into squares. But the new wave of demonstrations could not be addressed with police batons. The protests were too big, and the demonstrators were too influential: bankers, editors, iPhone-wielding socialites and the wives of prominent oligarchs.

It was a sign that the hyperreality of the Surkov era, with its grand imitation of politics by a succession of doubles and clones, had been exhausted. It was clear that a new form of politics had taken hold. The opposition was no longer a marginal force that could be addressed with fake, Kremlin-sponsored simulacra. Putin was fighting for his political life, or at least seemed to think he was, and the Kremlin was using new language, and new politics – in other words, real politics.

This was symbolized by Surkov's apparently forced resignation in December. The maestro of domestic politics quipped 'stabilization has eaten its young', paraphrasing French revolutionary Georges Danton standing in front of the guillotine. He was transferred to a new, less influential post.

In his Victory Park speech, Dugin again used rhetoric that Putin would adopt only later. He blamed 'fifth columns' and 'internal agents' who were working 'to weaken Russia from within so as to open the door to external control'.[7] The Victory Park demonstration was the Kremlin's counterattack, the first major pro-regime demonstration following the opposition successes. And it featured all the nationalists (who were not on the side of the protesters) that the Kremlin could lay its hands on: Dugin, Kurginyan, Shevchenko, Prokhanov – all delivered full-throated defences of Putin, blaming subversion by dark foreign hands. When I asked Pavlovsky about this spectacle, he replied that Putin had chosen the group to address protesters because 'they were all that was left'. The meeting was a stark warning that, shorn of its liberal wing, Putin's third term was going to be very different. Instead of tacking back and forth between liberals and conservatives, Putin was now entirely reliant on the latter.

The proximate reason for the protests was Putin's decision, announced the previous September, to return to power. Mounting a podium at the annual United Russia Party congress that month, he and Dmitry Medvedev had suddenly sprung the decision on party delegates, who were thoroughly unprepared for the move. Medvedev's relatively liberal circle had clearly not been informed beforehand; his economic adviser Arkady Dvorkovich had tweeted 'there is no cause for celebration' following the announcement. Meanwhile, Minister of Finance Alexey Kudrin, who had had his eye on the prime ministership and had clearly not been told what was coming, made a number of intemperate comments about the government and was sacked by Medvedev days later.

In the run-up to the parliamentary elections, Putin felt more and more pressure. In November 2011, stepping into the ring of a martial arts match to congratulate the winner, he was abruptly booed by the crowd. He stammered through his lines, but was clearly flummoxed by the reaction. A few days later, his staff cancelled a similar public appearance in St Petersburg, according to news reports. 'Putin had been assured that once he announced his return, his popularity would shoot into the heavens. The opposite happened', said Pavlovsky, who by this time had been sacked by the Kremlin for his too-open support for Medvedev.

The parliamentary elections on 4 December added fuel to the crisis. Marred by fraud, they were followed by street demonstrations which culminated in a peaceful protest that drew an unheard-of 50,000 people onto Bolotnaya Square near the Kremlin; and then 100,000 showed up to demonstrate against the Kremlin on 24 December. Swelling the numbers at demonstrations, and providing street muscle, were disciplined formations of nationalists led by Demushkin and Belov. Though their organizations by this point had been banned, they nonetheless fielded tens of thousands of marchers.

What made these protests different was the legal permission granted for tens of thousands to gather – something that had never happened under Putin. Even to those at the very summit of the regime it was never clear whether Medvedev's circle, including possibly Surkov, had intended the legal demonstrations as a way of allowing protesters to let off steam, or whether they had an altogether different objective – of undermining Putin's re-election. All this fed paranoia in Putin's circle. According to Pavlovsky: 'From the standpoint of a large part of Putin's circle, and likely, Putin as well, the December demonstrations were inspired by Medvedev's circle. Perhaps not by Medvedev personally. But I think that is what Putin was thinking as well.'

Putin himself seems to have had some suspicions that the protests were the work of unseen foreign hands: '[Opposition leaders] heard the signal and with the support of the US State Department began active work', he said after US Secretary of State Hillary Clinton expressed concern about the conduct of the parliamentary elections. Putin's rhetoric grew more paranoid, more national-istic and more confrontational, perhaps reflecting his mindset. He told a stadium audience in February:

> We will not allow anyone to interfere in our internal affairs! We will not allow anyone to force their will upon us, because we have our own will, and it has always helped us to win! . . . We are a victorious people! It is in our genes, in our genetic code. It is transferred from generation to generation, and we will have victory!

There was never any danger that Putin would lose the election: he won easily in March 2012, and immediately steered a more conservative course. Politics under Surkov's successor Vyacheslav Volodin have been more confrontational, more nationalistic, more brutal.

After Putin's re-election, he rolled back Medvedev's limited liberal political reforms (such as elections for regional governors), and simultaneously appealed to Russian spiritual traditions, attacking Western values. He put a new emphasis on the loyalty of the political elite, bringing in a series of laws against owning foreign property (which was neutered on its third reading by a careful Duma). He hamstrung the opposition with a series of repressive laws, while simultaneously emphasizing Russia's national greatness and rapidly increasing military spending. The sort of rhetoric pioneered by the marginal nationalists in the 1990s became the standard jargon of state policy a mere decade and a half later.

As Putin said in his September 2013 speech at the Valdai summit:

> We can see how many of the Euro-Atlantic countries are actually rejecting their roots, including the Christian values that constitute the basis of Western civilisation. They are denying moral principles and all traditional identities: national, cultural, religious and even sexual. They are imple- menting policies that equate large families with same-sex partnerships, belief in God with the belief in Satan.[8]

Putin's new metaphysics contrasted Russia's romantic attachment to its iden- tity, the virtue of its humanitarian values, with the cyborg-like rationalism of a West that has lost touch with its inner human nature, its spirituality, its fraternal family bonds.

Duma deputies raced to outlaw or severely limit anything foreign that they could get their hands on. The Duma outlawed the adoption of Russian children by Americans; moved to limit the distribution of foreign films; and restricted the use of foreign driving licences, foreign study (for the children of officials), foreign assets (for officials) – even foreign travel. Many of these initiatives were subsequently overturned, but that was not the point. As political scientist Alexey Makarkin told the *New York Times* bureau chief Ellen Barry:

> . . . there is a principle in questions of patriotism or protecting the interests of the country, as the authorities see it, that it's better to overdo it than to show weakness . . . If you try too hard, and come up with some exotic, scandalous draft law, you are in any case one of us. Maybe you are too emotional – you're a patriot.[9]

The Orthodox Church received new prominence. A July 2013 law outlawed blasphemy, which is carefully phrased as 'offending religious beliefs', while the Kremlin flirted precariously with religious law in the strange prosecution of female punk band Pussy Riot in 2012.[10] After the three women performed a punk rock song 'Holy Virgin, Throw Putin Out!' in Moscow's Christ the Saviour cathedral, they were given two-year prison sentences for 'hooliganism motivated by religious hatred' (though they were formally pardoned in 2013). Prosecution documents state that the laws broken by the three defendants were articles 62 and 75 of the Quinisext Council, held under the Emperor Justinian in the seventh century, according to which access to the solea and ambon (the altar area of Orthodox churches) is reserved for clergy. While the judge in his final sentencing made no reference to the Quinisext Council, he did cite as expert opinion the fourth-century Council of Laodicea – according to which 'The solea and ambon have special religious significance for believers.'

Nightly broadcasts on state TV channels became more and more surreal: the West was in flames, fascism was on the march in Europe, while Russia was an island of stability and good governance. The fiery anchorman Dmitry Kiselev emerged as the *enfant terrible* of Russian television for his anti-gay and anti-Western rants. 'I think that just imposing fines on gays for homosexual propaganda among teenagers is not enough', he said in one characteristic rant about a new law outlawing 'gay propaganda'. 'They should be banned from donating blood, sperm. And their hearts, in case of an automobile accident, should be buried in the ground or burned as unsuitable for the continuation of life.'[11] ITAR-TASS, the former Soviet news agency, symbolically changed its name back to simply TASS, its Soviet-era name.

With the merciless attacks on liberals, it finally appeared that, 20 years after the end of the Cold War, a new official ideology was taking shape in which liberalism had replaced capitalism as the official enemy of the people.

With the Kremlin in the grip of a new conservative nationalism, it was only a matter of time before its expansionist ideas began to be tested in Russia's former imperial domains. Many dismissed Putin's October 2011 *Izvestiya* article proposing a 'Eurasian Union' by 2015 as an election stunt. But the signal was clear. Published a week after he had announced his intention of returning to the presidency, the article spoke volumes about Putin's priorities, laying out his plans for a Eurasian Union 'which won't be like other previous unions', as he put it. After Putin's return to power, it became clear that this was a deadly serious endeavour, intended as a future rival to China, the United States and the European Union. The present era, Putin told the Valdai forum in 2013, foresees:

> ... the formation of major geopolitical zones, as well as financial and economic, cultural, civilisational, and military and political areas. That is why integrating with our neighbours is our absolute priority ... Eurasian integration is a chance for the entire post-Soviet space to become an inde-

pendent centre for global development, rather than remaining on the outskirts of Europe and Asia.[12]

The Union had begun as a customs union with Kazakhstan and Belarus, signed in 2010. But following this article, Putin began filling the Eurasian Union with institutions along the lines of the European Union: a supranational executive branch was launched in 2012, along with a Eurasian Court based in Minsk. Eventually, it was not excluded that there would be a monetary union and a 'political component' to the Union.

Russia's political class read the message loud and clear: Putin was to be a 'gatherer of the lands', who would make his legacy the restoration of Russia's lost territorial patrimony; lands that his ancestors had shed their blood for; lands that Russia lost 20 million lives defending in the Second World War. Eurasia was a 'dog whistle', a cipher, a deniable but clear goal: to remake the Russian Empire in all but name. Hillary Clinton issued a stern warning, accusing the Kremlin of 'a move to re-Sovietize the region':

> It's not going to be called that. It's going to be called a Customs Union, it will be called the Eurasian Union and all of that. But make no mistake, we know what the goal is and we are trying to figure out effective ways to slow down or prevent it.[13]

Indeed, soon enough the West appeared to challenge Putin's plans. In 2013 the European Union offered an Association Agreement trade pact to former Soviet republics. The Kremlin saw this immediately as a threat that would complicate accession to its own Eurasian Union project and at the same time smooth the way for integration with the EU, which over the previous two decades had become a conveyor belt to NATO. The Kremlin was not simply going to give up.

Putin immediately set about pulling various geopolitical levers to prevent the states of the former USSR from joining. He is thought to have offered Ukraine lower prices for gas supplies and soft credits if it did not sign up to the EU partnership programme – and to have threatened crippling trade sanctions if it did. Putin's determination to keep the former Soviet republics out of Brussels' orbit was evident in Armenian President Serzh Sargsyan's sudden decision, after talks with the Russian president in September, to join the Customs Union. Diplomats suggested that Putin had threatened to withdraw military support for Armenia – support that it needs in its territorial dispute with Azerbaijan. Belarus, shortly before signing up for the Eurasian Economic Union, got a $2 billion loan.

Ukraine, the largest of the former Soviet republics, is also one of the most divided: it has a Russian-speaking east and a Ukrainian-speaking west which was added to the country only in 1939 by the Molotov–Ribbentrop Pact. Since independence in 1991, Ukraine's rulers had tacked back and forth between Russia and the West in an effort to keep every constituency happy. However, according to Timothy Snyder of Yale University: 'By 2013, oscillating between Russia and the West was no longer possible. By then, Moscow had ceased to represent simply a Russian state with more or less calculable interests, but rather a much grander vision of Eurasian integration.'[14]

Kiev's refusal to sign the EU treaty ignited protests in Kiev, where the educated intelligentsia and the western ethnic Ukrainians form a sizeable pro-European lobby that is not to be trifled with. Demonstrations starting in November grew in scope until revolutionaries had permanently occupied Independence Square in downtown Kiev. The protest turned into a three-month-long stand-off, with protesters barricading themselves on the square behind barricades of tyres and sandbags. The attempt to force Ukraine into Russia's Eurasian sphere of influence produced exactly the opposite result, as protests turned massive, and increasingly violent, with pitched battles between protesters and riot police.

CHAPTER FIFTEEN

EXPORT OF THE PASSIONARIES

A deep voice crackled over the radio. 'Work, on my mark. With a three-second countdown.'

The silence was broken again seven seconds later as a second voice came on the frequency. 'Okay, ready.'

'Ready', said a third voice.

'Three. Two. One.'

There followed the echoed sound of high-velocity rifle shots.

'Three. Two. One.'

More shots.

'Forty-fifth. Fire!' Crack crack crack.

This radio transmission recorded what is possibly the bloodiest day in Kiev's post-1945 history. The voices were those of a sniper team, perched in buildings high above Independence Square, the centre of the massive street protest against the government. In the streets below, there was carnage. Dozens of protesters, most carrying nothing more than wooden shields and helmets, lay in pools of blood in rain-soaked Institutskaya Street as they struggled up the hill from their protest camp towards police positions. All told, 53 protesters and 18 police were killed by snipers in a three-day period at the climax of protests in Kiev in February 2014.

The 'sniper massacre', as it came to be known, was the culmination of a months-long political crisis sparked by old-fashioned great-power rivalry between Russia and the West over the destiny of Ukraine. It was the bloody collision of two world-views: Putin's Eurasian vision and the opposing Western-sponsored course of European integration.

The violence reached its climax with the bloody and one-sided street battle, the details of which are still debated. Intercepts of police radio communications revealed the existence of at least three sniper teams operating in the area that day. Hours of video footage, along with radio communications intercepted and placed on the internet, allow a more complete picture of the events.

That police special units participated in the killings is not in doubt: dozens of witnesses and at least ten cameras recorded footage of men in Special Forces uniforms firing on the crowd with high-velocity rifles from various positions occupied by the police. They appeared to be covering a withdrawal by unarmed 'Berkut' riot police, who themselves were under sniper fire from the opposition (18 Berkut riot police were killed by gunshot wounds between 18 February and 20 February).

Most laid the blame for the killings of the protesters at President Viktor Yanukovich's door. He was under Russian pressure to end the protests, and possibly gambled that a show of overwhelming force would send the protesters home. However, the Kiev sniper massacre has since taken on the familiar characteristics of similarly decisive moments in post-Soviet history, becoming obscured in an immense tangle of conspiracy theories.

A very different narrative of these events, for example, has played out on Russian TV screens. During a news conference in March, Putin addressed the issue in response to a reporter's question, suggesting that the snipers in fact 'may have been provocateurs from opposition parties'. In Russia, the snipers were portrayed as a shadowy fifth column, deployed by the Euromaidan's foreign paymasters as an enormous provocation, shooting at both sides in an effort to escalate the situation and orchestrate the collapse of Moscow's client Yanukovich and the ushering in of a pro-NATO fascist junta. The physical battlefield of the streets of Kiev had been replaced with a virtual battlefield in which two simulacra of reality competed for the eyeballs and attention-spans of the world. While Russia lost the fight for terrain, it was the latter battlefield that mattered more.

The history of the massacre has since become akin to a fork in the road of history: two completely different realities emerged following the sniper massacre. And these continue to bedevil efforts to resolve the Ukraine crisis. To the West, it symbolizes the savagery of the Yanukovich regime, justifying its overthrow. But to their opponents, particularly Russian television viewers, it bears all the hallmarks of a false flag, a monstrous conspiracy, designed to discredit Yanukovich's pro-Russian regime.

To be fair to the Russian version, there is some evidence to suggest that the massacre was more complicated than it at first seemed: a leaked phone call between Estonian Foreign Minister Urmas Paet, visiting Kiev, and EU foreign policy chief Catherine Ashton recorded Paet as saying that police and protesters had been killed by the same type of bullets from the same guns. 'So there is now stronger and stronger understanding', Paet told Ashton, 'that behind the snipers, it was not Yanukovich, but it was somebody from the new coalition.'[1] His evidence was called into question by the chief witness he cited, Olga Bogomolets, head of the protesters' medical service, who said she had never told Paet what he attributed to her – that the same weapons had been used on both police and protesters. However, interim Health Minister Oleh Musiy has made a similar claim – that protesters and police alike were shot with the same rifles: 'I think it wasn't just a part of the old regime that [plotted the provocation], but it was also the work of Russian special forces who served and maintained the ideology of the [old] regime.'[2]

If such a force existed, its motives can only be guessed at. Opposition snipers might have had an interest in hanging an atrocity around the neck of the regime and discrediting Yanukovich (this is the version put forward by the security service chief blamed for the atrocity, for obvious reasons). A second theory is that regime snipers, firing at both police and protesters, could have been trying to quickly escalate the situation in order to justify a massive armed crackdown and the introduction of tanks to force an end to the protests (the version put forward by former Deputy Interior Minister Hennady Moskal).[3] Musiy, meanwhile, says he believes the 'third force' scenario might have been carried out by Russians in an effort to drive Yanukovich from power and justify an invasion.

These allegations have to be taken with a pinch of salt. Like any conspiracy theory, it relies on the *ex post facto* argument that what actually happened was indeed the goal of the plotters. But it attributes to the plotters the almost Einstein-like capacity to foresee the result of their actions in an extremely complex and unpredictable situation. Indeed, it would have been almost impossible to reasonably predict the consequences of massacring dozens of protesters in Kiev.

The reality is probably simpler. Rather than a 'third force' shooting at both protesters and police, it increasingly appears that what happened was that protesters shot at police, and police shot at protesters. Three police and commando sniper units were in the area during the massacre. The first, filmed with Kalashnikov assault rifles as well as sniper rifles, and wearing telltale yellow armbands, was an Interior Ministry unit named 'Omega', which appeared to be giving cover to retreating Berkut police. Three members of this unit, wearing the yellow armbands and shoulder patches, had been filmed firing Kalashnikovs from a police barricade on 20 February, down Institutskaya Street in the direction of Independence Square.[4] This is also thought to be the unit whose radio communications (reproduced above) were captured and uploaded to the internet, apparently by a radio enthusiast with an iPhone. We clearly hear snipers being given orders to fire and then firing. Later in the recording, an after-action report makes the result clear: 'Movement on the rooftop has ceased.'

Another unit, 'Alpha', under the command of the SBU (Ukraine's version of the KGB), had taken up positions in the Cabinet of Ministers building, with a clear line of sight down Institutskaya Street. The radio communications of this unit were also recorded and posted on the internet, but these contain no evidence that its members actually used their weapons: there are no orders to fire, no after-action reports from snipers, and no sounds of gunfire on the recording.[5] Six days later, Ukrainian TV station TVi interviewed a masked man who identified himself as Colonel Bychkovsky, commander of the Alpha unit, who insisted during the half-hour interview that his team had arrived at 10 a.m., after the violence. Bychkovsky also alluded to the existence of a different sniper team, a unit named 'Bulat', under the command of the State Guards Agency. This unit was alleged by parliamentarian and former defence minister Anatoly Hrytsenko to have participated in the killings; he offered no evidence for his assertion, however.

The only pieces of hard evidence showing what is possibly opposition snipers firing at opposition demonstrators comes from a video of the shooting of one protester on a terrace with a direct line of sight from the Hotel Ukraine, then under the control of the opposition. In addition, an unedited video recording posted on YouTube (but since removed) shows a BBC camera crew, along with correspondent Gabriel Gatehouse, being fired on from a window of the Hotel Ukraine. The tape is ultimately inconclusive, however; one of the camera crew is heard to say 'Fuck knows who it was.'

Ivan Siyak, a Kiev-based journalist who has worked tirelessly for the website Colta.ru to document the various claims and counter-claims,[6] writes that the 'third force' accusations have to be regarded sceptically: 'everyone has a reason to like this theory'. The Ukrainian opposition – which has since come to power – likes it because it 'gives them a convenient explanation for why a dozen and a half policemen were killed by gunshot wounds' during the supposedly peaceful protest. Russia, meanwhile, likes the theory because 'it can blame the blood-bath on Right Sector [a Ukrainian ultra-nationalist movement], the current Ukrainian government, or Western special services'. And Ukraine's security services like the theory because it 'allows them to hang blame for at least a portion of the victims on someone else'. Siyak, however, has come to the conclusion that the 'third force' was most likely a myth:

> Firing at both sides, the snipers of the 'third force' would have had to hide not only from thousands of opposition members and police, but also from dozens of cameras, which would have been astonishingly hard in the small patch that is downtown Kiev where Euromaidan stood.

Even so, the detention in early April 2014 of a dozen Interior Ministry soldiers charged with committing the murders is probably not the end of the story, though it is clear that many would like it to be.

It was not the first time that mysterious snipers had changed history. But instead of crushing the opposition and consolidating central control, as the Ostankino massacre had in Yeltsin's case, it shocked the Ukrainian political class and immediately destroyed Yanukovich politically. His bodyguards melted away, loyal oligarchs headed for the airports, and Yanukovich himself was forced to flee to Russia. On 28 February he held a press conference in Rostov on Don to call on President Putin to 'restore order'.

* * *

In the midst of the constitutional vacuum following Yanukovich's hurried exit, Putin struck quickly. With the events in Kiev bringing Ukrainian nationalists to power, one place in particular – the ethnically Russian Crimean peninsula – was an obvious place of concern.

On Friday, 28 February, dozens of unmarked military vehicles suddenly appeared on the roads of the Crimean peninsula, ferrying soldiers in uniforms without insignia to take control of chokepoints and airfields, and to man roadblocks. Ukraine's military on the peninsula were confined to their barracks, hemmed in by these troops. Aside from a single incident on 18 March, which killed one, the takeover was nearly bloodless. The Russian invasion was pulled off flawlessly as Kiev, in the midst of a constitutional vacuum, flailed helplessly. It was an infiltration, not an invasion, in the words of the BBC, and Russian occupiers were welcomed by much of the ethnically Russian populace. A lightning-quick referendum on seceding from Ukraine and joining the Russian Federation then won overwhelming support.

The whole operation was a tactical masterstroke, which left Western critics fuming but unable to respond to Russia's new 'asymmetric warfare'. It cost virtually no lives and appeared to be in line with the wishes of most of the population. Taking a page from the postmodern playbook of Kremlin political technology, in a documentary aired a year after the Crimean campaign Putin claimed that the first orders he had given in the effort to seize Crimea had been to sociologists, who then conducted secret public opinion polls to seek to ensure that the referendum would achieve the desired result.[7]

But, following the events in Kiev and Crimea, Putin's rhetoric slowly darkened. In his speech about Crimea's accession to Russia he spoke of a 'fifth column' and 'national traitors' – rhetoric straight from Dugin's speech in

Victory Park in February 2012. In April, Putin concluded his annual phone-in show (known as 'Direct Line') with a long monologue about the meaning of the Russian nation, in which he referred to the 'Russian cultural code', as well as a 'powerful genetic code', as:

> . . . one of our main competitive advantages in today's world. This code is very flexible and enduring. We don't even feel it but it is certainly there . . . It seems to me that the Russian person or, on a broader scale, a person of the Russian world, primarily thinks about his or her highest moral designation, some highest moral truths. This is why the Russian person, or a person of the Russian world, does not concentrate on his or her own precious personality . . . Western values are different and are focused on one's inner self. Personal success is the yardstick of success in life and this is acknowledged by society. The more successful a man is, the better he is. This is not enough for us in this country . . . I think only our people could have come up with the famous saying: 'Meeting your death is no fear when you have got people round you.' How come? Death is horrible, isn't it? But no, it appears it may be beautiful if it serves the people: death for one's friends, one's people or for the homeland, to use a modern word. These are the deep roots of our patriotism. They explain mass heroism during armed conflicts and wars and even sacrifice in peacetime. Hence there is a feeling of fellowship and family values. Of course, we are less pragmatic, less calculating than representatives of other peoples, and we have bigger hearts. Maybe this is a reflection of the grandeur of our country and its boundless expanses. Our people have a more generous spirit.[8]

Amplified by the mass media, the message was hammered home over and over again: Russia is unique, Russia is different, Russia is superior, Russia is under attack, Russia must defend itself.

Or, as the novelist Vladimir Sorokin put it in a *New York Review of Books* op-ed devoted to the Crimea speech: 'The huge iceberg Russia, frozen by the Putin regime, cracked after the events in Crimea; it has split from the European world, and sailed off into the unknown.'[9]

* * *

Beginning in April, pro-Russia paramilitary units fanned out across Russian-speaking eastern Ukraine, seizing government buildings and security facilities. On 17 April, during his annual phone-in, Putin referred to eastern Ukraine as *Novorossiya* or 'New Russia' – a term which dates from the eighteenth-century conquest of Ukraine:

what was called Novorossiya (New Russia) back in the tsarist days – Kharkov, Lugansk, Donetsk, Kherson, Nikolaev and Odessa – were not part of Ukraine back then. These territories were given to Ukraine in the 1920s by the Soviet government.[10]

He thus appeared to predict that more than just Crimea would eventually fall into Russian hands.

The pro-Russia militias that moved into eastern Ukraine appeared to be split into two groups. One, fairly harmless, was loyal to Donetsk-based oligarch Rinat Akhmetov, who ran the province's steel industry (and who has since switched to opposing the separatists). The other, more serious group, appeared to have had proper military training and advanced weapons, and it took control of several strategic towns in Donetsk Oblast: Slavyansk and Kramatorsk. Western diplomats and military analysts said the 'professional coordinated nature' and the weaponry they carried suggested that a core group consisted of Russian Special Forces. They were led by two shadowy figures, Igor Strelkov and Alexander Boroday. They became the core of Moscow's efforts to bring eastern Ukraine under its sway.

Strelkov's real name was Igor Girkin. He was a professional mercenary and die-hard ideological nationalist who found time (in between battles) to write for Prokhanov's newspaper *Zavtra*. Strelkov, also known as Strelok ('shooter'), had fought in most of the dirty wars around the Russian periphery since the fall of the Soviet Union: he served in Transdniester until 1992, Bosnia in 1993 and Chechnya in 1995; and from 1999–2005 he was a *kontraktnik*, or non-conscript professional soldier, serving in the Russian army. In 2005 he had also, intriguingly, boarded an aircraft showing an ID badge as an active officer in the Federal Security Service, according to Moscow journalist Sergey Kanev, who found the information in a pirated civil aviation database. Fond of vintage military gear, Strelkov has been photographed in modern battle-dress uniforms, Red Guard civil war-era *shinel* greatcoat and *papakha* Astrakhan hat, 1940s-era tunics and jodhpurs . . . There is even one photo of him wearing a suit of armour! His soldiers wear ribbons and chevrons of some of the most prominent regiments of the tsar's army. 'Historical reconstruction buffs gone to war' was how *Novaya Gazeta* journalist Kanev described these militia groups. 'It is impossible to imagine that this is a real representative of the Kremlin with a mandate for partisan warfare.'

The novelist Dmitry Bykov described the phenomenon of mad Red Brown ideologues going to fight across the border as the 'export of the passionaries', referring to Gumilev's famous phrase. It also turns out that part of the operation may have been financed by Konstantin Malofeev, the enigmatic Orthodox oligarch close to Putin's reputed godfather Archimandrite Tikhon. Known for large charitable contributions to conservative and Church causes, Malofeev is also close to Sergey Aksenov, the current prime minister of breakaway Crimea. He met Aksenov a month before he took power.

There is a further fascinating detail which, while it does not indicate direct state involvement, nonetheless provides a window onto how the Kremlin's arm's-length deniable operations such as this work. Russia's state bank VTB had accused Malofeev of misusing a $225 million loan, and threatened to sue him in a London court. Coincidentally or not, the two parties reached a resolution on 27 February – the day before the Crimea operation – and VTB declined to sue. That must have removed a major cloud hanging over Malofeev's future, at precisely the moment the Kremlin was seeking his financial help in securing Crimea. In other words, Malofeev was, however deniably, a private citizen spending his own money – one or two places removed from the Kremlin, which could claim it had no finger in the pie and that Crimea's decision to secede and to join Russia was spontaneous.

From 2005, Strelkov/Girkin had worked in Malofeev's security detail, a position secured for him by his friend and collaborator Alexander Boroday (son of Yury, whom we met earlier). Alexander Boroday, who had also worked for Malofeev, was appointed prime minister of the Donetsk Republic with Strelkov as defence minister. In fact, the Donetsk rebel Ukrainian government was almost entirely Russian.

The takeover of east and south Ukraine, financed by Malofeev using money he appears to have owed VTB, is an example of a 'public–private partnership', according to Moscow journalist Oleg Kashin:

> Crimea was taken over by the Kremlin and the oligarch Malofeev. The situation is now looking like a literal quotation from the film *Wag the Dog*. A spin doctor has been put in charge of actual soldiers.[11]

But rather than revealing Moscow as the master puppeteer behind the scenes, the critical mass of Russians among the supposedly indigenous separatist movement instead symbolized the slightly amateurish nature of the whole operation. 'Let's be precise', wrote Kashin:

> the appointment to the job of prime minister of the Donetsk Republic was given not just to any spin doctor, but to a bad spin doctor [Boroday], because a good spin doctor would try to behave in such a way that he didn't stick out so much. Even the Soviets, less experienced in such matters, always had a routine: from the Baltic states in 1940 to Afghanistan in 1979 they

always managed to find a local Babrak Karmal [Soviet-backed prime minister of Afghanistan]. It never occurred to anyone to give an official post to a Soviet emissary.[12]

Eventually the Russian leaders of the Donetsk Republic were prudently replaced by Ukrainians. First Strelkov resigned, disappearing into Russia after behaving too independently off his Kremlin leash. Then Boroday was replaced by the Ukrainian Alexander Zakharchenko, an appointment that was meant to neutralize accusations that the prime minister of the Donetsk Republic was a puppet. Nonetheless, Zakharchenko insisted on coming to cabinet meetings dressed in camouflage and sporting the Cross of St George (4th Class), a Russian military decoration. On 28 August he told Vesti.ru news agency that between 3,000 and 4,000 active-duty Russian soldiers were fighting in Ukraine while they were 'on vacation': 'Among us are fighting serving soldiers, who would rather take their vacation not on a beach but with us, among brothers, who are fighting for their freedom.'

* * *

Ukraine's 'separatists' are a fun-house mirror of contemporary Russia. Bearded Cossacks in parade dress, tattooed skinhead bodybuilders, bearded philosophers, camouflage-wearing, beer-bellied mercenaries, priests in cassocks, Chechens ... All passed through Donesk airport – until it was eventually reduced to rubble.

Alexander Proselkov was Dugin's representative in the Donetsk People's Republic cabinet – before he was mysteriously killed, apparently by his own troops, on 31 July 2014. In 2012 he had infamously staged a mock firing-squad execution of 'traitors' in the town of Rostov: dressed in the uniform of a tsarist officer, he had shot a row of balloons bearing the names of prominent anti-Kremlin politicians, like Navalny and Boris Nemtsov.

Dugin raised money for the revolutionaries, offered strategic advice and campaigned for Putin to send troops in to aid the rebels. Dugin's take on Putin shifted, however, after he was summarily fired from his post as chairman of the sociology of international relations faculty at Moscow State University. The proximate reason was an interview he had given to a Russian news agency, in which he reportedly said, on the subject of Ukraine: 'Kill! Kill! Kill! There can be no other discussion. This is my opinion as a professor.'

In a rambling post on the St Petersburg-based social network site Vkontakte, he blamed 'certain circles' for his dismissal, including 'lunar Putin' – a concept he seems to have concocted in the midst of his social-media rage:

There are two identities to Putin – the patriotic, heroic (solar) and the one inclined toward liberalism and compromises of the West (lunar). Therefore it is impossible to rule out that the decision to dismiss me was taken by one half, obviously the lunar . . . The solar Putin is the saviour of Russia during the Second Chechen Campaign, liberator of Ossetia and Abkhazia, and hero of the Crimea. The lunar . . . Let everyone himself guess where the lunar is . . . But it is still important that this decision was confirmed by Putin himself, even if lunar. Otherwise, it will be deprived of the ideological definition which will emerge from him. In this case, I will accept this decision without reservation. But information has reached me that Putin – and in fact even 'lunar' Putin – did not have anything to do at all with this decision, he did not sanction it.[13]

Dugin's standing did not seem to suffer: the same month he accompanied Malofeev on a trip to Vienna to introduce him to right-wing politicians, such as Marion Maréchal-Le Pen (granddaughter of Jean-Marie Le Pen of France), members of the Austrian Freedom Party, and other figures from Spain, Switzerland, Croatia and Bulgaria. The trip was on the occasion of the 200th anniversary of the Congress of Vienna, which ushered in the Concert of Europe – a Europe of sovereign national states, where balance and stability were guaranteed by the Holy Alliance of 1815: an alliance of Russia with German-speaking Europe in the form of Prussia and Austria-Hungary.

The meeting raised the spectre of an entente between the Kremlin and Europe's far-right political parties, who warmed to Putin's anti-gay and Christian-values rhetoric. Much as the USSR had manipulated European politics with the Comintern and via leverage with the left wing, today Putin's Kremlin has links with the radical right. 'Putin's Fifth Column Summit', blazed the headline in the Swiss newspaper *Tages-Anzeiger*.

Back in Ukraine, with the election of a legitimate president on 25 May 2014 the immediate danger to Ukraine's statehood appeared to have been removed. However, the logic of warlordism and state failure had already taken hold, as it had in North Ossetia, Abkhazia, Transdniester and other border territories that Russia has coveted since the fall of communism. While the population of Donetsk and Lugansk had never before been separatist, under the heavy bombardment of Ukrainian forces bent on retaking the lands from separatist forces, the population shifted allegiance. Many commentators see a long-term Kremlin objective of destabilizing Ukraine and eventually folding it into a new union, even if that does not happen immediately.

The Kremlin's cognitive-dissonance machine went into overdrive. In July, Dugin posted a story on Vkontakte about victorious Ukrainian soldiers crucifying a three-year-old child in the town of Slavyansk. It appears to have been utterly fabricated, but was dutifully picked up on Russia's First Channel prime-time news. 'One's mind refuses to understand how anything like that could happen today in the centre of Europe, while one's heart does not believe that such a thing is possible at all', said the First Channel anchor, commenting on the story with a hint of subversive doubt.

But that was nothing compared to the singularly awful propaganda machine that went to work following the tragic shooting-down of Malaysian Airlines flight MH17 over Donetsk, apparently by Russian separatists using a BUK missile system supplied by Moscow. All 298 civilians died, their bodies falling into fields, orchards and even houses around the town of Torez. While Western commentators initially believed that this would be a 'game-changer', the Kremlin blithely blamed Ukraine. All TV channels, newspapers and websites churned out conspiracy theories accusing Ukraine of downing the jet in a 'false flag' provocation designed to implicate Russia. Strelkov gave a bizarre press conference at which he said the plane apparently took off from Amsterdam full of corpses, apparently intended as a grisly provocation to war.

The truth is, in all likelihood, the most obvious version. Only one side in the conflict was shooting airplanes at the time. A few moments after the jet was shot down, rebels claimed credit for bringing down a Ukrainian AN-17 transport aircraft, and a website affiliated to Strelkov uploaded a video of the smoking crash site, which turned out to be the airliner. As soon as it became clear that what had been shot down was an airliner, the video and the announcement – which had also been put out over the TASS newswire – were removed.

With the help of geolocation work by Dajey Petros, a pro-Ukrainian blogger based in the Netherlands, *Daily Telegraph* correspondent Roland Oliphant interpolated online photos and Google maps to find the likely launch site of the missile that brought down the plane. It was, and continues to be, an area under Russian separatist control. But Russia's media noise machine was so effective that the badly contradictory version it spun – that the missile, according to the dominant version in the Russian press, had been launched from a Ukrainian fighter jet, or from a Ukrainian missile launcher – held together. According to the Levada Center, a public-opinion research group, 82 per cent of Russians surveyed a month after the tragedy believed that Ukraine had been responsible for shooting down the airliner.

Putin's dark thoughts about Western subversion, while initially a fantasy, probably were not far off the mark by the end of 2014. Western sanctions against Russia had led to a one-third drop in the value of the rouble.

The killing of opposition leader Boris Nemtsov, allegedly by Chechen militants who have since retracted their confessions, adds another tangled conspiracy theory to a rapidly proliferating total. The killing happened metres from the Kremlin, in one of the areas of Moscow under greatest surveillance, and it targeted a man who was himself an object of intense interest to the regime. Nonetheless, a poll by the Levada Center found that 58 per cent of Russians did not believe the Kremlin had played any role.[14]

* * *

It is hard to escape the idea that Putin's 'Eurasia' has become, in some sense, a geographical border around a separate truth. A century ago, the original Eurasianists gave birth to a new continent, a fictitious one, which over the decades has become more and more real; at the same time, Russia, a real entity, has become more and more fictional. There is a nagging feeling that this somehow represents two sides of the same coin.

Dugin – inventor, architect and impresario of Eurasia – has been prescient about Russia's approach to the Ukraine conflict since it started. He was the first of the nationalist crowd to use the term 'Novorossiya' in reference to eastern Ukraine in an interview on 3 March 2014, long before the occupation of Donetsk and Lugansk,[15] and one and a half months before Putin used the same term in his live broadcast. He predicted that militias in Donetsk and Lugansk would declare independence several weeks before they did, even correctly predicting the design of the flag of the Donetsk Republic: red with a blue St Andrew's cross. As mentioned in the Introduction, he also predicted that Russia would introduce ground troops on a large scale; it apparently started to do so in late August 2014, with more and more corpses coming back to Russia from the front. Relatives were told that they had been killed in training near the Ukrainian border.

Meanwhile, Dugin's long-held vision of Russia's Eurasian identity, which once seemed so mad and eccentric, finally came to pass via the May 2015 treaty creating Putin's 'Eurasian Union', signed in the Kazakh capital Astana, with Kazakhstan and Belarus as members.

By March 2015, Dugin had taken such a high profile in the Ukraine conflict that the US government imposed financial sanctions on him, along with other separatist leaders. Dugin himself is circumspect about his connection to the events of the last two years, insisting that he simply has a knack for getting it right, and is not some 'whisperer' in the ear of mandarins or a behind-the-scenes influencer.

In October 2015 he described the new expansionist phase of Russian nationalism as a 'diastole' (when the heart pumps blood through the body) with a regular pace and cycle. Rather than inspiring the expansionist phase, Dugin inists he simply waited for it to happen 'like I was waiting for a trolleybus':

> As a geopolitician I take the pulse of Russian history – it is my pulse as well, my heart beats with the same rhythm as the heart of my country, my people. I waited for the diastoles and systoles, the ebb and the flow, contraction and expansion.[16]

Dugin's clairvoyance may have something to do with his ties to hardliners in the Kremlin; but more than that, it appears to symbolize a dimensional shift in Russia, from a right-way-up world to an upside-down one. Having discovered the deterministic laws of an imaginary universe, this world is now slipping in and out of ours.

The creation of Eurasia is similar to the short story 'Tlön, Uqbar, Orbis Tertius' by Argentine surrealist author Jorge Luis Borges. In it he writes about the discovery of the planet Tlön, invented in the seventeenth century by a secret cabal of intellectuals known as the Orbis Tertius. The secret was handed down through generations of acolytes, each generation creating more and more artefacts and records. Their ultimate goal – to infiltrate Tlön into the real world:

> Almost immediately, reality 'caved in' at more than one point. The truth is, it wanted to cave in . . . Any symmetry, any system with an appearance of order – dialectical materialism, anti-Semitism, Nazism – could spellbind and hypnotize mankind. How could the world not fall under the sway of Tlön, how could it not yield to the vast and minutely detailed evidence of an ordered planet?[17]

A century ago, a similar group of scholars, like the Orbis Tertius, sought to infiltrate Eurasia into the real world, using a great heap of linguistic, anthropological and historical and geopolitical symmetries. After 80-odd years of life in books, they finally appear to have had their first successes – from somewhat tendentious scholarship, to popular history, to a political platform, and more recently to become the officially sanctioned national idea of Russia, articulated by its head of state.

Reality has 'caved in'. But it had wanted to 'cave in'.

The Eurasianist revolution represented the conquest of culture rather than politics. But via culture, it was a conquest of reality itself. And the scope of its victory and the reputation of its founders has only been enhanced by its arbitrariness, its flimsiness and its fakery. Eurasianism is a forgery that has superseded the original – not because it is a good forgery, but because it is so audaciously false that it undermines the true.

Eurasianism is testament to the audacity of the 'scribblers', to their ability and the extent to which it has now become possible to construct order entirely out of words and symbols. Eurasia, as Borges put it, is 'a labyrinth forged by men, a labyrinth destined to be deciphered by men'.

NOTES

Preface

1. http://globalthinkers.foreignpolicy.com/

Introduction

1. https://www.washingtonpost.com/news/monkey-cage/wp/2014/03/19/vladimir-putin-ethnic-russian-nationalist/
2. J.M. Keynes, *The General Theory of Employment, Interest, and Money*, https://ebooks.adelaide.edu.au/k/keynes/john_maynard/k44g/chapter24.html
3. Isaiah Berlin, 'The Birth of the Russian Intelligentsia', in Isaiah Berlin, *Russian Thinkers*, Penguin Books, 1979.
4. Sperry, quoted in James Gleick, *The Information: A history, a theory, a flood*, Vintage, 2012.
5. Richard Dawkins, *The Selfish Gene* (30th anniversary edition), Oxford University Press, 2006.
6. Ernest Gellner, *Nations and Nationalism*, Cornell University Press, 1983.
7. Yitzhak Brudny, *Reinventing Russia: Russian nationalism and the Soviet State 1953–1991*, Harvard University Press, 1998, p.192.
8. P.N. Savitskii, I. Vinkovetsky and C. Schlacks, *Exodus to the East: Forebodings and events: An affirmation of the Eurasians*, Charles Schlacks, Jr., 1996.
9. 'Pan-Eurasian Nationalism', in Anatoly Liberman (ed.), *The Legacy of Genghis Khan and Other Essays on Russia's Identity*, Michigan Slavic Publications, 1991 (hereafter LGK).
10. S. Lavrov, *Lev Gumilev: Sudba i idei*, Svarog i K, 2000, p.144.
11. www.youtube.com/watch?v=xqBxiqxHuTw
12. 'V strane idet voyna terminov', *Express Gazeta*, 3 March 2014.
13. 'Gosudarstvo predalo narod', www.youtube.com/watch?v=aL8rChMtUiQ
14. www.ft.com/intl/cms/s/0/a5b15b14-3fcf-11e2-9f71-00144feabdc0.html
15. www.ng.ru/politics/2012-01-23/1_national.html
16. http://en.kremlin.ru/events/president/news/19243
17. http://bd.fom.ru/pdf/d12ind15.pdf Robert C. Otto points out that 2 per cent is within the margin of error for the poll, however.
18. Edmund Griffiths, *Towards a Science of Belief Systems*, Palgrave Macmillan, 2014.

1: The most boring adventure ever

1. N.S. Trubetskoi and R. Jakobson, *N.S. Trubetzkoy's Letters and Notes* (Janua linguarum), Walter De Gruyter Inc., 1975, p.2 (henceforth NSTLN).

2. ibid.
3. Alexey Shakhmatov, *Ocherk Drevneyshego Perioda Istorii Russkogo Yazyka*, Indryk, 2002.
4. ibid., p.24.
5. Roman Jakobson, 'Responses', interview with Tsvetan Todorov, *Poetique* 57 (1984), pp.3–25.
6. Interview on French TV, quoted in F. Dosse, *History of Structuralism*, vol. 1: *The rising sign 1945–1966*, trans. Deborah Glassman, University of Minnesota Press, 1998, p.54.
7. S. Glebov, 'The challenge of the modern: The Eurasianist ideology and movement, 1920–29', PhD thesis, Rutgers University, 2004, p.8.
8. LGK.
9. Alexander Herzen, *My Past and Thoughts*, University of California Press, 1983, p.255.
10. Evgeny Trubetskoy, 'Vospominaniya', cited in M. Bokhachevsky-Chomiak, *Sergei N. Trubetskoi: An intellectual among the intelligentsia in prerevolutionary Russia*, Nordland, 1976, p.25.
11. Evgeny Trubetskoy, quoted in Henryk Baran (ed.), *Jakobsonian Poetics and Slavic Narrative*, Duke University Press, 1992, p.259.
12. Berlin, *Russian Thinkers*, p.126.
13. N. Trubetskoi, *Principles of Phonology*, University of California Press, 1969, p.309.
14. Translated by Lydia Pasternak Slater, 1957, posted on www.friends-partners.org/friends/culture/literature/20century/pasternak10.html
15. An icon.
16. Boris Pasternak, quoted in LGK, p.302.
17. LGK, p.298.
18. Nicholas Riasanovsky, 'The emergence of Eurasianism', *California Slavic Studies* 4 (1967), pp.39–72, fn. 38.
19. Olga Mairova, lecture on Russian Orientalism, University of Michigan, 2006.
20. In 1909–10, meanwhile, he was close to the Put movement, a liberal Christian movement that his uncle Evgeny had helped to found, which believed in the need to reform Russia's society along the principles of eastern Christianity, avoiding both capitalist and socialist models.
21. LGK, p.304.
22. Krystyna Pomorska, 'Autobiography of a scholar', in Krystyna Pomorska, Elzbieta Chodakowska, Hugh Mclean and Brent Vine (eds), *Language, Poetry, and Poetics: The generation of the 1890s: Jakobson, Trubetskoy, Mayakovskij. Proceedings of the first Roman Jakobson colloquium, at the Massachusetts Institute of Technology, October 5–6, 1984*, Walter De Gruyter, 1987, p.11.
23. Stephen Rudy, 'Jakobson – Aljagrov and Futurism', in Pomorska et al., *Language, Poetry, and Poetics*, p.277.
24. Roman Jakobson, quoted in Pomorska et al., *Language, Poetry, and Poetics*, p.8.
25. Richard Bradford, *Roman Jakobson: Life, language and art*, Routledge, 1994, p.6.
26. Email communication from Dr Omry Ronen.
27. Roman Jakobson, *Six Lectures on Sound and Meaning*, Harvester Press, 1978, p.19.
28. Jakobson, quoted in Jindrich Toman, *Letters and Other Materials from the Moscow and Prague Linguistic Circles 1912–1945*, Michigan Slavic Publications, 1994.
29. Interview with Patrick Sériot.

2: The short summer

1. NSTLN, p.310.
2. Roman Jakobson, *My Futurist Years*, Marsilio Publishers, 1992, p.77.
3. ibid., p.81.
4. Vladimir Nabokov, *Speak, Memory*, Vintage, 1989, p.282.
5. Toman, *Letters and Other Materials*, p.16.
6. ibid., p.17.
7. ibid.

3: Family trees

1. NSTLN, p.5.
2. LGK, p.295.
3. Email communication from Dr Omry Ronen.
4. André Martinet, *Économie des changements phonétiques*, Francke, 1955.
5. It must be said that, according to these theories, Dutch should have a [g], but it doesn't. Thanks to Liberman for pointing this out.
6. On Jakobson and Trubetskoy's debt to other Russian thinkers with teleological bent, see Toman, *Letters and Other Materials*.
7. NSTLN, letter 30.
8. N. Trubetskoi, 'The phonetic evolution of Russian and the disintegration of the common Russian linguistic unity', in Anatoly Liberman (ed.), *N.S. Trubetskoy: Studies in General Linguistics and Language Structure*, Duke University Press, 2001, p.120.
9. Hannah Arendt, *The Origins of Totalitarianism*, Harcourt, 1979, p.270.
10. Hannah Arendt makes this argument in ibid.
11. Glebov, 'Challenge of the modern', p.307.
12. Savitsky et al., *Exodus to the East*, p.122.
13. http://max.mmlc.northwestern.edu/mdenner/Demo/texts/scythians_blok.html
14. Trubetskoy to Suvchinsky, 15 March 1925, in N.S. Trubetskoy, *Pisma k P.P. Suvchinskomu 1921–1928*, Russkiy Put, 2008.
15. Trubetskoy to Suvchinsky, 28 March 1925, in ibid.

4: Coals to Newcastle

1. A. Liberman, 'N.S. Trubetskoy and his works on history and politics', in LGK, pp. 293–375. A samovar is a great metal pot with a spigot for pouring hot water. It is common in Russian households, where it is used for serving tea to guests. Tula, meanwhile, is a provincial Russian town famous for manufacturing samovars.
2. NSTLN, letter 16.
3. See Jindrich Toman, *The Magic of a Common Language*, MIT Press, 2003.
4. This section draws heavily on ibid. and Patrick Sériot, *Structure et totalité: Les origines intellectuelles du structuralisme en Europe centrale et orientale*, PUF, 1999.
5. Sériot, *Structure et totalité*, p.104.
6. LGK, p.93.
7. Roman Jakobson, 'K kharakteristike evraziyskogo yazykovogo soyuza', in *Selected Writings*, vol. I, Mouton, 1962.
8. Thanks to Liberman for pointing this out.
9. Savitsky et al., *Exodus to the East*, p.36.
10. LGK, p.93.
11. Jakobson, 'K kharakteristike', p.144.
12. Trubetskoi, *Principles of Phonology*; Claude Lévi-Strauss, *Structural Anthropology*, Basic Books, 1974, p.32.
13. Sériot, *Structure et totalité*, p.60.
14. Trubetskoy, *Pisma*, p. 120.
15. Glebov, 'Challenge of the modern', p.311–14.
16. Trubetskoy, *Pisma*, p.33–6.
17. Glebov, 'Challenge of the modern', p.314.
18. ibid.
19. A.F. Kiselev (ed.), *Politicheskaya Istoriya Russkoy Emigratsii, 1920–1940: Dokumenty i materialy*, vol. VII, Russkoe Nebo, 1999, p.248.
20. L. Nikulin, *Mertvaya Zib*, 1965.
21. S. Glebov, *Evraziystvo Mezhdu Imperiey i Modernom: Istoriya v dokumentakh*, Novoe izdatelstvo, 2010.
22. Nikulin, *Mertvaya Zib*.
23. N. Dolgopolov, *Genii Vneshney Razvedki*, Molodaya Gvardiya, 2004.
24. Kiselev, *Politicheskaya Istoriya Russkoy Emigratsii*, p.251.

25. S.S. Khoruzhy, 'Karsavin, evraziystvo i VKP', *Voprosy Filosofii* 2 (1992), pp.84–7.
26. To be published shortly by K. Ermishina. I thank her for showing me this.
27. Interview with Ivan Savicky.
28. Glebov, *Evraziystvo.*
29. V. Kozovoy, 'O Petre Suvchinskom i ego vremeni', in V. Kozovoy, *Taynaya Os*, NLO, 2003, p.39.
30. D. Brandenberger, *National Bolshevism: Stalinist mass culture and the formation of modern Russian national identity, 1931–1956*, Harvard University Press, 2002.
31. Glebov, 'Challenge of the modern', p.344.
32. A.B. Sobolev, 'Svoya svoikh ne poznasha: Evraziystvo, L.P. Karsavin i drugie', *Nachala* 4 (1992), p.56.
33. ibid., p.57.
34. During the Second World War, Jakobson met Lévi-Strauss while both were teaching at the Ecole Libre des Hautes Etudes de New York, which Lévi-Strauss has said was the key to his later development of the theory.
35. Lévi-Strauss, *Structural Anthropology*, p.33.
36. http://sm-sergeev.livejournal.com/120006.html
37. Roman Jakobson and Krystyna Pomorska, *Dialogues*, Cambridge University Press, 1983, p.34.
38. Catherine Andreyev and Ivan Savicky, *Russia Abroad*, Yale University Press, 2004, p.197.
39. Recollection of Ivan Savicky, elder son.
40. P.N. Savitsky, *Neozhidannye Stikhi*, Ruská Tradice, 2005, p.106.

5: Requiem

1. A.A. Akhmatova, *The Complete Poems of Anna Akhatova*, trans. Judith Hemschemeyer, Zephyr Press, 1997, p.388.
2. Emma Gerstein, *Moscow Memoirs*, trans. John Crowfoot, Harvill Press, 2004, p.56.
3. Amanda Haight, *Anna Akhmatova: A poetic pilgrimage*, Oxford University Press, 1976, p.28.
4. During the Bolshevik revolution, peasants drove Nikolay's family off their estate and they were forced to rent a three-room flat in the nearby town of Bezhetsk, which Lev hated.
5. Lavrov, quoted in Elaine Feinstein, *Anna of All the Russias: A life of Anna Akhamtova*, Weidenfeld and Nicolson, 2005, p.94.
6. Akhmatova poem 'I Drink to Loneliness', quoted in Vitaly Shentalinsky, *Prestuplenie bez Nakazaniya*, Progress Pleyada, 2007, p.306.
7. Nadezhda Mandelstam, *Hope Against Hope: A memoir*, Atheneum, 1983, p.135.
8. Haight, *Anna Akhmatova.*
9. Gerstein, *Moscow Memoirs*, p.169.
10. *Vspominaya L.N. Gumileva*, Memorialny Muzey Kvartira L.N. Gumileva, St Petersburg, 2003, p.104.
11. Gerstein, *Moscow Memoirs*, p.173.

6: The 'Big House'

1. Shentalinsky, *Prestuplenie*, p.294.
2. ibid., p.295.
3. ibid., p.302.
4. ibid.
5. Mandelstam, *Hope Against Hope*, p.72.
6. Trans. A.S. Kline.
7. Gerstein, *Moscow Memoirs*, p.64.
8. ibid., p.341.
9. Shentalinsky, *Prestuplenie*, p.297.

10. Mandelstam, *Hope Against Hope*, p.33.
11. Gerstein, *Moscow Memoirs*, p.342.
12. Shentalinsky, *Prestuplenie*, p.298.
13. ibid., p.317.
14. Alexander Titov, 'Lev Gumilev, ethnogenesis, and Eurasianism', PhD thesis, University of London, 2005, p.25.
15. Lavrov, *Lev Gumilev*, p.63.
16. Shentalinsky, *Prestuplenie*, p.309.
17. ibid., p.310.
18. *Vspominaya L.N. Gumileva*, p.320.
19. Gerstein, *Moscow Memoirs*, p.341.
20. ibid., p.209.
21. ibid., p.230.
22. *Vspominaya L.N. Gumileva*, p.92.
23. Shentalinsky, *Prestupleniye*, p.329.
24. T.A. Shumovsky, 'Besedi s pamyatyu', in *Vspominaya L.N. Gumileva*, p.93.
25. ibid.
26. ibid., p.95.
27. Lavrov, *Lev Gumilev*, p.67.
28. Arsenalnaya Naberezhnaya No. 7.
29. *Vspominaya L.N. Gumileva*, p.96.
30. ibid., p.99.

7: Gulag

1. *Vspominaya L.N. Gumileva*, p.102.
2. ibid., p.105.
3. ibid., p.106.
4. Lev Gumilev, 'Povodov dlya aresta ne daval', *Avrora* 11 (1991), p.19.
5. Savchenko in *Vspominaya L.N. Gumileva*, p.167.
6. Anne Applebaum, *Gulag: A history of the Soviet labour camps*, Penguin Books, 2003, p.318.
7. Lev Gumilev, 'Zakony vremeni', *Literaturnoe Obozrenie* 3 (1990), pp.5-6.
8. ibid.
9. ibid.
10. Gumilev, 'Povodov', p.19.
11. A description appears in ibid.
12. Life in Norlisk and other camps is described in Applebaum, *Gulag*, pp.212-14.
13. Lev Gumilev, 'Dovoennyy Norilsk', *Literaturnoe Obozrenie* 3 (1990).
14. *Vspominaya L.N. Gumileva*, p.116.
15. Lavrov, *Lev Gumilev*, p.73.
16. Gerstein, *Moscow Memoirs*, p.165.
17. Shentalinsky, *Prestuplenie*, p.372.
18. Gerstein, *Moscow Memoirs*, p.233.
19. M.L. Kozyreva, 'Lev i ptitsa', in *Vspominaya L.N. Gumileva*, p.154.
20. Isaiah Berlin, *The Soviet Mind*, ed. Henry Hardy, Brookings Institution Press, 2004, p.56.
21. Gerstein, *Moscow Memoirs*, p.98.
22. The *Kandidatskaya* – a first postgraduate degree.
23. Kozyreva, 'Lev i ptitsa', p.153.
24. Mandelstam, *Hope Against Hope*, p.34.
25. Kozyreva, 'Lev i ptitsa', p.154.
26. Lavrov, *Lev Gumilev*, fn. 20.
27. Gumilev, 'Povodov', p.27.
28. V.N. Voronovich and M.G. Kozyreva, *Zhivya v Chuzhikh Slovakh: Vospominaniya o L.N. Gumileve*, Rostok, 2006, p.143.
29. Kozyreva, 'Lev i ptitsa', p.161.

30. Lev Vosnesensky, 'Mozhno ya budu otvechat stikhami?' in *Vspominaya L.N. Gumileva*, p.42.
31. ibid., pp.42–3.
32. *Vspominaya L.N. Gumileva*, p.182.
33. ibid., pp.171–2.
34. ibid., p.173.
35. G. Von Zigern Korn, *Rasskazy o Svetlom Proshlom*, Peterburgskiy Pisatel, 2005, p.168.
36. Gumilev, 'Povod', quoted in Lavrov, *Lev Gumilev*, p.98.
37. He seems to have called them the Huns and not Xiongnu.
38. Gumilev, 'Povod', quoted in Lavrov, *Lev Gumilev*, p.98.
39. L.N. Gumilev, *Khunnu: Sredinnaya Aziya v drevnie vremena*, Izdatelstvo Vostochnoi Literatury, 1960, p.10.
40. Lavrov, *Lev Gumilev*.
41. Quoted in ibid., p.97.
42. Gerstein, *Moscow Memoirs*, p.455.
43. ibid., p.457.
44. ibid., p.328.
45. ibid., p.334.
46. ibid., pp.326–7.
47. Lavrov, *Lev Gumilev*, p.93.
48. ibid., p.95.
49. Gerstein, *Moscow Memoirs*, p.456.
50. ibid., p.326.
51. N.V. Gumileva, in *Vspominaya L.N. Gumileva*, p.15.
52. Gumilev told Savitsky this news in a letter of 7 July 1957, listing the titles as 'Istoriya Khunnu s drevneyshikh vremen do V veka n.e.' and 'Istoriya pervogo tyurkskogo kaganata VI–VII vv.'. However I have been unable to find these articles.
53. Lavrov, *Lev Gumilev*, p.152.
54. 'Hunnu: Sredinnaia Aziia v drevnie vremena [Hiung-nu: The innermost Asia in ancient times]. By L.N. Gumilev (Moscow: Academy of Sciences, USSR, Institute of Oriental Studies. 1960. Pp. 292. 11.50 rubles.)', *American Historical Review* 66:3 (1961), pp.711–12.
55. Lavrov, *Lev Gumilev*, pp.160–1.
56. ibid.
57. ibid., pp.180–1.
58. ibid.
59. ibid.
60. *Vspominaya L.N. Gumileva*, p.212.
61. Interview with Anatoly Anokhin.
62. Interview with Sergey Semanov, 2010.
63. Sergey Belyakov, *Gumilev Syn Gumileva*, Astrel, 2012.
64. ibid., p.346.
65. Vadim Kozhinov, '"Mongolskaya Epokha" v istorii Rusi i istinny smysl i znachenie kulikovskoy bitvy', *Nash Sovremennik* 3 (1997), p.176.
66. Dated 23 July.
67. Lev Gumilev, *Searches for the Imaginary Kingdom*, Cambridge University Press, 2009, pp.14–15.
68. Quoted in Lavrov, *Lev Gumilev*, p.225.
69. *Vspominaya L.N. Gumileva*, p.18.
70. Their correspondence is available at: http://gumilevica.kulichki.ru/articles/Article32.htm
71. Lev Gumilev, 'Etnogenez i etnosfera', *Priroda* 1–2 (1970), pp.46–55; 43–50.
72. Y.V. Bromley, 'K kharakteristike ponyatiya "Etnos"', in *Rasy i Narody*, Nauka, 1971, pp.9–33.
73. Interview with Anokhin.

74. Y.V. Bromley, *Ocherki Teorii Etnosa*, LKI, 2008, p.17.
75. ibid.
76. Lev Gumilev, 'O lyudyakh na nas ne pokhozhikh', *Sovetskaya Kultura*, 15 September 1988, available at: http://gumilevica.kulichki.net/articles/Article77.htm
77. Y.V. Bromley, 'K voprosu o sushchnosti etnosa', *Priroda* 2 (1970), pp. 51–5, available at: http://scepsis.ru/library/id_836.html#_ftnref16
78. Brudny, *Reinventing Russia*, p.89.
79. N.A. Mitrokhin, *Russkaya Partiya: Dvizhenie Russkikh Natsionalistov v SSSR 1953–1985*, Izdatelstvo NLO, 2003.
80. Brudny, *Reinventing Russia*, p.93.
81. A. Cohen, *Russian Imperialism: Development and crisis*, Praeger, 1996, p.104.
82. Alexander Yakovlev, 'Protiv antiistorizma', *Literaturnaya Gazeta*, 15 November 1972, available at: http://users.livejournal.com/amk_/2391.html
83. See: www.pseudology.org/information/Ganichev_int.htm
84. Interview with Sergey Semanov, 2010.
85. Lev Voznesensky, in *Vspominaya L.N. Gumileva*.
86. *Vspominaya L.N. Gumileva*, p.48.
87. Interview with Anatoly Lukyanov, 2009.
88. ibid.
89. ibid.
90. Alexey Bondarev, *Istoriya i Osnovnye Napravleniya Razvitiya Otechestvennykh Teoreticheskikh Issledovanii Kulturgeneza*, Avtoreferat, 2009, p.19.
91. Lev Gumilev, *Ethnogenesis and the [Human] Biosphere*, online version of chapter 6 available at: http://gumilevica.kulichki.net/English/ebe6a.htm
92. The text of the interview with Kozhinov is available at: http://kozhinov.voskres.ru/articles/pereplet.htm
93. Voznesenski, in *Vspominaya L.N. Gumileva*, p.54.
94. Lavrov, *Lev Gumilev*, pp.302–303.
95. *Voprosy Istorii* 12 (1974), p.72.
96. Interview with Marina Kozyreva.
97. Lavrov, in *Vspominaya L.N. Gumileva*, pp.209–15.
98. Bromley, *Ocherki*, pp.20–1.
99. Interview with Sergey Cheshko.
100. Brudny, *Reinventing Russia*, pp.181–91.
101. ibid., p.182.
102. Quoted in Lavrov, *Lev Gumilev*, pp.297–300.
103. ibid.
104. Belyakov, *Gumilev Syn Gumileva*, pp.586–610.
105. Brudny, *Reinventing Russia*, p.189.
106. ibid., p.187.
107. Text of letter available at: http://rutenica.narod.ru/lng.html
108. Interview with Anatoly Lukyanov, 2009.
109. Interview with Anatoly Chistobaev, 2009.
110. *Moskovskaya Pravda*, 24 May 1990.
111. V.A. Tishkov and D.D. Tumarkin (eds), *Vydayushchiesya Otechestvennye Etnologi i Antropologi XX veka*, Nauka, 2004, p.624.
112. Rogers Brubaker, 'Nationhood and the national question in the Soviet Union and post-Soviet Eurasia: An institutionalist account', *Theory and Society* 23:1 (1994), pp.47–78.
113. Interview with Anatoly Lukyanov, 2009.
114. Interview with Sergey Cheshko.
115. Gerstein, *Moscow Memoirs*, p.xvii.
116. Lavrov, *Lev Gumilev*, p.311.
117. *Chas Pik* 3 (1991).
118. Titov, 'Lev Gumilev', p.216.

8: A Soviet Virgil

1. A. Rovner, *Vsompinaya Sebya: Kniga o druzyakh i sputnikakh zhizni*, Izdatelstvo Zolotoe Sechenie, 2010, p.84.
2. Yury Mamleev, at: http://zavtra.ru/content/view/2008-04-0271/
3. Rovner, *Vsompinaya Sebya*, p.86.
4. ibid., pp.109, 115.
5. Natalya Tamruchi, 'Bezumie kak oblast svobody', *NLO* 100 (2009), available at: http://magazines.russ.ru/nlo/2009/100/ta33-pr.html
6. Rovner, *Vsompinaya Sebya*, p.106.
7. Sovdep was a White Russian epithet for the Bolshevik leadership, dating from the 1920s.
8. Konstantin Serebrov, *The Mystical Underground of Moscow*, ed. Robin Winckel-Mellish, Serebrov Boeken, 2006, p.162.
9. ibid., p.103.
10. Mark Sedgwick, *Against the Modern World: Traditionalism and the secret intellectual history of the twentieth century*, Oxford University Press, 2009, p.226.
11. Franco Ferraresi, 'The radical right in postwar Italy', *Politics and Society* 16 (1988), p.84.
12. Alexander Dugin, *Pop Kultura i Znaki Vremeni*, Amfora, 2005, pp.82–3.
13. Vladimir Pribylovsky, 'Natsional-patrioticheskoe dvizhenie: istoriya i litsa', in A. Verkhovsky et al., *Nationalizm i Ksenofobiya v Rossiyskom Obshchestve*, Panorama, 1998, p.45.
14. A nineteenth-century forgery, which purported to describe a worldwide Jewish conspiracy.
15. Alexander Yakovlev, 'Rossiyskikh fashistov porodil KGB', *Izvestiya*, 17 June 1998, p.5.
16. Georgy Urushadze, *Vybrannye Mesta iz Perepiski s Vragami*, Izdatelstvo Evropeyskogo Doma, 1995, p.290.
17. Alexander Yakovlev, *Sumerki*, Materik, 2005.
18. Vladimir Kryuchkov, *Lichnoe Delo*, Moscow Eksmo Algorithm Kniga, 2003.
19. Yakovlev, *Sumerki*.
20. John Dunlop, *The Rise of Russia and the Fall of the Soviet Empire*, Princeton University Press, 1993.
21. Edith Clowes, *Russia on the Edge: Imagined geographies and post-Soviet identity*, Cornell University Press, 2011.
22. Alexander Dugin, *Osnovy Evraziystva*, Arktogeya Tsentr, 2002, p.85.

9: Paris 1990

1. Thomas Sheehan, 'Myth and violence: The fascism of Julius Evola and Alain de Benoist', *Social Research* 48:1 (1981), p.62.
2. Alain de Benoist, *Europe: Tiers monde, même combat*, R. Laffont, 1986, quoted in Pierre-André Taguieff, 'From race to culture: The New Right's view of European identity', *Telos* 98–99 (Winter 1993–Spring 1994).
3. Henry Rousso, *The Vichy Syndrome*, Harvard University Press, 1994, p.196.
4. Roger Griffin, 'Between metapolitics and apoliteia: The Nouvelle Droite's strategy for conserving the fascist vision in the "Interregnum"', *Modern and Contemporary France* 8:1 (2000).
5. Alain de Benoist, 'The idea of empire', available at: www.gornahoor.net/library/IdeaOfEmpire.pdf
6. Alexander Dugin, *Osnovy geopolitiki: Geopoliticheskoe budushchee Rossii*, Arktogeya, 1997.
7. De Benoist, email communication with the author.
8. Alain de Benoist, 'What is racism?', *Telos* 114 (1999), pp.46–7.
9. Quoted in Tamir Bar-On, 'A response to Alain de Benoist', *Journal for the Study of Radicalism* 8:2 (2014), pp.123–68.
10. See Andreas Umland, 'Alexander Dugin and post-Soviet uncivil society', PhD thesis, Cambridge University, 2009, pp.72–5.

11. Robert Steuckers blog, available at: http://robertsteuckers.blogspot.com/2014/02/answers-to-questions-of-pavel-tulaev.html

12. This according to Dugin's website arctogaia.com

13. Marlene Laruelle makes a very persuasive case that Dugin's Eurasianism owes more to the New Right than to the original Eurasianists. See Marlene Laruelle, 'Aleksandr Dugin: A Russian version of the European radical right?', Occasional Paper No. 294, Woodrow Wilson International Center for Scholars.

14. Holger Herwig, 'Geopolitik: Haushofer, Hitler and Lebensraum', in Colin S. Gray and Geoffrey Sloan, *Geopolitics, Geography and Strategy*, Frank Cass, 1999, p.218.

15. Dugin says these trips occurred in 1989; de Benoist says 1990.

16. Vladimir Pozner interview with Prokhanov, 3 March 2013, available at: www.1tv.ru/sprojects_edition/si5756/fi21881

17. Dunlop, *Rise of Russia*, p.170.

18. Brudny, *Reinventing Russia*, chapter 8.

19. *Literaturnaya Rossiya*, 30 March 1990.

20. Charles A. Ruud and Sergei Stepanov, *Fontanka 16: The tsar's secret police*, Sutton Publishing, 1999, p.125–51.

21. Alexander Dugin, *Konspirologiya: Teoriya zagovora, sekretnye obshchestva, velikaya voyna kontinentov*, ROF Evraziya, 2005, p.19.

22. It is a point which could scarcely have been better made by Hannah Arendt, who writes in her scathing indictment of European facism, *The Origins of Totalitarianism*, that 'if a patent forgery like the Protocols of the Elders of Zion is believed by so many people that it can become the text of a whole political movement, the task of the historian is no longer to discover a forgery'.

23. Dugin, *Konspirologiya*, p.19.

24. ibid., p.6.

25. Kathryn S. Olmsted, *Real Enemies: Conspiracy theories and American democracy, World War I to 9/11*, Oxford University Press, 2011, p.8.

26. Alexander Dugin, 'Posledniy prygun imperii', internet essay available at: www.arctogaia.com/public/txt-prohan.htm

27. Charles Clover, 'Last days of the USSR', *Financial Times*, 19 August 2011.

28. John Dunlop, email communication with the author.

29. John Dunlop, 'The August 1991 coup and its impact on Soviet politics', *Journal of Cold War Studies* 5:1 (2003), p.94.

30. Clover, 'Last days of the USSR'.

31. Dunlop, 'The August 1991 coup'.

32. 'Byvshy shef KGB Kryuchkov ubezhden v pravote del GKChP', newsru.com, 16 August 2001, available at: http://newsru.com/arch/russia/16aug2001/putch.html

33. 'KGB borolsya s videomagnitofonami i prosmotrel raspad SSSR', *Izvestiya*, 13 December 2006, available at: http://izvestia.ru/news/319885

34. 'Marshal Sovetskogo Soyuza Dmitriy Yazov: Vozmozhno, GKChP byl klubom samoubiyts', *Komsomolskaya Pravda*, 16 August 2001, available at: www.kp.ru/daily/22613/11455/

35. Interview with Dugin, 2005.

36. Dugin, 'Posledniy prygun'.

37. As he put it to me in a 2010 interview.

38. The Sobchak commission later determined that the orders for the suppression of the demonstration had originated with Defence Minister Yazov, who himself was likely carrying out orders from government-level officials.

39. Here I am not referring to de Benoist, but to others of the aforementioned thinkers. De Benoist objects to being identified as being of the extreme right.

40. 'Perspectives géopolitiques eurasiennes', *Vouloir* 87/88 (1992), p.14.

41. Quoted in Laruelle, 'Aleksandr Dugin'.

42. Alexander Dugin, 'KPRF i Evraziystvo', in Dugin, *Osnovy Evraziystva*, p.579.

43. Marlene Laruelle, *Russian Eurasianism: An ideology of empire*, Woodrow Wilson Centre Press, 2008, p.11.

10: Satan's ball

1. Shapova retaliated two decades later with an autobiographical *It's Me, Elena*: 'I'm writing this story about how much I hate you', she writes on the second page, without naming Limonov. 'Here is a story for your kids, if you ever have any. If you don't, so much the better.'
2. Edward Limonov, *It's Me, Eddie: A fictional memoir*, Pan Books, 1983.
3. Eduard Limonov, *Anatomiya Geroya*, Rusich, 1997.
4. Bruce Clark, *The Empire's New Clothes: The end of Russia's liberal dream*, Vintage, 1995.
5. ibid.
6. Ivan Ivanov (pseudonym), Anafema-2 website at: www.duel.ru/publish/ivanov_i/anafema2.html
7. Nikolay Anisin, 'Rasstrel napokaz', *Zavtra* 40:514 (1 October 2003), available at: http://panteon-istorii.narod.ru/sob/93a.htm
8. Alexander Dugin, 'Dykhanie dukha pod pulyami v Ostankino', Arctogaia website, available at: http://arctogaia.com/public/v4/v4-1.shtml
9. Anisin, 'Rasstrel'.
10. Interview with Leonid Proshkin, 2011.
11. ibid.
12. Alexander Korzhakov, *Boris Yeltsin: Ot rassveta do zakata*, Interbook, 1997.
13. 'Tayny rasstrela "Belogo Doma"', *Komsomolskaya Pravda*, 3 October 2008, available at: http://m.kp.ru/daily/24174/385092/
14. Interview with Gennady Zaytsev, 2010. Also see Zaytsev's autobiography – G.N. Zaytsev, *Alfa: Moya Sudba*, Slavia, 2006.
15. 'Tayny rasstrela "Belogo Doma"'.
16. Eduard Limonov, *Moya Politicheskaya Biografiya*, St Petersburg, 2002.
17. However, I have never seen anyone in the NBP do this salute, despite hanging around with them a fair bit.
18. https://wikileaks.org/plusd/cables/08MOSCOW916_a.html
19. Umland, 'Post-Soviet uncivil society', p.74.
20. www.apn.ru/publications/print1286.htm
21. Interview with Eduard Limonov, 2010.
22. Limonov, *Moya Politicheskaya Biografiya*.
23. ibid.

11: Heartland

1. John B. Dunlop, 'Aleksandr Dugin's "Neo-Eurasian" textbook and Dmitrii Trenin's ambivalent response', *Harvard Ukrainian Studies* XXV:1/2 (2001).
2. Brudny, *Reinventing Russia*, p.259.
3. Dugin, *Osnovy geopolitiki*.
4. Anton Shekhovtsov, 'The palingenetic thrust of Russian neo-Eurasianism: Ideas of rebirth in Aleksandr Dugin's worldview', *Totalitarian Movements and Political Religions* 9/4 (2008), pp. 491–506, available at: www.mod-langs.ox.ac.uk/russian/nationalism/shekhovtsov1.html
5. Dugin, *Osnovy geopolitiki*, p.6.
6. Dunlop, 'Aleksandr Dugin's "Neo-Eurasian" textbook'.
7. Dugin, *Osnovy geopolitiki*.
8. ibid.
9. ibid.
10. ibid.
11. ibid.
12. And still is, as far as I can tell.
13. Irek Murtazin, '"Orekhovskie" soberutsya snova', *Novaya Gazeta*, 19 August 2013, available at: www.novayagazeta.ru/inquests/59562.html. The testimony was later disqualified by a lie detector test. An investigation was relaunched in 2013.

14. 'Povest o veshchem Olegoviche', *Moskovskaya Komsomolka*, 26 March 2001, available at: www.newlookmedia.ru/?p=7529
15. Interview with Gleb Pavlovsky, 2009.
16. ibid.

12: The chess piece

1. Statement by the Ryazan Regional Federal Security Service (FSB) of 24 September quoted in Alexander Litvinenko and Yuri Felshtinsky, *Blowing Up Russia*, Encounter Books, 2007, p.72. The book claims (pp.74–5) that the FSB operatives involved in the operation were detained first and only after they produced the FSB IDs, and after those IDs were confirmed they were released. The FSB statements however do not say this: 'The [Ryazan] department of the FSB had identified the places of residence in Ryazan of those involved in planting the explosive device and was preparing to detain them.' Felshtinsky, in email communication with the author, asserts that the FSB would not have said that it detained the operatives, as then it would have had to release their names.
2. In 2002, the newspaper *Sovershenno Sekretno* carried an article based on anonymous interviews with what it said were the FSB operatives who carried out what they described as a training exercise. 'A gorod ne znal, chto ucheniya idut', *Sovershenno Sekretno* 6 (2002).
3. Olga Kryshtanovskaya and Stephen White, 'Putin's militocracy', *Post-Soviet Affairs* 19:4 (2003), pp.289–306.
4. ibid.
5. Charles Clover, 'Will the Russian bear roar again?', *Financial Times*, 2 December 2000.
6. Dunlop, 'Aleksandr Dugin's "Neo-Eurasian" textbook'.
7. Interview with Petr Suslov, 2011.
8. Thanks to Robert C. Otto for pointing this out.
9. Limarev confirmed this to me in a phone conversation in 2012.
10. Litvinenko and Felshtinsky, *Blowing Up Russia*, p.41.
11. 'Zagadki Maksa Lazovskogo', *Moskovskaya Pravda*, 14 March 2001.
12. Interview with Valery Korovin, 2005.
13. Alexander Maksimov, quoted in Dunlop, 'Aleksandr Dugin's "Neo-Eurasian" textbook'.
14. I am indebted to Eduard Ten Houten, Nukayev's biographer, for pointing this out. It should be noted that Umar Dzhabrailov, owner of the Radisson Slavyanskaya hotel in Moscow, also claims to have been the prototype for Gunaev.
15. Pavel Khlebnikov, *Razgovor s Varvarom*, Detektiv Press, 2003, p.76.
16. Anna Politkovskaya, *A Dirty War: A Russian reporter in Chechnya*, Harvill Press, 1999, p.148.
17. 'Konstitutsionalist po klichke Khozha', *Russkaya Mysl*, 15 April 1999.
18. Interview with Petr Suslov, 2010.
19. Interview with Petr Suslov, October 2009.

13: Political technology

1. Charles Clover, 'Russians "adopting illiberal ideas"', *Financial Times*, 16 May 2001.
2. Interview with Sergey Kurginyan, 2011.
3. http://evrazia.org/article/164
4. http://evrazia.org/article/1876
5. Elena Tregubova, *Bayki Kremlevskogo Diggera*, Ad Marginem, 2003.
6. Ilya Zhegulev and Lyudmila Romanova, *Operatsiya Edinaya Rossiya: Neizvestnaya istoriya partii vlasti*, Eksmo, 2011.
7. ibid.
8. Alexander Dugin, 'Good bye, golden boy (ob ukhode Surkova)', Livejournal post, available at: http://dugin.livejournal.com/4237.html
9. Interview with Pavel Zarifullin, 2005.

10. www.washingtonpost.com/opinions/who-is-the-bully-the-united-states-has-treated-russia-like-a-loser-since-the-cold-war/2014/03/14/b0868882-aa06-11e3-8599-ce7295b6851c_story.html

11. 'Zamestitel glavy administratsii prezidenta RF Vladislav Surkov: Putin ukreplyaet gosudarstvo, a ne sebya', *Komsomolskaya Pravda*, 28 September 2004.

12. This was published originally by journalist Dmitry Popov on the website Nork.ru; however, the link has since died. Other versions of the speech are on the Evrazia website at: www.evrazia.org/modules.php?name–ews&file=article&sid=2255

13. Interview with Valery Korovin, 2009.

14. According to the Nashi website.

15. Valery Korovin, *Nakanune Imperii*, Izdatelstvo Evraziyskoe Dvizhenie, 2008.

16. ibid.

17. Andrei Soldatov and Irina Borogan, *Russia's New Nobility*, Public Affairs, 2011.

18. Peter Pomerantsev, 'Putin's Rasputin', *London Review of Books*, 20 October 2011, available at: www.lrb.co.uk/v33/n20/peter-pomerantsev/putins-rasputin

19. Alexander Dugin, *The Fourth Political Theory*, Arktos, 2012.

20. I do not pretend to understand what Heidegger was saying, or whether Dugin got it right.

21. Dugin, *Fourth Political Theory*.

22. Konstantin Voronkov, *Alexey Navalny: Groza zhulikov i vorov*, Eksmo, 2012, p.65.

23. www.gazeta.ru/social/2011/05/16/3619317.shtml

24. ibid.

25. http://zona.media/online/born-dopros-hasis/

26. Thanks to Robert C. Otto for pointing out this article.

27. Edward L. Keenan, 'Muscovite political folkways', *Russian Review* 45:2 (1986), pp.115–81.

28. See, for example, Donald N. Jensen, 'Are the Kremlin hardliners winning?', 1 October 2014, available at: http://imrussia.org/en/analysis/world/2041-are-the-kremlin-hardliners-winning. See also a 2014 report by Minchenko Consulting, 'Vladimir Putin's Big Government and the "Politburo 2.0"', available at: http://minchenko.ru/netcat_files/File/Big%20Government%20and%20the%20Politburo%202_0.pdf

29. 'Putin eto Dugin': 2007 interview on Russia.ru, published on Evrazia.org website at: www.evrazia.tv/content/putin-eto-dugin-2007; also available at: https://www.youtube.com/watch?v=ZcVwGBsrS_g

30. Tsentr problemnogo analiza i gosudarstvenno-upravlencheskogo proektirovaniya pri Otdelenii obshchestvennykh nauk RAN, tema 'Rossiya i Zapad: chto razdelyaet?', 7:16 (2009).

31. Marshall Capital sold its Rostelekom stake in 2013.

32. In 2008, Kılınç was arrested along with a number of other members of the Ergenkon group, allegedly a right-wing cell accused of plotting terror attacks. Asked today about this trip, Dugin is circumspect, saying that he indeed did make the trip on behalf of 'some officials' in the Kremlin, but declining to name them.

33. Yigal Liverant, 'The prophet of the new Russian empire', *Azure* 35:5769 (2009), available at: http://azure.org.il/include/print.php?id=483

34. www.mid.ru/brp_4.nsf/sps/17568BA16D3AB9CCC32573E600594626

35. Interview with Modest Kolerov, 2013.

14: Wag the dog

1. Pavel Zarifullin, *Russkaya Sakralnaya Geografiya*, Limbus Press, 2010.

2. Interview with Alexander Dugin, 2010.

3. https://www.youtube.com/watch?v=ZlY5aZfOgPA

4. Stefan Wagstyl, Charles Clover and Isabel Gorst, 'Georgia fired first shots in war – report', *Financial Times*, 30 September 2009.

5. Thanks to Andreas Umland for pointing this out.

6. www.apn.ru/publications/article22117.htm. Thanks to Robert C. Otto for pointing this article out.
7. https://www.youtube.com/watch?v=AVzithktyJY
8. 'Meeting of the Valdai International Discussion Club', kremlin.ru website, 19 September 2013, available at: http://en.kremlin.ru/events/president/news/19243
9. www.nytimes.com/2013/01/13/world/europe/russian-lawmakers-move-to-purge-foreign-influences.html
10. www.themoscowtimes.com/news/article/activists-fear-repercussions-of-blasphemy-bill/481657.html
11. Kiselev defended the speech saying, accurately, that the United States bans the donation of blood and organs by gay men.
12. 'Meeting of the Valdai International Discussion Club'.
13. Charles Clover, 'Clinton vows to thwart new Soviet Union', *Financial Times*, 6 December 2012.
14. www.newrepublic.com/article/117692/fascism-returns-ukraine

15: Export of the passionaries

1. www.rt.com/news/ashton-maidan-snipers-estonia-946/ Paet has confirmed that the recording is authentic.
2. Mike Ecke, 'Russia, Ukraine feud over sniper carnage', Associated Press, 8 March 2014.
3. ibid.
4. www.youtube.com/watch?v=B4OgynH-7Is
5. www.youtube.com/watch?v=2IcMmpXhRIw&app=desktop
6. www.colta.ru/articles/society/2393
7. 'Krym: put na rodinu', Rossiya 1 Channel, 15 March 2015, available at: http://russia.tv/brand/show/brand_id/59195
8. http://en.kremlin.ru/events/president/news/20796
9. Vladimir Sorokin, 'Let the past collapse on time', *New York Review of Books*, 8 May 2014, available at: www.nybooks.com/articles/2014/05/08/let-the-past-collapse-on-time/
10. http://kremlin.ru/news/2079
11. Oleg Kashin, 'Iz Kryma v Donbass: Priklyucheniya Igora Strelkova i Alexandra Borodaya', *Slon*, 19 May 2014, available at: http://slon.ru/russia/iz_kryma_v_donbass_priklyucheniya_igorya_strelkova_i_aleksandra_borodaya-1099696.xhtml
12. ibid.
13. http://vk.com/duginag?w=wall18631635_3186
14. www.newsru.com/russia/19mar2015/nemtsov.html
15. 'V strane idet voyna terminov', *Express Gazeta*, 3 March 2014.
16. 'Voyna na Donbasse budet navyazana nam Vashingtonom i Kievom', Novorosinform.org website, 29 October 2015, available at: www.novorosinform.org/comments/id/828. Thanks to Robert C. Otto for pointing this out.
17. Edwin Williamson, *The Cambridge Companion to Jorge Luis Borges*, Cambridge University Press, 2013, p.12.

SELECT BIBLIOGRAPHY

Andreyev, Catherine and Ivan Savicky, *Russia Abroad*, Yale University Press, 2004

Applebaum, Anne, *Gulag: A history of the Soviet labour camps*, Penguin Books, 2003

Arendt, Hannah, *The Origins of Totalitarianism*, Harcourt, 1979

Belyakov, Sergey, *Gumilev Syn Gumileva*, Astrel, 2012

Berlin, Isaiah, *Russian Thinkers*, Penguin Books, 1979

Bradford, Richard, *Roman Jakobson: Life, language and art*, Routledge, 1994

Bromley, Y.V., *Ocherki Teorii Etnosa*, LKI, 2008

Brudny, Yitzhak, *Reinventing Russia: Russian nationalism and the Soviet State 1953–1991*, Harvard University Press, 1998

Clark, Bruce, *The Empire's New Clothes: The end of Russia's liberal dream*, Vintage, 1995

Clowes, Edith, *Russia on the Edge: Imagined geographies and post-Soviet identity*, Cornell University Press, 2011

Dosse, F., *History of Structuralism*, vol. 1: *The rising sign 1945–1966*, trans. Deborah Glassman, University of Minnesota Press, 1998

Dugin, Alexander, *Osnovy geopolitiki: Geopoliticheskoe budushchee Rossii*, Arktogeya, 1997

Dugin, Alexander, *Pop Kultura i Znaki Vremeni*, Amfora, 2005

Dugin, Alexander, *Konspirologiya: Teoriya zagovora, sekretnye obshchestva, velikaya voyna kontinentov*, ROF Evraziya, 2005

Dunlop, John, *The Rise of Russia and the Fall of the Soviet Empire*, Princeton University Press, 1993

Gellner, Ernest, *Nations and Nationalism*, Cornell University Press, 1983

Gerstein, Emma, *Moscow Memoirs*, trans. John Crowfoot, Harvill Press, 2004

Glebov, S., 'The challenge of the modern: The Eurasianist ideology and movement, 1920–29', PhD thesis, Rutgers University, 2004

Glebov, S., *Evraziystvo Mezhdu Imperiey i Modernom: Istoriya v dokumentakh*, Novoe izdatelstvo, 2010

Gray, Colin S. and Geoffrey Sloan, *Geopolitics, Geography and Strategy*, Frank Cass, 1999

Gumilev, Lev, *Searches for the Imaginary Kingdom*, Cambridge University Press, 2009

Haight, Amanda, *Anna Akhmatova: A poetic pilgrimage*, Oxford University Press, 1976

Jakobson, Roman, 'K kharakteristike evraziyskogo yazykovogo soyuza', in *Selected Writings*, vol. I, Mouton, 1962

Jakobson, Roman, *Six Lectures on Sound and Meaning*, Harvester Press, 1978

Jakobson, Roman, *My Futurist Years*, Marsilio Publishers, 1992

Kiselev, A.F. (ed.), *Politicheskaya Istoriya Russkoy Emigratsii, 1920–1940: Dokumenty i materialy*, vol. VII, Russkoe Nebo, 1999

Korovin, Valery, *Nakanune Imperii*, Izdatelstvo Evraziyskoe Dvizhenie, 2008

Kryuchkov, Vladimir, *Lichnoe Delo*, Moscow Eksmo Algoritm Kniga, 2003

Lavrov, S., *Lev Gumilev: Sudba i idei*, Svarog i K, 2000

Lévi-Strauss, Claude, *Structural Anthropology*, Basic Books, 1974

Liberman, A. (ed.), *The Legacy of Genghis Khan and Other Essays on Russia's Identity*, Michigan Slavic Publications, 1991

Liberman, A. (ed.), *N.S. Trubetskoy: Studies in General Linguistics and Language Structure*, Duke University Press, 2001

Limonov, Eduard, *Anatomiya Geroya*, Rusich, 1997

Limonov, Eduard, *Moya Politicheskaya Biografiya*, St Petersburg, 2002

Mandelstam, Nadezhda, *Hope Against Hope: A memoir*, Atheneum, 1983

Mitrokhin, N.A. *Russkaya Partiya: Dvizhenie Russkikh Natsionalistov v SSSR 1953–1985*, Izdatelstvo NLO, 2003

Nikulin, Lev, *Mertvaya Zib*, 1965

Politkovskaya, Anna, *A Dirty War: A Russian reporter in Chechnya*, Harvill Press, 1999

Pomorska, Krystyna, Elzbieta Chodakowska, Hugh Mclean and Brent Vine (eds), *Language, Poetry, and Poetics: The generation of the 1890s: Jakobson, Trubetskoy, Mayakovskij. Proceedings of the first Roman Jakobson colloquium at the Massachusetts Institute of Technology, October 5–6, 1984*, Walter De Gruyter, 1987

Pribylovsky, Vladimir, 'Natsional-patrioticheskoe dvizhenie: istoriya i litsa', in A. Verkhovsky et al., *Nationalizm i Ksenofobiya v Rossiyskom Obshchestve*, Panorama, 1998

Riasanovsky, Nicholas, 'The emergence of Eurasianism', *California Slavic Studies* 4 (1967), pp.39–72

Rovner, Arkady, *Vsompinaya Sebya: Kniga o druzyakh i sputnikakh zhizni*, Izdatelstvo Zolotoe Sechenie, 2010

Ruud, Charles A. and Sergei Stepanov, *Fontanka 16: The tsar's secret police*, Sutton Publishing, 1999

Savitskii, P.N., I. Vinkovetsky and C. Schlacks, *Exodus to the East: Forebodings and events: An affirmation of the Eurasians*, Charles Schlacks, Jr., 1996

Sedgwick, Mark, *Against the Modern World: Traditionalism and the secret intellectual history of the twentieth century*, Oxford University Press, 2009

Serebrov, Konstantin, *The Mystical Underground of Moscow*, ed. Robin Winckel-Mellish, Serebrov Boeken, 2006

Sériot, Patrick, *Structure et totalité: Les origines intellectuelles du structuralisme en Europe centrale et orientale*, PUF, 1999

Shentalinsky, Vitaly, *Prestuplenie bez Nakazaniya*, Progress Pleyada, 2007

Soldatov, Andrei and Irina Borogan, *Russia's New Nobility*, Public Affairs, 2011

Titov, Alexander, 'Lev Gumilev, ethnogenesis, and eurasianism', PhD thesis, University of London, 2005

Toman, Jindrich (ed.), *Letters and Other Materials from the Moscow and Prague Linguistic Circles 1912–1945*, Michigan Slavic Publications, 1994

Tregubova, Elena, *Bayki Kremlevskogo Diggera*, Ad Marginem, 2003

Trubetskoi, N., *Principles of Phonology*, University of California Press, 1969

Trubetskoi, N.S. and R. Jakobson, *N.S. Trubetzkoy's Letters and Notes* (Janua linguarum), Walter De Gruyter Inc., 1975

Trubetskoy, N.S., *Pisma k P.P. Suvchinskomu 1921–1928*, Russkiy Put, 2008

Urushadze, Georgy, *Vybrannye Mesta iz Perepiski s Vragami*, Izdatelstvo Evropeyskogo Doma, 1995

Von Zigern Korn, G., *Rasskazy o Svetlom Proshlom*, Peterburgskiy Pisatel, 2005

Voronkov, Konstantin, *Alexei Navalny: Groza zhulikov i vorov*, Eksmo, 2012

Vspominaya L.N. Gumileva, Memorialny Muzey Kvartira L.N. Gumileva, St Petersburg, 2003

Yakovlev, Alexander, *Sumerki*, Materik, 2005

Zhegulev, Ilya and Lyudmila Romanova, *Operatsiya Edinaya Rossiya: Neizvestnaya istoriya partii vlasti*, Eksmo, 2011

ILLUSTRATION CREDITS

1 Monoskop. 2 An-Poluhin. 3, 9, 13, 20 Sputnik. 4 Akhmatova.org. 5 *Ogonyok*. 6 Johnny Cirucci. 7 Boehhoe. 8 CODOH. 10 Diane-Lu Hovasse. 12 photo-chronograph.ru. 14 N. Makheeva. 15 Anna Artemyeva/*Novaya Gazeta*. 16 Reuters/Itar-Tass/Presidential Press Service (Russia). 17 Gumilev-Center.ru. 18 Apostrophe. 19 Reuters/Sergei Karpukhin. 21 Political Hotwire. 22 Russia Insider. 23 Sean Gallup.

INDEX